Praise for Advertising Strategy

"Where most business books limit themselves to text (my own included), *Advertising Strategy* is packed with images and artifacts that chronicle the most fascinating inflection points for some of the world's greatest brands. Between the covers is a rich course in business history of what happened, when, where, and why."

Scott Bedbury, author of *A New Brand World* and
former Chief Marketing Officer for Starbucks

"This book strikes me as different and more accessible. It also SHOWS students how to write for ads rather than preaching to them. It's written in a casual, conversational style. It makes it easy and inviting to read. Sounds like the authors are just talking to the students. Geez, isn't that what we tell them to do when writing copy?"

Sheri J. Broyles, University of North Texas

"This book really does a great job of showing and helping illustrate the importance of creative strategy."

Cynthia M. Frisby, University of Missouri–Columbia

"I wish I'd had this book when I got into the business. It drops you off right at the door. Where you go from there depends on whether you get it or not. And, if you do, whether you've got the talent and insight to add a few points of your own."

John Melamed, Executive VP, Cramer Krasselt

"Will this book make a contribution? Definitely. The organization, included examples, and tone of the work will make it especially attractive to advertising educators."

Jason Chambers, University of Illinois at Urbana–Champaign

"It's refreshing to read a book on advertising with insight and work from the industry's most talented. If you read this book and your portfolio still sucks, perhaps you should read 'How to Become a Plumber'."

Tony Calcao, VP/Associate Creative Director, Crispin Porter + Bogusky

"Well written, entertaining, and informative. The examples provided good insight into the 'real world.' It is a strong 'how to' book that can help empower students to actually learn how to write copy."

Sally J. McMillan, University of Tennessee

"*Advertising Strategy* by Tom Altstiel and Jean Grow is a comprehensive, considerate, and motivational book that seeks to discover the muse behind creativity. The authors have not only done their homework, they've done it astonishingly well. With meticulous detail they dispel some of the myths rife within our business, and lay some secrets bare.

They now know more about what makes great advertising than most of us in the business do. It's 408 pages long. And I may actually read the whole darn thing."

Janet Champ, winner of 5 Kelly Awards for her work on Nike women's advertising for Wieden + Kennedy

"I find the approach of the text to be appropriately focused, businesslike and approachable. The War Stories and Words of Wisdom are just about the right touch for 'advice from on high.' . . . I especially appreciate its 'more how/less why' approach."

Greg Pabst, University of San Francisco

"I am a big fan of their 'more how/less why' approach. . . . You can tell the authors have real-life experience, which is a plus. I think the Words of Wisdom are great. By the nature of the layout of the book, the quotes are sure to be read, and there are some real gems here. They match the tone of the book and contain worthwhile perspectives."

Lara Zwarun, University of Texas at Arlington

"Basic concept approaches are very straightforward and provide students a much more concrete place to begin than just 'make an ad.'"

Kendra L. Gale, University of Colorado–Boulder

"I welcome a text that is informative, instructive, and a text with energy."

Peggy J. Kreshel, University of Georgia

"I give a hearty 'Concept approved!' to the writers of *Advertising Strategy*, a thorough, concise, honest, 'tough-love' guide to the businesses of advertising and marketing communications. An easy-to-follow and complete compendium of lessons for the person who aspires to be in the creative seat, *Advertising Strategy* instructs as a textbook must, without ever falling into the textbook category 'boring.' Instead, it inspires. With hundreds of visual examples and war stories from people on the inside of the business, it teaches with relentless wit and candor, making one feel inside the sometimes goofy, always stimulating world of advertising. I even found myself using the book as a means of assessing work I'd already done, and hoping that I'd accomplished the goals and objectives it sets forth. If there were a Gold Pencil for textbooks, this would earn one."

Charlotte Moore, former Co-Creative Director, Wieden + Kennedy, Amsterdam

Advertising Strategy

Creative Tactics From the Outside/In

Tom Altstiel
Jean Grow

Marquette University

SAGE Publications
Thousand Oaks ▪ London ▪ New Delhi

For information:

Sage Publications, Inc.
2455 Teller Road
Thousand Oaks, California 91320
E-mail: order@sagepub.com

Sage Publications Ltd.
1 Oliver's Yard
55 City Road
London EC1Y 1SP
United Kingdom

Sage Publications India Pvt. Ltd.
B-42, Panchsheel Enclave
Post Box 4109
New Delhi 110 017 India

Printed in the United States of America.

Library of Congress Cataloging-in-Publication Data

Altstiel, Tom.
Advertising strategy : creative tactics from the outside/in / Tom Altstiel, Jean Grow.
    p. cm.
Includes bibliographical references and index.
ISBN 1-4129-1796-4 (pbk.)
   1. Advertising. I. Grow, Jean. II. Title.
HF5823.A758 2006
659.1—dc22   2005012623

Acquisitions Editor:	Margaret Seawell
Editorial Assistant:	Sarah Quesenberry
Production Editor:	Denise Santoyo
Designer:	Gary Hespenheide
Typesetter:	C&M Digitals (P) Ltd.
Indexer:	Pam Van Huss
Cover Designer:	Dan Augustine

Contents

Preface

Why This Book?

Finding that *one* text that educates and motivates students is the holy grail of advertising instructors, especially in the creative field. Many books cover theories and principles, but not much about how to create an ad. Others feature great examples that are helpful for illustrating the state of the industry ten years ago but hold little relevance for today's students. Still others provide a wealth of anecdotes by the giants of our industry, but very little advice that applies to the struggling novice. So, after searching for the perfect book, we decided to write one, knowing full well it will never be just right. Even for us.

The subtitle of this book comes from the 2003 Marquette university team in the National Student Advertising Competition. Their "Outside/In" campaign hit all the right buttons for creative strategy and tactics. Outside/in also describes our approach to teaching. As a working professional, Tom brings an outsider's point of view while working inside academia. Jean draws on her years of experience in the outside world in addition to the discipline and in-depth analysis of our business that comes from earning a Ph.D. Each of us brings a unique blend of real-world and academic perspectives. In other words, *outside/in.*

Our approach is to share what we've learned in this business, what has worked well for us in teaching classes, and what we've observed from others who are more talented and successful. The rest we've just stolen from other authors (with every attempt to give credit where it's due).

This book has several other differences from traditional textbooks:

- *More how, less why:* The focus here is on creative strategy and tactics. We skip most of the principles and history of advertising. Instead, we offer more tips and techniques, checklists and how-to stuff. We recognize that creativity does not come from reading a list or following some formula, but the presentation of some concepts may help readers get organized or trigger a burst of creative thinking.

- *Up-to-date examples:* About 90% of the examples we present here are less than five years old. Those that are older are used to illustrate key points, not to represent the latest trends.

- *Student-created ads:* This is your competition. These examples not only illustrate particular points, they show the incredible untapped resources in our colleges and design schools.

- *War stories:* We offer short case histories and anecdotes from our personal files and from other people in this business.

If you learn nothing else from this book or from an advertising class, remember this: Never stop learning. Never stop growing.

Let's get started.

Acknowledgments

We'd like to thank the following people, without whose help this book would never have gotten this far: Mary Altstiel and Terry Doyle, for their proofreading skills and incredible patience while we were holed up with a computer instead of spending quality time with them. Scott Bedbury, who graciously provided a wealth of insight about branding. Anna Morris and Iliana Aleman, who provided valuable perspectives on African American and Hispanic advertising. Janet Champ and Charlotte Moore (formerly with Wieden + Kennedy), Bill Wright (Crispin Porter + Bogusky), and Andrew Meyer (Leo Burnett), who contributed great war stories. Peter Noble (Southern Methodist University), who was the adviser for the 2004 NSAC championship team, provided valuable perspectives on NSAC and connected us with former students who provided even more information. Mike Trinklein, Dan Early, Johnathan Crawford, Jeff Ericksen, and John Melamed, all Milwaukee-area professionals, who provided a world of great information on broadcast, the Internet, and advertising in general. Dan Augustine, who took many hours out of his blossoming career to create illustrations for several chapters of this book. Our students, who offered constructive criticism and also provided some of the samples used in this book.

Finally, we would like to gratefully acknowledge the support and encouragement of our editor, Margaret Seawell, who saw in our book a unique contribution to advertising education. Along with Margaret, a number of others at Sage patiently guided us through the publishing process, including Sarah Quesenberry, Deya Saoud, Denise Santoyo, and Judy Selhorst. Finally, we wish to thank our colleagues who supported our efforts by giving us the freedom to pursue our dream and finish this book.

Copy and Creativity

N o one can teach you to be creative. But you may be surprised how creative you really are. You may not have been an A+ English student. But you may find you're an excellent copywriter. In reading this book, you will discover a lot about creative strategy and tactics and probably a lot about yourself. At the very least you should learn the following:

- The correct format for writing copy for each medium.
- The basic rules of copywriting and when to break them.
- How to put more sell into your copy.
- How to connect the reader or viewer with the advertiser.
- How to keep continuity throughout a campaign.
- The importance of presenting your work.

Who Needs Copy (and the People Who Write It)?

At the beginning of each semester, we ask our students, "Who wants to be a copywriter?" When we first began to ask this, we expected the majority to raise their hands, or at least lift them a few inches off their desks. Sad to say, only about one in six expresses any interest in becoming a copywriter, at least at the beginning of the course. These are the most common reasons students give us for *not* pursuing a writing career:

"I want to be an account exec."

"I want to be a media director."

"I want to be a designer—I do pictures, not words."

"I'm not sure I can write."

"I'm not sure I even want to be in advertising."

1.1. When other cars represented conspicuous consumption, VW countered with a sensible economic approach.

These are legitimate reasons, but we can make a case for learning about creative strategy and tactics to answer every one of them.

Account executives need to know how to evaluate creative work. Does it meet the objectives? What's the strategy? Why is it great or not so great? When account executives and account managers understand the creative process, they are more valuable to both their clients and their agencies.

Media folks need to recognize the creative possibilities of each medium. They need to understand tone, positioning, resonance, and the other basics pounded into copywriters.

Designers, art directors, producers, and graphic artists should know how to write or at least know enough to defend their work. Why does it meet the strategies? Do the words and visuals work together? Does the font match the tone of the ad? Is the body copy too long? (It's *always* too long for art directors.) Design can't be separated from the process.

There is English and there is advertising copy. You're not writing the Great American Novel. Or even a term paper. You are selling products and services with your ideas, which may or may not include your deathless prose. What you say is more important than how you write it. Ideas come first. Writing with style can follow.

Creativity is still useful outside of advertising. You can put the skills you learn through developing creative strategy and tactics to work in many other fields. The ability to gather information, process it, prioritize the most important facts, and develop a persuasive message is useful in almost every occupation.

Even if you don't aspire to be the next David Ogilvy, you might learn something from this book about marketing, advertising, basic writing skills, and presenting your work. Who knows, you might even like it.

The history of creative advertising (don't worry, it's not long)

You can find other books that outline the history of advertising, probably going back to cave paintings. We'll concentrate on the advent of the Creative Revolution, one of many uprisings that took place during the turbulent 1960s. Unlike any other era before or since, the focus was on youth, freedom, anti-establishment thinking—and, let's face it, sex, drugs, and rock 'n' roll. So it's not surprising that some of the world's most recognized ads (some of which are included in this book) were created during that time.

What made these ads revolutionary? First, they began to shift the focus from the product to the brand. They developed a look, introduced memorable characters, and kept a consistent theme throughout years of long-running campaigns. All of these factors built brand awareness and acceptance. Second, they twisted conventional thinking. When most car companies were touting tail fins and chrome, VW told us to "Think Small." When Hertz was bragging about being top dog, Avis said, "We try harder," because they were number two. When Levy's advertised "our Jewish rye bread," they used an Irish cop and a Native American as models. Third, they created new looks, using white space, asymmetrical layouts, minimal copy, and unique typography—all design elements that we take for granted in today's ads.

The driving forces of this revolution included such giants as Leo Burnett, David Ogilvy, and Bill Bernbach, all of whom are quoted heavily in this text. First and foremost, they were copywriters. Even though they chaired mega-agencies, their first love was writing. In this age of rapidly changing technology and Integrated Marketing Communications, maybe *you* could become a leader in the next creative revolution.

The Copywriter's Role

Most copywriters do a lot more than just write ads. In fact, writing may be only a small part of their jobs.

The creative quarterback

Traditionally, a creative team includes a copywriter and an art director, with participation by interactive designers, Web developers, and broadcast producers. This team usually answers to a coach—the creative director.

Every player has his or her role on the team, but in many cases, the copywriter drives the creative process. The copywriter is usually the quarterback or, if you like, the point guard—the person who sets up the action. Why? Because the writer has to know the product frontward and backward, inside out. The writer knows who uses the product, how it compares to the competition, what's important to the consumer, and a million other facts. (We'll cover later *how* he or she knows this.)

1.2.

1.3.

Source: Illustration by Dan Augustine.

Every member of the creative team should have a good understanding of the product, but the copywriter should know more than anyone else. Just as a quarterback needs receivers and running backs, the copywriter has to rely on other skilled players. No one does it all. And no one person always has the best idea. Sometimes art directors write the best headlines. Or writers come up with killer visuals. Although the writer should drive the creative effort, he or she does not have to dominate it.

So, what else does a writer do?

In small shops, the writers wear so many hats, it's no wonder they develop big heads. Some of their responsibilities, aside from writing copy, include the following:

- *Research:* Primary and secondary research really matters.

- *Client contact:* Writers should get the facts direct from the sources, rather than filtered through account executives; they also present those ideas and defend the work.

- *Broadcast production:* Finding the right directors, talent, music, and post-production houses makes a writer's visions come to life.

- *New business:* Often writers gather data, organize the creative strategy, work on the pitches, and present the work.

- *Public relations:* Some copywriters also write news releases, plan promotional events, and even contact editors.

- *Internet/interactive content management:* The Internet has become an integral part of a total marketing communication effort. A lot of "traditional" media writers are now writing for Web sites and interactive media.

- *Creative management:* Much has been written about whether copywriters or art directors make the best creative directors. The answer: yes.

Controlling the Creative Process

If the writer drives the creative process, how does he or she keep it on the right path? We've developed some checkpoints for the creative process. They don't always evolve in the order shown below, but in most cases, you'll have to reach these mile markers before the work is ready to produce. If you let someone else take the lead, you may not be able to guide him or her in the right direction.

Step 1: Getting the facts. If you have a research department and/or account planners, take advantage of their knowledge. But don't settle for someone else's opinion. Talk to people who use the product as well as those who don't or won't even consider it. Talk to retailers who sell the product. Look at competitive advertising: What's good? Where are they vulnerable? In short, know as much as you can about the product, the competition, the market, and the people who buy it. Try to make the product part of your life.

Step 2: Brainstorming with a purpose. If you've done your homework, you should know the wants and needs of the target audience and how your product meets those needs. From that base, you can direct the free flow of creative ideas. Thanks to your knowledge, you can concentrate on finding a killer creative idea rather than floundering in a sea of pointless questions. But you must also be open to new ideas and independent thinking from your creative team members.

Step 3: Finding the reference/visuals. You may have a clear vision of the creative concept, but can you communicate that to your art director, creative director, account exec, and client? You can help your art director by finding photos, artwork, or design elements—not to rip off those ideas, but to make your point. The finished piece may not look anything like your original vision, but at least you can start with a point of reference. Browse the Web, stock photo books, and awards annuals. We can't emphasize this enough, especially for beginning writers—even if you can't find what you want, the search might trigger a new idea. The visual selection is a starting point, not the endgame.

Step 4: Drawing a writer's rough. This is critical, even if you can only draw stick people. Where does the headline go? How much copy do you think you'll need? What's the main visual? How should the elements be arranged? Even though art directors may ridicule your design, they will appreciate having the raw elements they can massage into a great-looking ad.

Step 5: Working with the art director and the rest of the team. For most writers, the happiest and most productive years of their careers are those spent

Why should lunch be as boring as the rest of your day?

It doesn't have to be at Zorba's. Not when you can have our spicy, slow roasted gyro on fresh fluffy pita bread, with Greek seasoned potatoes and a feta and veggie garnish–for about the same price as a boring McMeal. Who knows? Lunch at Zorba's may be the most exciting part of your day.

ZORBA'S

6th and Green
Urbana
(Across from McDonald's)

1.4. Even though art directors may mock your artistic ability, a writer's rough will give them a good idea of how the ad should look.

collaborating with art directors or broadcast producers. When two creative minds click, the whole really is greater than the sum of the parts. A great creative partnership, like any relationship, needs to be nurtured and has its ups and downs. Although as the writer you may want to drive the whole process, it's best not to run over your teammates. They may come up with some ideas that will make you look like a genius.

Step 6: Preselling the creative director and account executive. Chances are you will not be working directly with the client, and even if you are, you probably won't be the sole contact. That's why you need the people who interface with the client to buy into your ideas. Maintaining a good relationship with the creative director not only protects your job, it also gives you an ally when you pitch the account executive and client.

In many cases, the account executive represents the client in these discussions. He or she may try to poke holes in your logic or question your creative choices. That's why you must be able to back every creative choice with sound reasons. In the end, if the account executive is sold, you have a much better chance of convincing the client.

Step 7: Selling the client. We've been in far too many meetings where the account executives were "1,000%" behind the concept but started backing away at the first hint of a client's frown. As the writer who developed the idea, you have to be prepared to defend your work, using logic rather than emotion. Many times your brilliant reasoning will fail, since clients usually think with their wallets. Over time you'll know how far you can push a client. The trick is to know when to retreat so you can fight another day. Most clients don't mind being challenged creatively, as long as there are sound reasons for taking chances.

The three things you *never* want to hear from a client:

- "That looks just like the competitor's ads. I want our ads to stand out."
- "I was looking for something a lot more creative. Take some risks."
- "You obviously don't understand our product or our market."

You won't hear those things if you take care of Steps 1–6.

Step 8: Getting it right. OK, you've sold the client—now what? You have to hand your creation to the production team, but your responsibilities don't end. Does the copy fit the way it should? If not, can you cut it? Can you change a word here and there to make it even better? Are the graphics what you envisioned? Your involvement is even more critical for broadcast. Did you have a specific talent in mind for voice or on-camera roles? Does the director understand and share your vision? Does the music fit?

If you remember nothing else, keep this in mind and follow it through Step 10: *Nothing takes the guts out of a great idea like bad execution.*

Step 9: Maintaining continuity. Almost everyone can come up with a great idea. Once. The hard part is extending that great idea in other media and repeating it, only differently, in a campaign. Over time, elements of a campaign tend to drift away from the original idea. A client usually gets tired of a look before the consumer does. Art directors may want to "enhance" the campaign with new elements. Someone on the creative team needs to monitor the elements of an ongoing campaign continually to make sure they are true to the original idea.

Step 10: Discovering what worked and why. If the ad or series of ads in a campaign achieve their objectives, great! If they win awards but the client loses market share, look out. You need to keep monitoring the efficacy of the campaign. What are the readership scores? What do the client's salespeople and retailers think? How are sales? If you had to make any midcourse corrections, what would you do? If you never stop learning, you'll never miss an opportunity to make the next project or campaign even better.

Where Do I Go From Here?

A lot of entry-level copywriters set lofty career goals—most often the coveted title of creative director. However, many junior writers don't consider the other exciting possibilities. We list a few below for you to consider. You may actually take several of these paths in your career.

Copywriter for life: It could happen. Some people are happy to write their whole careers. You can do it if you continue to improve and never stop growing.

Management/creative director: A great job with great responsibilities. It often involves more personnel management than creative talent, requiring the skills of a head coach, sales manager, and kindergarten teacher.

Account manager: Many writers are drawn to "the dark side." It makes sense, especially if you like working with clients and thoroughly understand the product, market, and consumers. In some small shops, the copy-contact system gives account execs an opportunity to create and creative types a reason to wear suits.

Account planner: This is a natural for many writers who like research and enjoy being the conduit that connects the account manager, creative team, and consumers. It involves thorough knowledge of research, marketing, creative, and media, and a lot of intuition. Most successful advertising copywriters already possess those skills.

Promotion director: Writers are idea people, so it makes sense to use that creativity to develop sales promotions, special events, sponsorships, specialty marketing programs, displays, and all the other marketing communication tools not included in "traditional advertising." This is a rapidly growing area with a lot of potential for creative people.

Public relations writer: Although most PR people won't admit it, it's easier to write a news release than an ad. Most advertising writers won't admit that editorial writing is usually more persuasive than advertising. PR writing involves much more than news releases, though. You may become an editor for a newsletter or an in-house magazine. You may produce video news releases or schedule events, press conferences, and any number of creative public relations efforts.

Writer in an internal advertising department: So far, we've outlined agency jobs, but other companies also need talented creative people. In small companies, you may handle brochure writing, PR, trade shows, and media relations in addition to advertising. In larger companies, you may handle promotional activities not covered by your ad agency. You may even write speeches for your CEO.

Web/interactive media writer: The Web is so integrated into most marketing communication programs it seems ridiculous to consider it nontraditional media. Any writer today should be Web savvy. You should know the terminology and capabilities of the Internet just as well as you understand magazines or television. You don't have to be a whiz at Flash or HTML, but having some technical expertise is a huge plus. As with any phase of advertising, creativity—not technology—is the most precious commodity.

Freelance writer: A lot of people like a flexible schedule and a variety of clients. Being a successful freelancer requires tremendous discipline and endless self-promotion, plus the mental toughness to endure constant rejection, short deadlines, and long stretches between assignments.

Producer/director: Like to write broadcast? Maybe you have a knack for writing scripts, selecting talent, editing, and other elements of audio and video production. As with writing for the Web and interactive, creative talent and a logical mind are the keys. Technological expertise can be learned on the job.

1.5. Even though there is no copy in this ad, the copywriter gets the credit for the concept.

Agency owner: Any one of the previously mentioned career paths can lead to an ownership position. Many of the top agencies in the United States were founded by copywriters. Or course, running even a small shop requires more than writing ability. If you want to pursue this route, make sure you understand finance, accounting, marketing, personnel management, business and tax laws, insurance, and other critical areas that can make or break a business. If you don't know that stuff, make sure you hire someone who does.

Consultant: Too often, *consultant* is another word for unemployed. A select few actually make a living as creative consultants. Sometimes they are no more than repackaged freelancers. Sometimes they are "rainmakers" who help with a new-business pitch. Still, a number of downsized companies and agencies will pay consultants for skills and contacts they don't have in-house. Keeping current and connected is the key to success as a consultant.

Instructor: Want to give something back to the next generation? Want to interact with eager students? Want to earn a couple extra bucks for a nice vacation or a new motorcycle? If so, you may consider teaching. Some schools hire working professionals as adjuncts, providing a small dose of the real world to academia.

What's in It for Me?

You've probably already discussed the role of advertising in society and explored ethical issues. You've reviewed theories of communication and might have even read about the great copywriters of all time. That's all good, but let's be honest—if you want a creative career, you're only interested in three things: Fame, Fortune, and Fun. And not necessarily in that order. Let's look at each one in a little more detail.

- *Fame:* Everyone wants recognition. Since advertising is unsigned, there are only two ways to get it: awards and having people say, "You're *really* the person who did that?" If they're judged good enough, writers and art directors are immortalized in *Communication Arts* annuals. Last time we looked, there are no books showcasing account execs and media buyers.

- *Fortune:* Depending on experience, the economy, the results they generate, and a million other factors, creative people can make as much as or more than any other people in advertising. Recent salary surveys show

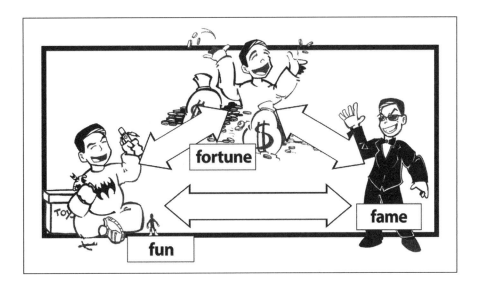

1.6.

Source: Illustration by Dan Augustine.

salaries for top creatives and top account supervisors are pretty much the same. But as a writer or art director, you get to wear jeans, have tattoos, pierce your nose, and spike your hair. If you want to. Even though creatives are given wide latitude in dress and behavior, never forget: It's still a job.

- *Fun:* You can be famous and rich and still be unhappy in any business. Even if you're not well-known or a millionaire, you can still get a kick out of solving problems for clients. It's still a treat to work with other creatives, interact with musicians and actors, win presentations, and travel to exotic locales such as Sardis, Mississippi. No matter how much you're earning, when it stops being fun or if you lose your edge, you should probably consider getting out.

Knowing the Rules and When to Break Them

We won't dwell on too many of the rules of advertising writing and design, but we will look at some accepted practices. These are the tips and techniques that have proven successful over time.

One "rule" will always be true: Advertising is a business. A business populated by a lot a crazy people, but still a business. Although the slogan "It's not creative unless it sells" has lost its impact, you still have to persuade someone to buy something. This reality leads to what we call "creative schizophrenia"—the internal conflict between the stuff you *want* to do and the stuff clients *make* you do. For example, if you want to get a job you need really cool, cutting-edge stuff in your portfolio, stuff that usually isn't usable in the real world. When you land that job, you'll probably be forced to do a lot of boring stuff that sells products but looks terrible in your book. That's the nature of this business, and unless you can live with a split personality, it's hard to survive. As famous copywriter Carl Ally said: "There's a tiny percentage of all the work that's great and a tiny percentage that's lousy. But most of the work—well, it's just there. That's no knock on advertising. How many great restaurants are there? Most aren't good or bad, they're just adequate. The fact is, excellence is tough to achieve in any field."[3]

Think of three circles. The first and smallest is the edgy stuff you'd like to do, but usually doesn't sell anything. You see a lot of this in art magazines and at awards shows. Most of it is produced *only* for art magazines and awards shows. The next circle contains ads that actually sell. They may be great or just average, but they work for a living. The last and largest circle is "Planet Schlock"—a

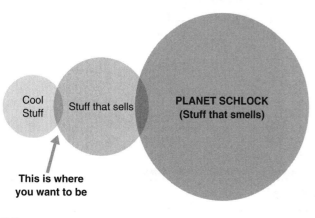

Cool Stuff

Stuff that sells

PLANET SCHLOCK (Stuff that smells)

This is where you want to be

1.7.

dreadful place populated by local car dealers, personal injury attorneys, and Chia Pets. Some of these ads sell like gangbusters, but most just lay there and stink.

You don't have to be crazy, but it helps

Psychologists have spent years studying creativity. Tests have proven to be "mediocre predictors" of creative achievement. That should reassure some students studying for final exams in writing or design classes. Collectively, studies have shown that creative people "are more autonomous, introverted, open to new experiences, norm-doubting, self-confident, self-accepting, driven, ambitious, dominant, hostile and impulsive" than noncreative people. At the core, they are independent and nonconformist. If that describes you, perhaps you're suited to be a writer or art director. Other studies have found that creative people, particularly writers, suffer more from "mood disorders," especially depression.[4] Anecdotal evidence supports that theory. Many of the best writers are privately dissatisfied with their work while they defend it unflinchingly to clients and colleagues. Although it's not exactly creative schizophrenia, it can drive a person a little nuts at times. But, as Jimmy Buffett said, "If we weren't all crazy, we would go insane."

WAR STORY:

GOLD PENCILS VERSUS MEAT AND POTATOES

In another life, I was VP/creative director at a small Milwaukee shop. The owner (who had promised to turn over the place to a few of us execs) decided to sell it all to a big Minneapolis agency. Not just any big agency, but one of the acknowledged creative powerhouses of the universe. They had enough gold pencils to become a second Fort Knox. So when I met with the president of the big shop, I was naturally a little apprehensive. How could our meager creative efforts stand up against the darlings of the CA annuals? First, he reassured me that the best of

our work was pretty damn good (whether that was a compliment or damning with faint praise, I don't know). What really struck me was his second comment: "You never see most of the crap we have to do for clients. Sure, we win a ton of awards, but that's only a fraction of what we do. We're lucky to have enough great clients that let us do a lot of good work. The rest of the world thinks all we do is produce award-winning ads, while in reality, most of what we do is not much better than the meat-and-potatoes stuff everyone else cranks out."

—Tom Altstiel

Keeping It Legal . . . and Ethical

Sometimes a number of issues come together to make the "perfect storm" of marketing silliness and political incorrectness. The Great Beer Wars of 2004–5 is a prime example. After a decade of sagging sales, Miller Lite rebounded when they claimed to have fewer carbs than archrival Bud Light. Budweiser, violating the cardinal rule that Number One doesn't mention the competition, weakly replied that *all* light beers are low in carbs and that taste is all that matters.

Feeling frisky, Miller launched a campaign to poke fun at the King of Beers, claiming that real Americans don't "kowtow to a bunch of tiara-wearing crumpet eaters" and that Miller is the "President of Beers." Budweiser responded by taunting Miller as the "Queen of Carbs"—a not-so-subtle attack on the manhood of red-blooded beer drinkers. This triggered outrage by feminist and gay/lesbian groups. Bud continued the offensive by pointing out that Miller was owned by a South African company, while Bud was "American owned since 1852." Bud went so far as to slap stickers on Miller products asserting Miller's South African ownership (actually, SABMiller is a British-based company). Budweiser even brought back Louie and Frankie, the Bud lizards, to promote the brand's American roots and deride Miller's South African connection.

Some industry observers predicted a backlash of sympathy for Miller given Bud's sledgehammer approach to competitive marketing. Even Bud marketing executives admitted they wanted to get back to positive brand promotion rather than the "current silliness."

1.8. So many issues, so little time. As part of the Great Beer Wars of 2004–5, Bud challenged the patriotism and manhood of Miller drinkers. This Memorial Day ad claimed (incorrectly) that Miller was a South African company and seemed to say the best way to honor our country is to show bikini-clad women holding Buds. The copy reads, "Show your colors this holiday weekend with a true American beer. Unlike Miller, who was bought by South African Breweries, Anheuser-Busch has proudly been AMERICAN OWNED SINCE 1852."

Good taste, good sense, and good business

As you'll see in later chapters, perceptions of ad messages can vary widely depending on audiences. You may find it's worth taking a creative risk to persuade one small group, knowing full well it will turn off most everyone else. You have to weigh the risks (which may include loss of overall sales, adverse publicity, and even lawsuits) against the benefits (higher sales to a select group, publicity, and creative recognition). We do not advocate doing anything creatively for the sake of shock value. Nor do we recommend using sexist, racist, or homophobic messages, sleazy gimmicks, or gutter humor to gain attention. Some of the examples in this book may go beyond the threshold of acceptable taste for some people. They are what they are, and even if we don't always agree with their content, they are part of the real world.

The American Association of Advertising Agencies has established a creative code of ethics for its members. Even if you're not a 4A member, it's good advice:

Knowing what *not* to do does not absolve you of responsibility. While you might not be able to change the world through advertising, you can certainly avoid adding to the current problems. We encourage you to find ways to include positive images of minorities and marginalized

Creative Code of Ethics of the American Association of Advertising Agencies

We the members of the American Association of Advertising Agencies, in addition to supporting and obeying the laws and legal regulations pertaining to advertising, undertake to extend and broaden the application of high ethical standards. Specifically, we will not knowingly create advertising that contains:

False or misleading statements or exaggerations, visual or verbal.

Testimonials that do not reflect the real opinion of the individual(s) involved.

Price claims that are misleading.

Claims insufficiently supported or that distort the true meaning or practicable application of statements made by professional or scientific authority.

Statements, suggestions or pictures offensive to public decency or minority segments of the population.

We recognize that there are areas that are subject to honestly different interpretations and judgment. Nevertheless, we agree not to recommend to any advertiser, and to discourage the use of, advertising that is in poor or questionable taste or that is deliberately irritating through aural or visual content or presentation.[5]

groups in mainstream advertising. Overall, the philosophy of "enlightened self-interest" works best. When you do good, you'll do well.

We hope we've got you thinking about some of the ethical issues involved in what you, as copywriter, actually do. How can you make a difference for you, for your client, and for society? It really does matter how you frame an issue, highlight a benefit, select an image, take on the competitor, and choose your words. It's about ethics, but it's also about legality, because the law kicks in where ethics ends.

Legal concepts that really matter

Whole books have been written on the subject of the law and advertising. We have no intention of even trying to compete. Rather, we want to focus very briefly on two aspects that we think really matter to copywriters: claims and copyright.

Stake Your Claim

Copywriters make all kinds of claims, and most of them are perfectly legal. Yet it's worthwhile to consider briefly what *legal* really means. All fact claims in advertising are viewed very seriously under the law. There can be no deception. If you're making a fact-based claim, you'd better have research data to back it up. However, advertisers have a fair amount of wiggle room in the three types of nonfact claims that are routinely used: puffery, obvious falsity, and lifestyle claims. Most of us write claims that fall into one of these three categories, and thus we escape the scrutiny of the law.

- *Puffery* is the use of superlatives to tout the greatness of your brand—making it so obvious that consumers are bound to know the claims are exaggerated. "Nestlé's makes the very best chocolate" is incredibly amazing puffery—and so is our commentary on it.

- *Obvious falsity* usually involves spoofs, spins, or metaphors. Consumers can't miss the obviously false nature of the claims. The Altoids tagline "Curiously Strong" is a great example of a claim with obvious falsity, with a dose of puffery.

- *Lifestyle claims* are claims that are based on subjective assumptions about how consumers feel about the product or its effects. Think of ads for Viagra. They are making some big assumptions—one ad implied more than an assumption about lifestyle and had to be pulled.

You walk a fine line, but as long as your nonfact claims fall somewhere within the bounds of these three categories, you're probably safe.

Copyrights and Copywriting

WORDS OF WISDOM

"The creative person wants to be a know-it-all . . . because he never knows when these ideas might come together to form a new idea. It may happen six minutes later, or six months, or six years down the road."

—CARL ALLY[6]

It's very important that copywriters understand and respect copyright law. As students and instructors, most of you know that under the "fair use" doctrine you can reproduce nearly anything—just as long as it's for educational purposes. In fact, the ads in this book are being used for educational purposes and thus fall under the fair use doctrine.

When you are concepting ads, fair use also applies. Since the advent of computers and the massive expansion of the Internet, art directors and copywriters have been borrowing images and pasting them into layouts to illustrate concepts for their clients. The fact that you are not reproducing these images for profit is what allows you some wiggle room. That's where fair use ends, however. You must either buy the images you want to use in actual ads or re-create the borrowed images in ways that are substantially different so as not to be construed as copying the images.

What about words? Most slogans and taglines are considered protected by copyright. So are brand names. In fact, most brand names are trademarked and aggressively protected. Using someone else's slogan or tagline will get you into legal trouble, and it won't do much for your career either. You need to do your homework to be sure that the brilliant tagline is not already used by another brand. When in doubt, run it by a colleague or do an online word search. If you're still in doubt, contact legal counsel. Many large agencies have their own legal staff. If you work for an in-house agency, you might have access to legal counsel through the corporation.

In short, don't make assumptions, and do your homework.

A Word about Awards

Luke Sullivan explains the attraction of awards in his book *Hey Whipple, Squeeze This:*

> Our work isn't signed. And when you're new in the business, there's no better way to make a name for yourself than getting into "the books." Awards shows allow tiny agencies to compete with the behemoths. They serve as great recruiting tools for agencies. And they expose us to all kinds of work we'd not see otherwise.[7]

We can't think of another industry that congratulates itself as much. There are probably more than 50 national advertising awards programs and hundreds of awards in local, regional, and industry-specific venues. While it's always fun to win, many awards programs have experienced problems with bogus entries and fraudulent documentation. Some entries have been created just for the awards and never appeared in any media. The hunger to win can turn into a feeding frenzy. One of the most notorious examples involved a near riot at an awards ceremony where the nominees stormed the podium and looted the awards.

We've also been on the judges' side of the table. It's a tough job. There's no time to read all the copy. No one wants to listen to all those radio spots. In most cases, you never know if an ad is real or was produced just for the show. Sometimes judging panels arbitrarily decide that nothing is good enough to win in certain categories.

The toughest and the most valuable of the award competitions in advertising include the One Show, ANDY, ADDY, EFFIE, *Communication Arts Advertising Annual*, D&AD Awards (United Kingdom), and Cannes.

Winning awards can earn you some short-term fame and maybe a little fortune, but over time, you'll have to sell something. If you keep moving from one award-hungry shop to the next, you might have a great career. But if you stay put, eventually a client will demand that your creativity puts some cash into the company as well as plaques on your wall.

1.9.

Before You Get Started

Most texts on advertising will tell you that you can't just start writing an ad from scratch. Of course you can. And you just might get lucky the first time. But can you repeat that success? What about the next project? And the one after that? No one hits a home run every time at bat. But those who study the fundamentals of the game, take batting practice, and play every day have a much better chance when they step up to the plate. That's why we need to discuss the foundations of marketing communications. First, a few definitions.

Advertising, MarCom, IMC, IBP, or what?

Everyone knows what advertising is, right? George Orwell called it "the rattling of a stick inside a swill bucket."[8] H. G. Wells claimed, "Advertising is legalized lying."[9] For a less cynical take, Professor Jef Richards of the University of Texas says, "Advertising is the 'wonder' in Wonder Bread."[10] He should know. He teaches advertising.

You've probably learned that advertising is paid communication to promote a product, service, brand, or cause through the media. Is direct mail advertising? Well, if you consider mail a medium, yes. How about a brochure? Probably not; however, it can be mailed or inserted into a magazine as an ad. Internet content? Yes and no. A Web site by itself is not really advertising, but a banner or pop-up ad on that site is. Public relations? No, because the advertiser is not paying the editor to publish an article (at least not directly).

Confused? Don't feel alone. Many marketing professionals can't distinguish between advertising and other forms of promotion. That's where the term *MarCom* arose. Some people view MarCom as taking in every form of marketing communication. Others describe MarCom as every form of promotion that's not traditional advertising. Traditional advertising usually covers print (newspapers, magazines), television, radio, and some forms of outdoor media. "Nontraditional" promotion includes direct marketing, sales promotion, point of sale, public relations, the Internet, and everything else you can slap a logo, slogan, or ad message on. These divisions evolved as large agencies discovered that they could make money beyond earning media commissions for "traditional" advertising. So they created MarCom units or separate interactive, direct, and sales promotion divisions. Sometimes these are set up as separate entities under the corporate umbrella of a large agency.

IMC, or Integrated Marketing Communications, unites the MarCom elements into a single campaign. IMC has become a buzzword, especially for agencies that recently set up MarCom divisions. Actually, IMC is nothing new. Smaller full-service agencies and in-house ad departments have been doing it for years under the banner of "doing whatever it takes to get the job done." With limited budgets, companies need to get the most mileage possible from their promotional dollar with a variety of tools, including advertising.

Elements of IMC can include the following:

- Trade and professional journal advertising
- Direct mail
- Conventions/trade shows
- Incentives for sales force
- Public relations/publicity
- Event marketing
- Sales promotion (contests, rebates, and so on)
- Point-of-sale displays
- Brochures and catalogs
- Sales meetings
- Trade show support
- Newsletters
- Corporate ID
- Package design
- Co-op ads
- Banner ads
- Viral marketing

- Customer relationship marketing
- Videos
- Interactive CD-ROMs
- Web pages
- Search engine marketing
- Permission marketing
- Product placement
- Movie trailers

1.10. IMC is a big part of many business-to-business campaigns. Here direct mail, collateral, premiums, and print advertising were all used to bring prospects to a trade show booth, where the real selling took place. Response rate: a remarkable 98%.

IBP (integrated brand promotion)

Like its counterpart IMC, IBP, or *i*ntegrated *b*rand *p*romotion, is another way to approach the elements of MarCom. Here the focus is on strategic brand building. Thomas O'Guinn, Chris Allen, and Richard Semenik define IBP as "the use of various promotional tools, including advertising, in a coordinated manner to build and maintain brand awareness, identity and preference."[11] Their approach focuses on coordinated efforts to build and maintain a brand.

No doubt you will encounter many other acronyms and buzzwords that all mean pretty much the same thing: marketing communications. For the sake of simplicity, we use the terms *advertising* and *MarCom* interchangeably in this text. Most of the organizational principles that apply to advertising, in its strictest definition, also apply to direct mail, the Internet, and sales promotion. We'll make distinctions in special cases. So as you read, when you see "advertising," think "marketing communications."

Convergence

As of this writing, "convergence" has become the latest buzzword for integrating the Internet with other marketing communication methods. Although in later chapters we separate promotion from the Internet, and print from direct mail, in today's blurred marketing communication environment, most of these have to work together for a complete campaign—not unlike the way integrated marketing has always functioned. Since this is primarily a book about copywriting, we need to address the specific requirements of writing for each medium rather than "converging" them into a single discussion.

Advertising's Role in the Marketing Process

If you really want to understand how advertising works as a component of the whole marketing process, get to know DAGMAR. She isn't a Danish exchange student. DAGMAR stands for "*d*efining *a*dvertising *g*oals for *m*easured *a*dvertising *r*esults."[12] The basic premise is that the effectiveness of advertising can be measured at all phases. If you can measure effectiveness, you don't need to watch the cash register to know whether your advertising is working.

WORDS OF WISDOM

"Creativity without strategy is art. Creativity with strategy is advertising."

—JEF RICHARDS[13]

The key components of DAGMAR are awareness, comprehension, conviction, and action. In addition to providing a way to quantify advertising effectiveness, DAGMAR provides a great model for the way advertising works:

- *Awareness:* How do you get viewers' and listeners' attention? They have to remember a brand or product name.

- *Comprehension:* What does the brand mean to them? Do they understand the product benefits? Can they differentiate your product from the competition? What is the present position of your brand?

- *Conviction:* Conviction is the bridge between knowing and doing. When the prospects are aware of the product and perceive a benefit or at least a difference, what do you want them to do? Ideally, you'd like them to have warm and fuzzy thoughts about your brand. You'd like them to compare your product to the competition, look for it in the store, and send for information. Depending on the type of product, this process may take seconds or months.

- *Action:* Ultimately, this means sales—even though it usually takes more than advertising to close the deal. But it can also involve several steps, such as a test-drive for a car or a meeting with a sales representative. It depends on the type of product. Trying a new brand of gum usually doesn't require much involvement. Buying a million-dollar machine tool does. One of the key lessons of DAGMAR is that advertising can be very effective, but it can only bring the potential customer to the seller. If the product doesn't meet the buyer's wants and needs or the salesperson blows the sale at the dealership, you can't blame it on the advertising.

TABLE **1.1**   **The Relationship between Strategy and Tactics**

Strategy	Tactics
Increase awareness and comprehension of new arthritis medicine in 50- to 80-year-old women from 5% to 20% in 12 months.	Four-color full-page magazine ads in *AARP*, *Arthritis Today*, and *Arthritis Self-Management*. Create Web site to discuss trends in arthritis, treatments, and results.
Expand database of potential lawn mower buyers in top 25 DMAs (designated market areas) from 50,000 to 200,000 names by January 31 next year.	Hold sweepstakes to win a free lawn mower as incentive to send in direct mail questionnaire. Promote sweepstakes on radio, TV, point of sale in stores.
Encourage 50,000 20–30-year-olds to test-drive the new Honda Element from April 1 through June 30.	Offer free backpack for test-drive. Promote with network and cable TV, spot radio, and magazine ads in *Maxim*, *Cosmopolitan*, and *Rolling Stone*.

Creative Strategy in the Marketing Mix

WORDS OF WISDOM

"Brilliant creative isn't enough. You must be creative and effective. It's a time for the strategic thinker, not just the creative rebel."

—**HELAYNE SPIVAK**[14]

The difference between strategy and tactics stumps a lot of clients and their agencies. They usually mix them up and throw in a few goals and objectives for good measure. Typically, the net result is a rather random laundry list of what they'd like to happen—about as specific and realistic as wishing for world peace. Other than drafting a mission statement by committee, listing strategy and tactics can be the most confusing and worthless task in marketing.

Don't get us wrong. A copywriter needs to follow a strategy. Otherwise, you're creating for the sake of creativity rather than solving a problem. Think of strategy development as picking a destination, such as "I want to go to Cleveland." The strategy is to make the trip. The tactics are how you get there. If I drive, which roads should I take? Should I fly? If so, which airlines have the best rates? Where will I stay? How long will I be there? You need to ask these and a bunch of other questions that deal with the specific actions you must take to get to Cleveland and back.

Another analogy comes from the military: Strategies deal with achieving objectives, like capturing a city. Tactics are the means used to achieve strategies, such as using a combination of close air support, flanking maneuvers from infantry, frontal assaults by tanks, and constant artillery bombardment.

Strategy often deals in long-term solutions, such as building brand share. Strategy is concerned with continuity, growth, and return on investment. Strategies are very specific and almost always measurable. Tactics are all about getting results quickly and effectively—for example, running a sweepstakes to boost sales in the fourth quarter. Tactics are the tools we use to achieve our goals—the strategies.

Theories, Schmeories

Looking for a single theory that explains how people process advertising? Keep looking, because no one has a one-size-fits-all solution. The search for new ways to explain why advertising makes any sense is the main justification for advanced studies in mass communication (other than being a ticket to a professorship).

Left brain/right brain/no brain

Psychologists have discovered that people have a right brain and a left brain, each with very different functions. We won't spend a lot of time dissecting brain tissue, but we can apply those findings to advertising. The left brain likes words, logic, and reasons. The right brain likes pictures, emotions, and feelings. This is all very interesting, but unless you can find a defined target audience composed of people whose heads are lopsided on either the left or right, it doesn't help you to develop an ad concept. However, it is interesting to note that the bridge that connects the left and right halves of the brain is larger in women than in men. Does this mean women do a better job of balancing emotion with logic? Uh, we won't go there.

The [your name here] creative process

Large agencies have developed their own systems for thinking about the audience, the product, and the marketplace. All of them are good, but we don't want to get into specifics about them here; if we were to recommend the Foote Cone & Belding planning grid model, for example, you'd have to unlearn it if you got a gig at Leo Burnett. However, there are a few theories worth noting. Actually, they started as theories and are now considered rock-solid facts of marketing communications. These are *positioning, brand character,* and *resonance.*

Assume the Position

Al Trout and Jack Ries revolutionized marketing in the late 1970s and early 1980s with their theory of positioning. Their book *Positioning: The Battle for Your Mind* introduced a new way of thinking about products and how they fit into the marketplace. The best definition of positioning we've found is this one from George Felton:

> Simply stated, positioning is the perception consumers have of your product, not unto itself, but relative to the competition.[15]

Like most new religions, positioning loses some of its orthodoxy over time. It seems everyone has a little different spin on what it means and how it's used. One approach is to look at it as the evolution of advertising; as Bruce Bendinger notes, "The search moves from 'within the product' (USP) to 'within the ad' (image) to 'within the prospect's mind.' That's where you create your position."[16]

The key to understanding and using positioning lies in the consumer's mind. The consumer files product considerations into two broad categories: garbage ("nothing there for me") and maybe-I'm-interested. In the second category, the consumer uses subcategories for different products, often aligning those positions with heavily promoted brand images. For example, BMWs are fast. Volvos are safe. Jeeps are rugged. And so on. So if you asked most consumers to "position" or rank those brands in various categories, you'd probably find some resistance to the idea that a BMW is as safe as a Volvo, or that a Jeep can be as fast as a BMW, or that a Volvo can be as rugged as a Jeep. All true in some cases, but not universally believed. Once a position is established, it takes a lot of effort to change it.

Before you develop the position of your client's product, you have to ask:

- What is the current position?

- What is the competitor's position?

- Where do you want to be?

- How are you going to get there? (That's strategy.)

Sometimes it's useful to describe the current and desired positions graphically. You can use any two categories for *x* and *y* coordinates. Before you begin, try to figure out where you are now. What's your position? How does that compare to the competition? Do you have any unique advantages? Does the competition have any unique advantages? Have you left any positions undefended? Start small and keep expanding your vision until you have the big picture.

Repositioning your product

If you don't like your product's position, you may want to change it. Your grandfather bought Old Spice aftershave for its manly seafaring image in print and TV. Today, 18–24-year-olds have made it a hot brand for deodorants and antiperspirants. Procter & Gamble launched splashy marketing campaigns for Old Spice High Endurance deodorants and Old Spice Red Zone antiperspirant and teamed up with video-game maker Electronic Arts to create a gaming tie-in. The hook? The football video game NCAA 2004 has a "Red Zone" theme with the tagline "When performance matters most." According to a recent article in *Business Week,* TV ads for Old Spice deodorant had the "highest return on investment of any marketing element in the past three years of Old Spice. The product now holds the number one spot in the deodorant market, with a 20% share, besting Right Guard and other underarm giants. Old Spice is also the leading aftershave brand, with 10% of the market."[17]

Rolling Stone magazine gained wide acceptance as the first mass-market counterculture publication. The Woodstock Nation grew up, cleaned up, and found that Wall Street was cooler than Haight-Ashbury. Yet they still read *Rolling Stone*. However, the magazine's advertisers were still stuck in the sixties. *RS* needed mainstream advertisers, not smoke shops and Earth Shoes. Fallon McElligott Rice (the precursor of today's Fallon) did the trick with their famous "Perception/Reality" campaign. By using icons for the perceived image of *RS* readers next to a symbol of the real readers, *RS* attracted big-bucks advertisers. This not only kept the magazine in business, it helped make it slicker and ultimately pushed it into the mainstream.

Volvo had always promoted the durability of their cars. The boxy old things just lasted forever. That's great for a few moss-covered college professors, but most people don't associate car ownership with tenure. Since Volvos were not going to win any styling awards, the company wisely chose to reposition the cars as safer than the competition. They produced a long-running campaign of well-crafted, intelligent ads that effectively changed the brand image. Now when someone says "safe car," you think Volvo.

Repositioning the competition

You can also try to change the consumer's perception of the competition through repositioning. One way is to describe the competition's products in a different

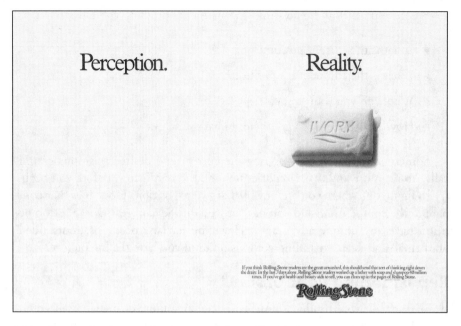

1.11. Who says business-to-business can't be cool? This famous trade campaign won a ton of awards and, more important, generated a ton of new advertisers for *Rolling Stone*. The copy explains that *Rolling Stone* readers really aren't all part of the "great unwashed" generation.

way—not necessarily in a negative light, but using different connotations. For example, where the word *compact* might be positive, *tiny* is less desirable. However, you have to do this legally. In the early days of advertising, Schlitz beer said they used "live steam" to clean their bottles. This implied that their product was cleaner and healthier. Without saying it, the ads also positioned Schlitz's competition as careless slobs who gave their customers dirty bottles. The fact was, all brewers steam cleaned their bottles. While they were the only ones that talked about it, Schlitz offered no real competitive advantage, and they were forced to cease this deceptive repositioning. The beer wars were renewed in 2004, when Budweiser positioned Miller as a "South African" brand.

WORDS OF WISDOM

"Good advertising does not just circulate information. It penetrates the public mind with desires and belief."

—LEO BURNETT[18]

Positioning Redux

Although Trout and Ries opened a lot of minds to a new way of thinking, many critics have taken issue with their premise that creativity makes no difference. Sometimes it's the only difference. Creativity can create the product's position or reposition the product.

Another caveat is that Trout and Ries analyzed successful campaigns from the past and made them fit their theory. Did the 7-Up creative team really think about positioning when they launched the "UnCola" campaign, or did they just want to do great advertising? Often the creative is the only thing that makes a brand memorable. Remembering a brand's position usually happens over time.

Jumping on the Brand Wagon

It has become fashionable to focus on brands—brand character, brand image, brand values, brand equity, brand management, integrated brand promotion, brand blah, blah blah. Why the obsession with brands? Some people theorize that the proliferation of ad messages makes it impossible for consumers to remember detailed product information. People are lucky to remember a few select brand names. In addition, some observers see a shift from tangible things to information, making the image of a brand more important than the product itself. Another explanation is that advertisers have always stressed brand names, only now we're a lot more sophisticated in managing brand image. Still others say the current focus on the brand is all part of a new crop of marketing buzzwords, like *po-mo, CRM,* and *click-through rate.*

WAR STORY:

SAVING THE SWOOSH

A few years ago, while conducting some interviews at Nike, I came across a very interesting anecdote—one that perfectly expresses the value of a brand and the power of an icon. The Nike swoosh, in many ways, embodies the "Just do it" spirit—the essence of the Nike brand. During the mid- to late 1990s, when Nike was struggling with labor issues, they significantly reduced the use of the swoosh in their advertising. During this same period, signs began to appear in the common corporate spaces at Nike, such as conference rooms. The signs read, "Protect the Swoosh." Surely this was a concerted effort to protect the icon that had come to define the brand. Clearly, the equity of the Nike brand was, and still is, rooted in the swoosh.

—Jean Grow

Before you start supporting a brand, you first have to understand what a brand is and what it does. Authors on advertising have their own ideas about brands, and they're all good. They can be summarized into two main thoughts:

- *What it is:* A brand is shorthand for all of a product's attributes, good or bad.

- *What it does:* A brand conveys a product's personality, which reflects on the people who buy the product.

Luke Sullivan expands those thoughts when he says, "A brand isn't just a name on the box. It isn't the thing in the box either. A brand is the sum total of all the emotions, thoughts, images, history, possibilities and gossip that exist in the marketplace about a certain company."[19]

If you think he's exaggerating a bit, consider the fact that brands (at least those with positive images) are assets to their companies, sometimes worth billions of dollars. Some companies protect their brands like a momma bear guarding her cubs. Put yellow arches on a taco stand or an unlicensed Harley logo on a T-shirt and you'll quickly find out how sharp those claws can be.

WORDS OF WISDOM

"I believe brands have karma. If brand awareness was once a standard measure of brand strength, and brand resonance and relevance are the new yardsticks, I suspect that brand karma will one day become the ultimate definition of brand strength. Hard to measure, but dangerous to ignore."

—SCOTT BEDBURY[20]

Companies spend millions to establish and nurture brand images. Brand image advertising (and promotion) sells the personality, the mystique, the aura surrounding or emanating from the product, not the product itself. Think of the old cliché, Sell the sizzle, not the steak.

Every product has a brand image. Some are stronger than others. Think of the brand images or brand characters of some well-known products. How does the brand image of BMW differ from the brand image of Cadillac or Lexus? All these cars cost about the same, but they all have different characters, as do their customers. How did Apple differentiate itself from IBM? Not as a technically superior and more expensive computer, but rather as one with an easy-to-use operating system favored by right-brain types. IBM told people to "Think." Apple said, "Think Different."

Luke Sullivan states, "Most of the time we're talking about going into a customer's brain and tacking one adjective onto a client's brand. That's all. DeWalt tools are tough. Apple computers are different. Volvos are safe. Porsches are fast. Jeeps are rugged. Boom. Where's the rocket science here?"[21] Think about that "one adjective" for the brands on the next page.

You may think of more than one adjective, but focus on the first thing that comes to mind. Now think about these brands' competitors and the one adjective each inspires. Are the adjectives different? If not, then the brands on the following page have not "won the battle for your mind."

1.12. This ad from Mexico proves that "Just do it" works in any language, and you don't even have to say it. The ubiquitous swoosh precludes the need for any other brand support. The visual puzzle may take a few microseconds longer to process in the brain, but once that "aha!" moment comes, you remember it.

1.13.

1.14.

1.15.

1.16.

1.17.

Mercedes-Benz

1.18.

1.19. Rather than show a new storefront or company logo, L. L. Bean used their products to represent the brand, tying them in beautifully with a Washington, D.C., icon. They could have also put tents on the White House lawn, a flannel shirt on the Washington Monument—you get the idea. Once they found the visual connection, the campaign strategy became a lot easier to execute.

To support a brand's image, advertisers use simple, unique, and easily recognized visuals. Over time, the brand (and all its attributes, good and bad) comes to consumers' minds whenever they catch even a glimpse of these visuals. Quick, name that brand:

1.20.

1.21.

1.22.

1.23.

1.24.

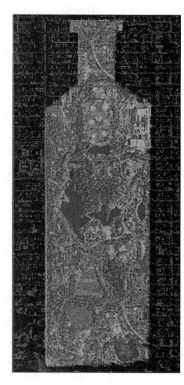

1.25.

FROM THE BEAN TO THE EXPERIENCE: HOW STARBUCKS BECAME A MEGABRAND

Scott Bedbury was instrumental in helping Starbucks grow from a local coffee bean merchant to a global brand. This is what is he told us about the transformation:

Originally, Starbucks would have spent their marketing money on coffee—the bean. We shifted that to the experience. The experience goes way beyond the cup. So originally the Starbucks story was all about roasting the beans. The big moment for me came when I was hiking up the side of this volcano in East Java with Dave Olsen (no relation to Mrs. Olsen of Folgers). Dave and I are out there and it's predawn in this amazing place and I say to Dave, "What do you say will be the biggest opportunity for us?" Now remember, this guy lives for coffee. He's been with Starbucks 15 years and he literally worships the beans. He turns to me and says, "Everything matters. It's not just about coffee. It's a whole story about the place, the store, the people, the employees, the sound, the music—it's everything." It was a turning point in the collective mind of management. There was something much richer here than just the coffee cherry. "Let's really pull the stops and make the most amazing experience possible." After this only half went to the beans. The other half went to experience.

Resonance: Did You Just Feel Something?

When you achieve resonance, your external message connects with internal values and feelings. As Tony Schwartz notes, "Resonance takes place when the stimuli put into our communication evoke meaning in a listener or viewer . . . the meaning of our communication is what a listener or viewer gets out of his experience with the communicator's stimuli."[22]

Resonance requires a connection with feelings that are inside the consumer's mind. You don't have to put in a new emotion, just find a way to tap what's already there. In other words, to get your idea to resonate in the consumer's mind, you must trigger some internal experience with your communication and connect that with your message. This will strengthen awareness, begin building comprehension, and lead to conviction and possibly action. How's that for connecting multiple streams of psychobabble?

Want an even simpler explanation?

$$1 + 1 = 3.$$

That is, your message + internal experience = resonance, which is greater than the sum of its two parts.

Writing From the Consumer's Point of View

If you remember nothing else from this chapter, remember this:

People do not buy things. They buy satisfaction of their wants and needs.

You may have studied Maslow's theory of the hierarchy of needs, which includes the following:

- Biological needs (the needs for food, water, shelter)
- Need for belongingness and love (the need to be esteemed by others)
- Need for self-actualization (the need to realize one's full potential)

This model is often depicted as a pyramid, with the most basic needs at the bottom and progressing to the most complex and sophisticated at the top. According to Maslow, an individual's needs must be met at each level before he or she can progress to the next level. Maslow considered less than 1% of the population to be truly self-actualized.[24]

Communication theorists have expanded on Maslow's list, and today some texts list more than 30 needs. To simplify matters, we can probably sum up human wants and needs from a marketing communication standpoint as follows:

- Comfort (avoid pain and discomfort, convenience)
- Security (physical and financial)
- Stimulation (aesthetic, physical)
- Affiliation (belonging)
- Fulfillment (self-satisfaction, status)

Daniel Starch, one of the pioneers of advertising testing, noted in the 1920s:

The business of the advertiser or the seller is not to create fundamentally new desires. That is not necessary and really cannot be done. Man already has certain desires present from birth, which are a part of his fundamental make-up. All that a seller can do is to direct these desires in certain directions, or stimulate them to action, or show by what new ways an old desire may be satisfied.[25]

You have to discover the wants and needs of the people you want to buy your product. Then you have to communicate with them in a way that convinces them your brand can satisfy those wants and needs. One of the best explanations of a consumer's wants and needs can be found in this simple declarative sentence:

Don't tell me about your grass seed, talk to me about my lawn.

Think about that. People aren't really looking for seed. They need a play area for their kids. They want a calm green space for relaxing or a yard the neighbors will envy. Security. Comfort. Fulfillment. Wants and needs. A $50 Timex will probably tell the time just as well as a $3,000 Rolex. (Well, close enough for most folks.) So what wants and needs does the Rolex buyer satisfy by spending 600% more? Hint: It's really not about telling time.

Here's an exercise in thinking about wants and needs versus things:

WORDS OF WISDOM

"If you can't turn yourself into your customer, you probably shouldn't be in the ad writing business at all."

—LEO BURNETT[26]

Don't sell me insurance, talk to me about _____.

Don't sell me beer, show me _____.

Don't sell me a car, tell me about _____.

Don't sell me a soft drink, make me think about _____.

Don't sell me a house, talk to me about _____.

Don't sell me perfume, make me feel _____.

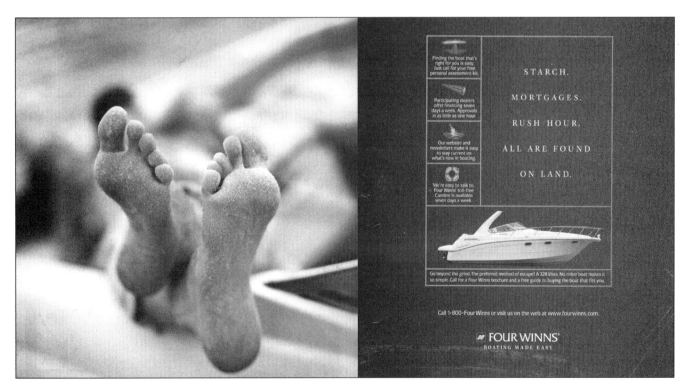

1.26. The headline reads, "Starch. Mortgages. Rush Hour. Are all found on land." Boating isn't about transportation. It's about kicking back and relaxing on the water. So rather than show a glamour shot of the boat, Four Winns chose to evoke a feeling of relaxation.

Sources of Information (Don't Just Take Our Word for It)

Textbooks can provide only so much information. As current as we try to make this text, we're bound to miss some really important bit of information that comes out just after it goes to press. But you don't have to. Throughout this volume, we promote some very good books that are great sources of information. Beyond that, you have access to weekly and monthly publications about advertising and creativity. Then there's the Internet—an incredible resource you can use to see student advertising, learn about marketing trends, view classic ads, download TV commercials, and check out the latest award winners. Dozens of new sites seem to pop up every month. Check them out, and bookmark the ones you find helpful.

Here is a list of some useful and interesting periodicals, Web sites, and books to get you started:

Periodicals

- *Advertising Age*
- *Advertising Age Creativity*
- *AdWeek*
- *Archive*
- *BrandWeek*
- *CMYK Magazine*
- *Communication Arts*
- *One: A Magazine*

Books

- *A Big Life (in Advertising),* by Mary Wells Lawrence
- *Defining Advertising Goals for Measured Advertising Results,* by Russell Colley

1.27. "Talk to me about my lawn." This ad from Scott's is not exactly about grass seed, but it's more than a load of fertilizer. The first part of the copy is almost poetry: *"Green is part of the dream. It gives kids the courage to leap. Cushions their falls. Softens the edges of our lives. Welcomes our visitors with open arms. Green says we're committed to something. Something the whole neighborhood believes in. Something good. Something the world, even on its best days, could use more of."*

1.28.

Source: Illustration by Dan Augustine.

- *Eating the Big Fish: How Challenger Brands Can Compete against the Brand Leaders,* by Adam Morgan
- *Truth, Lies and Advertising: The Art of Account Planning,* by Jon Steel
- *Soap, Sex and Cigarettes: A Cultural History of American Advertising,* by Julian Sivulka
- *The Art of Writing Advertising: Conversations with Masters of the Craft: William Bernbach, George Gribbin, David Ogilvy, Leo Burnett, Rosser Reeves,* by Denis Higgins
- *A New Brand World: 8 Principles for Achieving Brand Leadership in the 21st Century,* by Scott Bedbury
- *The Do-It-Yourself Lobotomy: Open Your Mind to Greater Creative Thinking,* by Tom Monahan
- *Ogilvy on Advertising,* by David Ogilvy

General Advertising Web Sites

- *Advertising Age* magazine: adage.com
- adflip (archive of classic print ads): adflip.com
- *AdForum* magazine: adforum.com
- *AdWeek* magazine: adweek.com
- *BrandWeek* magazine: brandweek.com
- *CMYK Magazine:* cmyk.com
- CommercialArts: comarts.com

Advertising Awards Web Sites

- International ANDY Awards: andyawards.com
- Cannes Lions International Advertising Festival: canneslions.com

- Clio Awards: clioawards.com
- D&AD Awards (U.K.): dandad.org/awards
- Athena Awards (newspapers): athenaawards.com
- Radio-Mercury Awards: radiomercuryawards.com

University and Portfolio School Web Sites

- Adcenter, Virginia Commonwealth University: adcenter.vcu.edu
- Texas Advertising, University of Texas at Austin: advertising.utexas.edu
- Brainco: The Minneapolis School of Advertising, Designing, & Interactive Studies: braincomsa.com
- The Creative Circus: creativecircus.com
- Portfolios.com: The Online Source for Creative Talent: portfolios.com
- Portfolio Center: portfoliocenter.com

Who's Who?

In this and future chapters, you'll see some "Words of Wisdom" floating around. Who are the wise guys and gals we quote? At the ends of most chapters we provide some very brief biographical sketches on some of the best-known voices in advertising as well as other innovators featured in the "Words of Wisdom" and "War Stories."

Scott Bedbury—Scott Bedbury helped make Nike and Starbucks two of the most successful brand stories of all time. Now one of the world's most sought-after brand consultants and speakers, Bedbury brings to his clients and audiences brand development practices that can help any enterprise strengthen its business. He contends that a powerful brand has to transcend the features of a product and create a personal and lasting relationship with consumers. Bedbury wrote the modern guide to brand strategy, *A New Brand World: 8 Principles for Achieving Brand Leadership in the 21st Century.*

Leo Burnett—Founder of the agency that still bears his name, Leo Burnett established a new creative style of advertising along with many memorable characters still working today, including Tony the Tiger, the Jolly Green Giant, the Keebler Elves, the Marlboro Man, and the Pillsbury Doughboy. Burnett believed that creativity makes an advertisement effective, but at the same time, the creativity requires believability.

Jerry Della Femina—Founder of Della Femina Travisano & Partners, Jerry Della Femina is one of the most creative and irreverent talents in the business. He worked on such accounts as Isuzu (Joe Isuzu), Meow Mix (singing cat), Beck's Beer, Blue Nun Wine, Chemical Bank, Dow Brands (Fingerman), and Pan Am. He sold his agency, became a successful restaurant owner, and then formed a new agency that later merged with Ketchum. He wrote *From Those Wonderful Folks Who Gave You Pearl Harbor* and tons of award-winning, hard-selling ads.

Jef Richards—A professor of advertising at the University of Texas, Jef Richards is a very innovative and creative educator who concentrates on advertising law and regulation. He has also written extensively about visual communication, advertising ethics, new technologies, and consumer comprehension/belief of marketing claims.

Notes

[1] Quote from University of Texas at Austin, Department of Advertising, http://advertising.utexas.edu/research/quotes (accessed May 19, 2005).

[2] Jerry Della Femina, *From Those Wonderful Folks Who Gave You Pearl Harbor: Front-Line Dispatches from the Advertising War* (New York: Pocket Books, 1971), 256.

[3] Quoted in Luke Sullivan, *Hey Whipple, Squeeze This: A Guide to Creating Great Ads* (New York: John Wiley, 1998), 17.

[4] Wayne Weitten, *Psychology Themes and Variations* (Belmont, CA: Thomson Wadsworth, 2005), 255–56.

[5] See the AAAA Web site at http://www.aaaa.org.

[6] Quote from Born to Motivate Web site, http://www.borntomotivate.com/FamousQuote_CarlAlly.html (accessed May 19, 2005).

[7] Sullivan, *Hey Whipple,* 101.

[8] Quote in Angela Partington, ed., *The Oxford Dictionary of Quotations* (New York: Oxford University Press, 1992), 501.

[9] Quote in Michael Jackman, ed., *Crown's Book of Political Quotations* (New York: Crown, 1982), 2.

[10] Quote from University of Texas at Austin, Department of Advertising, http://advertising.utexas.edu/research/quotes/Q100.html#Advis (accessed May 19, 2005).

[11] Thomas O'Guinn, Chris Allen, and Richard Semenik, *Advertising and Integrated Brand Promotion* (Mason, OH: Thomson, 2002), 13.

[12] See Russell Colley, *Defining Advertising Goals for Measured Advertising Results* (New York: Association of National Advertisers, 1969), 5.

[13] Quote from University of Texas at Austin, Department of Advertising, http://advertising.utexas.edu/research/quotes/index.asp (accessed May 19, 2005).

[14] Quote from the Clio Awards Web site, http://www.clioawards.com/html/wsj/spivak.html (accessed January 10, 2005).

[15] George Felton, *Advertising: Concept and Copy* (Englewood Cliffs, NJ: Prentice Hall, 1993), 60; see also Al Trout and Jack Ries, *Positioning: The Battle for Your Mind* (New York: McGraw-Hill, 1981; repr. 2001).

[16] Bruce Bendinger, *The Copy Workshop Workbook* (Chicago: Copy Workshop, 2002), 51.

[17] Pallavi Gogoi, "Old Brands, Renewed Appeal," *BusinessWeek Online,* December 21, 2004, http://www.businessweek.com/bwdaily/dnflash/dec2004/nf20041221_6747_db016.htm (accessed May 19, 2005).

[18] Leo Burnett, *100 LEO's: Wit and Wisdom from Leo Burnett* (Chicago: NTC Business Press, 1995), 47.

[19] Sullivan, *Hey Whipple,* 28.

[20] Scott Bedbury, *A New Brand World: 8 Principles for Achieving Brand Leadership in the 21st Century* (New York: Viking, 2002), 20.

[21] Sullivan, *Hey Whipple,* 28.

[22] Bendinger, *The Copy Workshop Workbook,* 105.

[23] Scott Bedbury, interview by authors, December 3, 2004.

[24] See "Maslow, Abraham Harold," in *Microsoft Encarta Online Encyclopedia,* 2005, http://www.encarta.com (accessed May 19, 2005).

[25] Daniel Starch, *Principles of Advertising* (Chicago: A. W. Shaw, 1923), 255.

[26] Burnett, *100 LEO's,* 23.

Getting Started

Congratulations! Your agency was invited to pitch the Winslow Widget account. Your job is to develop a creative strategy and build a marketing communication campaign that will knock the socks off the Winslow management. You really need this account, because if you don't win, half of your agency will be laid off, including you. Right now, you know nothing about the company, its products, its customers, its competition, or its market. By the way, you've got two weeks until the presentation. Once again, congratulations!

The above scenario happens every day somewhere. The good news is you're invited to the dance. But there are very few "gimmes" when it comes to new business, and if you're lucky enough to win an account, the euphoria quickly dissolves into the daily grind of keeping the business.

Solving the Client's Problem

If you were working on the Winslow Widget account, where would *you* start? The first thing to do is ask, "What's their problem?" Every client has a problem. Otherwise they wouldn't need to promote their products. Some clients state the problem as a broad objective, such as "Sell more Widgets in the next fiscal year." That's not the problem. The problem is: What's going to make it difficult to sell more Widgets and how can we overcome those difficulties? The client may tell you, but these may not be the only problems. An even more challenging situation emerges when the client can't even identify the problem.

WAR STORY:

A Curiously Strong Approach (Just Don't Tell the Boss)

Andrew Meyer had a dream assignment—working on Leo Burnett's incredibly successful Altoids account. However, sometimes it's hard to convince others in the agency that you can make a good thing even better. Here's his solution to solving a client's problem (that the agency management didn't know existed):

When I began working on the Altoids campaign, the original print and outdoor work had already been established as a perennially award-winning campaign. But as an outsider, it seemed apparent to me that there was a missed opportunity to bring the brand into other media. My partner, Art Director Noel Haan, agreed. Creative management at the time, however, was skeptical. The net result: We had no money, and no permission from the powers that be to pursue new work along these lines. Of course, that didn't stop us. Noel and I secretly wrote scripts and lined up a director and production company willing to foot the bill and shoot spec film for us. Management "didn't want to know a thing about it"—until we surprised our client with a finished educational film parody campaign for Altoids Sours. And they loved it. They gave us more money to create more and better spots, and ran them on TV, the Web, and cinema. Sometimes, risk does equal reward.

Get the Facts

The first step is gathering and organizing information. You have to answer the basic questions listed in Table 2.1. Notice that these creative development questions include some of the basic questions of journalism, such as who, what, and why. Where and when are media questions, the answers to which may also influence your creative strategy. For example, an ad in the *Sports Illustrated* swimsuit edition may inspire a look that is far different from that of an ad in the regular edition.

Where to look for information

Research can be divided into two basic categories: *primary*, where you gather the facts directly, and *secondary*, where you assemble research done by others. We'll look at secondary research first, because that's usually more accessible.

TABLE 2.1   **Getting the Facts**

Marketing Task	What It Means
Define the target audience.	Who are we talking to?
Identify features and benefits.	What makes this product better?
Clarify the current position.	What do people think about the product?
Align wants and needs with the product.	Why should people buy it?
Determine the call to action.	What do we want people to do?

Secondary Research

You can find a wealth of information about markets, products, and consumers. A lot of it is available for free on the Internet. However, most of the really good stuff comes from subscription services. Most university libraries offer the same information that costs companies thousands of dollars, although it is usually slightly out-of-date. Buying current data is often prohibitively expensive.

One of the most commonly used sources is Simmons, a multimedia research company specializing in marketing information. The Simmons database encompasses more than 8,000 brands, 400 product categories, all media venues, and the most detailed lifestyle descriptions currently available. Simmons has evolved into a multimedia research company with information on adults, teens, kids, and Hispanic consumers.[3]

WORDS OF WISDOM

"Our job is to bring dead facts to life."

—**WILLIAM BERNBACH**[2]

A quick search on the Internet will reveal hundreds of other marketing research firms. One organization that provides some great insight into consumer behavior is SRI and its VALS marketing and consulting tool. VALS categorizes consumers based on their lifestyles and income or "motivation" and "resources" (for more information, visit the SRI Web site at sric-bi.com/VALS).

Once you have identified your target market, you can start developing messages that appeal to that segment. While VALS is extremely helpful for defining a target market, never forget that you are writing to an individual, not a segment.

You can also find a lot of information on various government agency Web sites. For starters, visit FirstGov, the U.S. government's "official Web portal" (firstgov.gov) and use its search engine to find the information you need.

In addition, many clients belong to trade organizations that provide their members with lots of great market information. Ask the client to share that with you. You might also find some useful secondary research on the Web sites of the client's competition.

Primary Research

When primary research is mentioned, most people think of formal types of research, such as focus groups and mail surveys, but this research can also be very informal and personal. The following are just a few ways of conducting primary research:

- Visit a store and see how your product is displayed. Check out the competitive products. How does the shelf appeal of your product compare?

- Talk to the salespeople, retailers, and others who sell your product. What do they tell customers about it? Where do they place the product in the marketplace?

- Sometimes it's helpful to take a factory tour. However, you should be aware that you'll usually get the view of the manufacturer instead of the consumer. Take the tour, but also see where and how the product is used.

- Review ads and other promotional materials for your product. Check out the competition. Study their claims. Where are they weaker or stronger compared to your product?

- Read the publications your media department is considering. Watch the TV shows they recommend.

- Talk to the people who buy your product. Why did they buy it? Would they buy it again? If not, why not?

- Talk to people who considered buying your product but did not. Why not? What would make them change their minds?

You can find people to interview in a number of places—stores, malls, sporting events, trade shows, basically anywhere members of your target audience may gather.

You can conduct more formal research with focus groups of members of the target audience. These groups, moderated by professionals, can explore attitudes and opinions in depth.

Other types of research might include mass mailings of questionnaires and telephone surveys.

Interpreting research findings

Funny thing about research—if it confirms the client's opinions, it really wasn't needed; if it contradicts the client's opinions, it's flawed. While the "facts" may be gathered and presented objectively, the interpretation is highly subjective.

WORDS OF WISDOM

"The overquantification of business is removing any sense of personal accountability for mistakes. It's much easier to blame a focus group in Des Moines for approving an unremarkable or boring commercial than to take personal accountability."

—SCOTT BEDBURY[4]

Sometimes research reveals information about something you're not even measuring. For example, a survey for a business-to-business client revealed a strong negative opinion of the brand in the Southeast. Why did they love the brand in Ohio but hate it in Georgia? The client considered running some image ads in the South to build a more favorable opinion. Further investigation revealed that the problem was not with the brand, but with the person selling it. In this case, no amount of brilliant advertising could solve the problem. A quick realignment of the sales force did.

Another observation we can offer based on our years of gathering information and testing concepts: Clients focus on verbatim comments rather than numbers. They pay attention to a few video interviews rather than a mountain of statistics. Clients, like consumers, want to see and hear real people. They may analyze all the facts and figures, but a few memorable quotes usually help them form opinions. Knowing how clients respond to research can put the agency in the driver's seat.

Who is the target audience?

Who are you talking to? Your client may tell you. Your account planner should tell you. Your secondary and primary research will tell you. If you're lucky, the marketing objectives will be very specific, such as 35–65-year-old married men, living in the top 10 markets, earning $100,000 or more. Usually, though, the client tells the creative team about the product. Period. It's up to the agency to find out who is most likely to buy it and why. Unless you know who's buying the product and why, your creative strategy will be a classic example of "ready-fire-aim" planning. You need to find out:

- Who's buying the product now and why?
- Who is not buying the product and why not?

Outside/in the product

The object of your effort may not be a tangible product at all. It may be something you can't hold in your hand, like the local bus company, an art museum, or a government agency. It may be about corporate image—a campaign that promotes the integrity or strength of a company, but doesn't highlight products. Good examples are utility and telephone companies and multinational megafirms like General Electric. You could also develop creative for an organization such as the American Cancer Society or Amnesty International. For the sake of simplicity, we will call the object of promotion *the product* no matter what it may be.

From the Inside: Features

Products have characteristics and personality traits, just like people. By themselves, these features are not good or bad. They're just there. That's why listing product features without putting them in the context of a benefit to the customer usually wastes time and space. Sometimes the benefit is so obvious the reader or viewer will make an instant connection. But other times, writers just include lists of features and hope someone will figure out why they're important. On a luxury car, for example, features can be technical, such as a GPS navigation system; functional, such as side curtain air bags; or aesthetic, such as

2.1. This ad for Reebok is not selling mall walking shoes to seniors. While it resonated with the intended market in *Slam* magazine when it was introduced, ideas about who's "Fabulous" and "Classic" change almost daily.

TABLE 2.2 The Relationship between Features and Benefits

Feature	Benefit	Wants and Needs
Contains fluoride	Prevents tooth decay	Saves money, saves time
Automatic shutoff	Shuts off unit if you forget	Safety, saves money, convenience
Electronic ignition	Easier starts in cold weather	Convenience
Slow release of nutrients	Greener plants, more flowers	Aesthetically pleasing, convenient

brushed aluminum console trim. In most cases, the more technical and abstract the feature, the greater the need to tie it to a benefit to the consumer.

From the Outside: Benefits

Not all products have features you can promote, but all have benefits. A benefit leads to the satisfaction of a consumer's wants and needs. "Cool, crisp taste" is a benefit (it quenches thirst and tastes good). "Firm, smooth ride" is a benefit (it pleases the senses and gives peace of mind). "Kills 99.9% of household germs" is a benefit (you're protecting your family).

WORDS OF WISDOM

"Provide a benefit . . . you're not making wallpaper; you're making advertising."

—PHIL DUSENBERRY[5]

Anyone can write a feature ad. All you need is a spec list. As a writer, you have to translate those features into benefits that resonate within the customer. Sometime it's as simple as listing a feature and lining up a benefit. That's the old FAB (*features-advantages-benefits*) approach used for years in industrial brochures. However, if you want to blast off from Planet Schlock, you'll think of more subtle and clever ways to promote the benefits.

As we'll discuss shortly, you should think in terms of an overriding benefit. Remember the adjective you need to tack onto the brand name. If that adjective is positive, such as *economical, stylish, effective, safe,* or *powerful,* you've established an overall benefit.

Features and Benefits: Know the Difference

Beginning writers have a hard time separating features from benefits. Too many times their ads include features and benefits lumped together in a disjointed stream of consciousness. The examples in Table 2.2 show how features lead to the benefits, which lead to satisfaction of wants and needs.

Assembling the Facts

You've gathered a lot of information. Now it's time to organize it into something you can use. Below we describe three basic ways to organize this information: the copy platform, the creative brief, and the consumer profile.

Copy platform

The copy platform is also known by several other names, including the *creative strategy statement.* It can be as simple or as detailed as you like. No matter what you call it and how complicated it can be, a good copy platform should cover the product's features/benefits, competitive advantages/weaknesses, information about the target audience, the tone of the message, and a simple, overriding statement about the product. We call the last of these the *One Thing.* It could also be called the *central truth,* the *unique selling proposition* (more on this later), the *big idea,* or the *positioning statement.*

In Chapter 1, we discussed attaching an adjective to a brand. The best way to develop that connection is to finish this sentence:

"If you could say just *One Thing* about this product, it would be _____."

It's not an easy sentence to complete. When we begin working with new clients, we sometimes ask them to complete that statement. You'd be surprised how many times they struggle with their answers. The most common response is, "Gee. Nobody really asked that before. It's really so many things. I can't think of just one." Then they provide a laundry list of features. No wonder they needed a new agency!

You'll find an example of a copy platform in the appendix to this volume. The example is a composite of several forms used by different agencies. Each firm has its own way to organize the information in a copy platform, but the format in our example does a pretty good job most of the time.

To summarize, you need a copy platform for the following reasons:

- *Provide a framework for your ad:* In the copy platform you have all the basic facts about the target, the product, the competition, and the marketplace. If you have some blank lines, you know you need more information.

- *Identify the One Thing that's most important:* You could include a position statement. Or the single adjective to attach to the brand. Or you could write a long sentence that describes what you want the consumer to believe about this product.

- *Support that One Thing with believable information:* You could list features and benefits that support product claims. In the case of a copy-free ad, only the visual supports that overriding image of the product.

- *Connect people with the product:* In your copy platform you should ask, What do you want the reader/viewer/listener to do? What is the desired "conviction and action" step? Do you want the reader/viewer/listener to take a test-drive? Ask for more information? Visit a Web site? Or do nothing?

WORDS OF WISDOM

"Our best work has always begun with a marketing solution, not a creative solution. The ads flowed from the strategy, not the strategy from the ads."

—JAY CHIAT[6]

- *Organize the client's thoughts:* A good copy platform is a collaborative effort between client and agency. The client can provide a lot of information, and together you can clarify and prioritize it. This should not be done by a large committee—at least not by a committee larger than one or two people per client and agency. When the copy platform is completed, both the agency and the client have the same road map for creative strategy.

- *Justify your creative decisions:* If the client has signed off on the copy platform, he or she will be less likely to criticize your creative efforts if you can prove you're on strategy. If the client says you're off target, you can ask where and why, based on your collaboration on the copy platform.

Creative brief

A creative brief may be prepared from a copy platform or directly from the assembled information. Compared with the copy platform, the creative brief describes a more linear progression, from where you are to where you want to be and how you will get there. The strategy is more clearly defined in the creative brief than in most copy platforms. One of the best creative brief formats we've seen is the one used by Virginia Commonwealth University's Adcenter. The

Sample Creative Brief

The following is a sample creative brief written by a student for Q-Tips:

What do we want to accomplish?

The main objective of my campaign will be to introduce Q-Tips Cotton Swabs to the next generation of adults, showing them the many uses as well as the quality that distinguishes Q-Tips Cotton Swabs over the generic competition.

Who are we talking to?

We are speaking to people who value a good product and want the best. More importantly, we are targeting the emerging twenty-something crowd to sway their future buying habits.

What do they think now?

The majority of our new audience is indifferent to Q-Tips Cotton Swabs. They consider this a very menial purchase and usually pick the cheapest package on the rack. They have always depended on others to pick up this item, so this will be a brand-new purchase for them.

What do we want them to think?

We want to instill a brand image into their minds, when they walk into a grocery store for personal care products; we want them to think Q-Tips. We want them to pass over the generic products and choose Q-Tips because Q-Tips are a personal product as well as a practical one.

Why should they think this?

Because Q-Tips will be presented in a very edgy and fun way, we will be able to connect to our audience. This will carry over to the point of purchase and influence their buying habits. We want them to realize the importance of taking care of themselves with the highest quality of cotton swabs.

What is our message?

Q-Tips Cotton Swabs are a personal item with practical applications.

questions are very simple, but if you answer them correctly, you've got just about everything you need to know to start concepting an ad:

- What do we want to accomplish? (objective)
- Who are we talking to? (target audience)
- What do they think now? (current position)
- What do we want them to think? (reinforce position or reposition)
- Why should they think this? (features/benefits)
- What is our message? (How do we say it and show it—what is the One Thing?)

Consumer profile

The consumer profile takes the copy platform and creative brief a step farther by putting a human face on the target audience. Think of journalism's "five Ws" in terms of the consumers: Who are they? What are their wants and needs, their buying intentions, their attitudes toward the product and competitors? What do they do for a living? What are their hobbies? Where do they live and work, and how does that affect their buying patterns? When are they planning to buy? When do they watch TV or use other types of media? Why should they consider your product or a competitor's?

Meet Maria

Maria Sanchez is a modern 35-year-old working mom with a husband and two children, ages 5 and 8. She graduated from the University of Illinois with a degree in management, which helped her get a job in the human resource department of a large insurance company in Chicago. She has steadily advanced to become assistant department manager. She earns $65,000 and expects to continue moving up the corporate ladder. Her husband, Carlos, is a sales representative for a large manufacturing firm. His income varies greatly from year to year, so Maria's large and stable income is extremely important to their family.

In her spare time, Maria likes to ride her bicycle, play tennis, and shop. She and Carlos enjoy traveling, with and without the kids. They try to set aside at least one weekend a month as "date night" to recharge their marriage.

After work and dinner at home with the family, Maria usually reads the mail and watches her favorite TV programs—*Survivor, Will & Grace,* and *Law & Order.* She rarely has time to read the newspaper, except on weekends, when she relaxes with the Sunday *Chicago Tribune.* Maria and Carlos subscribe to *Time, Chicago,* and *Midwest Living,* but they seldom read every issue.

Maria and Carlos live in a four-bedroom home in Hoffman Estates, which is a 45-minute commute one-way (when traffic is moving). Maria loves her job, but the stresses of caring for a family, commuting, and the usual pressures of a human resources department can sometimes trigger a migraine headache. With her busy schedule, Maria can't take time off from work and family when she has a migraine. The increased frequency of her migraines creates even more stress, but she doesn't have time to visit a doctor or make an extra trip to the pharmacy.

Allergy Season?   Allegra Season!

Seasonal allergies can make you feel miserable. Only once-daily Allegra 180 mg tablets have fexofenadine for long lasting, non-drowsy allergy relief, so you can feel more like yourself again. For people 12 and older. Side effects with Allegra 180mg are low and may include headache, upper respiratory tract infection and back pain. Please see additional important information on the next page. 1-800-ALLEGRA www.allegra.com Call your doctor or pharmacist now for more information.

Enjoy your world™

2.2. Get to know the person to whom you're writing. Instead of telling him about allergy medicine, show him what he'd rather be doing without allergy symptoms.

Based on the demographic, psychographic, lifestyles and values, and other research, a consumer profile puts some flesh on the bare bones of the copy platform. You might consider summarizing the demographics in the first paragraph of your consumer profile and describing the psychographics in the second paragraph, while you weave the lifestyles and values information through the whole profile.

The example of a consumer profile on page 43 was written by a student to describe the ideal prospect for Excedrin Migraine.

From this profile we know that an advertiser can reach Maria through radio (drive time), billboards (along her commute), direct mail, television, and, in a more limited way, newspapers and magazines. The approach must be intelligent (she's smart and successful) and to the point (she doesn't have a lot of spare time). The benefit of a nonprescription remedy without a doctor's visit may be the main selling point.

In the end, you have to use judgment. The ad will not write itself based on a compilation of facts. Sometimes a great creative idea stems from a minor benefit and blooms into a powerful image that drives a whole campaign. Our advice: Get the facts and use them, but don't be a slave to data.

WORDS OF WISDOM

"You must make the product interesting, not just make the ad different. And that's what many of the copywriters in the U.S. today don't yet understand."

—ROSSER REEVES[8]

So what?

When you see a feature or even a rather vague benefit, be sure to ask, So what? What does that feature do for the consumer? Keep asking "so what?" until you get to the benefit that satisfies a basic want or need. Think about the questions you'd ask if you were buying something. You may not always get something you'd include in the body copy, but if you keep probing, you might get an idea for a whole campaign. For example:

> Dove soap is one quarter cleansing cream.
>
> *So what?*
>
> It's creamier, less harsh to the skin.
>
> *So what?*
>
> Your skin looks younger, less dry.
>
> *So what?*
>
> You feel better about yourself.

Now you've got a hook. Don't tell her about your soap, talk to her about feeling young, beautiful, free, and sexy.

Put yourself in the target customer's shoes. As Luke Sullivan says: "Ask yourself what would make you want to buy the product? Find the central truth about the product . . . hair coloring isn't about looking younger. It's about self-esteem. Cameras aren't about pictures. They're about stopping time and holding life as the sands run out."[9]

Tone

You know what you want to say, now you have to figure out how to say it. Whether you create a formal tone statement or just think about it, you really do need to define the tone of your creative effort.

In this po-mo era, the tone of many ads smacks of irony, inside jokes, and a hipper-than-thou attitude. Sometimes the message is so abstract you risk confusing or alienating 99% of the audience to connect with that critical 1%. That's fine for Skyy, but don't use that tone for Welch's Grape Juice.

As with everything else, you have to know the target audience from the outside/in. Then find the right tone to communicate your message.

2.3. This Winston smoker said, "Yeah, I smoke. What are you gonna do about it?" Rather than justifying smoking or even saying why Winston tastes better, this ad challenges anyone to criticize Winston smokers.

2.4. Another look at smoking, this time with a quite different tone. A mom dying of emphysema says goodbye to her family.

2.5. The "Call to Action" should grab the viewers' attention.

Source: Illustration by Dan Augustine.

Call to action: What do you want them to do?

You need to expect some kind of outcome from your advertising. What do you want to happen, aside from immediate and colossal sales? Depending on the type of product, the purchase cycle may take seconds or years. Promoting an impulse item like a pack of gum doesn't require much of a call to action. Everyone knows what it is and where to buy it. But if you're considering a car, you need more information. So the call to action in the ad would include a Web site address, a toll-free phone number, an invitation to take a test-drive, a suggestion of a visit to the friendly dealer, and the option of sending for a free brochure.

The main idea is to connect the reader, viewer, or listener with the advertiser. Make it easy to get more information if it's needed. If personal selling is critical to a purchase, find a way to connect the prospect with the salesperson. Making these connections can take the following forms:

- Web site address
- E-mail address
- Reply card
- Toll-free phone number
- Coupon (for the technologically challenged)
- Invitation to visit the store/retailer
- Invitation to take a test-drive

Putting It All Together

You've done your homework on the audience, the product, and the competition. Now you're ready to talk to a prospective customer. Imagine you're talking to a neighbor over the fence instead of writing an ad or a TV spot. Could you tell him or her the One Thing to know about your product? Could you give reasons that support that One Thing? Do you have answers to your neighbor's objections or misconceptions about your product? Could you convince that neighbor to seek more information or to visit a store to compare or just buy the product? It's all about making a personal connection. Here are a few samples:

- *Objective:* Introduce new category of car—crossover utility vehicle

- *Type of product:* Considered purchase, high-involvement durable good

- *Target audience:* 20–30-year-old women in top 25 markets, $25–50K income

- *Possible creative strategy:* Use lots of pictures to show features, styling, captions to explain benefits (dependable, lots of space, mileage)

- *Tone:* Convey fun, independence, adventure

- *Objective:* Reinforce established brand of computer

- *Type of product:* Considered purchase, very high-involvement technical product

- *Target audience:* 25–45-year-old creative professionals

- *Possible creative strategy:* Show side-by-side comparisons to competition; use screen displays instead of copy, bullet points of specs/features

- *Tone:* Peace of mind (Aren't you glad you have this one?), superior attitude (Don't you feel smarter than the people who bought the competition?)

- *Objective:* Encourage contributions to animal rights group

- *Type of product:* Emotional issue, high involvement for select few

- *Target audience:* 18–64-year-old women

- *Possible creative strategy:* Show animal suffering in lab tests, long copy telling story of animal and how you can help

- *Tone:* Emotional, urgent, call to action (send money)

- *Objective:* Promote new identity for manufacturer of heating system components

- *Type of product:* Highly technical products, selected by price, specs, reputation

- *Target audience:* Design engineers at 250 original equipment manufacturer (OEM) companies who specify components to be used in building complete systems

- *Possible creative strategy:* Feature logo and slogan, tie in photos of products and/or applications

- *Tone:* Professional, helpful, friendly

- *Objective:* Introduce new style of brace for arthritic knees

- *Type of product:* Considered purchase, high involvement

- *Target audience:* 45–80-year-old men and women with arthritis

- *Possible creative strategy:* Position as alternative to surgery and drugs, show active seniors, possible testimonials or before/after photos

- *Tone:* Create peace of mind (postpone surgery, relieve pain, resume active lifestyle)

Who's Who?

William Bernbach—Although he was the third name in Doyle Dane Bernbach, there was no doubt who was in charge of the creative process. Bill Bernbach revolutionized advertising from the late 1950s through the 1970s, suggesting that advertising is an art and not a science, with groundbreaking campaigns for Volkswagen, Alka-Seltzer, Polaroid, Avis, Orbach's, and many others. His simple yet sophisticated commercials generated huge sales for his clients as they wove their way firmly into the popular culture. Doyle Dane Bernbach not only changed advertising forever, it also spawned many of the creative superstars of the 1970s, 1980s, and 1990s who formed their own shops.

Mary Wells Lawrence—While CEO, chairman, and president of the legendary Wells, Rich and Greene agency, Mary Wells was the highest-paid, most well-known woman in American business. She was also the first female CEO of a *Fortune* 500 company. Her innovative campaigns for Braniff, Alka-Seltzer, Benson & Hedges, and American Motors brought a fresh new look to established brands. At age 40, she became the youngest person ever inducted into the Copywriters Hall of Fame (until Ed McCabe several years later).

G. Andrew Meyer—Andrew Meyer has created advertising campaigns that have been recognized by the Kelly Awards, the ANDYs, the Art Director's Club, *Communication Arts Advertising Annual,* the One Show, the British D&AD Awards, the Clio Awards, and the OBIEs, among others. Meyer came into advertising as a designer and art director, eventually morphing into a copywriter before becoming executive creative director at Leo Burnett in Chicago.

Rosser Reeves—As chairman of the Ted Bates agency, Rosser Reeves originated the concept of the unique selling proposition, or USP, which dominated advertising strategy until the Creative Revolution of the 1960s. His no-nonsense technique of hammering a single message home was very effective in turning features into benefits consumers could easily understand.

Notes

[1] Mary Wells Lawrence, quoted in *Vogue,* February 15, 1972.

[2] William Bernbach, *Bill Bernbach Said . . .* (New York: DDB Needham Worldwide, 1989).

[3] See the Simmons Market Research Bureau Web site at http://www.smrb.com.

[4] Scott Bedbury, interview by authors, December 3, 2004.

[5] Quote from the Clio Awards Web site, http://clioawards.com/html/wsj/dusenberry.html (accessed December 20, 2004).

[6] Quote from the Clio Awards Web site, http://clioawards.com/html/wsj/chiat.html (accessed December 20, 2004).

[7] David Ogilvy, *Ogilvy on Advertising* (New York: Random House, 1985), 166.

[8] Quoted in Denis Higgins, *The Art of Writing Advertising: Conversations with Masters of the Craft: William Bernbach, George Gribbin, David Ogilvy, Leo Burnett, Rosser Reeves* (New York: McGraw-Hill, 2003), 125.

[9] Luke Sullivan, *Hey Whipple, Squeeze This: A Guide to Creating Great Ads* (New York: John Wiley, 1998), 35.

Issues in a Changing Marketplace

We're all the same . . . only different. Look around. Does everyone look like you?

Until the late 1960s, advertisers must have thought everyone in the United States was a straight, uptight, well-dressed white suburbanite. Because that's all they showed in their ads. It took time, but marketers finally discovered that African Americans actually own homes. Women buy cars. Gays and lesbians like vacations. People who don't speak English as their primary language still know that money talks. Integrating advertising was not only the right thing, it was the smart thing.

As of 2005, one in every three Americans is a person of color. Women make up 51% of the total population, with 40–64-year-old women representing the single largest U.S. market segment.[1] Another demographic shift is the aging of America. The generation that created the youth culture of the 1960s is shifting not so gracefully into retirement. All these groups and many others have special wants and needs, and smart advertisers will find ways to address them.

3.1. Who's the prisoner here? Or is this ad saying we're all prisoners to racism? This is one of a series of ads from Benetton that got people talking—and thinking—about issues more important than clothes.

Today, it's not a question of whether to appeal to multicultural audiences and specialty markets. It's more a question of how to do it. How do we show people of color and special target market segments in our ads without using stereotypes? If we avoid the obvious, do we deny their identities? Can we keep it real without alienating other audiences?

3.2. As these ads show, in the early 1950s the only people of color in advertising were servants or less . . .

3.3. . . . Imagine the reaction these ads would provoke today.

3.4. You can call Tiger Woods an incredibly gifted golfer, a multimillionaire, or a very savvy businessperson. But don't call him an African Asian American, because he doesn't accept the labels that might define his parents.

Advertisers also need to be responsive to a cultural shift that suggests many people see themselves as multiethnic or multicultural. In fact, in the last U.S. Census, more than half of the people who identified themselves as "black in combination with at least one other race" were under 18 years old.[2] New magazines such as *Mavin* and *Fader* celebrate cultural diversity. This trend will undoubtedly continue to grow. Some of the hottest models today have an indefinable ethnic look. Tiger Woods is a great example of a celebrity who chooses to define himself as multiethnic, refusing to be categorized as African American or Thai or Asian American, ethnicities that define his parents. Woods embraces his multicultural heritage and fully expects advertisers who hire him to do the same. How will postmodern conceptions of identity influence the way you define and speak to your target audience?

It's All There in Black and White

As advertising began to integrate in the late 1960s, the trend was to make African Americans look like "dark-skinned white people." If they look "just like us," they'll want to drive a Buick, eat at Denny's, and get their dishes clean with Lemon Joy. In reality, back then even white people in ads didn't look like real people. While some African Americans were happy to finally be represented in mainstream advertising, others resented the lack of realistic models, situations, and limited media placements.

Ad professionals such as Thomas Burrell, founder of Burrell Communications, the largest African American ad agency in the United States, and Al Anderson, founder of Anderson Communication, Inc., have long argued "blacks aren't dark-skinned whites."[3] Forty years ago, before minority-owned agencies existed, the industry really lacked for messages that reflected cultural experiences beyond a white world. Today, according to Anderson, the *multi* in multicultural marketing has gotten a bit blurred: "Last time I checked, all marketing is targeted at somebody. Now how you construct this young, black, Latino, Asian person, I don't know. I've never met one of these folks."[4] Reaching multicultural audiences means creating a connectivity between the message and the audience, and using all avenues of integrated marketing to deliver that message. For Burrell and Anderson, success has come by tapping into the unique cultural experiences of African Americans and slipping that message into channels that resonate with their audience.

Just how much are African Americans represented in advertising today? Of all ethnic groups, African Americans have the highest representation in mainstream magazines ads. Yet only 14% of the ads in mainstream magazines feature diverse groups of people. Does the advertising industry really embrace the diversity reflected in American culture? Although some brands, including Skechers, Maxwell House, and Toyota, have been at the forefront of multiethnic marketing trends, this is not necessarily the norm. When it comes to television, African Americans make up 36% of the models in spots running during prime time. Many of these ads feature celebrities such as Dominique Wilkins (tortilla chips), Venus and Serena Williams (Wrigley's gum), and Ken Griffey, Jr. (Pepsi).[5] One could argue that because these people are

This is when you want something more than a soft drink. Nothing soft about the taste of Coca-Cola...lifts your spirits—boosts your energy.

things go better with Coke

3.5. 1965: Even the cars were white.

3.6. Today: Coke learned to use more colors than red.

3.7. A revered organization fuses a celebrated tagline ("A mind is a terrible thing to waste") with powerful imagery in an award-winning campaign created by Y&R, New York.

3.8. Does this portrayal of a black worker stereotype African Americans as blue-collar laborers or merely show a rugged guy who needs tough boots?

3.9. This product is targeting young men. When you can put yourself in the same situation, it doesn't matter what color you are.

major sports figures, their celebrity transcends race. But consider this: Overall advertising budgets targeting African Americans increased 67% from 1997 to 2002.[6] What's really happening here?

The African American population is expected to grow at twice the rate of European Americans in the next 20 years. Further, African Americans are younger than the general U.S. population, with a median age of 30, and nearly half live in married households.[7] In all, 55% of African Americans live in the South. Yet the largest concentrations of African Americans are found in nonsouthern DMAs: New York, Chicago, Los Angeles, Philadelphia, and Washington, D.C. Don't assume they all live in cities. In fact, 39% live in the suburbs.[8]

WORDS OF WISDOM

"You know why Madison Avenue advertising has never done well in Harlem? We're the only ones who know what it means to be Brand X."

—DICK GREGORY[10]

Tapping into the African American market

- Community involvement is a huge part of life for African Americans. Consider using IMC elements to enhance the reach of your campaign.

- Women play a prominent role in family life. Don't underestimate their influence or their buying power. African American women have the highest spending power among women of color.[9]

- Avoid using slang. It's often insulting.

- African Americans' preferences, habits, and attitudes reflect a broad range of sensibilities.

McREALITY

For many years, I was creative director at the world's largest African American agency, where McDonald's was one of our major clients. In the late 1980s, when McDonald's was changing its theme line, yet again, I decided to jump into the "here and now." I asked my creative group to come up with something that reflected modern reality. The result was two spots that pushed the envelope. "Momma's Date" addressed a divorced (or widowed) mother who was getting back into the social swim, much to her young son's chagrin. He was totally disapproving until the gentleman caller treated them to a visit to McDonald's, where the son ran into his classmates, including a little cutie pie. (I had to respond to a letter that accused us of promoting juvenile sexual promiscuity. Go figure.)

The other spot, "Second Chance," introduced Calvin, an ex–juvenile delinquent. In his walk through the neighborhood, a voice-over conversation pointed out the noticeable changes in his personality and behavior. At the end it is revealed that he has been employed by the Golden Arches. Some members of McDonald's Marketing Department tried to kill it (too street), but the big kahuna loved it. Calvin was an immediate hit with consumers, as well as the owners and operators of McDonald's, so we did a series of commercials with him as the hero. When we finally bid good riddance to Calvin, we thought he was history.

Two decades later, Calvin resurfaced on *Chappelle's Show*. In a devastating send-up, Calvin [played by Dave Chappelle] gets a job at "Wack Donald's." At first he is the pride of the neighborhood, but things rapidly go downhill. Chappelle's series of spoofs mirrored the original Calvin's progression, so it had to have made an impression on him. (I wonder if he got turned down for the role.)

—Anna Morris

- Media matters. Eight out of 10 African Americans are heavy magazine readers—and that's more than the U.S. average.[11] But television is also important.

- Fashion is often a form of personal expression for African Americans.

¿Cómo Se Dice Diversity en Español?

Today more than 32 million Latinos live in the United States, representing Mexico, Cuba, Puerto Rico, the Caribbean, and Central and South America, not to mention the blended Anglo-Latino cultures along the border from California to Florida. Look at the differences between the English spoken in the United Kingdom, the United States, and Australia, then multiply that by the 19 countries that speak Spanish, and you'll realize you can't treat this market as one group. For example, an exterminator in Mexico will remove your *bichos* (bugs), but the same word in Puerto Rico refers to a man's private parts.[12]

You have to do more than just find the right slang. You have to understand the culture. Here are some examples:

- A Coca-Cola ad may use the slogan *"y su comida favorita"* ("and your favorite food"), but for Miami Cubans the ad shows pork loin, for south Texas Mexicans it's tacos, and for New York Puerto Ricans they use chicken and rice.

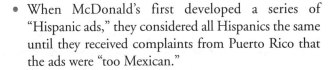

- When McDonald's first developed a series of "Hispanic ads," they considered all Hispanics the same until they received complaints from Puerto Rico that the ads were "too Mexican."

- A telephone company tried to market its products to Latinos by showing a commercial in which a Latina wife tells her husband to call a friend and tell her they would be late for dinner. The commercial bombed since Latina women generally do not give orders to their husbands and their cultural concept of time would not require a call about lateness.[14]

- When translated literally into Spanish, the famous "Got Milk?" slogan means "Are you lactating?" Fortunately, the California Milk Board realized this before it was launched. The new slogan, "Familia. Amor. Leche" ("Family. Love. Milk"), not only avoids the problems of the literal translation, it also fits the culture better. Although Anglos might find the concept of milk deprivation funny, a Latino audience would consider it insulting. Running out of milk means not providing for your family.[15]

Dígame más (tell me more)

As of 2005, Latinos outnumber African Americans in the United States, and they're a young audience. The median age of Latinos is 27, and one in three is under 18. Latinos tend to live in urban areas, but you'll find small communities popping up in unexpected places. Los Angeles, Miami, Chicago, and many cities in Texas have large, vibrant Latino communities. As you might expect, the Spanish language is a big part of their cultural experience. Half of all adult Latinos speak Spanish at home. According to Louis Nevaer, bilingual Latinos are influenced more by advertising in Spanish than by advertising in English. Needless to say, Spanish language media is hot! And so are multicultural ad agencies, where Latino agencies account for more than 60% of the total revenues. African Americans might be big readers of magazines, but Latinos are huge consumers of television, with more than 63% of media buys going to television and a mere 11% going to print. Univision and Telemundo are the top two Spanish-language networks. In all, Latino purchasing power is a whopping $581 billion annually. Procter & Gamble, Sears, and General Motors represent the top three advertisers in Latino media.[16] But when it comes to creativity, Citibank and its agency La Comunidad are big winners. Why? Because Citibank's first foray into Spanish-language creative spoke with strong cultural resonance of the immigrant experience and the pursuit of the American dream. Citibank and La Comunidad struck gold at the Advertising Age 2004 Hispanic Creative Advertising Awards. More important, their integrated Spanish-language campaign generated a growth in new business of 169%.[17]

Tapping into the Latino market

- Family-focused activities are a central element of Latino life, and it's not uncommon for multiple generations to share the same household. For Latinos, familial concerns often trump individual needs.

3.10. Translation: "Eliminates grease—with the new formula removing grease is easier." Notice the sensuous curve of the stacked plates. Does it remind you of anything?

3.11. Translation: "The only thing worse than losing a child to AIDS is to discover that it could be avoided." The power of language is apparent in this ad concerning pediatric AIDS, and it transcends cultures.

- Spanish is often spoken rapidly, at least to the ears of English-only speakers. But don't feel like you have to cram in more words. Rather, consider this a cultural variation.

- Everyday life is a bit slower paced within Latino culture. Family-centered obligations often supersede outside commitments.

- Music is a big part of Latino life, and it often blends mainstream American culture with a multitude of Latino sensibilities. Consider the fact that *American Idol* is the top English-language TV program among Latinos.

- While the majority of Hispanic television originates in Mexico, Latino culture is far more diverse. Considering the specific heritage of your Latino audience will make for a more resonant campaign.

- Latinos are Web savvy, but few Web sites use Spanish. How can you use the Web to your strategic advantage when reaching out to Latinos?[18]

In our discussions with Iliana Aleman, we discovered the debate over what to call Latin Americans is still raging. She told us that a recent poll indicated about 65% prefer to call themselves *Hispanic,* which is how the business world identifies the target audience. She said *Hispanic* is accepted primarily by older, more established residents in the United States. Younger, more liberal types prefer *Latino* or *Latina,* which is less corporate and more personal. Overall, though, people prefer to identify themselves by their countries of origin. They are more likely to be proud of being *Chicano* or *Argentino* or *Cubana* than of being "Hispanic."[19]

HISPANIC HYPERREALITY

Iliana Aleman at BVK/MEKA, a Hispanic advertising agency in Miami, explains that there is no single Hispanic culture, but rather a "hyperreality" that blurs the difference between the symbolic and real:

> *Hispanic* is really just a marketing term coined by the advertising industry in the U.S. This hyperreal market lumps together people of Latin American and Spanish heritage under one "ethnic" classification, when in fact the 19 Latin groups under the Hispanic umbrella can be drastically different from one another.
>
> One of our clients, a top telecom, was launching a new international calling plan for mobile phones. Another opportunity to practice those hyperreal Hispanic Spanish skills, right?
>
> I started by asking Sandra, a Mexican coworker, "How do you answer the phone?" We say, "*¿Bueno?*" (by the way, *bueno* literally means "good"). Nereyda said Cubans answer *"Oigo"* ("I hear"). The Venezuelans told me they say, *"Aló"* (which has no meaning). Puerto Ricans say, *"Hello"* (pronounced "jel-ó"). The Argentine said she had the only legitimate, polite, correct, and perfect phone greeting: *"Hola."* From there on everyone had a say, visiting clients opined . . . *"Buenas," "Dígame," "Sí."* It was Babel.
>
> A little later, the client called to "remind" us that we should use the proper Mexican "dialect" for the West Coast and "generic" Spanish for the rest. That's exactly what we did. We created a pun for the West Coast version where one character answered the phone by saying *"¿Bueno?"* ("Good") and the caller replied, *"Bueno no, buenísimo"* ("Not only good, but very good"). We sent a creative rationale explaining that literally *bueno* means good, but that in context it really means hello. That it was a play on words to introduce the retail message (great prices), etc., etc. . . . of course. She never got it. The cultural divide was insurmountable. On the other hand, we never found a Pan-Latin way of saying hello. The hyperreal had turned surreal.
>
> We ended up creating a funny, clever, and very effective campaign where people call their countries of origin, but no one answers the phone by saying hello. We just started the spots midway through the calls. In the world of Hispanic Hyperreality, definitely less is more.

3.12. This billboard was created by Lápis, a Hispanic ad agency. Yet the boards were pulled after protests from some Latino groups who claimed the campaign was racist and sexist. What do you think?

Women in Advertising: Have We Really Come a Long Way, Baby?

Advertising has been called a meritocracy, a place where gender and race often don't affect advancement. We won't debate that here, except to say that 53% of the jobs in our industry are held by women, and female owners and CEOs are far more common in advertising than in other businesses. Nonetheless, women still hold only 28% of the top management positions in advertising.[20] Women in advertising have made great inroads into account management and media, where they equal or outnumber men in similar positions. However, women are underrepresented on the creative side, holding only about a quarter of the creative jobs.[21] It surely can't be that women are not as creative as men. Having said all this, perhaps the most compelling question to consider is: Have we moved away from the stereotyping of women in advertising?

Rob Walker, who writes the "Ad Report Card" column in *Slate* online magazine, has commented on the trend for advertisers to have it both ways when they portray women—titillating images and noble intentions:

> Typically, when advertisers do something that they suspect will offend a portion of the audience, they claim that they aren't actually *committing* the offense, they are *critiquing* the offense. So, for example, the Miller Lite "catfight" spots aren't exploiting sexy girls in their underwear; they are simply making fun of advertising that stoops to such levels and those who respond to it. The inclusion of the actual sexy girls in their underwear happens to be the only way to make this sophisticatedly ironic point.[22]

What do you think about the argument he makes? Do you think he's equating "sexy" behavior with "girls"? Last time we saw those ads, they looked like women to us. Word choice really does matter.

On one hand, it seems ironic that women are so often considered a specialty market when they make up 51% of the U.S. population and influence 85% of all purchases, including making 80% of all health care decisions and 65% of all new car choices.[23] Yet women do view the world through a different lens. Just ask Mary Lou Quinlan, CEO of Just Ask a Woman and author of a book by the same title. Or ask Faith Popcorn, coauthor of *EVEolution,* a book that forecasts trends among women.[24] Both of these experts suggest that women are indeed unique. Reaching them requires doing your homework and not making assumptions (especially if you are male).

Women take brands seriously, but be careful—they tend not to bond with brands they perceive as aggressively targeting them. The best way to reach women is to consider the unexpected and to pay attention to details—women do. Even the subtlest nuance can mean more. Give them time to make their decisions. If you plan on impulse buys, you've got the wrong target in mind. Consider that three-quarters of all women in the United States work full-time, and women over 40 have some of the highest spending power in the nation.[25] Now think about this from a multicultural perspective. There are 32.7 million women of color, and they have $723 billion in purchasing power. While there are a lot of similarities

3.13–3.15. Whole books have been devoted to how women have been depicted in ads. Here's a pretty good cross section from the 1950s and 1960s that illustrates three long-running stereotypes: sex symbol, mindless ditz, and dedicated homemaker. Have we really come all that far since then?

along the gender line, cultural groups have their own distinct buying patterns. The really interesting thing is that most women of color embrace their American culture while still holding fast to their ethnic identity.[26]

Women are also considered the leading indicators of social change. To reach them, we "must deeply understand the meaning, significance and direction of large social changes."[27] Women have a high preference for personal networking. They prefer dispersed or shared authority. And they thrive on conceptual thinking, consensus building, and flexible lifestyles.

If there's one thing we can say about women, it's that they want and deserve respect. Don't talk down to them and don't assume you know everything about them. Respect them and their differences.

Maybe women really are different

OK, we're not talking about which planet women come from. We're talking about how women view the world of consumer goods and how we, as advertisers, can reach them.

- Women are relationship focused; men put a high value on competition.
- Women are driven by people and family; men are driven by action and outcomes.
- Under stress, women think "support"; men think "respond."
- Women take more time making purchase decisions than men.
- Women earn only 75 cents to every dollar earned by men.[28] They are not very happy about it.
- Women are more educated than men: 29% of U.S. women have a college degree, compared with only 26% of men. Further, 56% of all college students are women, and that percentage is expected to grow.[29]

Women have come a long way, and so have the images we see of them in ads. Prior to World War II, women where shown as keepers of home and hearth. During World War II, images of women integrated both home and work. Women were shown as powerful and strong as they responded to the needs of a nation at war. But the 1950s brought images of women back to the home—this time to the suburbs. During the 1960s, while the sexual revolution was flourishing, images of women were still fairly homebound. It was not until the 1970s that images of women in advertising began to show the effects of the sexual revolution. During this time the use of more overt sex appeals began to appear. Interestingly, so did the "natural" look. Both kinds of images speak to the seeds sown by feminism. During the 1980s, they were often depicted as superwomen—women who could have it all.

During the 1990s, images of women finally began to find a balance with the reality of their lives. Images of empowerment and equity began to appear. Unfortunately, even more sexualized images also thrived. Some say these highly sexualized images, along with the use of abnormally thin body types (not to mention huge breasts), in advertising as well as in other forms of media, have led to a significant rise in eating disorders and unwarranted dissatisfaction among women with their bodies. We could write an entire chapter about this. And a lot of great books are available on this topic, such as Jean Kilbourne's *Deadly Persuasion* and Alissa Quart's *Branded: The buying and selling of teenagers*.[31] We urge you to consider the impact the images you create, as advertisers, have on girls and women.

WORDS OF WISDOM

"The consumer isn't a moron. She is your wife."

—**DAVID OGILVY**[30]

3.16. At the beginning of the women's liberation movement in the 1960s, Virginia Slims positioned their cigarettes just for women. Why should men have all the lung cancer and heart attacks?

3.17. Betty Crocker. She's had eight extreme makeovers since her visual debut in 1936—the brand was launched in 1921 without her image. Betty's look evolves to reflect the trends of the times, and she's still going strong.

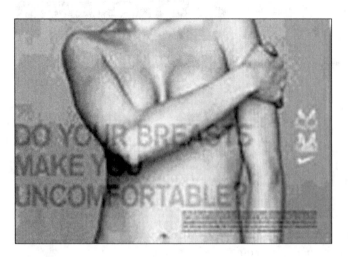

3.18. An earlier version of this 2000 Kelly Award-winning Nike ad ran with the breasts uncovered. Nike caught flak and soon pulled it. Why are these Nike bra ads controversial when Victoria's Secret ads are readily accepted?

3.19. Is the secret that you can sell clothing by showing models not wearing it? Do sexy images give women a sense of empowerment or are they degrading? Or is there some middle ground?

Tapping into the women's market

- Listen to her. She's got a lot to say—most of which you won't be expecting.

- Give her details. She'll respect you, and respect translates into loyalty.

- Talk to her like you'd speak to a friend. Testimonials can have real power.

- Move past stereotypes. She has.

- If you think she's one-dimensional, you're wrong. Women juggle a lot. Target your brand to her lifestyle and you just might reach her.

- Tell the truth. She'll catch you if you don't.

- Use other women to find her and connect to her. Think unconventionally.

- She'll hold you accountable for your actions. Be a good corporate citizen.

Don't Ask, Don't Tell, Just Sell

3.20. Dove launched the "Campaign for Real Beauty" in an effort to spark a debate about current definitions of beauty. Consumers can even go to a Web site (campaignforrealbeauty.com) and cast their votes.[32] Talk about engaging your audience!

Depending on the survey, anywhere from 6% to 10% of the American population identifies as gay, lesbian, or bisexual. Smart marketers know they can't ignore

18 to 30 million people. Aside from the sheer numbers, the gay and lesbian segment offers marketers other advantages: They tend to have more money than other Americans, and they spend it. Simmons Market Research Bureau reports that more than 20% of gay/lesbian households exceed $100,000 in annual income. Simmons also notes that this market is exceptionally loyal, with 89% stating that they'd buy products and services advertised in gay publications.[33] While some advertisers may fear a conservative backlash, many mainstream consumer product marketers feel confident in targeting all market segments. As with other specialty markets, the question is not should we do it, but how?

WORDS OF WISDOM

"In advertising, sex sells. But only if you're selling sex."

—JEF RICHARDS[34]

A poll of 5,000 readers of *The Advocate* revealed that 54% want ads that address gay and lesbian themes. However, 33% said their opinions depended on how the content is handled, and 13% wanted advertisers to concentrate on the product, not the consumer's sexual orientation.[35]

Tapping into the gay/lesbian market

If your assignment is to reinforce brand preference among gays and lesbians, you have several options:

- Run your "mainstream" ad in gay-oriented publications, especially if the content is gender neutral. You don't change the creative, but the media selection indicates that you're interested in their business.

- Incorporate gay themes into your campaign, using visuals, copy, or both, and run them in gay publications. This really shows your commitment to gay and lesbian customers. Just be careful not to fall victim to stereotypical images.

- Use your gay-themed ads across the board. Ikea, for example, has used gay-oriented themes in television commercials that also reached the straight market. This demonstrates that you believe your brand is for all consumers and you're willing to risk a possible backlash.

- Run gay-oriented ads in traditional mainstream media, but in areas with high concentrations of gays and lesbians. There's less chance of a backlash or of being identified as a "gay brand."

- Keep your mass-media advertising mainstream or gender neutral and run promotions and public relations programs to target gays and lesbians, such as sponsorship of a gay pride parade.

Depending on your perspective, Christmas 2004 brought glad or grinchly tidings to Target a brand that actively targets gays and lesbians. In an effort to maintain consistency in their policy concerning solicitation, Target prohibited Salvation Army volunteers from setting up their red kettles outside Target stores. Now here's the backlash we talked about: That decision was lambasted by conservative groups, who suggested that Target "buckled under pressure from gay-rights advocates." Target denied any motive other than the need to "consistently apply our no-solicitation policy."[36] Procter & Gamble (P&G) found itself in a similar situation when the American Family Association (AFA), a conservative media watchdog group, took aim at a P&G commercial that had been running in Canada for four years.

AFA called for a boycott of P&G products, citing among the reasons that P&G advertises in gay and lesbian media and sends employees to diversity training programs. P&G responded by stating that they "are pro-P&G consumers and pro-P&G employees. It is wrong to suggest that P&G has any special 'agenda' beyond this. As a company, we don't advocate any particular lifestyle. That is simply not our business."[37] According to Bob Witeck, president of the gay marketing firm Witeck-Combs Communication, and Michael Wilke, executive director of the Commercial Closet Association, an organization that archives gay and lesbian–oriented advertising, Target and P&G could benefit from the backlash.[38] Just remember, *could* is the key word. Knowing what's in the best interest of your brand, while acknowledging your own personal boundaries, will help you weigh opportunities against possible consequences.

3.21. This Miller Lite ad got a lot of attention for its positive use of gay themes to market the product to all adult beer drinkers.

Other brands, such as Pottery Barn, Absolut Vodka, and Subaru, don't mind their position as gay-oriented products. On the other hand, Miller beer tried a two-track approach: catfighting models ripping off each other's clothes for the straight guys and a totally different approach with two women unwittingly flirting with two gay guys. It may seem counterintuitive for beer companies,

3.22. These guys are successful small businessmen who happen to be gay. It's a good example of talking about the product or service and not the lifestyle.

3.23. European advertisers have used same-sex couples in mainstream media for years. Now more American firms are joining the trend.

whose product is usually associated with stereotypical masculine attributes, to freely embrace gay themes. But that's exactly what they've been doing for some time now, says Wilke. "Some years ago, beer companies were heavily criticized for their use of sexist commercials," he explains. "So they started looking elsewhere for materials and have found both humor and great success in utilizing gay themes." He adds, "Gay themes are easy to respond to and to many people's surprise, they have seen a great degree of acceptance."[39] (If you're interested in learning more on this topic, check out the Commercial Closet's Web site at commercialcloset.org.)

Back in the mid-1990s, Nike ran an ad, "Canoeists," featuring two lesbians as a part of the "Just do it" campaign for the women's brand. Ironically, no one at Nike knew they were lesbians. That fact was not lost on the creative team, who consciously chose the two women because they felt they epitomized the empowerment theme and spoke to an often-ignored audience, not to mention it silently pushed a few buttons at Nike. Today using lesbians in an ad doesn't have to be a silent response.

You're Never Too Old to Buy Something

Rob Walker discusses a recurring stereotype in advertising:

> Hilarious Old People—Clara "Where's the Beef?" Peller being the archetype—have been in a bit less demand in recent years, as the ad business has figured out that there are a lot of "mature" consumers who happen to have money to spend and don't think of themselves as (barely) living punch lines. (Although Madison Avenue has not quite figured out how to deal with this. Are older consumers adventurous? Are they horny? Do they have a sense of humor?)[40]

If it's true that mature Americans tend to think of themselves as 10 to 15 years younger than they really are, does it make sense to turn off a huge potential market by showing a bunch of wacky geezers in your ads? Plain and simple, it doesn't.

Mature consumers are a more dynamic group than you might think, and they've got a lot of money to spend. According to J. Walter Thompson's Mature Marketing Group, this segment controls 75% of our nation's assets as well as 70% of the nation's net worth—more than half of which is available for discretionary spending. They travel a lot, often taking more than three trips a year. In fact, mature travelers account for 31% of all domestic trips. And this might surprise you: Mature Americans represent the fastest-growing segment of Internet users in the United States. Mature users actually spend more time online than college students do—and they buy more, too. More than half own cell phones as well. People over 55 are living full, active, and adventurous lives. And they live in "homes," not "the home." Less than 5% of Americans over 65 live in nursing homes; 86% own their own homes, and most of them are mortgage-free.[41] They've always been young at heart, and now they have time and a lot more money to spend. It's about time advertisers gave them a little more respect in the way they are depicted.

The mature market is very diverse. Although it skews heavily female, mature Americans have varying incomes, education, life experiences, and much more.

Two distinct groups emerge within the mature market. One is the *65-plus group.* These individuals remember World War II. They have a strong work ethic, and they are self-sacrificing, tolerant of authority, comfortable with conformity, loyal, and patriotic; they'll happily spend what they've earned and appreciate a good value. On the other hand, the 55–65 group, the *Baby Boomers,* are well educated, hedonistic, focused on self-improvement, and nonconformist; they believe work should be fulfilling, feel a sense of entitlement, tolerate differences, and seek adventure and new experiences. Despite their differences, people nearing or in retirement have a lot in common. No matter what group they fall into, those in the mature market love to spoil their grandkids, spending an average of $500 a year on them.[42]

Tapping into the mature market

- *Get to know them:* They are multifaceted. Don't make assumptions.

- *Give them facts:* Be clear and straightforward. Let them know the benefits.

- *Build relationships:* They value personal relationships and are unlikely to make quick decisions. Above all, don't pressure them.

- *Use life-stage marketing:* They respond strongly to the life-changing events in their world. Make these events the defining moments of your campaign.

- *Educate the market:* They have a lot of time to read, listen, and learn.

- *Design with their eyes in mind:* Make your ads visually accessible; use 11- or 12-point type, plenty of white space, bold headlines, and clear subheads, and break your copy into columns.

- *Avoid scare tactics:* Scaring them won't work anyway. Instead, celebrate the joys of aging and retirement.

- *Don't call them names:* If there's one word they hate, it's *senior. Old* and *elderly* won't get you very far either. We saw one ad promoting investment seminars for "Greedy Geezers"—which was either very gutsy or just plain rude.

- *Demonstrate your credibility:* They want to trust you, so give them a chance. Consider testimonials, use research, and try endorsements.

- *Remove the risk:* Offer a guarantee or free trial to gain their trust and loyalty.[43]

Now that you have an overview of the mature market, here are a few specifics to consider related to each advertising medium, courtesy of AgeVenture News Service:[44]

3.24. While Michelob's TV ads show athletic Gen Xers flirting at the gym and pool, the company is going after healthy, active Baby Boomers in this ad placed in AARP. The split headline, "If this is your idea of a pleasure cruise, this is your beer," is consistent with the rest of the campaign.

3.25. This ad shows very little sensitivity toward the mature market. Remember what we said about humor? Well, let's just say we're not so sure this works.

- *Business cards:* Is the print legible? Is the type large enough?

- *Brochures:* Avoid glossy stock because it glares. Remember to use larger type and go for high contrast.

- *Newsletters:* Mature Americans take the time to read them cover to cover as long as the topics interest them.

- *Print ads:* Keep it simple and avoid clutter. They respond well to "how-to" copy.

- *Radio:* Keep background music to a minimum and remember they are heavy early-morning listeners.

- *Television:* Nobody watches the news like they do (notice all the mature market products advertised during the national network news programs?). Watch the background music and keep titles on the screen just a bit longer.

- *Direct mail:* They like getting mail. It's not all junk mail to them.

- *Promotion:* If something can save them money and the offer doesn't expire too soon, they'll participate.

It's a Global World

Multinational companies demand global campaigns from their advertising agencies. They stress conformity in brand names and advertising images. Unfortunately, one look does not fit all countries, even if they speak the same language. Some famous examples of losing it in translation:

- Ford has had a series of problems in marketing cars internationally. Their low-cost truck, the Fiera, means "ugly old woman" in Spanish. The Ford Caliente in Mexico was found to be slang for "streetwalker." The Pinto subcompact was a hit in the United States, but in Brazil, *pinto* means a small penis.

- In Germany, the Sunbeam Corporation did not test the name of their "Mist-Stick"—a mist-producing hair curling iron. In German, *Mist* means "excrement," and a "manure-stick" did not draw much interest.

- United Airlines headlined an article in their in-flight magazine about the star of *Crocodile Dundee* "Paul Hogan Camps It Up." Unfortunately, in Australia, "camping it up" is slang for "flaunting homosexuality."

- When PepsiCo advertised Pepsi in Taiwan with the tagline "Come Alive with Pepsi," they had no idea that this would be translated into Chinese as "Pepsi brings your ancestors back from the dead."

- In Japan, Procter & Gamble used a television commercial that was popular in Europe. The ad showed a husband entering the bathroom and touching his wife as she takes a bath. The Japanese considered this ad to be in very poor taste because it depicted an invasion of privacy and inappropriate behavior.[45]

- In Mandarin Chinese, the literal translation of *Coca-Cola* is "bite the wax tadpole."

3.26. McDonald's globalized their brand to be consistent no matter where you see it. However, in India they use no sacred cows in their burgers. Note the "Maharaja Mac" and "Vegetable Burger with Cheese."

You may have noticed that we haven't included on this list the infamous story of the Chevy Nova, which has been said to have failed in South America because in Spanish *no va* means "won't go." This urban legend has been debunked; as many writers have pointed out, the name Nova, spelled and pronounced correctly, had already been well accepted for other products in South America by the time the Chevy model came along.[46]

While it's true that companies stress conformity in branding, there are two approaches to consider: the standardized approach and the globalized approach. The *globalized approach* takes the view that consistent branding supersedes most cultural differences. With the exception of language, campaigns are virtually identical from country to country. The *standardized approach* suggests consistency, but only to a point. Brands that adopt a more standardized branding approach internationally keep their logos and other branding elements consistent, but they make other changes to accommodate local cultures. While the globalized approach focuses on maintaining brand consistency to a much higher degree, neither approach can afford to completely ignore local customs and cultures. Regardless of which approach works for your brand, you must understand local laws and regulations, as they vary greatly from country to country.

In the global marketplace, advertisers usually think in terms of four levels:

1. *Local:* A local brand is advertised within a single location or country.

2. *Regional:* A regional brand is advertised within a specific geographic area, such as North America, Europe, or Southeast Asia.

3. *International:* International brands are advertised across the globe but tend to use the standardized approach to advertising and thus reflect local culture.

4. *Global:* Global brands are those that embrace the globalized approach, described above, as they stretch their brand names worldwide. McDonald's and Marlboro are great examples of global brands.

Tapping into global audiences

Wells, Burnett, and Moriarty offer a few tips for globalized and standardized advertising that we think are good—plus we've added a few of our own ideas.[47]

Globalized

- You can save money with economies of scale.
- Ensure that your advertising messages are complementary and consistent.

- The company can maintain control over its advertising image.

- Global media creates more opportunities for global marketing.

- Converging buyers' wants and needs across the globe can increase desire for the same product.

- There is limited competition in many foreign markets.

- Graphics and visual approaches can (sometimes) overcome cultural differences.

Standardized

- There's a better fit with the local marketplace and advertising will be less likely to overlook variations in buyer behavior.

- Involve a local professional in the decision-making process to enhance local acceptance.

- Any cost increases resulting from a more culturally specific approach are often offset by off-target ads.

- Culturally respectful and strategically bound advertising can often be highly successful.

- The chances of cultural blunders decrease.

- Honoring local customs can lead to good PR.

As we move deeper into the 21st century, the global marketplace offers advertisers ever-increasing potential. For now, the growth is slow, similar to ad spending in the United States. Global brands look to the international market-place for strategic growth, but not to the exclusion of the U.S. market, which still accounts for 45% of advertising spending.[48]

Companies such as Procter & Gamble, Unilever, and General Motors have been aggressive players on the global stage for years. For instance, Unilever—think Axe, Slim-Fast, and Ben & Jerry's—buys media in 72 of the 78 countries tracked by *Advertising Age*.[49] Yet, across the board, advertising media spending has been down while spending on sales promotion, sponsorship, interactive, and PR increases.[50] As global brands look for ways to expand markets, advertisers need to improve their measurement of advertising's effectiveness and efficiency as well as continue to be respectful global corporate citizens. As the global marketplace grows more competitive, IMC will rule and advertising will continue to compete against the other forms of marketing communication—and it had better do so effectively, efficiently, and with global consciousness.

Companies that ignore global consciousness pay a high price. Consider Nike's labor woes in the mid-1990s, or Johnson & Johnson's attempt to sell floor wax in countries where the majority of the people had dirt floors, or Nestlé's advertising of baby formula in countries where clean water was scarce and breast-feeding was the norm. When advertising a global brand, you can't afford to ignore the multitude of possible pitfalls.

Another factor to consider is the backlash against American consumer products. Whether it's a reaction to U.S. foreign policy, revival of social and cultural traditions, or resistance to the Americanization of local culture, a lot of people around the world don't like us or the goods that represent America. French consumers cheered the destruction of McDonald's restaurants by angry mobs. In the Arab world, locally bottled Mecca Cola is becoming the alternative to Coke. Recently, the Chinese government lambasted a Nike commercial featuring LeBron James fighting a kung fu master and various other Chinese characters, stating that the spot contained "content that blasphemes national practices and cultures."[51]

Did We Miss Anyone?
You'd Better Believe It

What about Asian Americans? While there are some cultural similarities, you can't use the same tactics for Chinese, Japanese, Korean, Indian, Pakistani, Thai, and the dozens of other Asian American ethnicities. And remember, Asian Americans may be a small market segment, but in general they are also a well-educated and highly affluent segment.

What about Arab Americans? Not all Arabs are Muslim. Not all Muslims are Arabs. How do we address them while not alienating other groups of Americans? The challenges can be daunting.

Then there are Native Americans. We've come a long way from using the most offensive stereotypes, but we still have a long way to go to integrate them into the mainstream. The same is true for disabled people. Every disability presents different wants and needs. Like African Americans before the 1970s, disabled people are nearly invisible in today's advertising.

Then there are children and teens. Teens speak a language anyone over 30 can't possibly comprehend. So how do you write ads to reach them? Children might well be the most interesting and perhaps the most controversial market segment to discuss. There just isn't enough time or space. However, we can offer a few overall tips that apply to most situations:

- Don't make assumptions.

- Do your homework.

- Always remember that even within a market segment there can be huge variation.

- Market segments, like subcultures, are culturally bound.

- Social context matters.

- We'll steal an old slogan: "Act globally and think locally."

- Above all, be respectful.

This last point needs some more discussion. John Kuraoka, a freelance copywriter, offers some advice regarding diversity and copywriting:

Racism, sexism, and other us-against-them motifs are not funny. It is no more acceptable to poke fun at a middle-aged white man than it is to poke fun at a young black lesbian. It makes no difference that you, personally, are either a middle-aged white man or a young black lesbian. On reflection, it's questionable whether poking fun at anybody helps sell anything.[52]

WORDS OF WISDOM

The following was written by Charles Hall, an African American copywriter and film director. While some of it applies specifically to people of color, it's good advice for anyone starting out:

to the blacks browns reds and yellows periwinkles teals and fuchsias

if you want to be in advertising, there is one thing to remember.

don't be afraid.

of hard work, rejection, racism, responsibility, sexism.

don't be afraid of being the only one in the room.

don't be afraid to ask questions, find answers. listen. hear. trust.

don't be afraid to follow. don't be afraid to lead.

don't be afraid to learn. to grow. to mature. to change.

don't be afraid to try. to fail. to try again. fail again. try again and fail again. don't be afraid to ask for help.

don't be afraid to be smart. clever. witty. funky. hard. street. elegant. beautiful. you.

don't be afraid to be fired.

don't be afraid when you hear the word nigger.

don't be afraid to remind them that right after the black jokes come the jewish jokes the polish jokes and the fat jokes.

don't be afraid to master the craft. to master the game.

don't be afraid when they don't understand your accent, dialect, or slang. your heroes, your sex symbols. your style. your music. your people. your culture. your you.

don't be afraid to take criticism.

don't be afraid to be wrong. to be right.

don't be afraid to speak your mind. stand up for what you believe and pay the consequences.

don't be afraid to be a team player. don't be afraid to be the peon. the rookie. the junior. the helper. the pair of hands. the intern. the student.

don't be afraid to not be the victim. don't be afraid to not take it personally. don't be afraid to call a spade a spade.

don't be afraid to have a personality. an opinion. a point of view. a perspective. an objective. a positive attitude.

don't be afraid of those who are threatened by your presence. or feel you don't belong. or those who need you to fail for them to succeed.

don't be afraid to understand the difference between racism and insecurity. between racism and power. between sexism and chauvinism.

don't be afraid to forgive. to apologize. to be humble.

don't be afraid to surrender. to win. to lose. to fight.

don't be afraid of titles, awards. salaries. egos. offices. windows. ponytails. clothes. jewelry. degrees. backgrounds. lifestyles. cars. beach houses.

don't be afraid to compete.

don't be afraid of not being popular.

don't be afraid to work weekends. holidays. birthdays. sick days. personal days.

don't be afraid to work twice as hard. twice as long. twice as good.

don't be afraid to get more out of this business than this business ever intended on giving.

p.s. and under no circumstances whatsoever are you to be intimidated. because some will try.[53]

On the other hand, don't let political correctness overrule common sense. Kuraoka has some good advice on this, too: "**There is a difference between race and racism, sex and sexism.** It is foolish, for example, to make a pantyhose ad gender-neutral. Be aware of cases in which neutering the character of your copy will degrade its effectiveness."[54]

It's Also about the People Who Make the Ads

It's also about the corporations who hire us. It's about who we work for, whether it's the agency or the client. It's about the decisions we make. Would you be willing to do liquor ads if you grew up with an alcoholic father? Would you work for Planned Parenthood if their message conflicts with your beliefs? We might go out with the "girls" or catch a beer with the "boys," but in our ads do we really want to call grown people "boys" or "girls"? It's all a matter of sensitivity. It's a judgment call—your judgment.

WORDS OF WISDOM

"To be sure, men and women approach things differently. . . . But I'm not sure those differences create barriers. In advertising, the issue isn't who did it, but how good is it."

—HELAYNE SPIVAK[55]

Advertising, perhaps more than any other type of business, draws from a wide and varying range of personality types. It can be a very exciting business. It can also be extraordinarily challenging. We could write another chapter on this alone. But as this is a creative strategy book, we'll keep it short and sweet. Our best piece of advice is this: Get to know yourself *before* you get into this business. A lot will be asked of you, and you had better know where you stand before you have to make tough decisions. We can't help but close with the Golden Rule: "Do unto others as you would have them do unto you." We suggest that you take the Golden Rule to heart. It will take you far in this business—and in life.

A final note: In preparing to write this chapter, we talked with a diverse group of advertising practitioners and also conducted extensive secondary research on diversity and on legal and ethical issues as they relate to diversity and creative strategy. We tried to be sensitive and unbiased regarding the various issues discussed here. Yet, in the current supersensitive PC environment, some people may take issue with our content or the tone. Some might say we spent too much text on one issue and not enough on another, or that we totally missed the point on others. The best we can do is to bring these issues out in the open and encourage you to be sensitive to them. How you handle them depends on your own perception and sensitivity.

Who's Who?

Al Anderson—Al Anderson began his career working for the black-owned Citizen's Trust Bank, where one of his first decisions was to reject an outside advertising pitch because it just didn't speak to his customers. The rejection changed his career and led him into the agency world. Today, he is CEO of Anderson Communication, Inc., in Atlanta, the second-oldest African American–owned ad agency. Anderson's clients include Chevrolet, Kraft Foods, Pillsbury, Procter & Gamble, and Reebok. He is perhaps best known for what he and Thomas Burrell preached during the 1970s: "Black people aren't dark-skinned whites."[56]

Thomas Burrell—After starting in the mailroom of a Chicago agency, Thomas Burrell was promoted to copywriter in 1961. During the 1960s, as the race issue gained significance on Madison Avenue, Burrell became a leader in addressing race in advertising. He eventually opened his own agency, Burrell Communications, the first African American ad agency. By 1980, Burrell had become the largest African American agency in the United States, stressing the unique experiences of African Americans. Burrell's client list includes Coca-Cola, McDonald's Corp., Procter & Gamble Co., and Sears, Roebuck & Co. and surpassed $168 million in billing in 1998.[57] Burrell has since retired, leaving a legacy that continues to inspire innovative young advertising professionals.

Anna Morris—Anna Morris is an award-winning creative who began her career with Burrell Communications, where she specialized in targeted radio and television commercials for clients such as Procter & Gamble, Coca-Cola, and McDonald's. Morris later founded an independent production company that specializes in television, targeting African American audiences. In addition to her evolving role as a producer, Morris is a part-time instructor in the Marketing Department at Columbia College in Chicago.

Tere Zubizarreta—A Cuban-born entrepreneur, Tere Zubizarreta spent the first 12 years of her career working for mainstream ad agencies. After her experiences in the late 1960s and early 1970s, she came to believe that mainstream agencies didn't understand how to speak with resonance to Latino consumers. It was clear to her that taking an English spot and dubbing it was just not enough. In 1976, she established her own agency, Zubi Advertising. As of 2003, Zubi had gross billings of $147 million; the agency counts American Airlines, Ford, S. C. Johnson, and Wachovia Bank among its clients.[58]

Notes

[1] A. Jerome Jewler and Bonnie Drewniany, *Creative Strategy in Advertising*, 7th ed. (Belmont, CA: Wadsworth, 2001), 29.

[2] From *American Demographics Forecast*, April 21, 2001, http://www.magazine.org/ Advertising_and_PIB/ad_categories_and_demographics (accessed May 25, 2005).

[3] C. Stone Brown, "African Americans Aren't Dark-Skinned Whites," *DiversityInc*, December 6, 2004. (This and other articles from *DiversityInc* magazine can be accessed online at http://www.diversityinc.com.)

[4] Quoted in ibid.

[5] See "Diversity," n.d., Magazine Publishers of America (MPA) Web site, http://www. magazine.org/diversity (accessed May 25, 2005).

6 PIB (Publishers Information Bureau), 2002.

7 William D. Wells, John Burnett, and Sandra Moriarty, *Advertising: Principles and Practice,* 6th ed. (New York: Prentice Hall, 2003), 107.

8 U.S. Census Bureau, "Forecast Analysis 2000," *Population Today,* May/June 2001.

9 Peter Ortiz, "Women of Color Are on a Buying Spree," *DiversityInc,* July 1, 2004.

10 This 1962 quote from comedian and civil rights activist Gregory comes from Stephen Donadio, ed., *The New York Public Library Book of Twentieth-Century American Quotations* (New York: Stonesong, 1992), 70.

11 Mediamark, fall 2002.

12 Jewler and Drewniany, *Creative Strategy in Advertising,* 31.

13 Quoted in Peter Ortiz, "Calling the Shots—in Spanish," *DiversityInc,* December 13, 2004.

14 Jewler and Drewniany, *Creative Strategy in Advertising,* 31.

15 This information comes from http://css.edu./users/dswenson, October 8, 2001.

16 "Hispanic Fact Pack," *Advertising Age* (suppl.), June 21, 2004, 36.

17 Laurel Wentz, "Heineken, Citibank Are Big Winners," in "Hispanic Creativity" (special report), *Advertising Age,* October 4, 2004, S-2.

18 Angela Johnson, "The Truth about Marketing Urban Legends," *DiversityInc,* January 12, 2004.

19 Iliana Aleman, e-mail correspondence with authors, July 13, 2004.

20 *The Advertising Age Encyclopedia of Advertising,* vol. 3 (New York: Taylor & Francis, 2003), 1655.

21 Ibid.

22 Rob Walker, "The Return of Hilarious Old People: Ads That Make Fun of the Elderly," *Slate,* May 26, 2003, http://www.slate.com/id/2083463 (accessed May 25, 2005).

23 Mary Lou Quinlan, *Just Ask a Woman: Cracking the Code of What Women Want and How They Buy* (Hoboken, NJ: John Wiley, 2003), 1.

24 Faith Popcorn and Lys Marigold, *EVEolution: The Eight Truths of Marketing to Women* (New York: Hyperion, 2000).

25 New Strategist Editors, *American Men and Women: Demographics of the Sexes* (Ithaca, NY: New Strategist, 2000), 247.

26 Ortiz, "Women of Color."

27 Charlie Hess, "Women Lead Way in Profound but Quiet Revolution," *Advertising Age,* January 24, 2000, 26.

28 Hillary Chura, "Failing to Connect: Marketing Messages for Women Fall Short," *Advertising Age,* September 23, 2002, 14.

29 New Strategist Editors, *American Men and Women,* 64.

30 David Ogilvy, *Confessions of an Advertising Man* (New York: Ballantine, 1971), 84.

31 Jean Kilbourne, *Deadly Persuasion: Why Women and Girls Must Fight the Addictive Power of Advertising* (New York: Free Press, 1999); Alissa Quart, *Branded: The Buying and Selling of Teenagers* (Cambridge, MA: Perseus, 2003).

32 Silvia Lagnado, "Getting Real about Beauty," *Advertising Age,* December 6, 2004, 20.

33 Simmons research cited in Walker, "The Return of Hilarious Old People."

[34] Quote from University of Texas at Austin, Department of Advertising, http://advertising.utexas.edu/research/quotes/Q100.html#Advis (accessed May 24, 2005).

[35] Jewler and Drewniany, *Creative Strategy in Advertising,* 41.

[36] T. J. DeGroat, "Target Boots Salvation Army, Wins over Gay Consumers," *DiversityInc,* December 20, 2004.

[37] Quoted in T. J. DeGroat, "Call for Boycott Continues as 4-Year-Old Gay Ad Haunts P&G," *DiversityInc,* December 22, 2004.

[38] http://abcnews.go.com/sections/business/DailyNews/beerads_010530.html (accessed July 24, 2004).

[39] Ibid.

[40] Walker, "The Return of Hilarious Old People."

[41] All of the statistics cited in this paragraph come from Frank Kaiser, "Secrets of Successfully Advertising to Seniors," n.d., http://www.kaisercom.com/advertiseseniors.html (accessed May 25, 2005).

[42] Ibid.

[43] List adapted from http://www.eamet.com.

[44] Ibid.

[45] Information from http://css.edu./users/dswenson, October 8, 2001.

[46] Johnson, "The Truth about Marketing Urban Legends."

[47] Wells et al., *Advertising,* 107.

[48] Laurel Wentz and Mercedes M. Cardona, "Robust Ad Spending Growth Forecast for U.S. Next Year," *Advertising Age,* December 8, 2003, 8.

[49] "Global Marketing Expenditure," *Brand Strategy,* February 2004, 38.

[50] R. Craig Endicott, "Top Marketers Spend $74 Billion," *Advertising Age,* November 10, 2003, 26.

[51] "Advertising 101: U.S. Sensibilities Don't Always Translate Overseas," *DiversityInc,* December 19, 2004.

[52] John Kuraoka, "How to Write Better Ads," n.d., http://www.kuraoka.com/how-to-write-better-ads.html (accessed May 25, 2005).

[53] Quoted in Maxine Paetro, *How to Put Your Book Together and Get a Job in Advertising* (Chicago: Copy Workshop, 2002), 156.

[54] John Kuraoka, "How to Write Better Ads," n.d., http://www.kuraoka.com/how-to-write-better-ads.html (accessed May 25, 2005).

[55] Quote from the Clio Awards Web site, http://www.clioawards.com/html/wsj/spivak/html (accessed January 10, 2005).

[56] Brown, "African Americans Aren't Dark-Skinned Whites."

[57] "The Advertising Century" (special issue), *Advertising Age,* March 29, 1999, 66.

[58] Ortiz, "Calling the Shots."

Concepting (What's the Big Idea?)

The word *concepting* usually trips up spell-checkers. They often try to replace it with *conception*. We suppose in many ways it's similar to creating new life. Another way to say it is *ideation* or *the creative process*. In this book we define concepting as the development of the big idea. If you have a central thought, that One Thing you can say about the product, how do you say it and how do you show it? Right now we'll focus on print concepts, with the primary emphasis on magazine ads. Why magazine ads? They give you the space for copy if you want to write it, they work very well for multi-ad campaigns, and they fit into your portfolio nicely. The same processes are used for other media, except for radio, where the visual is implied.

Concepting is the bridge between strategy and tactics, taking you from gathering facts and getting organized to creating words and pictures. At this stage in your career, you don't have to be a great writer or an accomplished art director. But you should start working on becoming a great idea person.

How to Be Creative (Concepting Strategies)

You can find many theories and recommendations on how to be creative. However, it's not a nice, neat, linear process. In most cases, the only scientific principle that applies is "chaos theory." That killer idea may pop up in the shower. On the drive into work. When you're watching TV. Or in a dream. No one can tell you when and how to think it. Concepting a single ad or a whole campaign is like making sausage. The end result can be delicious, but the outside world doesn't want to see how it's done.

While there is no single process that works for everyone, most people rely on two basic methods:

1. Adapt the strategy to the creative.

2. Make the creative fit the strategy.

Working backward: There's got to be a strategy in there somewhere

We've all done it. In a sudden fit of inspiration, you come up with a great headline or find a really cool photo. Now, how can you use it? There's got to be some client this will work for. Maybe it's so great it doesn't matter if it solves the client's problem. Any of that annoying problem-solving stuff can be handled in the body copy. Heck, you can throw in a subhead to explain it. After it's done, you can always go back and rationalize a strategy. Who knows, it might even be on target when you work backward.

This approach is usually used in the following scenarios:

- Pitching new business ("We don't know much about your product but we can do wacky stuff.")

- Portfolio padding ("The ad looks great, and no one will know if it really didn't sell anything.")

- Awards competition (See above.)

- Advertising class work ("This was the only decent picture I could find so I had to build my ad around it.")

Concepting by the book

Great concepts begin with great strategy and great research. Garbage in, garbage out. Before you start scribbling, make sure you have the answers to the following questions:

- What is the client's real problem?

- Can I solve the problem creatively with marketing communications?

- Do I know the target audience?

- Do I know the product features/benefits?

- What is the One Thing I can say or show about this product?

- How much do I need to say or show? (Do I even need a headline?)

- Where is this product positioned? Where do we want to be positioned?

- Do I know the competition's strengths and weaknesses?

- What should the tone be?

Depending on the product and target audience, some of the answers to the above questions may be "not applicable." For a mature package good, such as deodorant, you really don't need an in-depth analysis. But you do need to understand the target audience and find the right tone to reach them.

Concepting Approaches

As we've mentioned, developing creative ideas is not a neat, orderly process. Many texts provide formulas for concepts, which usually work great to describe a completed ad, but don't help to develop a new one. At the risk of falling into the same trap, we offer several simplified approaches to concepting.

- *Show the product:* Establish or reinforce brand identity. Period.

- *Show the benefit:* What happens when you use it? What does it do for you?

- *Show the alternative:* What happens when you don't use it, or when you use the competition?

- *Comparison:* Compare it to other products or offer a metaphor.

- *Borrowed interest:* Introduce something seemingly unrelated.

- *Testimonial/case history:* Present an endorsement or description of what it's done for someone else, whether a celebrity or an ordinary person.

WORDS OF WISDOM

"Good advertising achieves whatever objectives are established at the outset. Some campaigns do this through sheer weight and repetition. Others do it by speaking to the consumer in an intelligent manner, as an equal, opting for the highest common denominator rather than the lowest."

—JEFF GOODBY[2]

Show the product

It sounds boring, but some of the most innovative ads just show the product or logo. The benefit may be buried in the copy, implied in a tagline, or missing entirely. The main purpose is to establish a brand image or reinforce that image. For example, with most packaged goods, it's probably better to show the package or label rather than describe it in a headline. After all, it's what the consumer sees on the grocery store shelf. Sometimes you can set up a concept in a modified "question/answer" format, where the question (or problem) is stated and the product/package/logo is the answer (solution).

Show the benefit

In many cases, this involves a straightforward declarative sentence proclaiming the main benefit. Usually the reader does not have to think too hard to get the concept. Sometimes this is the first thing you think of. From here you move on to more creative approaches. However, it may be exactly what's required, especially if you can pair your straightforward headline with a compelling, attention-getting graphic. For a soft drink, for example, you may not have any headline, but you show the can or bottle and people having fun. The benefit is implied: Your product is connected with good times.

4.1. Sometimes when you show the product, the headline and copy are the fun parts of the ad.

4.2. Look closely and you'll see this "pixilated" Honda Element is actually constructed entirely of Legos. So you can not only show the product, but you can also make the point that everything fits together just right.

4.3. This student ad does a great job of establishing the package as well as positioning the product as just water.

4.4. The benefit here is as plain as the hair on your head.

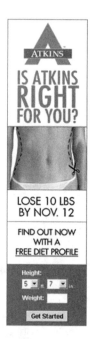

4.5. In this banner ad the benefit is not only shown, it can also be personalized. Of course, considering the already slim, headless women, it's also hard to miss the messages about perfection and objectification.

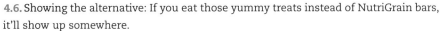

4.6. Showing the alternative: If you eat those yummy treats instead of NutriGrain bars, it'll show up somewhere.

4.7. This student-designed ad shows the alternative to wearing a new Hanes T shirt. ("Sometimes you need a plain white T-shirt.")

Show the alternative

This can be a lot of fun. One extreme example is a campaign for Terminex that shows outrageous ways people keep insects out of their homes—turning the living room into an ice-covered deep freeze, for one. That's a lot more interesting than showing a clean, bug-free house. When you go back to basic wants and needs of the target audience, it becomes easier to visualize the alternative concept. In most cases, you think of the opposite of basic wants and needs—hunger, thirst, embarrassment, loneliness, illness, pain, and so on. You can probably think of several extreme images for each of these that are far more interesting than their positive counterparts.

Comparison

You can compare your product to a competitor or, by using a metaphor, compare it to just about anything.

Competitive/Comparison Concepts

When you go head-to-head against the competition, keep these factors in mind:

- If you are the market leader, don't compare yourself to number two.
- When you compare product claims, make sure you are correct.

A few examples:

Avis claimed they were number two, so they had to try harder than Hertz to win your business. Seven-Up is crisp, clear, and citrus-based versus brown cola-nut sodas. It's the "uncola." Both claims were true. Both claims were made by competitors hoping to gain market share from the leaders.

4.8. In this ad, Lincoln compares their large Aviator SUV to their own titanic Navigator instead of to competitive brands, using the headline "Genes? Yes. Clone? No."

4.9. A competitive comparison that shows a tangible benefit—half the fat of the leading brand.

The "cola wars" of the 1980s and 1990s represent another component of competitive advertising. Pepsi was number two to Coke and pursued a very aggressive series of campaigns that involved taste tests, celebrity talent, catchy jingles, cutting-edge concepts, elaborate sales promotions, and take-no-prisoners marketing tactics. While Pepsi won the hearts and minds of ad critics with their creativity, they are still number two—probably because the consumer still can't perceive a real difference between Pepsi and Coke.

Here are some tips for comparison advertising:

1. Try to make sure that your claims are as factually bulletproof as possible.

2. Try to collect hard evidence in advance to support your factual assertions (your lawyer will thank you).

3. Consider the risk/reward ratio—how much incremental benefit you will get from making the specific comparison versus how much additional risk you court by doing so.

4. Consider including a footnote with additional factual data, such as (a) the applicable version numbers of the products in question and (b) the date as of which the information is current.[3]

4.10. This student visual puzzle says Oxydol gets any smell out of clothes. Look closely and you'll see the "skunk" is actually a pile of clothes.

4.11. Two ways to use white space. Banana Boat sunblock keeps you from turning red. Get it?

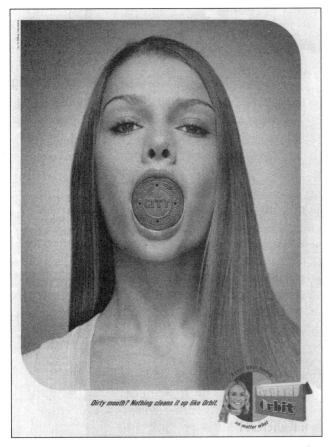

4.12. Look closely. That's a manhole cover, not a cookie, in her mouth. Can you think of a stronger metaphor for bad breath?

4.13. Visual metaphors work for business ads, too, especially when you're discussing rather intangible products, such as improvement in data-processing speed.

4.14. Everyone knows what a Hershey's bar looks like, so this ad uses borrowed interest to show why it would be bad to change it.

Metaphors

Favorites of English teachers and awards judges. Since grade school, you've been instructed to use metaphors to spice up your compositions. Use what you know about metaphors and apply them visually to your ad concepts. Visual metaphors can be very direct, such as a grumpy bear morphing into a normal-looking guy after his first cup of coffee in the morning. Or they can be more subtle. Some are very obscure and require a few mental leaps to connect the visual with a product. Sometimes readers appreciate the minor challenge of making that connection themselves. They know the advertiser gives them some credit for having a brain.

Judging by recent awards programs, the greater the distance from visual to benefit or brand value, the higher the ranking, especially if you dispense with headlines or copy to sell anything. Even though you may lose many readers with obscure visual puzzles, sometimes you'll really hook the committed few who take the time to study and understand your ads. You need to know if enough members of your target audience can solve your visual puzzle (unless your only goal is to pad your portfolio).

Borrowed interest

Sometimes you can use something seemingly unrelated to make a point. Like the visual puzzle, it relies on a visual for the bulk of the message, but unlike a metaphor, there's no obvious direct connection to the product name or benefit. Usually this approach involves some kind of attention-getting graphic and/or headline that snags readers. Once they're hooked, the body copy reels 'em in. Sometimes the only objective is brand recognition, and no copy is needed. Some texts call this the "indirect approach" versus a direct benefit. Whatever you call it, it can work very well as long as readers get your intended message and remember the brand favorably.

Testimonials/case histories

Years ago, celebrities not only allowed products to attach names to their fame, they actively pitched the products. Ronald Reagan, for one, breathlessly hawked cigarettes, soap, and General Electric. Another form of "testimonial" told a story, often in a comic strip format, of an ordinary Joe with a problem. His wife/best friend/boss tips him off about the wonderful product, and in the final frame he's happy as a clam, achieving inner happiness and financial success.

Today, testimonials, celebrity and otherwise, are still a popular concept. To be effective, they must have credibility—sort of like an editorial feature.

RON LORY *is an autoworker, a father of three and a lifelong St. Louis baseball fan. He and his family have strong ties to the Midwest. Here, he tells us why, despite the risks, he uprooted his family and left a secure job to come help build the brand new Saturn cars in Spring Hill, Tennessee.*

"…I'm a St. Louis boy, and my wife is a St. Louis girl. I raised my family there and worked at a car plant thirty miles out.

I enjoyed what I was doing, but you reach a point in your life when you look at the future and decide to do something for no other reason than just believing it's right.

For me, Saturn was the chance to make a difference. To prove I have a mind, that I'm more than just a pair of hands. **I wouldn't have moved my family four hundred miles just to fail. Then have to pack them up and move again.**

My wife had to leave a house she loved. A nice three-bedroom with a full basement and a patio in the back.

My 16-year-old was convinced we were

ruining her life. Her first serious romance, and all. I wouldn't have made the move unless the whole family said 'Let's go for it,' and my daughter knew it. So she decided to try. You know, I'm really proud of her for that.

Funny story. When I first heard about Saturn, I came home and we started hauling out the maps, looking for Spring Hill. 'Where's Spring Hill?' Sure enough, it's right in the middle of the fold and we couldn't find it.

Now, can you imagine trying to talk a couple of teenagers into moving to a town that's smaller than their high school?…"

A DIFFERENT KIND *of* COMPANY. A DIFFERENT KIND *of* CAR.

If you'd like to know more about Saturn, and our new sedans and coupe, please call us at 1-800-522-5000.

4.15. When Saturn introduced their brand, they didn't show cars. They told stories about the people who make them. This ad talks about a guy who moved his family to Tennessee to work for Saturn.

PIERCE BROSNAN'S CHOICE

SEAMASTER AQUA TERRA
Co-Axial Escapement
3 year extended warranty

The name Omega has always been closely associated with quality and reliability. The Seamaster Aqua Terra upholds this pioneering spirit. Its classic design features the latest in watchmaking technology, the unique Co-Axial Escapement movement, which offers unrivalled long term accuracy.

OMEGA

Brown & Co Roswell, GA 1-800-535-0620

4.16. Now that he's no longer 007, Pierce doesn't need a watch that turns into a cruise missile.

You might want to consider using a case history or testimonial in the following circumstances:

- The right celebrity can have a positive and plausible connection with the right product (Lance Armstrong promoting Trek bicycles).

- You can develop a case history that convinces the reader the product can solve a similar problem for the consumer (a farmer says, "I saved $4,000 this year by using a new automated milking system").

- You can connect an event or person to the product to leave a positive impression (a Buick dealer promotion tied in with Tiger Woods and the Buick Open golf tournament).

On the other hand, your testimonial or case history could be so outrageously fake that readers can see through the satire and create a positive image of the product. In other words, use a celebrity to convey an alternative message, such as the ad for a barbershop featuring Richard Nixon and the headline, "You can't cover up a bad haircut."

Gary Jobson puts his trust in classics.

WHIRLW...
Perpetual Spirit

Having completed successfully in a variety of boats, Gary Jobson's choice for himself is a classic Herreshoff 28-footer, whose graceful design will never go out of style. The same aesthetic is reflected in his timepiece.

ROLEX

4.17. "Gary Jobson put his trust in classics." He may not be as famous as Pierce Brosnan, but he's the kind of guy who appreciates things of value.

The Concepting Process

Now comes the fun part. Time is running out. Your assignment is due tomorrow morning. You're still sitting in front of a pile of white paper and your mind is as blank as the first sheet on the stack.

Say it straight, then say it great

If you're not blessed with a sudden bolt of creativity, how do you get started? One of the best pieces of advice comes from Luke Sullivan: "Say it straight, then say it great."[4] In other words, try a straightforward approach just to get the facts organized and trigger more ideas. You can start with "This ad is about. . . ." Then you can toss that and move on to a more creative way to say it and show it.

This is also a great way to test the strategy internally. Work up a number of straightforward concepts that look like ads. Then review them with the account team. The objective is to get the group to say, "Yeah. That's the main idea. Now how do we make it better?" This not only makes for better concepts, it helps build good relationships with your team. Take their input, then really go to work to do something great.

You may want to start scribbling down product features or other attributes of a product and keep asking "So what?" Those questions may lead to something interesting.

Brainstorming

Here's the recipe for a great concept: Combine two creative people, preferably a writer and art director; add stacks of blank paper, Sharpies®, pencils, and layout pads; mix in copies of *Communication Arts,* stock photo books, and popular magazines; turn up the heat with tight deadlines and client demands; let it simmer or boil over occasionally; if cooking process takes longer, add pizza, junk food, and beer; allow thoughts to cook until a number of rough ideas develop or one of the creative people has killed the other.

From our experience, we've found brainstorming works best with two people. Usually, the dynamic duo is the copywriter/art director team. But it may be two writers or two art directors. Or an art director/illustrator or writer/producer team. Sometimes a third or fourth party gets involved, but it's usually better to bring in other people to validate ideas rather than develop them.

Creating by committee is usually a bad idea, especially if a client is involved in the early process. Sometimes a creative team needs to really rip on the product or brand to get the silliness out of the way and/or really address some marketing problems. That's hard to do with a client in the same room. It's always better to ask a client, "What do you think of this idea?" instead of "What do you think we should do?" The process often isn't pretty. Most times you really don't want to know how it's done as long as the finished product turns out great.

Idea starters

Sometimes you don't have the luxury of brainstorming with another creative person. Your only companion is a blank sheet of paper, mocking every lame idea that pops into your fevered brain. In this case, don't wait for the perfect concept to develop. Just start scribbling. Write down anything. Even the stupid stuff. Jot down key words. Doodle different visuals. Write out headlines or taglines. Just keep working, and eventually you'll have a stack of ideas. Most of them will be junk. But there just may be a few keepers. Show these to the art director. He or she may be able to work some magic. Or he or she may twist your idea into one that's even better.

Ten tips for better concepts

Through years of trial and error (more of the latter), we've developed a few recommendations for developing creative ideas:

WORDS OF WISDOM

"I have learned to respect ideas, wherever they come from. Often they come from clients. Account executives often have big creative ideas, regardless of what some writers think."

—LEO BURNETT[6]

1. *Just do it.* Scribble down everything. Key words. Sketches. Stick people. At this stage, there are no stupid ideas. One key word or visual could trigger an entire award-winning campaign.

2. *Write, don't talk.* Keep scribbling. If something works, then describe it to your partner. If you can't explain it in a few well-chosen words, go back to scribbling.

3. *Throw it all on the wall and see what sticks.* Tack your ideas on a wall and stare at them for a while. If you have the luxury of time, come back the next day and see if they still look good. Invite a couple other people to look at them and ask for feedback.

4. *If you're on a roll, don't stop.* Once the creative juices get flowing, keep tossing out ideas. If you're lucky, you and your partner will get on a streak and come up with not only a killer theme, but enough concepts for a whole campaign.

5. *Does this look funny?* During your concept development you'll come up with a lot of silly ideas. Some may make you fall down laughing, either because they're so funny or you're totally sleep deprived. Humor is a powerful force, so if your idea still makes you and others chuckle a couple days later, find some way to use it. With that said, don't set out to be funny. Try to be interesting.

6. *Show it, don't tell it.* One picture may be worth a thousand sales. Find an image that grabs a reader. Then develop a tagline or headline that works in synergy with that image, rather than just describing it. Luke Sullivan says, "Try to solve the problems visually if you can. As larger brands become globally marketed, visual solutions will become even more important. Visuals translate better than words."[7]

7. *Don't be different just to be different.* To paraphrase Bill Bernbach, don't show a man standing on his head unless the ad sells something to keep things in his pockets. Sometimes an art director will go crazy with backgrounds, weird typography, and other bells and whistles that satisfy his or her creative muse. But if they don't add anything to the concept, don't do it.

8. *Keep it simple.* Don't lose sight of the main idea. You've got the concept burned in your brain, but does a casual reader get it? If not, adding

WAR STORY:

"START ME UP" AND SAY GOODBYE: SOMETIMES YOU CAN'T GO HOME AGAIN

At Wieden + Kennedy, Charlotte Moore was part of the creative team that helped win scores of prestigious awards for Nike and other clients. After a sabbatical, she returned to W+K, where she was assigned to the agency's newest client, Microsoft. Here's her story:

I had a creative person's pie-in-the-sky notions. I was exceedingly romantic about the possibilities, and why shouldn't I have been? What could lend itself to a wider and deeper (in fact, bottomless) dialogue than the world of communication, business, exchange, technology, creation? After all, isn't that what software really is? It's a tool, yes, but it's a tool that invisibly and, if well designed, intuitively serves our most basic human expressions. I was ready to delve into it.

I was not prepared for the client, for the phalanxes of "software people" who responded analytically, but utterly unemotionally, to creative work. I was appalled that the people who made the very tools I was so excited about could see only the "toolishness" of the tools, and not what they actually made possible on the bigger scale. I was frustrated that exciting work that addressed the big issues of communication and creativity and productivity was routinely shot down in favor of stuff that was more

blandly corporate or features oriented. And ultimately, I was incapable of accepting the results, which were (to me) un-Wieden + Kennedy-like to the extreme. Not radical. Not interesting. Not moving. Not what I wanted to be responsible for.

The final indignity was the production of a spot for the launch of Windows 95, which featured—in fact, was based on—the Rolling Stones song "Start Me Up" because it was linked, obviously enough, to the Microsoft Windows "start button" feature. My partner had suggested it. (I don't blame him; it was a solution in a tight squeeze, and perhaps from some point of view it was the right thing to do.) But I hated the cheapening of a rock classic. I hated the fact that the spot had no idea of its own, other than to throw mediocre visuals of people using computers against a $3 million sound track. And I hated the fact that in some way I was responsible, though I couldn't for the life of me figure out how.

So I resigned. It seemed that where the agency wanted to go was not where I wanted to go. And no one asked me to reconsider. I did go back to the agency a year later as the co–creative director in Amsterdam. I've since moved on. But it's still the agency I consider my workplace, and my professional home. I suppose it's no wonder that I've chosen, in its wake, to remain a free agent, taking projects here and there, but with no deep commitment.

subheads to explain the idea or cramming in extra inset photos won't help. Simple ideas break through the clutter; they are easier to remember, and sometimes they clarify the strategy.

9. *Don't second-guess the client.* Develop concepts that get attention and sell the product. Then worry about selling them to the client. Don't handcuff your creativity by worrying about what the client will like before you begin. The client hired you to be creative. Otherwise, they'd be doing their own ads.

10. *Build a "maybe" file.* Most of your ideas won't work, but don't throw them all away. File the better ones. They may be the answer for the next assignment. Keep a file of the scrap-stock photos, competitor ads, articles, and other stuff that can trigger some great ideas.

Concept Testing

You should test your concepts at three stages, starting with yourself.

Self-evaluation

You've narrowed your stack of rough ideas down to a single concept that you love. But before you start asking the creative director for a raise, make sure you do a little internal evaluation of your ideas.

Level 1: Gut check. The first level of testing begins with you. Ask yourself, Does this concept feel right? If you have the luxury of time, put it aside for a few days and then ask the same question. This means don't start thinking about it the night before it's due.

Level 2: Two quick tests. The first is the "matchbook test." Can you put your idea on the cover of a matchbook and still convey the One Thing about your product? Another quick test is the "billboard test." If you have written copy and laid out the ad, cover up the body copy so you see only the headline and main graphic. Would it make a good billboard? If so, your creative idea communicates quickly and effectively. If not, maybe you need to come up with some new ideas.

Level 3: Honest evaluation. Your idea looks good and feels good. But it still has to meet some objectives. Remember strategy? So before you fall in love with your idea, ask yourself . . .

- *Is this concept doable?* Can you pull this off within the budget constraints? Can you execute it correctly? Do you have the talent? Props? Locations? All the other things required to make this idea work?

- *Is it on target for this audience?* You love it, but will the intended buyer? You might want to try it out on a few people in the target audience—but don't rule it out if all of them don't get it.

- *Does it have legs?* Will this idea work in an extended campaign? Is it a one-hit wonder, or can you expand this concept for use in other media?

- *Can you sell this to the client?* Is this idea so far out of the box the client will have a heart attack? Can you justify this concept with sound logic?

Creative director/account executive evaluation

The creative director and account executive will also quickly run through the self-evaluation process listed above. They will also apply a higher standard of evaluation that includes the following questions:

- *Have I seen this before?* Chances are, your creative director and account executive have been working a few more years than you. It's much better for them to point out an unoriginal idea than the client.

- *Will it grab the reader?* What's going to catch the reader's eye and make him or her notice your ad? A former boss said it best: "We need a concept that's like a fishhook in the brain."

- *What is the visual-verbal connection?* Concepts are much stronger when the headline and visual work together. When the reader makes the connection, the ad is more memorable. When the headline describes the visual, you've wasted an opportunity.

- *What is the One Thing?* Is the central truth evident in this concept? A good CD can spot it immediately. If you have to explain a concept to him or her, you're in trouble. You can't rationalize an ad to every reader of the magazine.

Client evaluation

Clients are fond of telling their agencies to think outside the box. What is this "box," anyway? Typically, clients confine the box to features and benefits. Some engineering- oriented companies think in terms of specifications. Marketing-driven companies think in terms of solving problems for customers. Your box should be much larger. Once you start working within your bigger box, look for ways to step outside of it. It's always better to have a bunch of crazy ideas you can pull back into the box than having the client tell you to be more creative.

Sarah does not want to play with father.

Her father likes the kind of games that hurt.

Soon, Sarah will find some new friends.

They will give her drugs and money to make the pain go away.

4.18. Looks like an old-style first-grade reading book, right? Look closer: It's a very direct and disturbing ad about child abuse. The old-school graphic approach isn't aimed at kids. It's meant to attract Baby Boomers who might be hurting their children.

Do the Twist

Not to be confused with a dance from the 1960s, a twist is an unexpected element in an ad or commercial. The

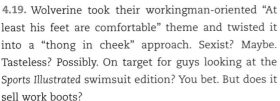

4.19. Wolverine took their workingman-oriented "At least his feet are comfortable" theme and twisted it into a "thong in cheek" approach. Sexist? Maybe. Tasteless? Possibly. On target for guys looking at the *Sports Illustrated* swimsuit edition? You bet. But does it sell work boots?

4.20. Sometimes being edgy just means being goofy. To promote their breakfast items, Burger King wanted people to "Wake up with the King." In this TV spot, a mascot with an absurd plastic head shows up in this guy's bed. BK's agency said the ad was designed to appeal to the ironic bent of cynical 18–35-year-olds.

most obvious example is the recent commercial for Pepsi Twist (the name is a fortunate coincidence) in which the Osbourne children unzip their skins to reveal they are really Donny and Marie Osmond. That's a twist. But there's one more. Ozzy wakes up from this nightmare to find his wife is really Florence Henderson. It's hard to figure out which of them should be more scared.

Here's another TV twist: A prosperous-looking retired couple relaxes on their sailboat in the Caribbean. It looks like an ad for a mutual fund, insurance company, or arthritis medication. The twist? It's actually a commercial for paper shredders. It seems that this sweet old couple stole your credit card number and are now living the high life because you didn't shred your receipts.

WORDS OF WISDOM

"Advertising needs to have a bit of an edge, whether it's aimed at the neighborhood or the world."

—PHIL DUSENBERRY[8]

4.21. From the infamous Abercrombie & Fitch Christmas catalog. Nothing expresses the spirit of the season like a bunch of flawless young white people sleeping under the tree buck naked. Future catalogs may be just as racy, but the models will probably be more diverse, after a 2004 court settlement that requires A&F to institute a range of policies and programs to promote diversity to prevent discrimination based on race or gender. The line between edgy and ethical is very thin indeed.

Finding the edge

It's starting to become a cliché, but people are still looking for an edge—some kind of creative device to separate their advertising from the rest of the pack. "Edgy" ads take risks. They may push the envelope (another overused term) to the breaking point. In summary, creatives who work on the edge:

- Risk offending general audience to appeal to target audience.

- Shock the reader/viewer into noticing.

- Drive a wedge between "our customers" and everyone else (us versus them).

Going for the edge may seem like the perfect approach. If you are willing to offend or confuse a large share of the total audience to make a stronger connection to a highly defined target audience, it might be OK. However, never forget the risks of pushing the envelope too far. Before you cross that line, you should review Chapter 3 and reconsider.

4.22. A nice play on words . . . but unfortunately a group of needlepointers took issue with being called "old bats." The billboard was modified so it would not offend.

4.23. One of a series of Nike ads supporting disabled athletes. The campaign uses what could be seen as disturbing photos and matches them to positive copy. The net result is you don't feel sorry for these guys, you admire them.

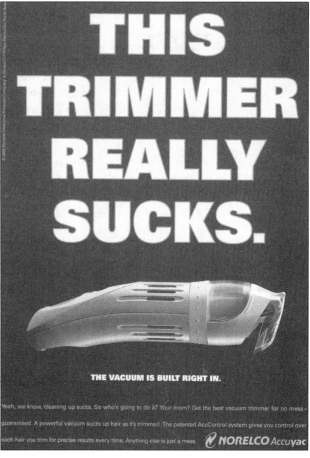

4.24. Sure, it's a play on words (because the trimmer cuts and vacuums), but does using vulgar slang grab your target audience or just seem like you're pandering to them?

How to give your ads an edge

The lazy way—*nudity, sex, violence, offensive language:* In an attempt to be edgy, some creatives use words and images that may be controversial to the general audience, without regard to the consequences. However, this approach may be on target for their intended audience. For example, an ad featuring gratuitous nudity in *Playboy* would not be very shocking. The same ad in *Reader's Digest* would be scandalous. Creating an ad just for shock value, rather than to sell something, is usually a losing proposition. So many TV commercials use crude bathroom humor, frat-house sexual jokes, and slapstick violence that they don't really create an edge anymore.

Music/sound effects: Using hip-hop or hard-core rap to promote a car to 20- to 30-year-olds makes sense, but don't expect Baby Boomers to dig it. Using Led Zeppelin for Cadillac was kind of edgy, since their primary owner base of

septuagenarians probably said, "What's with that hippie garbage?" But for aging Boomers, rock 'n' roll resonates.

Us versus them: Depending on your target market, you can pit young against old, men against women, slobs against snobs, gays against straights, jocks against nerds, or any group against another. The approach is, "We've got the product just for you, not those other people."

Inside jokes/slang: Talk to a snowboarder about "grabbing some really sick air" and you're cool. Say the same thing to his grandfather and he's thinking about his bathroom. It only works if your target audience believes the advertiser is one of them. Nothing bombs like a 45-year-old trying to talk like an 18-year-old.

Production values/design: The advent of MTV forever changed the way we produce commercials. Music video production techniques have found their way into all media. Jump cuts. Bizarre camera angles. Grainy, out-of-focus, blurred images. Unreadable type. Ambiguous messages. You'll find them wherever some writer or art director wants to push the edge.

4.25. When you're promoting a hard-core record label, you can get a little edgy—and a little messy, as in this student-designed ad.

Before you get edgy:

• Understand the tolerances of the total audience.

• Really understand how far you can push your target audience.

- Consider the risks (legal, ethical, business).

- Check your personal moral compass. Are you proud of the work?

- Be able to defend your idea logically, not just because you think it's cool.

- Have a backup idea.

- Don't try to be different just to be different.

- Get paid before the client goes bankrupt.

What to Do When You're Stuck

Everybody develops writer's block. Sometimes the slump lasts a few hours, sometimes a lot longer. Novelists have the option of waiting weeks and months for inspiration. Copywriters don't. So what happens when that blank sheet of paper becomes your worst enemy? We offer the following suggestions:

- *Back up.* Find out where you are, and you might know why you're stuck. Do you understand the product, the market, the target audience, the competition, and the tone? Did you miss something? Do you have enough information to "say it straight"? If so, you are very close to finding ways to "say it great."

- *Go back to the books.* Dig out old issues of *Communication Arts* and *CMYK*. Check out new Web sites that feature award winners. Leaf through the stock photo books.

WORDS OF WISDOM

"Rarely have I seen any really good advertising created without a certain amount of confusion, throw-aways, bent noses, irritation and downright cursedness."

—LEO BURNETT[10]

- *Talk about it.* Find a sympathetic ear and state your problem. Don't ask for ideas. Just explain what you know about the assignment and where you're stuck. You might find that by explaining it out loud, you'll find the solution yourself. Sometimes you'll mention an idea that seems kind of lame to you and another person loves it. They might give you just enough encouragement to turn it into a great idea.

- *Take a break.* See a movie. Watch TV. Play basketball. Dig in your garden. Do something totally unrelated to work. This will unclog your mind and may allow some fresh ideas to sneak in. (Just don't let your break extend to an hour before your assignment is due.)

- *Don't expect to find inspiration in drugs or booze.* You might develop a good idea by getting high. Under the influence, just about anything seems like a good idea. It's just not smart for your career long term. You're a professional doing your job. Deal with it straight!

4.26. Hitting a brick wall is every writer's worst nightmare.

Source: Illustration by Dan Augustine.

Who's Who?

Carl Ally—Cofounder of Ally & Gargano, Carl Ally is known for cutting-edge and risky advertising that spoke very bold truths. Some of his breakthrough advertising included work for FedEx, Hertz, Dunkin' Donuts, Volvo, Fiat, Saab, MCI Communications, Polaroid, IBM, PanAm, Piper Aircraft, and several others. He was the man responsible for winning a change in television rules against mentioning the competition in commercials. He was not afraid to take on corporate underdogs, and he changed many unknown companies into household names. He enjoyed taking on accounts that were new or troubled, and he built brands up from almost nothing.[11]

Phillip Dusenberry—Phillip Dusenberry joined BBDO as a copywriter in 1962 and developed into one of the world's most influential creative forces as he rose to vice chairman at BBDO Worldwide. His impact came chiefly from memorable General Electric and Pepsi-Cola campaigns (including a megamillion-dollar deal with Michael Jackson). Dusenberry also played a major role with advertising's volunteer Tuesday Team, whose "Morning in America" commercials helped reelect Ronald Reagan. His screenwriting credits include "The Natural," starring Robert Redford.

Charlotte Moore—Born in Chattanooga, Tennessee, and educated in Virginia, Charlotte Moore is a southerner who found a spiritual and professional home on the West Coast when she began to work for the creative hot shop Wieden + Kennedy. Over the course of almost eight years, she worked as art director and, eventually, group creative director on accounts that included Nike, Microsoft, and Coke. She did her most exceptional work with her partner of many years, Janet Champ, on Nike's print advertising for women. She left the agency in the fall of 1995 but returned as co–creative director of its European headquarters in Amsterdam. Ambition was interrupted by love, however, and she followed her heart to Italy, where she currently lives with her husband and children, and pursues creative projects sometimes for money, but more often for personal reasons. Along the way, she has been recognized by *CA,* One Show, and *McCall's* Advertising Women of the Year, and has received four nominations and two back-to-back wins in the MPA's Kelly Awards for best, most effective print advertising.

Luke Sullivan—An award-winning copywriter (twice named by *AdWeek* as one of the top writers in the United States), Luke Sullivan is also the author of a very nice book about copywriting, *Hey Whipple, Squeeze This,* which should be required reading for anyone who is serious about a career in copywriting.

Notes

[1] Quote from the Clio Awards Web site, http://www.clioawards.com/html/wsj/spivak.html (accessed January 10, 2005).

[2] Quote from the Clio Awards Web site, http://www.clioawards.com/html/wsj/goodby.html (accessed December 15, 2004).

[3] See "Allegedly Out-of-Date Comparative Advertising Triggers Lawsuit," August 14, 2003, on the By No Other Web site, http://www.bynoother.com/2003/08/comparative_adv.html (accessed June 3, 2005).

[4] Luke Sullivan, *Hey Whipple, Squeeze This: A Guide to Creating Great Ads* (Hoboken, NJ: John Wiley, 1998), 52.

[5] Morris Hite, *Adman: Morris Hite's Methods for Winning the Ad Game* (Dallas: E-Heart, 1988), 165.

[6] Leo Burnett, 100 LEO's: Wit and Wisdom from Leo Burnett (Chicago: NTC Business Press, 1995), 52.

[7] Sullivan, *Hey Whipple, Squeeze This,* 37.

[8] Quote from the Clio Awards Web site, http://www.clioawards.com/html/wsj/dusenberry.html (accessed December 20, 2004).

[9] Quoted in Cristin Burton, "The Life and Career of Carl Ally," March 31, 2004, http://www.ciadvertising.org/sa/spring_04/adv382j/cristin44/home.html (accessed June 3, 2005).

[10] Burnett, *100 LEO's,* 7.

[11] See Burton, "The Life and Career of Carl Ally."

Design for Writers

Why me?

I'm not a designer.

Ah! But your eye went right to what you hoped would be the answer. By the end of this chapter, you'll understand and appreciate why your eye traveled as it did and be able to answer the question, Why me?

Design for copywriters is in many ways just like design for art directors. The biggest difference is we won't hold you accountable for design and layout perfection. That's where your partner the art director comes in. However, in the classroom, or if you're not working in an agency, chances are you'll be both the copywriter and the art director.

Why Writers Need to Be Designers Too

Have you ever seen a copywriter's portfolio filled with nothing but copy sheets? Precisely. If you want to get a job, an internship, or even a foot in the door, you'd better learn how to put your concepts into visually interesting layouts. Copy doesn't exist in a vacuum. You need to marry copy to design within an engaging layout. Mind you, we didn't say *perfect*—we said *interesting* and *engaging*.

WORDS OF WISDOM

"Type, photography, illustration are tools. You need to know how they work . . . if you can't use the tools, you really can't make a good idea work."

—HELMUT KRONE[1]

Just what makes a layout interesting? We'll get to that a bit later. First, let's consider why copywriters need to understand design:

- Words and visuals do not exist in isolation.

- The creative should engage the audience visually and verbally.

- Design helps express the big idea and sell the product.

- Portfolios are important, and presentation matters.

- Multiple skills increase your value.

- Knowledge is power.

This last one deserves a little more discussion, even if you're never going to be a creative. Fine. Now, imagine yourself as an AE who can speak the language of creatives and clearly articulate their ideas to the client. Think you'll climb the ladder quicker?

Don't throw your pencils away

We know you all love computers and would rather start creating ads than reading this *text*book. But you need to pick up a pencil first. Believe it or not, it's also a design tool. Design starts in your head, flows onto paper via your pencil, and is executed using your computer. Yes, you'll use a computer, but you'll need to use it wisely.

Don't use the computer to go shopping for ideas. Your ideas (concepts) should first be expressed as thumbnail drawings. Remember the order: head, paper, computer. You're the genius, not the computer.

Use technology wisely. If you're seriously thinking about going into design or production, you'll need to be competent in the programs that are the current industry standards. Using the programs you already know, or simply like, just won't fly. At the very least, learn the basics and move on.

Or buy a Volkswagen.

5.1. This classic VW ad was actually the art director's rough. It was perfect because it ran as the finished ad in 1980, when gas rose to the outrageous price of $1.00 per gallon.

Basic Design Principles

Artists define design principles in their own way, and some write books about them. All those opinions might seem confusing, but in reality it's a matter of perception and preference. We each tend to be comfortable with slightly varying definitions. As you peruse design books, you'll begin to see how concepts and principles overlap. We've chosen to discuss the following *Four Principles of Design:*

1. Proximity

2. Alignment

3. Balance

4. Unity

yesterday i was doing

some grilling when my

neighbor came over and said,

"a cow was murdered

just for that steak!"

and i came to thinking,

she's right.

i can't sit by while

a whole cow is

killed just for a

juicy grilled t-bone.

so today i bought

a leather jacket.

i am a man.

a compassionate man.

a grilling man.

Match Light

charcoal

5.2. This beautifully written ad (by a student) uses text to create a vertical visual flow right to the logo.

Proximity

Robin Williams (not the actor), in a great design book for nondesigners, says, "The principle of proximity states that you group related items together, move them physically close to each other, so the related items are seen as one cohesive group rather than a bunch of unrelated bits."[2] Another way to think about it is grouping those items while considering both human emotions and your advertising objective. When you've tapped into the audience's emotions you've hooked them. Use proximity—that is, how elements are placed—as a hook.

The principle of proximity helps designers and art directors (we'll use these words interchangeably) work to bring the strategic concept to life. Physical closeness can bring the visual(s) and the copy together in a strategic way. Conversely, items can strategically be placed further apart, adding separation.

Proximity creates strategically designed associations that enhance visual flow. Let's take a moment to explain this concept and some design terminology.

Visuals are the images that support the copy. They are almost always either photographs or illustrations. Avoid using the word *picture*. It tends to connote a photograph, and this can confuse people or lock you into an unintended concept.

Visual flow refers to how readers' eyes follow the layout. As a designer, you're in charge of the visual flow based on strategic design objectives. More about this later.

Imagine how you might intuitively group the elements in your layout. How do you see them fitting together? When we speak of elements we are not just talking about the visuals in your layout. We are talking about type (copy), lines, space, and the visuals. The challenge with the proximity principle is to make all the elements work together strategically. Remember, the designer is in charge of how the ad is read—to graphically drive the One Thing home.

WORDS OF WISDOM

"I can't just write an ad. I care how it looks as well as what it says."

—**HAL RINEY**[4]

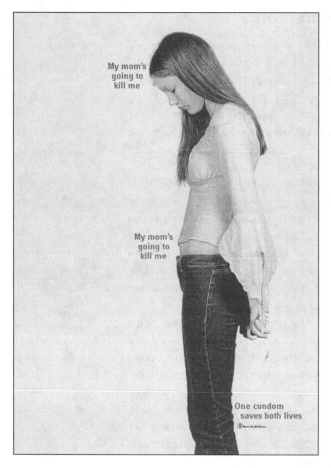

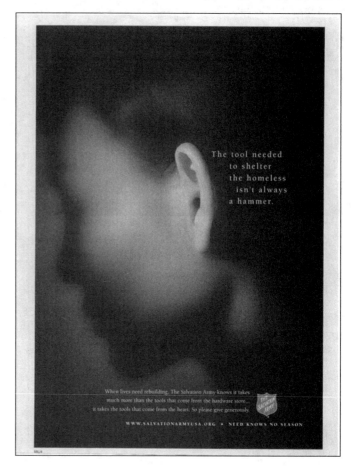

5.3–5.4. The proximity of the type to the visual makes these ads work.

Alignment

Consider alignment as expressing what is rhetorically important. In other words, *make the verbal visual.* Each element should have a visual connection to another element. Nothing should "hang" alone. Nothing should be placed arbitrarily. How will you align or organize the elements on the page?

Prioritize. It's an important concept across the creative process. Prioritizing helps you create alignment and thus stronger visual flow.

Some novice designers start by centering the headline or the visual and everything that follows. We are not suggesting that you never center anything, because sometimes a centered layout is perfectly on strategy and quite interesting. (The Matchlight ad on page 101 is a good example.) But centered layouts can be boring and predictable. Rather than following a formula, it's better to let the strategic message, the big idea, guide your alignment.

Lines are the basic tools of alignment. Lines are (a) the edges of visuals, (b) the ends of lines of copy, (c) the edges of blocks of copy, or (d) actual lines. Robin Williams explains how lines work: "In any well-designed piece, you can draw lines to the aligned objects, even if the overall presentation is a wild collection of odd things with lots of energy."[3]

In essence, the direction the reader's eyes move should be defined by the end of one line and the beginning of another. Take a close look at some layouts you admire. Try to trace the alignment. The more you practice this, the better you'll understand how using lines—that is, alignment—works.

Lines, of course, can be literal. They can, with linear motion, define space or give direction. Lines can be created by other elements of design, such as blocks of type. How type is justified, or how it fits within the text box, is an important part of alignment. In the end, remember: Nothing is placed arbitrarily, even in chaotic layouts.

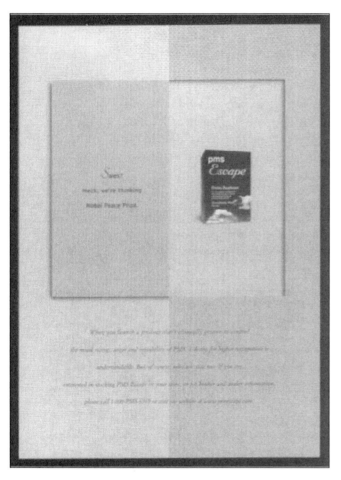

5.5. Lines contain, suggest space, give direction, and convey meaning.

5.6. Here lines convey meaning. The border and other lines define this as a blueprint.

Balance

Balance and its counterpart *contrast* are very important design concepts. Every layout you execute should reflect a clearly defined sense of balance. *Symmetry* and *asymmetry* are other ways to talk about balance. A symmetrical layout can be very calming and, for certain products, the perfect choice. But more often than not, a perfectly symmetrical layout is also boring. Asymmetry brings contrast, which creates visual interest and is one more way to hook the reader.

Contrast can be achieved through *size, type, weight, color, texture,* and *space.* All elements in a strong layout should be balanced in opposition to one another. You will always find contrast in a visually balanced layout. How much contrast is up to you.

If you're unsure about this principle, consider *mirroring.* Try to reflect the opposite weight, shape, or size in another part of your layout. Once you've mastered how to balance visual elements evenly, you can advance to create uneven or asymmetric layouts. *White space,* also known as *negative space,* is more than just the unused portion of the layout—more than just a background. White space has optical weight. Consider that weight when you're working toward balance or contrast. Why use white space? Our eyes sometimes need a rest. White space offers that. It can also frame elements or form a base on which an element can visually rest. White space can draw attention to a headline, copy block, or visual. Respect white space. It's an art director's and a copywriter's friend.

When it comes to balance, we suggest being adventurous. Make your choices matter. Opposites really do attract. Once you've taken a chance, stand back and take a look. The well-trained eye is more quickly able to judge balanced layouts. Peruse *CA, CMYK, Archive,* and the myriad other creative magazines available to you and become a visual professional.

Unity

As a design principle, unity probably has the closest relationship with alignment. When a layout is unified, all the elements form a visually cohesive whole. One of the fundamental ways to achieve unity is through repetition. Just as with writing,

5.7. White space: What you don't see is important. It draws the eye to the main graphic in this ad designed by a student.

5.8. Negative space puts the focus on the main graphic, which in this case is also negative space.

5.9. In a symmetrical design, each side of the ad is given equal weight. In this case it's up to the reader to decide if the car weighs more than the woman.

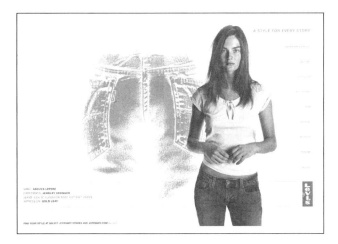

5.10. An asymmetrical design gives more weight to one side of the ad. Here the emphasis shifts to the right with the inclusion of the person endorsing the jeans. But the imprint of her jeans in the middle helps hold the spread together.

repetition can bring harmony and coherence, and thus unity. You can bring repetition into play with shape, color, type, line, and placement. Creating a thematic quality through repetition unifies a layout. Another way to enhance unity is by using the concept of image-dominant and type-dominant layouts. When deciding between an image-dominant and a type-dominant layout, your thoughts should be guided by your creative strategy. What will best convey the big idea? Once you determine the most dominant element of the layout, unity emerges as the other elements are placed in subordinate relationships to the dominant element. Remember how we keep talking about prioritizing?

For copywriters, a good way to think about unity is to consider thematic qualities in writing. You don't change the subject of a conversation in midsentence, so don't change your design theme in midlayout. Carry your visual concept throughout the ad. From top to

5.11. Repetition is a way to achieve unity. In this student-designed ad, the whole is greater than the sum of its parts. Not to mention great use of symmetry and white space.

bottom, left to right. When you design an ad, ask yourself, "How well does everything hang together?" If the answer is "Pretty darn well," you've probably achieved unity.

How to Develop Better Layouts

Robin Williams offers a very simple yet effective approach to creating better layouts: "See it. Say it. Sketch it."[5]

- *See it.* Start keeping a file, scrapbook, or morgue—in other words, a collection of ads that you like. Learn to file anything that strikes you. Your scrapbook will be a great resource for ideas. Use it before you start concepting. Or when you're stuck. It's bound to trigger some fresh ideas.

- *Say it.* Write down why you like the ads you've selected. What makes them sing? Which of the four design principles are strongest? What made each one stand out? What caught your eye? If you can articulate why you like a certain ad, you are well on the way to defending your own ideas.

- *Sketch it.* Remember Planet Schlock? Sometimes those dreadful ads inspire great new ads. Cut the schlocky ad apart and rearrange it. Or take a piece of tissue paper and draw over it. Make it better. This process may just inspire a great design for your next ad. The point is to put something on paper. You may be tempted to jump on the computer before you have a concept. Don't. Scribble something down first. Try some alternatives. When you're happy with your rough, then turn on your computer.

Typography

Like many of the design choices you'll make, the selection of type and color goes a long way toward enhancing awareness and building strategic comprehension. To begin, we'll address the basic components of type, also referred to as *typefaces* or *fonts*. Technically, these terms have slightly different meanings, but for copywriters we'll consider them interchangeable. No matter what you call them, do not mix too many fonts in the same layout. Multiple fonts, without any strategic purpose, often do nothing but tire the reader's eyes.

Typography has its own language, and if you're going to work in, or with, a creative department, you need to speak some of the language. We discuss a few of the most important terms in the following section.

LOOKING FOR INSPIRATION? TURN ON THE TUBE

While I was conducting research on Nike women's advertising, a copywriter from Goodby Silverstein, in San Francisco, shared a wonderful story with me. The strategy was to connect running to women's everyday life activities. He and the AD were stuck and had been for two days. One night while watching TV, he noticed *TV Guide* lying on his coffee table, and the idea hit him. Embed images of running into the documents of everyday life: time cards, e-mails, restaurant order forms, television program listings. The campaign not only worked for Nike, it earned a ton of awards.

—Jean Grow

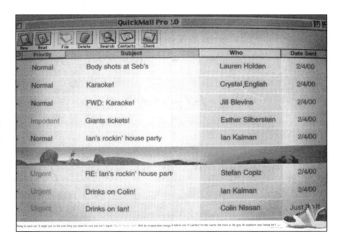

5.12.

Serif/sans serif. Serif typefaces have little tails (serifs) at the ends of the strokes. Sans serif fonts do not. Probably the most important thing to remember about serif versus sans serif is that the serifs tend to make the type appear more flowing and easier to read. Conversely, sans serif type tends to be more stiff or edgy and perhaps a bit more dramatic.

Weight. When we speak of the weight of type, we mean optical weight. One font may be much heavier than another. That is, the strokes are much more substantive, making each letter visually heavier. The most common designations of type weight are: light, regular, **medium**, and **bold**. You may also see terms such as **demi**, as in **demibold**, which is sort of in between medium and bold. You can also choose **extra bold**.

Size. Type comes in many sizes. In the world of graphics we refer to the size, or the height, of type as its point size. Interestingly, many styles of type vary slightly in height even if the point size is the same. Looking at these two fonts, both in 16-point type, can you see a variation in height?

Times New Roman and Arial

Generally the size range for body copy is anywhere from 8 to 12 points. Knowing your audience will help you decide what size is most suitable. Display copy (headlines and taglines) is often larger; 36 points and above is not uncommon. The main objective is to go beyond legibility and make your copy inviting to read. So resist the temptation to shrink your type size down to 8 points to make your copy fit. It's better to cut some of your copy than to make all of it hard to read. The point sizes suggested, like much of what you read in this book, are guidelines. They are not hard-and-fast rules.

Structure and form. A designer would undoubtedly separate these two elements. *Form* refers to shape of type, while *structure* refers to how the letters are technically built. To really get into the nitty-gritty details, we'd have to explain to you how types come in families, but that's a story for a design book. For now, let's just talk about four styles of type.

Styles of type

Old Style

This type represents the first generation of type. It emerged out of old hand-lettered type. It always has serifs.

Bookman Times Garamond

Modern

As the mechanisms of printing evolved, so did type. Modern type is a reflection of more sophisticated printing capabilities. It represents the evolution from hand lettering to mechanized printing. Modern type often has serifs

Perpetua Eurostile Trebuchet

Script

This family of type is designed to be reminiscent of hand-lettered type. Not hand lettering as with old style type—rather, it appears to be type done by a calligrapher using a brush, pen, or pencil. Script fonts are both serif and sans serif. A word of caution: Script fonts are fine for display type or special emphasis, but you'll probably want to avoid using them for text.

BrushScript *French Script* *Lucida Handwriting*

Decorative

In many ways decorative type is defined quite well by its name. These fonts are meant to be decorative, to stand out. Rarely will you see these types used in body copy. More commonly they are used as display copy.

Papyrus COPPERPLATE **Ad lib**

Placement

In short, we are talking about how type appears within your layout. As the designer, you have many choices. Every choice has the potential to alter the appearance of the type within the layout. Make each choice count. How you use type can convey messages far beyond the actual printed words.

Reverse and Overprinting

This has nothing to do with reading backward. Reverse type refers to type that is white (actually colorless) because it "reverses" out of a block of color. Beware of using reverse type on low-quality paper. It will tend to bleed, and you may not be able to read your copy clearly. For new designers we suggest using this technique sparingly.

Overprinting is just the opposite. It simply means the type (often black) is printed over a lightened (ghosted) image, texture, or tone.

Spacing. This refers to the spaces between the letters, which can vary from font to font. Spacing can also be varied mechanically through something called kerning, in which one stretches or contracts each piece of type across a line or within a single word. How spacing is used with type has many connotations. Consider how type can express the feeling of

C O L D & WARM

Leading. Typesetters used to work with individual letters cast in lead, with bars of lead between the lines of type. Leading (pronounced "ledding") is the space between rows of type. The amount of leading depends on the size of type, and the relationship between the two is indicated as type size/leading. In this text, it's 11/13, that is, 11-point type on 13 points of leading (see Table 5.1).

TABLE 5.1   Leading

10/12	12/16
The lines become more compact.	The lines become farther apart.

TABLE 5.2   Justification

Center justified simply means the type is centered.

Right justified (as in Arabic literature) means the type lines up on the right side of the page and is "ragged" on the left.

Left justified (as in Western literature) means the type lines up on the left side of the page and is "ragged" on the right.

Justified means that the type is spread evenly across the page, column, or copy block and forms smooth edges both right and left no matter how many characters there are per line (as you would see in most daily newspaper columns).

Justification and alignment. Like form and structure, alignment and justification are not exactly the same. However, once again we are taking liberties and lumping them together. Text *alignment* refers to where the type lines up in relationship to all the elements within a layout. *Justification* refers to where type begins and ends within the copy block, column, or line. There are four kinds of justification, as illustrated in Table 5.2.

Making type look better

Back in the 1980s, art directors would "send out" for type. A runner (often a guy on a bike) would pick up copy and return with "galleys" of typeset text, which the art director would literally paste into the layout. But even with professionally set copy, the layout artist usually had to do some fine tuning with an X-Acto knife to make it perfect. Now we do all of that electronically with a few keystrokes. But the basic idea is the same. The following are a few ways to ensure that the type in your layout looks its best.

Watch for Widows

When you see a line of type with only one or two words, it's what we call a widow.

As you can see above, a widow doesn't look good. it interrupts the flow of the copy and wastes space. You can get rid of widows by lengthening or shortening the copy, changing the font size, or adjusting the kerning.

Pick a Display Font That Matches the Tone of Your Ad

Type plays a big role in creating resonance in the reader. For example, which of the following best matches the brand image of a Chevy truck?

LIKE A ROCK   *Like a Rock*

Use Restraint When Selecting Fonts

Just because you have 1,200 fonts in your computer doesn't mean you have to put all of them in one ad. If you mix fonts, do it for a reason—for special emphasis of key words, captions, or other stand-alone copy blocks, or for display type for headlines and taglines. You don't have to use the same font for everything. When in doubt, print out several versions with different font choices and then decide.

Serif fonts are generally easier to read in long copy blocks. Most newspapers, books, and magazines use serif fonts because they are considered easier on the eye—something to consider for ads with long body copy. For short blocks of copy, headlines, and stand-alone copy, just about anything goes.

Reversed copy is usually more difficult to read

If you reverse copy (white on black or a dark color), make sure it's legible. You might have to increase the font size by a few points and use a heavier face.

Break Headlines
Sensibly

With large display type you can only fit a few words on a line. So be careful where you break longer headlines. It could change the whole meaning of the ad. Sometimes you can use that for dramatic effect, as 7-Up tried to do a few years ago with

MAKE 7

UP YOURS

Keep It Readable, Not Just Legible

Make it inviting to read. If you took the time to write copy, why make it hard for the reader? Leave enough margin (remember white space?) so the eye is drawn to the copy. Don't cram so much copy in that it becomes intimidating to read. Use enough leading so you don't have a "mass of gray" rather than distinctive lines of copy.

5.13–5.14. With literacy declining and attention spans becoming even shorter, it's not a good idea to make readers work hard to find a headline or decipher copy. The first priority is to make it inviting to read.

Color

Starting with the basics, think of colors as primary and secondary, warm and cool, or complementary or contrasting. From a designer's point of view, here are two key points:

- The human eye is most comfortable looking at warm colors.

- Complementary and contrasting colors should work for you to visually enhance your strategy.

Whether you're using warm or cool colors, or engaging complementary or contrasting colors, you also need to keep in mind the social and cultural connotations attached to each color. Just as with words, colors can have multiple meanings. Think of the social and cultural meanings of each color. Then weigh those meanings against the brand, the colors associated the brand, and its competitors. Also consider your audience's sensibilities when making color choices. Finally, remember color may be applied to many elements of a layout: type, line, and backgrounds. Visual images too have an expressed color pallet.

Make wise choices that you can justify. Some questions to help you select color:

- How will color enhance the big idea/that One Thing?
- Are your color choices in keeping with the strategy?
- Does the color support the brand?
- Will the audience relate positively to the colors?
- What is your justification for each color choice?

Color considerations

How an audience relates to color depends on many variables:

Culture

Depending on the culture, colors can have very different meanings. For example, in parts of Asia, white is the color of funerals, while in the West white is the color of weddings. Know and respect cultural connotations.

Age

Young children tend to prefer bright, solid colors, while adults tend to prefer more subdued colors. If you're designing an ad for a young audience and you're using muted pastels and shades of gray, their parents might like it, but the kids may ignore it.

Class

Class, like age, influences our perceptions because our experience of the world varies. Marketing research in the United States has shown that working-class people tend to prefer colors anyone can name (blue, red, green, and so on) while more highly educated people tend to prefer colors that are more obscure (such as taupe, azure, mauve). Some designers say this is why Wal-Mart uses bright red and blue in their logo. Another theory is that red and blue were Sam Walton's favorite colors. So, be aware of class differences, but don't overanalyze them.

Gender

In many cultures, men tend to prefer cooler colors (blues and greens) while women tend to prefer warmer colors (reds and oranges). Western men are also more likely to be color-blind and so unable to see some differences among colors. While it's important to note the difference between men's and women's perceptions of color, don't let obscure differences in color preferences take precedence over good creative ideas.

Trends

Color, like everything else in design, is influenced by trends. Consider the Web as a point of reference. Black was the rage a few years ago, and now you hardly see it (but it will surely come back into style as we write this). Colors also tend toward seasonality. In other words, color choices reflect the season they were designed for: blacks, whites, and grays for winter; greens and bright colors for spring; yellows for summer; and browns and golds for fall.[6] Try to stay on top of trends, but don't let them drive your color decisions.

Here are a few specific color terms you'll want to know:

- *RGB:* This stands for primary colors (*r*ed-*g*reen-*b*lue). It's an option when saving colors for Web use and Photoshop work in progress, but not for print-based material.

- *CMYK:* This acronym refers to the colors that printer use and also the way you will need to save colors in electronic layouts. It means *c*yan, *m*agenta, *y*ellow, and *b*lack—the colors of a four-color (not *full*-color) layout. The four colors are mixed in various percentages to create a color image. If you've ever had the yellow ink run out on your ink-jet printer, you already know how the four-color printing process works.

- *PMS colors:* PMS (acronym for the trademarked Pantone Matching System) describes a set of custom colors used by designers. PMS colors are standard across the printing industry (at least in North America—European

5.15.

printers like to use the percentages for CMYK). PMS colors are referenced by numbers, such as PMS 1032. The beauty of PMS colors is that they can be matched identically by any designer or any printer. PMS colors add consistency to corporate identities and campaigns.

- *Spot color:* This simply means the use of one (or more) color in an otherwise black-and-white layout. It often has a dramatic effect and is particularly common in newspaper advertising and low-budget collateral work. *Spot color* can also refer to one of the colors in the layout being a PMS color. For example, a four-color brochure may add a fifth color, which is a specific PMS color, for a corporate logo because it can't be matched exactly in the four-color printing process. When you hear "two-color" it actually means black and a second color.

- *Ghosting:* Ghosting, also called "screening back," means an image is reproduced at less than 100% of the color density. If you want to ghost an image and run copy over it, a good starting point is screening it back to 30% or less. The "busier" the background (lots of contrast in the visual), the more difficult it will be to read overprinted type. You can "knock back" the background, change the background visual, or use larger type that's easier to read.

- *Gradation:* This refers to the color shifting from a greater to a lesser intensity or completely fading as it moves across the visual element. For example, you may want a dark blue background at the top of the ad so you can reverse out a large white headline and then have the ad gradate to light blue toward the bottom because you want to overprint black body copy.

- *Bleed:* When the color or type runs to the very edge of the page, it "bleeds" off the page. When your background has no border, it "bleeds." Sometimes it's a problem to print a full-page bleed ad on an ink-jet printer. You either have to make the image smaller or find a printer that prints a larger sheet and trim it to a bleed.

AppleMusic.com

5.16. This top-down design draws the eye right to the Web site (with a tiny Apple logo in the upper right).

Layout Basics

Visual hierarchy, or *visual flow,* as we've been calling it, tends to be a problem area for many beginning copywriters who are forced to be their own art directors. Usually all the elements are there, but they just don't work together. The eye doesn't know where to go first, and so the whole layout looks confused.

In terms of layout design, there are three very commonly used visual flow patterns. First, there's the *top-down* layout, where the elements are centered and

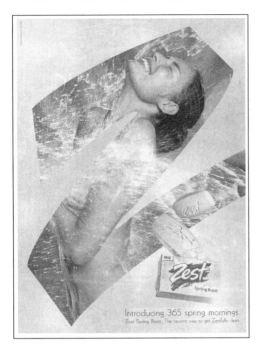

5.17. Even account execs can find the Z in this design.

5.18. Leave it to Porsche to take a shortcut with this upper left to lower right design.

flow from top to bottom. Sometimes it's very effective. You might want to start with this approach. Then experiment with something less predictable.

The second pattern is called the *Z* or *backward S* pattern. In Western cultures, our eyes tend to begin reading a page in the upper left corner. Next, our eyes naturally flow to the right side of the page, just like when we read a book. Then our eyes travel down and, in the process of scanning, move from upper right to lower left. Can you imagine the Z or backward S configuration? This classic pattern is the reason you so often see the logo anchoring the lower right corner of a layout.

The third visual flow pattern lets you take a shortcut. With the *upper left to lower right* layout, you basically start and end at the same place as with the Z—you just get there faster.

"Advertising is not a f—ing science! Advertising is an art. No question about it."

—**GEORGE LOIS**[7]

Layout patterns

Any given design text will list a number of common organizational layout systems or patterns. We've simplified it down to three:

1. Grids

2. Columns

3. Chaotic

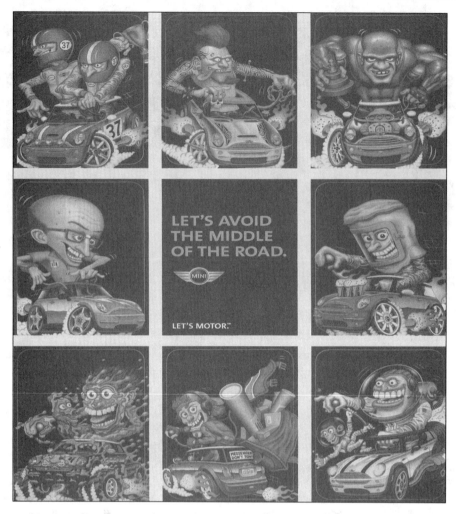

5.19. This grid design is also functional. The insert is printed on card stock and perforated so the reader can create separate cards.

You can experiment with each of these layout systems by using that wonderful design tool—the pencil. Quickly rough out four or five thumbnails, sketching in only copy blocks, display copy (as scribbles) and visuals (as solid shapes). Use any one of these systems as a jumping-off point. Before you know it you'll be on your way.

Grids (also know as *Mondrian* layouts) are simply a systematic way of dividing up space using geometric patterns, beginning with the basic rectangle that makes up your page. Grids allow us to see how elements of a layout might be organized. Consider how many elements you have in your layout. That will help you decide how many blocks you'll need to create within your grid.

Don't think of a grid layout as a stack of blocks or a boring "checkerboard" where you have to fill in all the squares. You have a bit more creative latitude. You can use white space and asymmetrical alignment, for example, to create visually interesting grid layouts. From a practical standpoint, grids are easier to build for both print ads and Web sites—which are really collections of interconnected tables.

Columns are much like grids. In fact, sometimes the terms are used interchangeably. We discuss them separately to help you see how columns are really just vertical grids. Sometimes, for beginning designers, thinking of columns and grids separately can help them conceptualize and organize more easily.

5.20. Another classic grid. Mondrian would be proud.

5.21. A grid design with a "violator" in the middle to break up the monotony.

5.22. Grids don't have to be perfectly symmetrical.

5.23. Columns can be visuals or text or both, as in this student-designed ad.

5.24. A newspaper ad with a column of text and product integrated into it.

Chaotic layouts (sometimes called *circus* or *field-of-tension* layouts) are usually not as crazy as they sound. Generally, the organizing principle that pulls chaotic layouts together is alignment. Thus the use of lines can bring organization to a chaotic layout. Proximity is another principle that brings order. You can organize the seemingly random placement of visuals, for example, by placing

5.25–5.26. The circus is in town! Despite the chaotic organization, these circus or field-of-tension layouts incorporate the four design principles.

5.27. Miller Lite's sleazy "Group Sex" ad (talk about chaotic). Do you see any design principles here? Do you care?

captions nearby. Some chaotic layouts, especially from novice designers, are just that—visual train wrecks. Unless you have a well-defined design strategy and use some organization principles, we suggest you stick to something simpler.

Building Your Layout

Learning about layout systems and creating thumbnails are just the first steps to creating layouts. Now let's talk about a few graphic considerations beyond the organizational systems we've already discussed.

Edges

Here we are referring to the negative space of edges, including the page edges and the gutter, as well as the visual design elements along the edges. The "gutter" is the inside edge of a magazine page—where the pages are bound. Because the binding takes space away from the ad, and since we read left to right, you don't want to draw the reader's eye into the gutter. When it comes to layout, as well as concepting, keep your mind out of the gutter. When laying out your ad, remember this technical but very important point: *Always honor your margins* (edges).

5.28. Look at the beauty of an edge within the margins. Notice how clean the layout is. Perfect for newspaper. Not to mention, a bit tongue-in-cheek.

5.29. This student-designed ad honors the margins. The eye is drawn into the copy, not off the page.

When laying out their ads, many beginners push text to the edge of the layout because (a) the copy is too long, (b) the type size is too large, (c) the space allotted to copy is not deep enough, or (d) they just don't have a clue how to put an ad together. Most likely, it's a combination of all four.

While backgrounds and visuals can bleed (remember, that means they run all the way to the outer border of the page), anything of value, such as copy or a strategic part of the visual, needs to remain inside the margins. For most single-page ads the margins are at least one-half inch. If you violate that half-inch rule, your ad not only looks unprofessional, but you could also lose your copy or visual when the ad is bound into the magazine.

Blocks and shapes

You can use blocks and shapes, as well as lines, to organize the elements in your layout. You can arrange and rearrange these blocks and shapes in a variety of patterns until you find the right combination. Organize them by grid, columns, or in a chaotic layout, but be sure to use the Four Principles of Design to guide you.

Copy as graphic

Think of copy as a block or shape, and then figure how it will fit with the other elements of the layout. Once you decide where it goes and the general proportion with the rest of the layout, you can begin to pick your font. Consider various qualities discussed earlier in this chapter. Then begin playing with the your options by drawing thumbnails. When you figure out what you want to do, it's time to use the computer.

The Design Process

In a nutshell, the process begins with your creative strategy. Work from your brief all the way through. Once you have a clear idea about what you need to convey and a darned good idea about how many elements might be in your layout, start sketching and collaging. If you're more comfortable with sketching, draw thumbnails until you run out of paper. It you're more hands-on, try collaging. Cut out shapes and move them around within the confines of your layout. Or combine both techniques. The bottom line is good designing takes a lot of work. When you brainstorm a headline, you may create 30, 40, 50, or even 100 ideas. Most of which will be schlock. The same process holds true with designing. Scribble, scratch, and cut and paste 30, 40, 50, or even 100 ideas. In the process, you'll come to see what works best for your specific project. One last bit of advice that bears repeating: Don't start shopping for visual images until you've nailed down your big idea.

Selecting your visuals

As you'll see in later chapters, certain words in headlines and copy pull in more readers. The same is true with visual elements—in print, on the Web, or on television. As with "proven" headline words, don't use cliché visual choices just because they've generated results over the last 50 years. Try to find a new approach that gets noticed. Below, we discuss a few of the visual choices that attract readers and viewers.

People, not things. Given a choice, people like to see other people. It's all about satisfying those wants and needs. Is that person in the ad benefiting from the product? Is that person suffering because he or she's not using the product? Will I look like that handsome/beautiful person in the ad if I use that product? If asked, any reader would say, "Nah, I don't look at people in ads." But they do. And so do you.

The choice of showing the product or people using the product depends a lot on the product category. For example, showing a medium-long shot of a sexy sports car racing through the night could be the most effective image for that vehicle. But showing a mom with her kids, and a lot of stuff to carry, may be the best image for a minivan.

5.30. What do you see first? If you're human, it's probably the person. If you saw this in color, you'd also notice the lemon-yellow background.

5.31. Want to sell sweaters? Why not show the people who design them rather than just the products? You still see the sweaters, but using the head designer and her apprentice make a much nicer story. Talk about warm and fuzzy.

Babies, puppies and kittens (actually children and animals, to be less specific). We know, this is lame. But think about your favorite ads and commercials. How many have kids and animals? Every Super Bowl ad Top 10 list is topped by animal acts. If you use this visual crutch, at least do it creatively, without being cute or patronizing.

5.32. Sometimes you can get away with a cliché. In this case the little kid resonates with a lot of moms who want to help him blow his nose.

5.33. Kids and puppies. It might be cheesy, but they still hook a lot of people.

Surprise! Men and women think differently. Psychologists suggest that there really are fundamental differences in the ways men and women process information. (Remember all that right brain/left brain stuff?) In general, women respond more to details, and men want the big picture.

A recent discussion on National Public Radio's "Talk of the Nation" brought out the following points from a panel of marketing experts. One participant said: "For women, ads often are more detailed. Take for example toiletry ads. For one thing, women are more concerned about grooming and appearance. And they appreciate very fine distinctions, such as five different variations of shampoo—for curly hair, straight hair, oily hair, dry hair, etc. For men, by contrast, toiletry ads focus on a single product." And here's a surprise: "Men seem to be much more sensitive to sexual signals. This fact has not been lost on advertisers. We all know how sex sells."[8]

For some male-oriented products, men like to see other men in ads. The theory is they see models as they'd like to see themselves. However, it gets confusing for other products, where ads for men feature women. The theory here is men like to see women, in many cases, wearing as little clothing as possible. It's even more confusing because the covers of men's magazines like *FHM, Maxim,* and *Playboy* show beautiful scantily clad women while the covers of women's magazines like *Cosmopolitan* show, well, beautiful scantily clad women. As you

WORDS OF WISDOM

"The best writers are conceptual. . . . They understand the ad as a whole, not as a patch of copy and a piece of photography. In the best work, the visual and the verbal are so complementary that neither would be as strong on their own."

—HELAYNE SPIVAK[9]

5.34. Who's the target audience—women looking for athletic shoes or art students?

5.35. Does the fact that this is a fashion ad in a women's magazine make it less objectifying? Imagine the outrage if this ran in a men's magazine and the photo of the dress were changed to a bottle of beer.

concept and design an ad, you have to walk a tightrope between attracting readership and pandering to baser instincts. Can you develop a visual that resonates with the intended target market and still shows respect for women (and men too)? The whole issue of how much sex sells and how we use it can't be answered here, if it can be answered at all.

More visual, less copy

You need to know how to write copy. But you also need to know when to leave it out. While people will read long copy if they're interested, for many consumer ads, you just don't need it. It's better to use a visual to capture their attention than a mass of intimidating text. Once again, the choice depends on the target audience and type of product. Soft drinks and chewing gum don't need 200 words of copy. A business-to-business product might. See page 124 for a comparison of copy dominant vs. image dominant ads.

Illustration versus photography

Years ago, illustration was much more common. Now with Photoshop, photo manipulation creates amazing effects that used to be available only with illustration. However, illustration is a valid option for a lot of reasons:

- *You can't show it any other way:* Cutaway drawings, blueprints, overlays, ghosted images, and many other graphic treatments are executed as artwork instead of photography when you can't show them any other way. Or sometimes as a combination of the two.

5.36–5.37. Nobody really wants to talk about life insurance anyway. But which ad would you read first?

- *Create a mood:* Illustrations create resonance too. Sometimes you need a painting or drawing to elicit an emotion you can't get from a photo.

- *Dramatic effect:* You can use illustration to exaggerate a feature, make a problem look bigger than it really is, or enhance a benefit. Such visual overstatements are more accepted as artwork than they would be as realistic photography.

- *Parody famous art:* Want to paint a moustache on the Mona Lisa? First you need a copy of the original painting (and permission). To mimic or modify an illustration, you need another illustration.

Finding your visuals

One of the biggest problems advertising students (and many professionals) face is where to get the visuals. Searching the Web and stock photo books for that perfect image often turns into a shopping trip. You might find something that looks cool but doesn't fit your concept. Try to stay true to your creative strategy, even if you can't find the perfect photo. Fortunately, with stock photo Web sites, your odds are greatly improved, even if the image is covered with watermarks.

5.38. Showing a real guy with bugs in his teeth would be gross. This exaggerated illustration is more fun and acceptable.

5.39. Another memorable campaign from Altoids. Their Strips featured delightfully disturbing illustrations. (Or would you call them curiously strange?)

- *Web sites:* Two of the best sites are fotosearch.com and Google images. They list most of the major stock photo and art sources and have very robust browsers to help you find the right image.

- *Stock books and disks:* Most of the major stock photo firms still publish color books. They also put their low-res images on disks. Ad agencies and design houses are always updating these books and usually throw out the old ones. Ask an agency if you can have a few of their rejects.

- *Magazines:* If you're looking for ideas or images you can scan or cut and paste into a collage, you might find them in magazines. For example, if you need an image of a glamorous model in an evening gown, start looking at some fashion magazines. Remember you are assembling images for a layout, not a real ad.

- *Digital photos:* Advances in digital photography and photo editing software have opened a lot of opportunities to creative people. Need a picture of a college student eating a pizza? Don't waste your time browsing stock photos. Just shoot your roommate (photographically, that is). With a little planning you can create all kinds of professional images on your own. This tactic also works very well to create photo storyboards for television commercials.

- *Draw it:* If you can't find it and can't photograph it, try drawing it. At the very least you'll have a rough that someone else might be able to turn into a nice-looking ad.

Design and campaign continuity

Design elements help tie a campaign together. The use of lines, type, color, and layout style in particular provide a certain look that's carried across a campaign. Pay special attention to logo treatment and taglines. They may have to work with a wide variety of executions in different media. It takes discipline

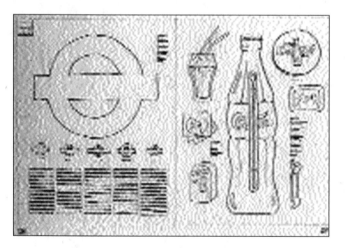

5.40–5.41. This well-thought-out thumbnail by Woody Pirtle of Pentagram shows how closely the final layout follows his drawing. Even though some of the elements are different in the final, you can see his organizing principles have been carried through from concept to completion. You don't have to be a great artist to noodle out a design. Just keep scribbling until you find the right look—then build it on the computer.

to maintain graphic continuity in a long-running campaign, especially when new ads are developed halfway through the campaign's run. This is when you really have to understand how the various elements interact to form the whole. Without that understanding, your campaign can visually fall apart.

5.42–5.44. This award-winning campaign for the *New York Times* featured three very different images yet used the same tagline and folded-back lower right corner to hold the campaign together visually.

5.45. A global brand requires global design continuity. Even if the language changes, you recognize the Coke design.

Putting It All Together

"'Maximum message, minimum means' means every message is best communicated with simplicity and a core concept that is manifested in a compelling manner and a degree of clarity that makes it easily understood."

—WOODY PIRTLE[10]

We've covered a lot of design concepts, but in reality, we've just scratched the surface. If you really want to become a designer or art director, you *must* take design classes, preferably taught by working professionals who deal with real clients every day. Learn the terminology. Learn the rules and when you can break them. Above all, practice, practice, practice. There is no substitute for experience, even if most of that experience is trial and error.

Writers can be designers, and vice versa. Even if you become an account exec or media director or can only draw a stick person, you should be able to evaluate design and have some good reasons for your opinions.

If you remember nothing else about this chapter, keep this thought in mind:

Keep it simple.

Don't add so many elements, styles, and fonts that no one can figure out what you're trying to say. Another way to say it: *Less is more.* Keeping it simple doesn't mean you can only put one element in an ad. It means you need to unify multiple elements into a cohesive design—so the reader is impressed by your idea, not your technique.

Another cardinal rule:

If you emphasize everything, you emphasize nothing.

A cluttered, confused, truly chaotic layout repels readers. No one wants to take the time to figure out your message. Once again: Less is more.

The following is a brief checklist of design tips and techniques. Use this to evaluate your work and the work of others. You may not follow every "rule" listed here. But if you don't, you should have a sound creative reason why you didn't.

Conceptual Considerations

- Does your layout convey the big idea?

- Did you design with your audience in mind?

- Did you prioritize elements? (The most important should be the most prominent.)

- Do your visuals and headlines work together?

- Overall, does your design catch the reader's eye?

- Did you keep it simple? (Less is more.)

Layout Considerations

- Did you consider alternatives? (You can never have too many thumbnails.)

- Did you consider the Four Principles of Design?

- Did you use white space effectively?

- Does your layout have a pleasing and logical visual flow?

- Did you choose display type that matches the tone of the ad?

- Is the body copy inviting to read—the right size and proportion?

- Did you honor the margins—allow enough space around critical elements?

- Did you keep it simple? (Less is more.)

5.46.

Source: Illustration by Dan Augustine.

Who's Who?

Helmut Krone—Helmut Krone developed a clean, uncluttered look in the 1950s that still sets the standard for modern advertising design. Working with copywriter Julian Koenig, Krone created witty, tasteful, intelligent masterpieces for Volkswagen and other Doyle Dane Bernbach clients. He sweated print details and advanced professionalism among creatives in his relentless pursuit of perfection. He was elected to the Art Directors Hall of Fame and has been a perennial award winner as he revolutionized advertising's "look."[11]

George Lois—George Lois gained fame and major awards with bold, clean work for Doyle Dane Bernbach, Papert Koenig Lois, and Lois Holland. He also became the youngest inductee into the Art Directors Hall of Fame. Lois's ads for Wolfschmidt vodka, Xerox, Allerest, MTV, Maypo, Wheatena, and Edwards & Hanly and his *Esquire* covers reflected his "loosey-goosey" style and exemplified his idiosyncratic "stun 'em and cause outrage" philosophy. Never an "establishment" model citizen, Lois is defined by his powerful early work.[12]

Woody Pirtle—Woody Pirtle began a very successful career in graphic design as an art director at Stan Richards and Associates, which later became the Richards Group, one of the leading agencies in the Southwest. Under Pirtle's direction, "single reactive projects would become well-conceived programs where design was pervasive and execution was critical."[13] After his stint at Richards, Pirtle founded Pirtle Design in Dallas and later became a director at Pentagram, one of New York's top design firms.

Notes

[1] Quote from the Clio Awards Web site, http://www.clioawards.com/html/wsj/krone.html (accessed December 20, 2004).

[2] Robin Williams, *The Non-Designer's Design Book* (Berkeley, CA: Peachpit, 1994), 15.

[3] Ibid., 35.

[4] Quote from the Clio Awards Web site, http://www.clioawards.com/html/wsj/riney.html (accessed December 20, 2004).

[5] Williams, *The Non-Designer's Design Book,* 71.

[6] Jennifer Kyrnin, "Color Symbolism Chart by Culture: Understand the Meanings of Color in Various Cultures around the World," n.d., http://www.webdesign.about.com/library/bl_colorculture.htm (accessed June 3, 2005).

[7] Quote from the Clio Awards Web site, http://www.clioawards.com/html/wsj/lois.html (accessed December 20, 2004).

[8] MelanieYarborough discusses this NPR program in "Gender-Pitched Advertising: Do Men and Women See the Same Thing?" n.d., http://village.fortunecity.com/carnival/383/adverts.htm (accessed June 3, 2005).

[9] Quote from the Clio Awards Web site, http://www.clioawards.com/html/wsj/spivak.html (accessed December 20, 2004).

[10] Woody Pirtle, contribution to *Graphic Design: Inspirations and Innovations,* ed. Diana Martin (Cincinnati, OH: North Light, 1998), 50.

[11] "Top 100 People of the Century," *Advertising Age,* March 29, 1999, http://www.adage.com/century/people.html (accessed June 3, 2005).

[12] Ibid.

[13] Jack H. Summerford, "Woody Pirtle: Completing the Circle," 2003, on the AIGA Web site, http://www.aiga.org/content.cfm/content?ContentAlias=woodypirtle (accessed June 3, 2005).

Campaigns

What is a campaign? Before you can create a campaign, you need to define it. In *Campaign Planner for Promotion and IMC,* Shay Sayre defines a campaign as "a themed series of planned brand messages delivered to a specific target audience through a variety of promotional media and activities during a fixed time period."[1] That's a good marketing definition, but from a copywriting standpoint we prefer Maxine Paetro's simpler description:

> A campaign is a series of ads for a product (or service or company) that work individually and cumulatively to communicate the advertiser's message to the consumer.[2]

In other words, each element of a campaign has to be effective on its own, because that may be the first and only exposure. All the elements also need to work together to build a cumulative image. In a well-executed multi-element campaign: the whole is greater than the sum of its parts. Another perspective comes from Jim Albright in *Creating the Advertising Message:* "A campaign is no more than putting together all the advertising skills you have learned in a concentrated, multi-pronged approach, based on the single strategy you developed."[3]

What makes a collection of marketing communication projects a campaign? In some cases a campaign can include the complete MarCom arsenal, or it can be as simple as a series of three fractional page ads, as long as it meets all of the following criteria:

- *Common objective:* It's aimed at a well-defined target audience and includes awareness, comprehension, conviction, and action goals within a given time frame. In other words, there should be a campaign strategy.

- *Unified theme:* Whether it's a tagline, graphic design, or copy message, a campaign needs to convey a single message so the consumer can connect that one adjective to the brand. This does not mean that all ads in a campaign have to look the same—but the overall message should be consistent.

- *Coordinated rollout:* Depending on the time frame, all elements can appear at once in a blitz, or new elements can be added depending on changing marketing environments, such as seasonality and competitive response. This involves media and promotion planning, but it certainly affects creative strategy.

Overall, if you remember nothing else about campaigns, know this:

The primary purpose of a campaign is to support the brand.

From the client's point of view, a campaign is a more effective, more profitable, and more stable situation for establishing his or her brand name.[4]

Campaigns and IMC

In Chapter 1, we outlined the concept of Integrated Marketing Communications. In a campaign, the operative word is *integrated*—all elements have to work together in a planned approach. Campaign strategy can involve the whole marketing communication toolbox, including public relations and media planning; however, we'll limit our thinking to creative elements.

Campaign components

Think about any recent soda or fast-food restaurant campaign. Where did you first notice it? Probably on television. But you also heard the radio commercials, saw the billboards, checked the coupons in the Sunday paper, got annoyed by the pop-up ads on the Web, and probably glanced at displays in stores or restaurants. Each individual component conveyed the message, and collectively they pounded it into your brain. So when you see that soda on the grocer's shelf or in a vending machine, you buy it, probably without realizing how many times you've been bombarded with different messages in the various media. What made you pull into the drive-through to try that new sandwich? Maybe it was the ad on your car radio or the billboard you just passed. Again, you probably don't realize how many campaign components were working together to influence you.

Here are a few of the components that can be part of an integrated campaign:

- *Advertising:* Consumer magazines, trade magazines, professional magazines, broadcast television, cable/satellite television, radio, local newspapers, national and trade newspapers, billboards, transit

- *Promotion:* Short-term sales contests, special offers, discounts, rebates, incentives, sweepstakes, cross-promotion with other products, publicity, and advertising of the promotion

- *Public relations:* Event planning, publicity of events, print news releases, newsletters, video news releases

- *Internet/interactive:* Web sites, Internet advertising, permission-based marketing, search engine marketing, customer relationship marketing, online and CD-ROM interactive programs and games

- *Direct marketing:* Database development, direct mail (letters, cards, dimensional mailers), fulfillment (mailing information or merchandise)

If all the above components are part of a campaign, they all have to work together, yet each must stand alone as an individual selling tool. Campaigns epitomize convergence.

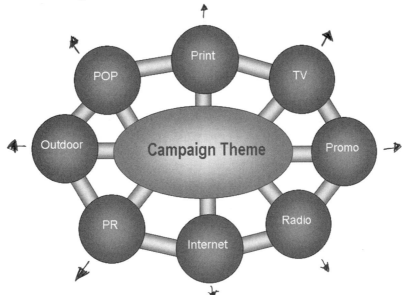

6.1. In an Integrated Marketing Communications program, all the elements work together so the whole is greater than the sum of its individual components.

How to Enhance Continuity

Continuity does not mean conformity

The biggest difference between a single-shot ad and a campaign is continuity. Continuity within a campaign means the various components of the campaign have enough commonality that the reader/viewer/listener should perceive a common theme and unified message. Continuity doesn't require that the TV spot uses the same dialogue as the radio commercial, or the billboards have the exact same graphics as the print ads. It's nearly impossible for us to give you one set of guidelines that works for every campaign, but remember this:

> Don't repeat the same idea in every part of the campaign—repeat the creative strategy with different executions.[6]

To create an effective campaign, you need to think in two dimensions: *extending* the creative strategy across the various media and *repeating* that strategy within each medium.

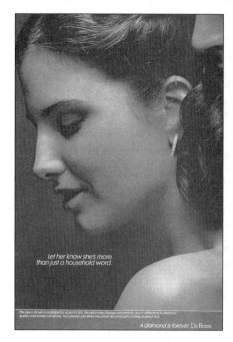

1982   1992

2004

6.2–6.4. A "Diamond Is Forever," and so is the DeBeers campaign. As long as women love jewelry and men love women, this campaign will probably never change.

Extendibility

The first dimension—extendibility—means you use the same theme and common elements in two or more media. For example, can you carry that creative message from print to TV? Will the direct mailers look like they came from the same company as the billboards? Does the advertising support the

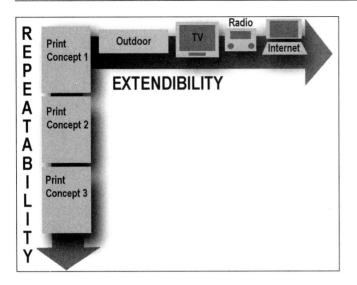

6.5.

promotion theme? Does the point of purchase material tie in with the campaign?

Repeatability

Repeatability is a little different from repetition. It does not mean rerunning the same ad or commercial until everyone is so sick of it they ignore it. That's a media decision. In a creative context, repeatability means using common elements to create a series of ads or commercials. The elements are not identical, but they are related—they can stand alone but also work cumulatively to convey a campaign theme.

6.6. In 1998, Apple launched their biggest campaign to date for the new iMac. In just five months, they spent more than $100 million in magazines, television, radio, outdoor, and the Internet to introduce a real product that supported their previous image-only "Think Different" campaign. The iMac introduction, plus subsequent campaigns for new Apple products, has helped to increase sales dramatically. However, Macs still own less than 5% of the personal computing market.

6.7–6.9. Three different headlines, one common theme: Applebee's will fill you up. This series was created by a student.

6.10. We can't think of a better example of repeatability. The formula for years has been to put a milk moustache on the flavor of the day (or from 25 years ago for Kiss) and drop in the tagline "Got Milk?" If you want to learn more about the evolution of this campaign, check out Jon Steel's *Truth, Lies and Advertising: The Art of Account Planning.*[7]

How to maximize extendibility and repeatability

We've already covered some of the creative tools you can use to provide continuity to a campaign. You can use one or all of them to help hold your campaign together.

Music

When people can't remember the words of a commercial but can sing the jingle, you know your campaign's music is holding it together. Music is far more memorable than any other commercial element. For example, you'd have a hard time finding anyone over 30 who doesn't know the Oscar Mayer wiener song. You have as many ways to use music in your campaign as there are songs—probably more, with today's sampling and mixing technology.

Original commercial music, also called jingles, has long been a staple of highly promoted consumer products, such as fast-food chains. When a tune catches on, it becomes part of the popular culture, and it's likely to stay around in one form or another for a long time. Everybody can sing "Like a good neighbor, State Farm is there" and "Sometimes you feel like a nut, sometimes you don't." When a mega-advertiser like McDonald's, Pepsi, or Coke unveils a new jingle, it's a major marketing event. In the 1970s a Coke jingle was adapted into a popular song that sold millions of records (and probably billions of Cokes, too).

In the last several years, *original popular music* has provided the sound tracks of many commercials. In the past, rights were considered too expensive, and artists didn't want to sell out to advertisers. Today, most artists don't own the rights to their music, and many would gladly take the cash, especially if they haven't had a hit in 15 years. We're sure Bob Seger never believed 10 seconds of "Like a Rock" would be played millions of times more than the full song. Turn on the TV and close your eyes—it sounds more like a classic hits radio station. It's been said the music you liked when you were 14 or 15 resonates the strongest. Pick your decade, and you can bet the top-selling artists from that time are in TV spots.

DILBERT

6.11.

WORDS OF WISDOM

"There's a difference between a campaign concept and an ad concept. Are the different ads different executions to illustrate the same point, or are they different ways of doing the same idea? The former is a campaign, the latter is probably just the typical either/or process creatives go through choosing which way to take an ad."

—**Tom Monahan**[8]

Some advertisers use *modified popular music* with their own lyrics. The tune's familiar, but the words can be a clever blend with the music or just plain awful. It can be a familiar old tune or a current hit. If you use current music, make sure you stay ahead of the popular culture curve.

Voice Talent

Using the same announcer throughout a TV and radio campaign helps establish a common sound. Here are a few examples.

Celebrity voice-over. A lot of very famous people provide voice-overs for commercials without identifying themselves. James Garner did Chevy Trucks. Lauren Bacall promoted cruise ships and cat food. Donald Sutherland has been the voice of Volvo, and Martin Sheen pitched Toyota. Using famous actors may be expensive, but they often have distinctive voices that connect with viewers or listeners.

Character voices. People are used to hearing smooth announcers, so a distinctive voice treatment can shock them into listening. Gilbert Gottfried's jarring "Aflac" quack is a prime example.

Announcers. Using the same announcer throughout a campaign, even if he or she is not a celebrity, can provide continuity. Be careful to maintain the tone and delivery style, even though the copy changes from spot to spot.

Animated Characters/Animals

For years, the Leo Burnett agency was known for its "critters"—those memorable animated characters that have been the common thread of many of their long-running campaigns. Before you dismiss these mascots as throwbacks to the 1950s, consider that they've been around for a long, long time. That means the agency has created long-term brand value and, in doing so, has retained clients much longer than most of their competitors. Some characters, such as Tony the Tiger, the Jolly Green Giant, and the Keebler Elves, are inseparable from the products.

While most advertisers hope to match the success of these established brand images, they usually give up when sales don't move as fast or as far as they'd like. For example, the Taco Bell Chihuahua was wildly popular, selling almost as many stuffed toys as tacos. However, after an initial increase, Taco Bell sales leveled off and declined slightly. The president of the chain resigned, the agency was fired, and the dog was out on the street. Was it the Chihuahua's fault, or the fact he drew a lot a customers into the restaurants to sample the food and they never came back?

Spokespersons/Celebrities

Celebrities. Back in the day when brands were the sole sponsors of radio and television programs, the star of the show was the brand spokesperson. For example, Ronald

6.12. Arby's Oven Mitt (voice of Tom Arnold) did not last as long as these other mascots.

6.13. This little guy has survived nearly 40 years of tummy pokes.

6.14. This campaign kept going, and going, and going, and . . .

6.15. Since the 1950s, Tony the Tiger has been a "G-r-r-eat!" mascot.

Reagan was host of the *General Electric Theater* television show, so Ronnie appeared in TV spots and print ads and at numerous speaking engagements promoting GE products.

In his prime, Michael Jordan was one of the top commercial spokespersons, starting with Coke, then Nike, before branching off to McDonald's, Hanes, and many others. His celebrity transcended his sports fame. Today, Tiger Woods is the symbol of Nike golf products and Buick, among others. George Foreman is better known for his cookware than as the former heavyweight boxing champ.

As we discussed in Chapter 4, using a celebrity works best when he or she has some reasonable connection with the product. Whether your celebrity is from the world of sports, show business, politics, or any other public venue, your main considerations should be:

- Can we afford this person?
- Does he or she have any skeletons in the closet—any future potential for embarrassing the client?
- Will he or she connect with the consumers?
- Will this person enhance the brand image?

Spokespersons/symbols. You can create spokespersons and, if things go right, they become celebrities. The "Dell Dude" was a prime example. For years, a guy wearing a black raincoat has been improving people's lives with Sprint digital phones. Or you can use a real person who's connected with the product, such as Wendy's did with the

6.16. Anna K's "15 minutes of fame" could describe most of her tennis matches. Now she's spokesperson and chief model for a line of sports bras. The tagline (we're not making this up)—"Because only the balls should bounce."

late Dave Thomas, who for years brought a likable, easygoing tone to his commercials.

Story Lines/Situations/Catchphrases

Story lines. Some advertisers use testimonials or case histories, all with a common theme to convey their message. State Farm Insurance has run campaigns that show people in risky occupations who won't take a chance on using another insurance company.

Situations. These are recurring themes or vignettes that involve (a) the same characters or (b) the same premise. For example, in a long-running series of commercials, Direct TV uses the same installer who interacts with different customers. Over the years Budweiser has featured their Clydesdales playing football while two cowboys watch the game. Imodium has created a series of print and TV ads with the theme "Where will you be when your diarrhea comes back?" In each case the victim is placed in a very awkward situation if the problem reoccurs.

Catchphrases. These can be official slogans, but more often they are lines that sometimes weave their way into the popular culture. For example, "Where's the beef?" from Wendy's even became a line in a presidential campaign. A few years ago, "Whassup!" ruled the airwaves and briefly enjoyed a few months of pop culture prominence. Any advertiser looking to stay on the leading edge of pop culture has to be aware when a catchphrase's 15 minutes of fame have expired. Rule of thumb: When middle-aged folks in Peoria start using your catchphrase, it's over.

6.17. One ad from a recent Coca-Cola campaign. The distinctive symbols of Coke are featured in every ad in the series.

Design and Tagline

As we discussed in Chapter 5, design elements can unify a campaign. Maybe it's a color, like the brown of UPS. They even built a slogan, "What can brown do for you?" around the distinctive color of the company's trucks and drivers' uniforms. Or a layout style, type style, or other graphic element could be the common thread. Once a look is established in the consumer's mind, extending it becomes a lot easier—until it stops getting attention. As we'll cover in Chapter 7, a slogan can also hold a campaign together.

Knowing the audience is job one for good campaign strategy

Even when your media mix is perfect and all the elements work together, your campaign can fail miserably if the basic idea—the One Thing—is wrong. Although the message seems right, it may be very wrong if you don't

6.18.

Source: Illustration by Dan Augustine.

understand your target audience. A classic example is the campaign by the U.S. State Department to encourage Muslims overseas to think kind thoughts about America after 9/11. They tapped Charlotte Beers, then the most powerful woman in American advertising, making her undersecretary for public diplomacy. Who better to craft a powerful message and deliver it to the right people? As it turned out, the campaign was a bust. Overseas, TV spots featuring Arab Americans saying nice things about this country were dismissed as crude propaganda. No matter what these people said, it couldn't compete with the images seen on Al Jazeera. After months of ridicule, the State Department pulled the plug, and in 2003 Beers left government service due to "health concerns." (Maybe the government got sick of wasting millions of dollars.) The moral: The success of your campaign starts with your understanding the wants and needs of the target audience.

NSAC: Like the Real Thing, Only More Fun

The National Student Advertising Competition, sponsored by the American Advertising Federation, provides an opportunity for college students to develop and present professional advertising campaigns for real clients. Some call it the World Series of college advertising. Each fall, teams begin work for the same client and then present their campaigns in the spring at regional and national competitions. For most college students, this is the closest thing to a real-world new-business pitch. They work with real objectives and real budgets with

6.19.

real guidelines, both from the client and from NSAC. Some schools make participation part of their advertising curricula; others participate as Ad Club members.

TABLE 6.1   NSAC

NSAC is like the real world because . . .	• You have to deal with budget, media, and creative restrictions imposed by a real client.
	• You work in small groups, sometimes with people you'd rather not work with.
	• The deadlines are crazy.
	• You pull a lot of all-nighters and eat a lot of junk food.
	• You face some really tough competition.
NSAC is not like the real world because . . .	• The 32-page plans book is usually far beyond the typical new-business effort.
	• The presentations are usually too slick for most new-business pitches.
	• You're evaluated by judges as well as by actual clients.
	• You do it all for free.
	• The losers party together.

NSAC consists of two main components: a plans book and a presentation. The plans book is the road map for a campaign. It includes an executive summary as well as sections covering situation analysis, research, media strategy and tactics, creative strategy and tactics, and sometimes promotion strategy and tactics. It also includes a budget, which makes the plan real, not just a creative exercise. The section devoted to evaluation is also important: What do you measure, how do you measure it, and when do you measure it?

How important is a plans book? In NSAC, it's given greater weight than the actual presentation. The judges are more interested in how you think than in how you present your thoughts.

The presentation is the fun part of NSAC. Four or five presenters introduce their team, walk through their recommendations, show the creative work, and, if they're smart, ask for the business. Following the 20-minute show-and-tell is a grueling 10-minute question-and-answer session. This is where the judges really test the presenters. It can make or break the whole presentation.

If you have the opportunity to participate in NSAC, do it! It's a great experience to develop a plan, execute the various campaign elements, and then sell it to a real client. It's also a great opportunity to see other college teams in action. What's more, NSAC participation looks great on your résumé, especially if you win.

Putting It All Together

Creative strategy for campaigns begins with marketing objectives. As always, you have to ask, "What do you want to accomplish?" The more specific the goals, the better your plan. When the objective is to introduce and reinforce a brand, start thinking campaigns.

Don't limit your thinking to repetition of the concept or even to how it will work in other media. Look at the big picture. The most famous one-shot ad of all time—Apple's "1984"—was actually part of a campaign that involved a huge amount of publicity and public relations. The commercial was shown many times—for free—after its one and only appearance on the Super Bowl, and the buzz put Macintosh on the map. It's interesting to note that the client was so nervous about the approach before the Super Bowl that the agency sold off their time for a scheduled second airing.

6.20. One of the magazine ads developed by the Marquette University team for the 2004 NSAC client: VISIT FLORIDA.

6.21. Creative can't exist in a vacuum. It has to be based on a sound strategy, executed properly, and distributed to the public through sound media choices. All those factors and more are outlined in a plans book. These are a few pages from the plans book of the 2004 NSAC champion, Southern Methodist University.

WAR STORY:

ALL-NIGHTERS, ADRENALINE, AND NAUSEA: WHAT IT TAKES TO WIN THE NSAC

Out of 16 schools at the finals, a team from Southern Methodist University won the 2004 National Student Advertising Competition in Dallas. The following is an account from Bethany Padnuk, one of the team leaders and presenters from SMU:

As a group of 18 students who barely knew each other, we faced the challenge of increasing the number of net leisure nights and paid lodging in Florida. "More heads on pillows" is what we called it. It seemed so fun and simple—getting people to visit Florida. Looking back, we had no clue what we were getting ourselves into.

We signed up to live, eat, sleep, and breathe Florida. Late nights, no free weekends, no spring break, and say goodbye to friends and loved ones. This project was anything but a vacation. Despite all these sacrifices, it was by far the best experience of my life, and it set me on the road to a successful career in advertising.

The day we got The Big Idea was one of the most memorable and exhilarating moments. We all just knew, "This is it. This is what we've been working for." It was the moment we linked travel to Florida with togetherness. This realization derived from our key consumer insight: People think of a Florida vacation as an "investment" in their relationships with loved ones. Our creative executions stood out both visually and strategically from every other leisure destination campaign, and our taglines spoke directly to relationship travelers: "This is friendship. This is Florida." And "This is family. This is Florida."

After countless all-nighters and a 15-minute power nap in the parking lot of Kinko's, our 32-page plans book was completed and sent off to the competition. It was time for the next challenge—the presentation. We'd done all the work; now it was time to tell our story. As one of five presenters, I can honestly say that I've never felt so much adrenaline and nausea than I did before our final presentation for the national competition in Dallas. Since we were regarded as the "team to beat," hundreds of people—parents, students, alumni, and recruiters—came to see our pitch. Not only were we standing just four feet in front of the judges' table, which included the CEO of VISIT FLORIDA, but sitting in the front row were four of my potential employers, whom I had invited to see me in action. My final interview was in two days. What a rush; we knew we had nailed it when the CEO said, "You guys really hit it out of the park."

The moment leading up to the announcement of the national winners was one of the most agonizing waits we've ever experienced. Hearts racing, palms sweating, eyes closed, and breath held, we finally heard "Southern Methodist University." And that was the moment we all knew it was worth it.

The rewards from taking part in this competition were numerous. While the end product of the NSAC experience—first place in the "College World Series of Advertising"—was important, the process required to get there was equally valuable. Nothing could have prepared me more for the real world. We learned to come together as a team in stressful situations. We learned how to fight for our work when pitching our business. We developed a unique point of difference from other students entering the job market. Most important, we established invaluable relationships. And that's what this business is all about.

—Bethany Padnuk, The Richards Group (SMU class of 2004)

6.22. Study advertising—good, bad—it doesn't matter. Seeing how other people solve the creative problem will help you become a better writer.

Source: Illustration by Dan Augustine.

Campaign tips

We've offered a lot of ways to improve the continuity and thus the effectiveness of campaigns. Here's some more good advice from Jim Albright:

- A campaign is a series of planned actions. Think big about a wide, multi-pronged attack on the marketplace.

- When assigned to write a one time ad, check to see if the client has an ongoing look and sound and slogan. If so, make the point of the ad under the umbrella of the ongoing look, sound and slogan.

- If the client has no continuity in its advertising, write the one-time ad so that it could be extended into a campaign, if necessary.

- When writing an advertising campaign, don't repeat the same plot in different media. Repeat the creative strategy with different executions.

- Think extendibility from the beginning. Sometimes a strategy is so narrow that only one or two good commercials or ads can be written under that strategy. Think ahead to all the different ways you can execute advertising under your creative strategy. You may have to write a song or have T-shirts printed.[9]

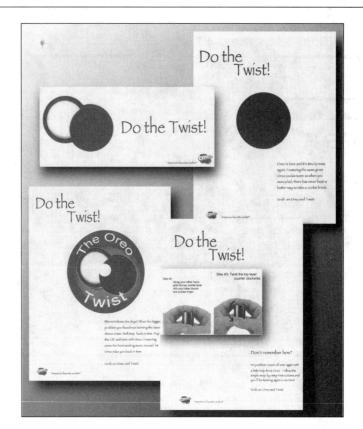

6.23. This mini-campaign designed by a student used a simple theme to add a little life to an old brand. The campaign included an offer for a CD of twist music and a booklet on creative twist techniques. It also included TV, Internet, and radio commercials.

According to the editors of *Advertising Age,* these are the 10 best campaigns of the 20th century:

1. Volkswagen, "*Think Small,*" Doyle Dane Bernbach, 1959
2. Coca-Cola, "The Pause That Refreshes," D'Arcy Co., 1929
3. Marlboro, the Marlboro Man, Leo Burnett Co., 1955
4. Nike, "Just do it," Wieden + Kennedy, 1988
5. McDonald's, "You Deserve a Break Today," Needham, Harper & Steers, 1971
6. DeBeers, "A Diamond Is Forever," N. W. Ayer & Son, 1948
7. Absolut Vodka, the Absolut Bottle, TBWA, 1981
8. Miller Lite beer, "Tastes Great, Less Filling," McCann-Erickson Worldwide, 1974
9. Clairol, "Does She . . . or Doesn't She?" Foote, Cone & Belding, 1957
10. Avis, "We Try Harder," Doyle Dane Bernbach, 1963[11]

Who's Who?

Charlotte Beers—A brilliant strategic thinker, Charlotte Beers rose to become the world's highest-ranked woman in advertising. The Texas native joined J. Walter Thompson Co. in 1969, and in 1979, she became COO, then CEO, of Tatham-Laird & Kudner. She tripled billings and merged with Europe's RSCG to create what is now Euro RSCG Tatham. Her performance led WPP Group to name her chairman-CEO of Ogilvy & Mather Worldwide and, later, chairman of JWT. Following 9/11, she served a brief stint as undersecretary of state for public diplomacy, during which she worked to improve the image of the United States in Muslim countries.

Marie-Catherine Dupuy—Marie-Catherine Dupuy is a third-generation ad agency executive. Her grandfather founded one of the first French advertising agencies (which later became Saatchi & Saatchi in 1986). Dupuy joined Dupuy-Compton as a copywriter in 1970. In 1984, she became a founding partner and executive creative director at Boulet Dru Dupuy Petit (later to become part of TBWA). As writer and creative director, she has won more than 200 awards in international competition for clients such as Virgin, BMW, McDonald's, Tag Heuer, Sony, and Bic.

Jeff Goodby—While working as a copywriter at Hal Riney, Jeff Goodby was freelancing with partners Andy Berlin and Rich Silverstein. Their freelance client eventually became Electronic Arts and got so big they decided to create their own agency, with EA as their first account. It wasn't their last. Their creative risk taking led to breakthrough campaigns for the California Milk Processor Board ("Got Milk?"), Budweiser (Louie and Frank the lizards and the "Whassup" campaign), Nike, E*TRADE, and the Winter Olympics. That campaign, among others, helped the once tiny agency gain significant recognition, including multiple Clio and Cannes awards. Goodby has been named "Agency of the Year" by *AdWeek* and has grown steadily with the addition of Unilever, Cracker Jack, Intel, and the *Wall Street Journal.*

Tom Monahan—Through his popular creative workshops, Tom Monahan has helped thousands of people master creative thinking. His consulting company, Before & After, has worked with clients such as Capital One, Frito-Lay, AT&T, and Virgin Atlantic. He is also the author of one of the top business-oriented books on creative thinking, *The Do-It-Yourself Lobotomy: Open Your Mind to Greater Creative Thinking.*

Jon Steel—One of the early leaders in the fast-growing field of account planning, Jon Steel is well-known for his innovative approach to focus groups, in which he elicited opinions from people where they lived, worked, and shopped, rather than in sterile interview rooms. As head of Goodby, Silverstein & Partners' planning department, Steel was named "West Coast Executive of the Year" by *AdWeek* in 2000. He also finds time to share his depth of knowledge in the world of academia at Stanford University's School of Business as a regular lecturer. His first book, *Truth, Lies and Advertising: The Art of Account Planning,* has become a must-read for anyone interested in account planning.

Notes

1 Shay Sayre, *Campaign Planner for Promotion and IMC* (Cincinnati: South-Western, 2002), 5.

2 Maxine Paetro, *How to Put Your Book Together and Get a Job in Advertising* (Chicago: Copy Workshop, 2002), 7.

3 Jim Albright, *Creating the Advertising Message* (Mountain View, CA: Mayfield, 1992), 41.

4 Thomas O'Guinn, Chris Allen, Richard Semenik, *Advertising and Integrated Brand Promotion* (Mason, OH: Thomson, 2002), 50.

5 Quote from the Clio Award Web site, http://www.clioawards.com/html/wsj/dupuy.html (accessed December 20, 2004).

6 Albright, *Creating the Advertising Message,* 49.

7 Jon Steel, *Truth, Lies and Advertising: The Art of Account Planning* (New York: John Wiley, 1998).

8 Tom Monahan, "When an Ad Is Not a Campaign," *Communication Arts,* May/June 2000, http://www.commarts.com/ca/colad/tomM_31.html (accessed May 27, 2005).

9 Albright, *Creating the Advertising Message,* 49.

10 Bob Garfield, "Top 100 Advertising Campaigns of the Century," *Advertising Age,* March 29, 1999, http://www.adage.com/century/campaigns.html (accessed May 27, 2005).

11 Ibid.

Headlines and Taglines

We can show you the easy way to get an A. Got your attention, right?

That's what a headline is supposed to do. It appeals to your self-interest. It can promise a reward. It makes you want to know more. It can draw you into the ad.

Why Have a Headline?

A headline is probably the most important element of copy. David Ogilvy said the headline is worth 80 cents of the client's dollar. Sometimes it's worth even more.

All forms of marketing communications use headlines, even when we don't call them headlines. In television it's the start of the commercial. In radio, it's the first few words of copy. In a letter, it may be a title or the first paragraph.

Ogilvy also stated that the headline is the "ticket on the meat,"[1] which sounds rather simplistic for someone who wrote, "*At 60 miles an hour the loudest noise in this new Rolls-Royce comes from the electric clock.*" He found a benefit (exceptionally quiet ride), included specifics (60 miles per hour), and twisted it with an unexpected comparison to an electric clock, probably the last thing you'd think about when buying a Rolls-Royce. At 18 words, it's very long by today's standards, but still memorable.

7.1. David Ogilvy discovered an obscure fact about Rolls-Royce and turned it into one of the greatest headlines of all time.

WORDS OF WISDOM

"All messages have headlines. In TV, it's the start of the commercial; in radio, it's the first few words; in a letter, the first paragraph."

—JOHN CAPLES[2]

Not all print ads have headlines, especially visual puzzles. However, it's important to know how to write a good headline first. Then you can decide if you need it. Some texts dissect and analyze headlines in great detail, but we'll boil their functions down to four primary points. A *good* headline does one or more of the following:

- Gain immediate attention (the old fishhook in the brain).
- Select the right prospect (appeal to self interest).
- Lead readers into the text (they want to know more).
- Complete the creative equation (synergy with visuals).

7.3. The visual is funny but doesn't make much sense by itself. The headline without the visual is weak. Together they're very effective.

7.2. By itself, this headline would probably get your attention. Paired with this disturbing graphic, it really grabs the reader. It reads, **"DON'T VOTE. Things are perfect just the way they are."**

7.4. Sometimes a great headline doesn't need a visual to communicate a powerful message. It's simple, clever, and makes a point without preaching.

7.5. *Synergy:* Headline and graphics working together to create a more memorable message. (The last line of copy is great too: "Even with available seating for seven, only one person can truly appreciate the Discovery. The rest have to go to school.")

7.6. Is the visual part of the headline or vice versa? Either way, it works with the subhead and pulls you into the body copy. It's also a good example of selecting the right prospect (this ran in a magazine targeting mature readers).

Types of Headlines

Categorizing headlines is usually more helpful for describing completed work than for helping you develop new concepts. Phillip Ward Burton has developed a list of categories that we like.[3] In Table 7.1 we've modified his list a bit and kept the descriptions brief.

7.7. *News:* A new salt company is born. Not exactly the Second Coming, but newsworthy to industrial users of salt.

WORDS OF WISDOM

"The headline is the most important element of an ad. It must offer a promise to the reader of a believable benefit. And it must be phrased in a way to give it memory value."

—MORRIS HITE[4]

Table 7.1   Headline Categories

Type of Headline	Use this when
News	. . . you want to introduce a new product, new brand, new feature.
Direct benefit	. . . you want to promise a reward or highlight the prime benefit in the headline.
Curiosity	. . . you want to intrigue the reader into finding the main idea in the body copy.
Emotional	. . . you want to sell the image and/or invoke resonance in the reader.
Directive (command)	. . . you want the reader to do something.
Hornblowing	. . . you want to impress the reader by being the biggest, the fastest, the first, etc.
Comparison	. . . you want to differentiate your brand from the competitor or use a metaphor to describe your product.
Label	. . . you want to focus on the brand name, product name, or campaign tagline rather than discuss features/benefits.

7.8. *Direct benefit:* This one tells the whole story in the headline and then supports it with the visual.

7.9. *Curiosity:* What does being a "foam peanut" have to do with insurance? Read the ad and find out. The goal in these types of ads is to make the headline so interesting you want to find out more.

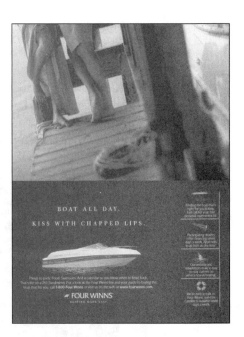

7.10. *Emotional:* Another indirect approach. This one promotes the fun of boating, not the features of the boat. "Boat all day. Kiss with chapped lips."

7.11. Directive: This B2B (business-to-business) ad challenges you to try to burn their ad. Actually, it's an insert coated with a fireproof material. The copy is directive too. "Hold this advertisement over an ashtray. Put a match or a lighter to it. Remove the flame, and page stops burning." We tried it, and it didn't burn.

7.12. Hornblowing: Sometimes a direct shot between the eyes gets the point across. In some cases, if you say it loud and often enough, eventually the reader or viewer might start believing you're the best . . . just because you say you are.

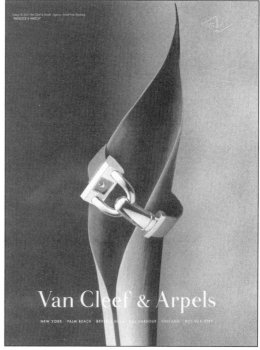

7.13. Comparison: Financial services as a safety line. This is a lot more interesting than a compound interest chart.

7.14. Label: If you don't want to say very much about the product, at least get them to remember the name of the store.

How to Write More Effective Headlines

The "magic words"

Let's take a few steps back to Chapter 1 and think about ideas that sell versus creativity for its own sake. Your choice of words can make a huge difference in the selling power of your ad. John Caples, the master of direct response (and member of the Copywriters Hall of Fame) developed a list of the most effective words to use in headlines. Over more than 40 years of copywriting experience, he found using these words significantly increased the response rate:

- Advice
- Announcing
- At last
- Free
- How
- How to
- New

- Now
- Reduced
- This
- Wanted
- Which
- Who else
- Why

The danger of cherry-picking words from this list is that you might forget what interests the reader. A headline that appeals to the reader and draws him or her into the copy is far more powerful than an empty phrase full of the "right words."

For example, using the above list, you might consider this to be the world's greatest headline:

At last! Announcing the free advice which you've always wanted. Who else would show you a new way how to do this at a reduced cost?

Proven styles of headlines

Additional research has shown that certain styles of headlines tend to pull better. Once again, it is far more important to write a headline that achieves one or more of its purposes than to write some empty bit of fluff that fits some formula. The three proven styles of headlines are:

- Question
- How-to
- Quote

The first two are effective because they involve the reader. If you ask a question (and the reader is interested), you stimulate involvement. The same is true with a how-to headline, but you have to finish the sentence with something that interests the reader. Quotations can be effective because they are usually connected to a person, and people are interested in other people, be they celebrities or ordinary Joes or Janes. A quotation hints at a story, which, if it interests the reader, fosters involvement. Table 7.2 shows some examples of each of the three styles.

TABLE 7.2   **Headline Styles**

Style	Headline	Visual	Client
Question	Do you really need more proof that drinking impairs your judgment?	Plain girl morphing into a fashion model as it gets later in the evening	MADD
Question	Ever see a grown man cry?	Broken whiskey bottle on floor	Crown Royal
How-to	How to convert liters into cups	Race car and racing trophies	Acura
How-to	How to write an obituary for your teenager	[All-type ad]	Partnership for a Drug-Free America
Quote	I told my dad I stopped raising hell and he called me a quitter.	Redneck-looking guy smoking a cigarette	Winston
Quote	These tables are my voice and I'm about to holla at the world.	DJ scratching two turntables	Mountain Dew Red

Using the creative tree for headlines

Think of an upside-down tree. The base is the basic positioning statement. The main branches are the various product attributes. Headlines sprout from each of these branches. First start with that One Thing you can say about the product. This is not a headline, but it will give you some idea starters to build one or several. Figure 7.1 on page 156 shows an example.

You can keep adding more branches based on other key copy points. This can go on forever. As with all creative writing, if you're on a roll, don't quit. Keep writing headlines even if 99% of them are awful. A real stinker may trigger a winner.

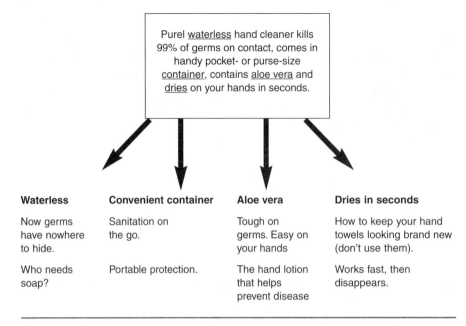

Purel <u>waterless</u> hand cleaner kills 99% of germs on contact, comes in handy pocket- or purse-size <u>container</u>, contains <u>aloe vera</u> and <u>dries</u> on your hands in seconds.

Waterless	Convenient container	Aloe vera	Dries in seconds
Now germs have nowhere to hide.	Sanitation on the go.	Tough on germs. Easy on your hands	How to keep your hand towels looking brand new (don't use them).
Who needs soap?	Portable protection.	The hand lotion that helps prevent disease	Works fast, then disappears.

Figure 7.1. The Creative Tree: Positioning Statements Branching Into Headlines

7.15. Question: This ad from the 1920s is considered one of the all-time classics. It ran at a time when people were actually concerned about appearing literate. If you want to improve your vocabulary and writing skills, you have to read further.

7.16. Question: This question could be used in a number of potentially uncomfortable situations.

7.17. How-to: This ad shows how to convey snob appeal in a fresh, nonconfrontational way.

7.18. Quote: In print, any headline written in the first person can be considered a quote. This is the print companion to a very funny TV commercial with the same theme.

WAR STORY:

FROM THOSE WONDERFUL FOLKS . . .

Jerry Della Femina developed one of the most famous headlines that was never used. Della Femina's agency had just won the Panasonic account, and they were stumped for ideas.

One guy said, "Well, what are we going to do about Panasonic?" And everybody sat around, frowning and thinking about Panasonic. Finally, I decided, what the hell, I'll throw a line to loosen them up—I mean, they were paying me $50,000 a year plus a $5,000-a-year expense account, and I thought they deserved something for all this bread. So I said, "Hey, I've got it, I've got it." Everybody jumped. Then I got very dramatic, really setting them up. "I see a Headline, Yes, I see this Headline." "What is it?" they yelled. "I see it all now," I said, "I see an entire campaign built around this headline." They all were looking at me now. "The headline is, the headline is: From Those Wonderful Folks Who Gave You Pearl Harbor."[5]

7.19. *Split headline:* The first part connects with the visual and also leads into the second part, which could also be a slogan.

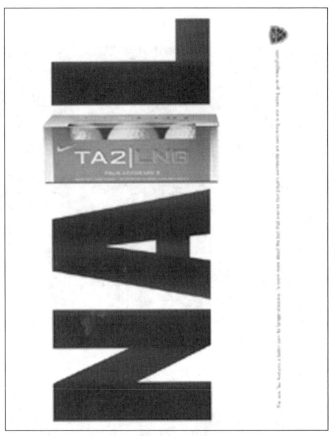

7.20. *Graphic in headline:* Nike is beginning to dominate the golf market the way they captured basketball, with simple, powerful messages.

Writing Headlines with Style

If you work on it, you can add a little spice to your list of headlines. We offer a few suggestions in this section. Try to work some of them into your long list and see if they lead to anything worth keeping.

Be specific. Let's go back to Ogilvy's classic. Do you think it would have been nearly as good with "This is one really quiet car" or "The clock is louder than the engine"? Without turning it into a laundry list of specs and features, see if you can work some details into your headline.

Rhyme, rhythm, alliteration. As with taglines, using rhyme, rhythm, and alliteration can make a headline more memorable. Some might say a rhyming headline is clever. Others may think the same headline is cheesy. If it's memorable and sells something, who cares? Rhythm usually employs connecting a few well-chosen short words, such as "Coke is it." Alliteration, for those who can't remember English composition, combines two or more words with the

PEOPLE: 6,000,000,000
WHO RUN: 562,810,398
THE 100 METERS: 729,227
IN 9.79 SECONDS: 1

USA TRACK & FIELD

7.21. This student ad promoting USA Track and Field is all specifics, and that's what makes it interesting.

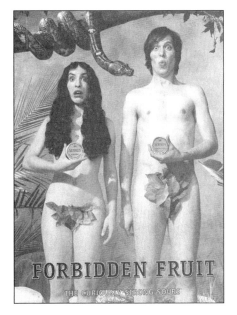

FORBIDDEN FRUIT
THE CURIOUSLY STRONG SOURS

7.22. Alliteration in a stripped-down version.

same initial sound, such as "The joint is jumping" or "Every kiss begins with Kay."

Judicious use of puns and wordplay. Sometimes puns work. We did an ad for a luxury boat company that showed our product docked at a marina with many other fancy boats. Some of the other owners were checking out our client's product. The headline: "Pier Pressure." Cute? Stupid? You decide. This tip could also include wordplay and double meanings. As with puns, be careful.

Parallel construction. This is just a fancy way of saying you're combining phrases or sentences with similar key words to make a point. A few years ago, VISIT FLORIDA used the line "When you need it bad, we've got it good." A student wrote an ad for Purel waterless hand cleaner making the point that money is full of germs and other nasty stuff. Her headline: "Dirty money. Dirty hands."

Boat Loans

7.23. Sort of a pun. Sort of a twist. Sort of a double meaning. Sort of an overstatement/understatement. Sort of a waste of time, since the client rejected it.

7.24. A "player" and a play on words. Sometimes you have to be very careful with wordplay. This ad probably works better on the back cover of *Maxim* than in *AARP*. The headline: "One Bad Mother pucker."

7.25. This ad not only features a clever headline with double meanings, it also makes good use of white space and lines to highlight the product.

7.26. This is one of a long-running series from Allen Edmonds that uses parallel construction headlines and the slogan "For all walks of life."

Try it with a twist. The headline is part of the concept, so give it a twist now and then. Another example from our luxury boat client: We showed the boat at a dock in front of a very nice house. The owners of our boat were hosting a fancy outdoor dinner party. The headline: "If your neighbors aren't impressed, move to a better neighborhood."

Understatement/overstatement. George Felton makes a good point in his book *Advertising: Concept and Copy* about headline/visual synergy and tone. "If your visual is wild and crazy or obviously excessive, then back off verbally. And vice versa. In other words, don't shout twice."[6]

Ineffective headlines

We can't tell you how to write the perfect headline. Unless it's an all-type ad, the headline usually doesn't stand alone. So the value of a headline is usually related to how well it interacts with the rest of the ad. The ultimate value of a headline depends on the expectations of the client and the results achieved. "Free donuts" may be the most effective headline to attract policemen, if that's your objective. A lot of headlines work very well

7.27. How do you promote a clothing optional resort tastefully? By twisting the traditional meanings of "button" and "suit."

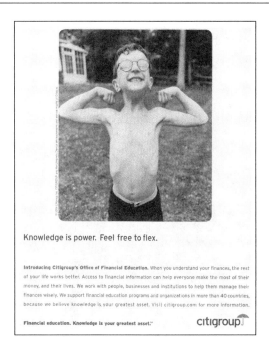

7.28. **Overstatement** = Wimpy but lovable kid flexing for the camera. **Understatement** = "Knowledge is power. Feel free to flex." This would not have worked nearly as well with a photo of a pumped-up weight lifter or a caption headline such as "Do you have a wimpy portfolio?"

on Planet Schlock, but there are some that just scream, "Think again!" Some things to look out for:

- Asking a question that can't be answered (confusing)

- Asking a question that can be answered with a simple yes or no (no involvement)

- Using a headline as a caption, describing rather than interacting (no synergy with visuals and limited involvement)

- Stupid puns ("stupid" defined as having absolutely no relation to the product or market)

- Insulting, condescending, patronizing (annoys intelligent readers)

- Being clever for the sake of cleverness (trying to impress rather than persuade)

Evaluating headlines

When writing headlines, you're faced with the same dilemma as with the overall concept. Do you write one that looks good in your portfolio or one that works hard at selling something? Once again, the answer is . . . that depends. Just as most people think they are experts on taglines, even

WORDS OF WISDOM

"I've done as many as 19 drafts on a single piece of copy. I wrote 37 headlines for Sears Roebuck last week and I think I got three good enough to submit."

—**DAVID OGILVY**[7]

7.29. This might have been a very effective ad, but would you buy expensive construction equipment from people who admit they might be insane?

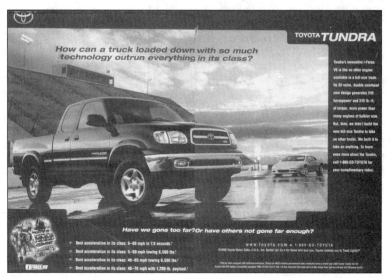

7.30. A weak question headline followed by a weaker question subhead. **"How can a truck loaded down with so much technology outrun everything in its class?"** (Maybe because it's loaded with technology?) Then the subhead, **"Have we gone too far? Or have the others not gone far enough?"** (You can't answer those questions either, and we'll never know from the copy.)

more have opinions on headlines. Some like straightforward news headlines, because there's no mistaking the message. Others like obscure references that hook a select group and leave the rest scratching their heads. Still others think silly puns are the height of creativity, while others just groan.

While there are infinite degrees of cleverness and clarity, our advice is:

If you can't be clever, be clear.

In other words, if you can't come up with a least one different, twisted, unusual, or interesting headline, then say it straight and always keep in mind the visual is there to work with the headline, not just to sit above a caption.

Headline Checklist

Before you settle on one headline, run through the following guidelines. Your headline doesn't have to meet all these criteria, but it should cover some of them.

1. Let your headline sit for a while. Do you still love it the morning after? (Or do you slap your head and say, "What was I thinking?")

2. Does your headline work with the visual or is it just a caption or, worse, completely irrelevant?

3. In your vision of the layout, does the headline look important? Is it readable? Does it have the proper proximity to the visual and body copy?

4. Can you do the "billboard test" and still have a concept that makes sense?

5. Does your headline appeal to the reader's self-interest?

6. Does your headline pull readers into the body copy?

7. Be honest. Is this the best you can do? Or can you start round two or three or four to come up with a list of great headlines? Keep running branches off that creative tree.

8. Do not use a strong subhead to "explain" a weak headline. Use a strong headline and you might not need a subhead. (Remember, less is more.)

9. Be careful with puns. There's a reason they're called the lowest form of comedy. Don't be cute just for the sake of cuteness. If a pun has a purpose, try it. Otherwise, find a more clever way to say it.

10. Think campaigns. How are you going to follow up that killer headline? Will your next five ads be just as good?

Subheads

As you would expect, the subhead is usually underneath the headline. Sometimes it immediately follows the headline, as if to say, "What we *really* meant to say is . . ." Other times subheads are used to separate long copy blocks or introduce new thoughts in an ad. In this context they are sometimes called *breakers*.

The four main purposes of a subhead are:

- Clarify the headline.
- Reinforce the main idea stated in the headline.
- Break up large copy blocks.
- Lead you into the body copy.

Subhead traps

Too often copywriters use subheads to "explain" the headline. You may feel the headline is too weak or the reader won't get it. So you add a straight line so there's no mistaking the benefit. Many times this is done to convince a skeptical client that a risky ad concept really is a serious selling effort. We don't like subheads used this way for two reasons: First, why write a weak headline and prop it up with a subhead? Write a strong headline in the first place. And second, use as few words as possible to convey your message. Adding a subhead can more than double the clutter in an ad.

Another subhead trap: Don't use the subhead to introduce a new, separate idea from the headline. Going back to our Ogilvy headline, you don't want to follow

7.31. In this student-designed ad, the headline catches the reader's attention and uses the subhead to lead you into the copy.

7.32. The headline promises a direct benefit, and the subhead reinforces it.

7.33. Here the subheads break up big blocks of copy. A reader can scan the subheads to get a feel for the copy and read in detail if it's interesting.

that beautiful headline with a subhead that says, "What's more, the new Rolls-Royce offers the highest horsepower of any luxury car."

Preheads

This is also called the overline. Whatever you call it, it precedes the headline. You can use preheads for a number of reasons, but the four most common are:

- Set up the headline.
- Define the audience.
- Identify the advertiser.
- Identify an ad in a series.

As with subheads, you need to decide if a prehead is needed to explain the headline. If so, rethink the headline and you may not need the prehead. In many cases, the prehead asks a question that the headline answers or starts a thought completed by the headline. In these cases, you could consider the prehead to be an integral part of the headline.

Taglines

We call them taglines, but you could also say they're slogans, signature lines, or theme lines. Usually, they are the catchphrases that appear after the logo in a print ad or at the end of the commercial, and, in most cases, they are very forgettable. However, if they're done right, taglines can be the most important element of a campaign.

Some clients expect too much from a tagline. They don't want a little blurb to sneak under their logo. They demand a "statement" that (a) defines the company, (b) positions the product, (c) denigrates the competition, (d) reassures the stockholders, and (e) will be approved by the CEO's wife. The more objectives a tagline tries to achieve, the more generic it becomes. When a tagline becomes generic, you can put it under any logo with negligible effect. Too many taglines are written by committees and tested by management panels. They're cobbled together with a few key words that by themselves mean nothing but, when used in a composite slogan, become completely irrelevant.

Before you start cranking out slogans you have to ask the client, "What's the One Thing you want to say?" Do you want to convey a general attitude or tone? Do you want something specific about the products? Do you want something relating to your customers? Just what the heck *do* you want? George Felton sums it up pretty well in *Advertising: Copy and Concept:* "Slogans . . . had better do more than just be clever . . . they need to be smart."[8] The smart taglines stick with you years after they first appear. They become part of the popular culture and define their place in time as well as the brand.

According to *Advertising Age,* these are the top 10 slogans of the 20th century:

7.34. Here's a case where the prehead is an integral part of the headline. The juicy beef and oddball "Macaroni Salad" catch your eye. Then you read the prehead for the complete message.

1. "A diamond is forever" (DeBeers)
2. "Just do it" (Nike)
3. "The pause that refreshes" (Coca-Cola)
4. "Tastes great, less filling" (Miller Lite)
5. "We try harder" (Avis)
6. "Good to the last drop" (Maxwell House)
7. "Breakfast of champions" (Wheaties)
8. "Does she . . . or doesn't she?" (Clairol)
9. "When it rains it pours" (Morton Salt)
10. "Where's the beef?" (Wendy's)[9]

Why Have a Tagline?

The primary purpose of a tagline is to establish or reinforce the brand name. To do this, the tagline should do the following:

- *Provide continuity for a campaign.* A tagline may be the only common component of a multimedia campaign. It can also be the link between campaigns with very different looks. A good tagline transcends changes in campaign strategy. No matter what BMW is doing with their ads, the cars are always "The Ultimate Driving Machines."

- *Crystallize the One Thing associated with the brand or product:* Whether it's staking out a position or implying an abstract attitude, the slogan is an extension of the brand name. When you can mention a brand name and someone else quotes the slogan, you know you've got something.

Going back to concepts discussed in earlier chapters, the tagline can help foster *awareness* and *comprehension* of a brand or product. A few well-chosen words can define the brand, separate it from the competition, and anchor it in the reader/viewer's brain. Think of M&M candies that "melt in your mouth, not in your hand." It's not only a statement of a real product benefit; nobody else can say this.

A good tagline increases your creative freedom. When the message ends with "Only in a Jeep," you can have a lot more fun with the content.

A few years ago, Cadillac wanted to stress their engineering expertise and styling panache. They developed the tagline "The Power of &," which did nothing to convince existing or potential customers they had anything new. The next year, they

7.35. In 2004, Chevy began to lead an American Revolution. This slogan was used as the headline in all Chevrolet car and truck advertising for the model year.

unveiled an entirely new attitude with "Break Through," which not only promoted a radical new car design, but also featured Led Zeppelin's "Rock and Roll" as the theme music. They still haven't captured all the Baby Boomers who prefer luxury imports, but at least they "broke through" to deliver a new message.

How to Write More Effective Taglines

The following are a few tips and techniques for writing better taglines. Of course, not every tagline is going to possess all these traits (unless you find the successor to "Just do it"). These guidelines are offered to help you evaluate your taglines before you submit them to the client.

Keep it short and simple. "Drivers wanted" sticks in the mind better than VW's older slogan, "It's not a car. It's a Volkswagen." Think billboards—no more than six words. Three words are even better. As a much better writer once said, "Brevity is the soul of wit." Just make sure your witticism makes sense.

Think jingle. Even if you never put your tagline to music, picture it in a TV commercial. You can use the old tricks of rhythm, rhyme, and alliteration to make it more memorable. For example, no one over 40 can forget "Winston tastes good like a cigarette should," even though cigarette advertising on TV ended in 1971. A modern example: Kay Jewelers says, "Every kiss begins with Kay."

Try to differentiate the brand. Can you come up with a simple way to separate yourself from the competition? Visa says they're "Everywhere you want to be," implying that American Express and MasterCard aren't. Currently Dodge is running "Take life by the horns," which only makes sense if you can pair it with their Ram logo. The ideal slogan can't be used by any other brand. Altoids established themselves as the "Curiously Strong Mint" so well they could extend the tagline to other products such as the "Curiously Strong Sour."

If you have to be generic, go global. Many brands use what could be called generic slogans. They're positive, easy to remember, and can be translated into most languages without changing their meanings. When they stand alone, these slogans could work for just about anyone. The difference is they're supported by millions of dollars of advertising and promotion. So if Joe's Burger Shack says, "i'm lovin' it," no one notices. When McDonald's does it, it becomes major marketing news. If you can remember the innocuous slogans for most mass-marketed packaged goods, it's because they've been beaten into your brain.

Play with words. A tagline can be more memorable if you take a common expression and twist it just enough to get attention. Chrysler promotes their preowned cars as "Brand Spanking Used." Years ago Panasonic promoted the ergonomics of their home electronics with "So advanced, it's simple." Sometimes you can give your slogan a double meaning. For example, a drug company targeted doctors with "Healthy concern for your practice," indicating that the drug company was successful and cared about their customers.

7.36. When someone says "beef," most people respond, "It's what's for dinner." They still use the slogan, but now it's tucked under their tiny logo. However, it's so well established that their Web site is beefitswhats fordinner.com.

7.37. In 2003, McDonald's unveiled their global slogan "i'm lovin' it" with a jingle sung by Justin Timberlake and "youth-oriented" images. Nothing screams "hip" and "cool" like a multinational corporation that specializes in mass-merchan-dized food and sketchy service.

7.38. Nissan developed several radical new car designs to jump-start lagging sales. Their new "Shift" slogan was also a radical departure. After the word "Shift" they added a series of attributes that flashed rapidly at the end of their spots and alternated on their Web site.

Don't confuse or mislead. In the effort to be creative, some writers forget that the rest of the world is not as clever as they are. An obscure one-word tagline could be misunderstood or, worse, ignored. Make sure the slogan fits the image of the brand and your overall message. A few years ago, United Airlines used

"Rising" as their slogan. It was certainly an appropriate word for an airline and, at the time, indicated bright prospects for the employee-owned company. However, given the financial status of United and the industry in general, no one would believe they are still "rising." Viagra used to say, "Let the dance begin." Maybe "Rising" would have been better for them.

Justify your choices. Everyone is an expert on taglines. So when you submit a list to the client, make sure everyone knows the parameters you were given. Too often the rules change after you've received the initial game plan.

The Creative Tree for Taglines

Writing taglines is a lot like developing whole concepts. Start with the One Thing. Then say it straight. From there you can veer off in several directions, each with a list of possible slogans. Figure 7.2 illustrates a brief template for a business-to-business client, although this technique works for any product or service.

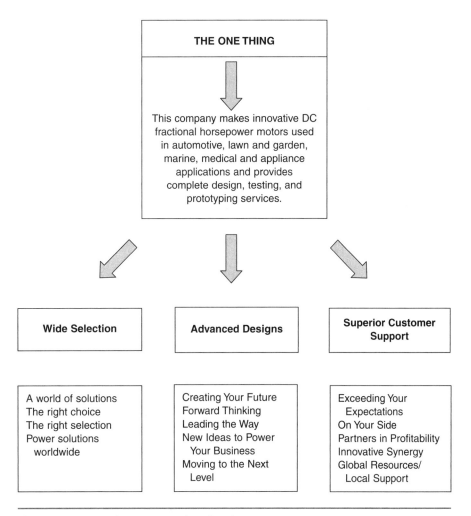

Figure 7.2. A Creative Tree Template for Slogan

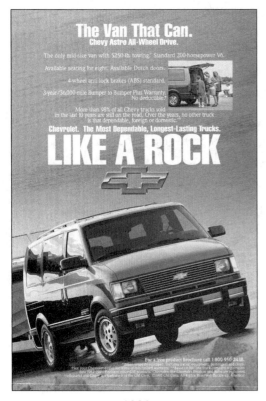

1993

2000

2003

7.39–7.41. Chevrolet used a phrase from an early 1980s Bob Seger song and turned it into one the longest-running slogans in company history. Originally used for large pickups, "Like a Rock" worked with their vans and lighter trucks, remaining the one constant through years.

As you've probably noted, the majority of the taglines in Figure 7.2 stink. Most of the time, you'll start with a generic slogan, but as you keep working, you'll branch out. You can have as many branches as you'd like. Don't worry if some of your slogans don't fit a defined category—just keep writing. Don't start editing until you get a huge list. Then weed out the obvious stinkers. Keep refining your list until you have a group of taglines you can live with. So you might come up with something a little better, such as:

The Power of Innovation

Solutions in Motion

We Power Your Ideas

OK, they're still not "Just do it," but don't stop trying. Keep sending out branches. You'll find one that works as long as it stays true to the values at the base of the tree.

Taglines Need Your Support

Even "Just do it" would not have made much sense if it had been launched in a campaign that highlighted the features and benefits of Nike shoes. It had to be paired with people dedicated to exercise. That synergy made it magic.

That's why writing taglines can be so pointless. They're usually evaluated by a committee in a vacuum, without the benefit of massive ad support or even a connection to the campaign. Once a slogan becomes established, you can vary the images and copy in the ads, but they have to be there when that tagline is introduced. Once it's established in the consumer's mind, it becomes part of the brand, transcending the creative execution that may change from year to year.

7.42. Taglines as we know them would cease to exist if it were up to the client.

Source: Illustration by Dan Augustine.

Who's Who?

Morris Hite—Morris Hite may well be the most significant figure in the evolution of advertising in the Southwest. He grew Tracy-Locke from a small Dallas-based advertising agency into a communications empire that included the Southwest's largest advertising agency, one of the country's five largest marketing research companies, a major public relations company, and an agency for smaller clients. (See, you don't have to be a copywriter to offer words of wisdom.)

David Ogilvy—Founder of Ogilvy & Mather, David Ogilvy was, first and foremost, a copywriter. One of the pioneers of image advertising, Ogilvy also wrote two best sellers, *Confessions of an Advertising Man* and *Ogilvy on Advertising*. He was one of the most eloquent and influential voices in advertising and today is still one of the most quotable.

Notes

[1] David Ogilvy, *Confessions of an Advertising Man* (New York: Ballantine, 1971), 92.

[2] Quoted in Phillip Ward Burton, *Advertising Copywriting* (Lincolnwood, IL: NTC Business Books, 1991), 16.

[3] Burton, *Advertising Copywriting,* 54.

[4] Morris Hite, *Adman: Morris Hite's Methods for Winning the Ad Game* (Dallas: E-Heart, 1998), 33.

[5] Jerry Della Femina, *From Those Wonderful Folks Who Gave You Pearl Harbor: Front-Line Dispatches from the Advertising War* (New York: Pocket Books, 1971), quoted on the Center for Interactive Advertising Web site, http://www.ciadvertising.org/studies/student/96_fall/femina/book.html (accessed June 30, 2005).

[6] George Felton, *Advertising: Concept and Copy* (Englewood Cliffs, NJ: Prentice Hall, 1993), 93.

[7] Quoted in Denis Higgins, *The Art of Writing Advertising: Conversations with Masters of the Craft: William Bernbach, George Gribbin, David Ogilvy, Leo Burnett, Rosser Reeves* (New York: McGraw-Hill, 2003), 92.

[8] Felton, *Advertising,* 99.

[9] "Top 10 Slogans of the Century," *Advertising Age,* March 29, 1999, http://www.adage.com/century/slogans/html (accessed June 15, 2005).

Body Copy

We've discussed so many issues involved with copywriting—maybe it's time we actually talked about writing copy. As you've seen in many of the examples in previous chapters, not all ads have body copy or any copy. In fact, many people believe that readers won't read copy in ads and the best we can do is get them to remember a brand name. That may be true, but a good creative person needs to know how to write body copy.

Who Needs Body Copy?

We asked this question in Chapter 1. Here are a few more answers:

You never know when you'll need it

Versatility is one of the keys to survival in the creative field, especially in a tight job market. You might write a cool tagline now and then, but what happens when the client wants a campaign with a series of 200-word spread ads? You should know how to write all varieties of copy well. If you can't write that well, you should at least be able to recognize and respond to good writing by others.

Ads aren't the only place you'll need copy

Remember Gossage's line about people reading what interests them and sometimes it's advertising. As we'll discuss a little later, there are many reasons to include copy in advertising. But there are many other varieties of marketing communication where good writing skills are just as important:

- *Web content:* An ad with one line of copy may drive a reader to a Web site that's chock-full of copy. Writing copy for the Web has its special rules, but a good portion of it is traditional advertising writing. The objectives are the same as with print ads: Grab readers, hold their attention, persuade them to consider your product, and tell them how to get it.

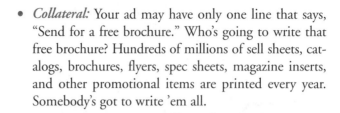

- *Collateral:* Your ad may have only one line that says, "Send for a free brochure." Who's going to write that free brochure? Hundreds of millions of sell sheets, catalogs, brochures, flyers, spec sheets, magazine inserts, and other promotional items are printed every year. Somebody's got to write 'em all.

- *Direct mail:* What makes you open a piece of junk mail? Somebody wrote something that caught your eye. Once you open it, you want to know more. Maybe it's a letter, or a brochure, or some other piece of information. Somebody wrote that too.

- *Reports, plans books, proposals:* Who says creative writing has to be limited to promotional material? Clients appreciate a well-written, crisply edited proposal or plans book. In fact, any manager would rather read something that quickly gets to the point and doesn't waste his or her valuable time. You can take entire courses on business writing, and, judging by some documents we've read, not enough people have taken these courses. Using some of the writing skills we'll discuss here will help make all your business writing better, not just your ad copy.

What you need to know . . . and use

No matter what the length or content of the body copy, you should keep a few basic concepts in mind. These apply to advertising, collateral, business documents, and basically any commercial form of writing:

1. Don't write to impress—write to persuade.

2. What you say is more important than how you say it.

3. Remember the rules of English, but don't feel forced to use them.

4. Above all, write to the individual, not the masses.

Why do we need copy in ads?

Some ads just work better with copy. Here are a few reasons:

- *Considered purchase:* Whether it's an industrial flow control valve or a power drill for the home owner, people want to know more about the product than its brand name. Go back to the foundations of the project and find out how the product features align with the wants and needs of the intended buyer. Prioritize them and string them together with style. That's body copy.

8.1. Collateral: Beautifully designed, beautifully written. Who says nobody reads anymore?

- *Differentiate products:* Why should a reader believe a Lincoln LS is a better value than a BMW 5-Series? Because the headline says it is or because the copy details independent testing that shows the Lincoln is faster, corners better, and overall performs better than the more expensive import? Sometimes you have to lay out the facts to make your case.

- *Multiple features:* We hammer that One Thing into your brain. But sometimes there's more than one thing to talk about. You may lead with the main point but then bring in other key benefits to build a more persuasive case for the product. If you don't have the luxury of producing single-feature ads, you may have to find a way to weave several key points into the copy.

- *Difficult, complicated, or controversial subjects:* If you want to change someone's mind or have him or her do something difficult, a catchy slogan isn't enough. For example, a recent anti-drug ad tells parents who smoked pot in their youth not to feel like hypocrites when they talk to their kids about drugs. That's much more effective than "Just say no."

The case for long copy

Writing good long-copy ads (200 words or more) is a fast-dying art. Reason 1: It's assumed no one reads ads, so why bother? Reason 2: No one knows how to write long copy well enough to hold a reader's interest . . . so see Reason 1.

Be honest. Even in textbooks that showcase the greatest ads ever written, do you actually read the copy? You probably don't even read the captions if they're more than five lines long. Before television shortened our attention span to 30 seconds and the Internet cut that to 2 seconds, magazine and newspaper ads had enough copy for a beginning, middle, and end. We could feature many wonderful classic ads that read like well-crafted short stories, so damn persuasive that even we want to run out and buy the products. But showing these great ads from another age won't be of much value if your creative solution is a three-word headline plus logo.

WORDS OF WISDOM

"There is no such thing as long copy. There is only too-long copy. And that can be two words if they are not the right two words."

—JIM DURFEE[2]

When we look at ads from the 1920s through the 1950s, we're amazed at the craftsmanship. The best ads had a rhythm and flow that sucked readers in, held their attention, and, in the end, left them convinced that the right brand of baked beans or laundry soap could improve their lives. Can you imagine a 400-word ad today for any kind of commodity packaged good like detergent, cereal, coffee, cigarettes, or whisky?

People will read long copy if they have a reason. John Caples said, "Don't be afraid of long copy. If your ad is interesting, people will be hungry for all the copy you can give them. If the ad is dull, short copy won't save it."[3]

The key to writing copy that's read, long or short, is to involve the reader. If the ad holds no reason to read on, don't expect anyone to get past a headline or visual. Here are a few examples where long copy can help capture attention and convince a reader:

- A cruise ship line outlines the daily activities for a typical family of four on their weeklong Caribbean cruise. You could look at a glamour shot of a big boat. Or you could read about snorkeling, rock climbing, wine tasting, whitewater rafting, theme parties, shopping, making new friends, and on it goes.

- A new brand of luxury car offers more horsepower, better handling, more interior room, more standard features, and a better warranty than the established leaders. You could show a pretty picture of the car, but how would you know you get so much more for the money?

- A company that sells plastic plumbing systems wants customers to know their product is cheaper and easier to install than copper pipe. But plumbers also want to know if it's certified safe, meets local plumbing codes, and is compatible with other systems. A single visual/caption won't cut it.

- A child welfare agency wants you to understand the suffering of impoverished children in developing countries. So they write a day-in-the-life profile of an individual child, detailing the struggles she faces just to stay alive.

"IT WAS A REAL BLESSING," Frances Vaughn said after volunteers from the Christmas in April program gave her house a face lift.

"A whole slew of people gave up their weekend to help me. They fixed my back porch. Painted every room. Gave me a stove. They even put a brand-new roof on. I could've kissed every one of them."

This neighborly love is being rekindled all over America, thanks to Christmas in April.

Thousands of people from all walks of life are banding together to help the poor, the elderly, the handicapped.

By repairing homes, these caring volunteers are doing more than painting and hammering. They're restoring dignity, hope and pride.

"TODAY I fell in LOVE with TWENTY perfect STRANGERS."

FRANCES VAUGHN
Washington, D.C.

The launch of Christmas in April ✲ USA was made possible through the commitment of many people and corporations, including a grant from the Toyota USA Foundation. We're proud to say we've been a supporter from the very start.

As a result, the national body has been able to help more communities start local programs. (The number has grown from 15 to 45 in just two years.)

Frances Vaughn is certainly thrilled the folks around Washington rallied behind Christmas in April.

In fact, she would have jumped through the roof with joy if it hadn't just been repaired.

TOYOTA
INVESTING IN THE INDIVIDUAL

8.2. One of a long series of corporate ads for Toyota. This one discusses a grant from Toyota to an organization that helps senior citizens renovate their homes. It's a story that can't be told in 25 words or less.

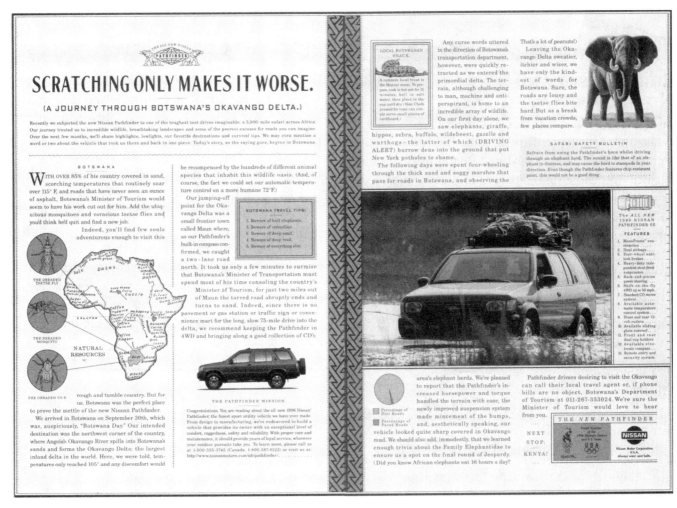

8.3. When Nissan introduced their Pathfinder SUV, they didn't just list features. Instead they put their vehicle on the road to some of the toughest places in the world and wrote a travelogue. This beautifully written series contains lots of interesting information about their exotic travels and, by the way, a little bit about the Pathfinder.

The story continues . . . on the Web

Long copy isn't dead. A lot of it just moved to the Internet. The purpose of many ads is to drive readers to a Web site. There they can read to their hearts' content without interrupting their magazine article. Or they can download and print the copy for future reference. Beyond print, the Internet can show video and animation, gather information, and do a lot of tricks you'd never get from a magazine ad. Plus it multiplies the impact of the message and, because the reader makes a conscious effort to contact the site, streamlines the awareness-comprehension-conviction-action process. Remember IMC? This is a big part of it.

EIGHT PAGES AND NO PRODUCT: WHO SAYS LONG COPY DOESN'T SELL?

When they developed Nike's "Empathy" campaign for women, Janet Champ (copy) and Charlotte Moore (art) decided to ignore the research and simply "talk to women as human beings." The campaign won a Kelly Award and the phones at Nike didn't stop ringing for months. Janet Champ told us:

> We used only one model. All the others were real people from a casting house in Texas. We were tired of being hemmed in to two or four pages. It bothered us that the men got big budgets. We said if we're going to be stuck with print let's do the longest ad we can. Charlotte had this idea—let's write a woman's life. So I wrote it too long and had to cut it in half. I took it to Nike and I got all choked up while reading it. Charlotte cried. Nike cried. Then they said, "Can you do it on a run of the press (magazine stock)?" We said, "No, absolutely not." Finally, they said OK. It was a hard sell because of the length (eight pages) and no product.
>
> Everyone went crazy once it ran. There were 500,000 letters and calls to the agency and Nike. This man whose wife suffered from depression for years called and said he showed the ad to his wife and she cried and said, "This is me." And then she started to run again.

Writing Structure

Types of copy

Knowing the various types of ad copy will never be as important as knowing how to write a good sentence. However, it can be useful to recognize several copy styles and know when to use them.

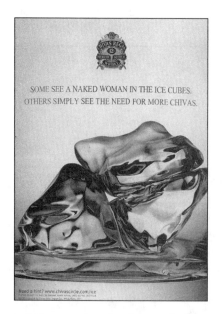

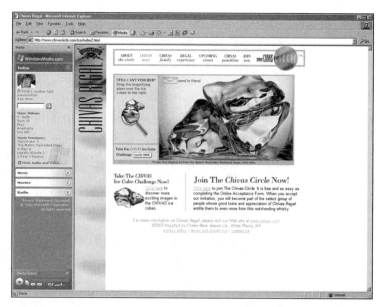

8.4. The promise of seeing a naked woman in the ice cubes doesn't require a lot of copy. But this Chivas Regal ad is a great example of using an ad to drive a reader to the Web to read more copy or, as in this promotion, involve the reader in an interactive game.

The Story

This is also called "traditional" copy and features three main components: a beginning, middle, and end. Usually the beginning establishes the theme, makes a promise, plays off the headline, and in general sets up the ad. The middle is typically the sales pitch, with reasons you should consider the product or service. The end is the summary and call to action. It wraps up the selling argument and encourages the reader to do something. A well-crafted story does not have to be a long-copy ad. But it should flow smoothly . . . as if you were telling a story that has a point.

Bullet Points

Many clients will say, "No one has time to read copy. Just list the key points." In many cases, this is just fine, especially if you can't think of One Thing to say and need to list a lot of features. Usually, the points are prioritized by the importance of the selling features, with the most important always going first. Too many times, the writer and client can't decide what's important, so they list everything and hope the reader will find something he or she likes.

You'll see a lot of bullet ads in retail newspapers, business-to-business magazines, and direct mail. This technique has sort of a "down and dirty" look, so it's usually not appropriate for a high-quality or brand image promotion. In addition, a long list of short bullet points takes up more real estate than a few well-written sentences in paragraph format. So if saving space is your only justification for using bullet points, measure carefully and reconsider.

One technique that can be very effective is a mix of traditional sentences and bullet points. The bullets highlight key points and, when done correctly, these draw the reader's eye to the most important selling messages.

One-Liner

Sometimes the headline is the only copy in the ad. Other times the headline and visual work together to convey the main message and a single copy line adds additional information. If you don't have to explain a lot about the product, need to direct the reader to a Web site for more detailed information, or just want to promote a brand image, one-liners (or no copy at all) work just fine.

Copy Format

While every agency or company may have a different format, most use something similar to the example shown in Figure 8.1 for manuscript copy. More and more, writers skip the manuscript phase and drop typeset copy directly into a comp layout.

8.5. This ad didn't have to say much because (a) it was reinforced by a TV spot with the same message, (b) it can communicate the main message without much copy, and (c) Mac users prefer pictures to words.

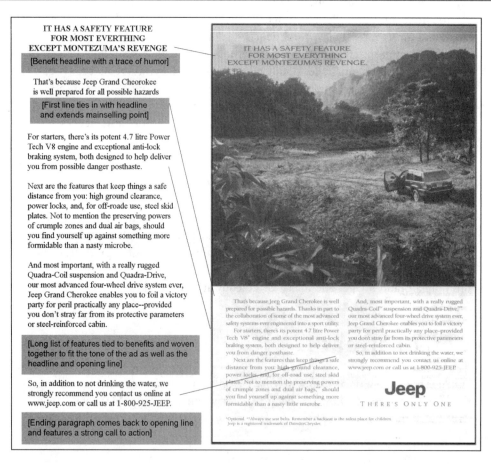

8.6. Jeep has a long history of creating clever, interesting, informative ads. Many use the classic beginning-middle-end approach. Here the first line of copy flows seamlessly from the headline. The main body copy weaves features, benefits, and the story line together. Finally, the closing paragraph ties it all together, comes back to the main theme, and asks the reader to take action.

8.7. This ad has more bullets than a Schwarzenegger movie. The theory must have been when you can't decide what's most important, say everything in bullet points.

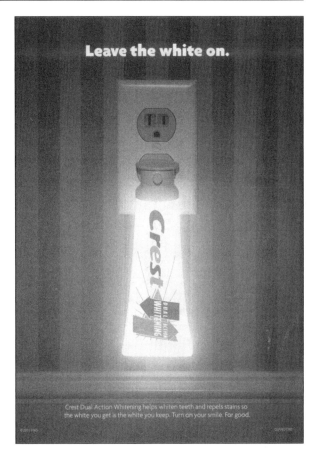

8.8. Just in case you didn't get the point, the one line of copy says, "Crest Dual Action Whitening helps whiten teeth and repel stains so the white you get is the white you keep."

Writing Style

Advertising is not English

In English classes you were told to write essays and reports with an assigned number of words, paragraphs, or pages. These were graded for spelling, composition, vocabulary, and comprehension. Your teachers were not looking for tight, get-right-to-the-point persuasion, but rather how you could expand a one-sentence idea into a four-page paper. That's fine for analyzing the existential philosophies of mid-19th-century German nihilism, but it ain't advertising.

In the real world, your writing will be evaluated on how well you communicate. Period. Using real words. In the way real people talk. Your writing must attract a jaded reader and hook him or her in the brain. You are appealing to a consumer's wants and needs. Not to teachers who get paid to grade papers by the pound. As Shakespeare said, brevity is the soul of wit. Good advertising is both witty and brief.

CLIENT PROJECT	Proctologists R Us Prostate Exam Ad ½-page newspaper
DATE REVISED	September 20, 2005 9/22/05 9/24/05 9/25/05 10/05/05 10/13/05
PREHEAD	
HEADLINE	Men, if you're over 45 . . . You don't need high tech for a digital exam
PHOTO	[CLOSE-UP OF RUBBER-GLOVED HAND WITH ONE FINGER POINTING UP]
SUBHEAD	Walk-in prostate exams now available.
COPY	The time to take care of your prostate is <u>before</u> you start thinking about it. Now, faster than you can say, "That wasn't so bad," we can check your prostate with a dependable digital exam. If we put our finger on anything suspicious, you'll know immediately. Before it becomes a real problem. Best of all—no waiting. Just walk in. And walk out with peace of mind. When it comes to digital exams, we give you the "white glove treatment." Call for an appointment today: **1-800-PROSTATE**
LOGO	PROCTOLOGISTS-R-US
TAGLINE	Here's looking up you, kid. www.upyerhiney.org

Figure 8.1. Example of Copy Format

Now this doesn't mean you can completely ignore grammar and spelling. You may be able to dress like a bum, but you can't write sloppy. Even though you may shatter a few rules of English grammar, the copy should be tight, easy to read, and clearly understood. Your copy style should be tailored to the target audience and the product. Remember tone? That should guide your style of writing. So an ad for a brand of chewing gum can be hip and informal, while a brochure for a million-dollar yacht should be more formal and elegant.

Persuade, don't impress

When it comes to ad copy, you don't have to impress readers with how many words you know. Or even with how much you know about the product. Instead, you have to persuade them your product meets their wants and needs. And you don't have a lot of time or space to do it.

A common error many novice writers make is to show the client how much they know about the product, especially for new products or new clients. As Julian Koenig said, "Your job is to reveal how good your product is, not how good you are."[7] Some ads don't say, "Buy me," they say, "Look how I can repackage what the clients told me so I can show them I was listening." That's OK for the first draft. But on the next round, take out the meat axe and start hacking away.

When you're given a creative brief or you write a copy platform, don't forget to keep looking for the "So whats?" Find out what's really important to the consumer, then see if the client's priorities mesh.

The "Seven Deadly Sins" of copywriting

A lot of teachers have told you how to write. Now we're telling you how to write better—by pointing out some common mistakes and how to correct them. We call these the Seven Deadly Sins. When you see them in your writing, make a brief confession and do penance by rewriting. Even experienced writers commit these sins. As with other transgressions, you can't feel guilty until you know it's a sin.

The Seven Deadly Sins are:

1. Advertising-ese
2. Bad taste
3. Deadwood
4. Generic benefits
5. Laundry lists
6. Poor grammar
7. Wimpy words

Let's explore each of these sins in detail and discuss ways to avoid them.

Advertising-ese

The native tongue on Planet Schlock. Don't confuse using proven selling words with the mindless clichés in some advertising. We've grown up with advertising jargon, so it's natural to write ads that way:

The best money can buy. You've seen the rest, now try the best. Isn't that amazing? Don't delay, call today. One call does it all. Nobody else offers this kind of

WORDS OF WISDOM

"I don't know the rules of grammar . . . if you're trying to persuade people to buy something . . . it seems you should use their language, the language they use every day, the language in which they think."

—**DAVID OGILVY**[6]

quality at such a low price. Hurry, these deals won't last forever. Unique. New and improved. Exclusive. State-of-the-art. Incredible. More for your money. You deserve the best. Get it now!

But wait, there's more . . . the list goes on and on.

Read your copy out loud. If it sounds like it should be on QVC, rewrite it.

In some cases, advertising-ese includes unsubstantiated claims or boasts of being the best without providing details to back them up. If you can't prove it, don't say it, because you'll lose all your credibility.

Advertising-ese also includes trite punctuation, especially the dreaded exclamation point. If you have to add ! to a headline or even a line of copy, you're shouting that you can't think of anything clever or memorable. For example, you used to see phrases like:

It's just wonderful! The all new 1965 Oldsmobile Vista Cruiser with the new improved smooth-as-silk Strato-Glide transmission!

Bad Taste

This includes sexist, racist, insensitive, offensive, and vulgar language. In this age of political correctness, people can find hidden meanings in the most innocent messages. When you look at some of the ads from the 1930s and 1940s, it's amazing how African Americans were portrayed. In the 1950s and 1960s, women were shown as mindless neat freaks, more concerned with whiter shirts than with careers. Today, writers who would never use stereotyped racial or sexist language think nothing of using sexual puns, vulgar language, and scatological humor. If you are appealing to a general audience, be careful what you say and how you say it. If you are going for an edgy concept that appeals to a very select group who won't be offended by your bad taste, try it, but be willing to accept the consequences.

Deadwood

This is one the most common sins committed by beginning writers. They say the same thing several different ways, time after time, in a very redundant fashion that wastes time and space, over and over again, ad infinitum. (Get the point?) Say what you mean. Then tighten it up. Look for ways to eliminate unnecessary words and phrases. Don't overstate the obvious. Don't include a description when a visual will work better. Your English composition teachers have stressed this since you were in grade school, but somehow, novice writers forget it.

- *Original copy:* Wamco engineers have developed several new ways to help original equipment manufacturers make products that are accepted better by their customers, which, in turn, makes them more profitable.

- *Better:* Wamco makes your products more profitable.

Generic Benefits

Also known as "weasel words," these benefits are so vague they could apply to almost anybody and anything. You may have attached a benefit to a feature, but have you gone far enough? Keep asking "So what?" and you'll eliminate generic benefits. Always lead with the strongest benefit. Readers may not get to it if you bury it at the end of the ad.

- *Original copy:* Our Super Life car batteries are superior to all other batteries. That's why they're the best value for your dollar.

- *Better:* Super Life batteries are guaranteed to deliver 850 amps of cold cranking power for up to eight years. You probably won't keep your car that long.

- *Even better:* Super Life: the last battery your car will ever need.

Laundry Lists

This sin usually involves grouping features without benefits and giving them all equal value. It's hard to find the One Thing. This is a crutch used by some writers who don't know much about the product so they throw every feature into the copy and string them together with no relation to each other or connection to a benefit. The temptation is to cram as many copy points into an ad as you can to let the client think you know the product. For example:

This sleek power boat features a powerful fuel-injected engine, two-tone gel coat finish, a tandem trailer, removable carpeting, lots of cup holders, an in-dash CD player, and a 5-year warranty. Who could ask for more in a family runabout?

While we provide many lists and "how-to" bullet points in this book, don't confuse our use of these features with writing body copy in your work.

Poor Grammar

You should make your copy easy to read, and sometimes that means using the proper mechanics of English, such as when to end a sentence and when to use commas, dashes, colons, and other punctuation. You should understand sentence structure, such as the need for a subject and a verb, and how to use prepositions, conjunctions, and phrases. Given that, don't feel compelled to follow every rule of English composition. However, you don't want readers to think you are an illiterate slob.

Speaking of punctuation, look out for these common problems:

- As we mentioned earlier, don't overuse the exclamation point!

- Also, don't overuse ellipses . . . they break up the flow and usually indicate you haven't figured out a good transition between sentences.

- Use commas only when it's necessary to provide a pause or improve readability.

- Some writers (David Ogilvy included) don't like to use a period in a headline, even if it's a complete sentence. Others believe a period adds deliberate emphasis.

As long as your copy reads well, punctuation is usually a matter of personal choice.

Wimpy Words

This category covers a lot of territory. Certain words rob copy of its vitality. Writing in passive voice also weakens copy. Beginning a sentence with a prepositional phrase or subordinate clause also dilutes the power. Some examples:

There. Usually you should never start a sentence with *There.*

- *Bad:* There are a lot of reasons why people visit their friendly Dodge dealer. First of all there's the large selection they have.
- *Better:* People visit their Dodge dealer for a lot of reasons: first, they offer the largest selection . . .

That. The word *that* is overused . . . try reading your copy out loud, with and without *that,* and see what sounds better.

Be verbs. "To be or not to be" is great for Shakespeare but not advertising copy. Derivatives of *to be* include *is, are, was, were,* and *being.*

- *Bad:* If you *have been* considering purchasing a luxury sport utility, then you *are* in luck.
- *Better:* Interested in a luxury sport utility? Lucky you.

Passive voice. Your copy should take action rather than being acted upon (even that tip reads awkwardly). Examples:

- *Bad:* Why do you think Sony computers *were chosen* by design engineers *who have held* senior positions in this industry?
- *Better:* Why the industry's top design engineers picked Sony.

Lead with phrases and clauses. Get right to the point. Don't put a phrase or clause in its path. Also, don't string a lot of phases together in the same sentence. Short, simple declarative sentences work best. For example:

- *Bad:* After shopping *for your family, on the way* home, stop in *for a cool* refreshing DQ Mister Misty.
- *Better:* DQ Mister Misty: a refreshing treat after a long day of shopping.

Make a copy of Table 8.1 and keep it handy when you're writing copy. It's also handy when reviewing other people's work.

WORDS OF WISDOM

"Taste and style are at the heart of selling."

—**HAL RINEY**[7]

Power writing

We've discussed what not to do. Now we'll offer some recommendations that will help make any ad read easier and communicate more effectively.

Mix short and long sentences. Sometimes short sentences work best, but you don't have to make every sentence three words. Mix up short and long sentences. Use the short

TABLE 8.1   **The Seven Deadly Sins of Copywriting and How to Correct Them**

1. Advertising-ese	Write the way people talk; eliminate clichés and useless phrases; keep it conversational (read it out loud).
2. Bad taste	Watch for sexist, racist, and other offensive language and symbols. If it feels wrong, it probably is.
3. Deadwood	Weed out weak, redundant, unnecessary words and phrases. Keep the flow of thought moving.
4. Generic benefits	Provide benefits in terms consumers understand. Appeal to their lives. Lead with the strongest benefit. Is one benefit so strong that it is the central truth or One Thing about this product?
5. Laundry lists	Don't list features without reference to what they mean to the consumer. Weave benefits into the ad and prioritize them based on the consumer's point of view.
6. Poor grammar	Watch for errors in spelling, punctuation, and verb tense. Know the rules and when to break the rules. Use fragments if it improves readability.
7. Wimpy words	Use power words, active voice, short simple sentences. If it doesn't feel strong, it's not.

ones for the sales message or, if you'd like, use the long sentence for the setup and the short one for the "punch line."

Use simple words if you can. If you're writing a technical brochure for orthopedic surgeons you're not going to talk about the "shinbone." But in most consumer work, simple language usually communicates best. Remember you are writing to persuade, not to impress readers with your vocabulary. Again, we quote the venerable John Caples: "Simple words are powerful words. Even the best educated people don't resent simple words. But they're the words many people understand. Write to your barber or mechanic or elevator operator."[8] *(We told you he was old.)* Caples found a simple word change had an immediate impact on response rates.

Write the way people talk. Most people use contractions and speak in sentence fragments. Try to write copy as if you're talking to a friend. Read your copy out loud. Does it sound like a normal person talking or an announcer from a 1960s game show?

Match the copy style to the product tone. More sophisticated products require more formal approaches (you'll never see "Yo. Check out Rolls-Royce. We got yer luxury right here!"). Copy for technical products should indicate some level of technical competence. But for the vast majority of consumer products, an informal, conversational style works best.

Use active verbs and positive attitude. Don't tiptoe into a benefit. Get right to the point. Use active voice and show excitement for the product. You can't do this with every sentence, but try to make an effort to activate your writing.

Be specific. "Flat-faced, bug-eyed, pig-snorting Boston terrier" conveys a stronger image than "dog." Rather than using "soon," say "today." Instead of "It's been stated by many physicians . . ." write "Doctors say . . . ."

Use parallel construction. As with taglines and headlines, you can use parallel construction in ad body copy. But use it judiciously and only to emphasize a point. Otherwise, it can become annoying or something even worse—poetry.

Use alliteration, rhythm, and rhyme. These techniques can spice up body copy. But use them carefully. You can emphasize key points, but you don't want your text to look like a string of slogans or a Dr. Seuss book. (So, you do not like rhyming text today, try it and you may I say.)

Tighten it up. The old rule is if you want 100 words, write 200. ~~As opposed to most good things in life, shorter is better. Find a way to say things in fewer words. Don't waste your reader's time. This is very important so if we could say it~~ in two words, "write tight."

Write out loud. Read your print copy out loud. Does it sound as good as it reads? If you need inspiration, read some of the great speeches of all times—fireside chats by

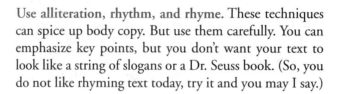
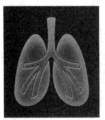

For a change, we'd like to talk about *your* air bags.

Take a deep breath. Relax. Get comfortable. You are about to read some good news.

Recently, Honda brought its advanced Low-Emission Vehicle (LEV) technology to everyone in America. All fifty states. Voluntarily.

It arrived in the form of the all-new 1998 Accord and the Civic. Both offer engines which meet California's strict Low-Emission Vehicle standard. But now you can buy one not just in California, but in Michigan. Texas. Ohio. Georgia. Wherever you live.

Both cars meet a 70-percent-lower emission standard for smog-contributing non-methane organic gases than is required by the most stringent federal standard. With no performance sacrifice or cost penalty.

Plus, in California and specific states throughout the Northeast, we're now offering our new Accord Ultra-Low Emission Vehicle (ULEV). It's the first auto certified by the California Air Resources Board as a ULEV, making it the cleanest gasoline-powered production car sold in the U.S. Ever.

That means, based on last year's sales figures, more than 60 percent of all new Accords and Civics, some 450,000 cars, will now be more environmentally friendly.

Historically, Honda has continually been a leader in fuel-efficiency and low-emission technology. Because we always think about more than the products we make. We think about the people who use them, and the world in which they live.

Which, in the end, helps us all breathe a little easier.

HONDA
Thinking.

For more about environmentally friendly Honda products, call 1-888-CC-HONDA ext. 109 or visit www.honda.com. © 1997 Honda North America, Inc.

8.9. This is what we mean by power writing. Notice the mix of long and short sentences, the use of specific information, the conversational style, and the smooth flow from beginning to end.

PUTTING IT ALL ON THE TABLE

Ed McCabe began his advertising career at the age of 15 in the mail room of McCann-Erickson and eventually wrote his way into the Copywriters Hall of Fame. McCabe describes his unique approach to writing body copy:

I work with pencils. I'll write with someone's lipstick or eyebrow pencil. In extremis, give me a twig and some dirt, a stone and a sidewalk, a fingernail and anything it can be scratched into. For years, I had a table in a restaurant in New York. I wrote some of my best ads and the body copy for them on tablecloths. Every morning, the cloth from the night before would arrive at the agency, oily with dinner drippings and blackened with notes. We'd copy the tablecloth, then send it back so they could launder it fresh and white, only to be assaulted again.[10]

Franklin Roosevelt, Winston Churchill's messages during World War II, Kennedy's inaugural, Martin Luther King's "I Have a Dream" speech, and Ronald Reagan's tribute to the *Challenger* astronauts. No matter how you feel about politics, these speeches were powerfully written. They featured simple eloquence, memorable catchphrases, and vivid imagery. Most of all, they resonated in the hearts of listeners long after the speeches were delivered.

Checklist for Better Copy

After you've written what you think is your final draft, use this checklist. You might find that you're not done writing.

- *Strong opening line (pull through):* Is the first line good enough to be a headline? It's got to pull the reader through. Readers take the path of least resistance—make it easy for them.

- *Appeal to consumer's POV:* Why do I want to buy this product or service? Appeal to the reader's self-interest—what's in it for him or her? Remember the "So whats?" Is the style appropriate for the audience? *Tell me about my yard, not your grass seed.*

- *Clear central idea (the One Thing):* After reading your ad, will the reader be left with the one main idea you want to convey? Does your copy provide mixed messages? Go back to your copy platform to check.

- *Strongest sales point first:* Lead with the strongest selling point. The reader may not get to it if you bury it.

- *Strong supporting information:* Is the information persuasive, presented in a logical order? Does it support the main idea?

- *Easy reading:* Is the message clear? Does the copy say it in as few words as possible and as many words as necessary? Even the most intelligent people appreciate simple language. People will read long copy if they are interested in the subject.

- *Power writing:* Can you use active voice rather than passive? Do you start any sentences with "There are . . . ?" Ruthlessly weed out unnecessary words. Get rid of the deadwood. "Avoid clichés like the plague." Strip away the ad jargon and "me too" phrases.

- *Call to action:* What do you want the readers to do? Where can they get more information? Where can they buy the product? For well-known widely distributed consumer products a call to action may not be necessary. But for retail it's mandatory. For technical products and other considered purchases, you need to establish a connection that may require several more contacts. The ad is merely a conduit to more meaningful communication.

You're not done yet

You've just written a modern masterpiece of ad copy. You've avoided all the Deadly Sins. It's passed the checklist with flying colors. So what's next? Honest evaluation.

WORDS OF WISDOM

"I don't think I am a good writer, incidentally, but I do think I am the best damn editor in the world. I can edit anybody well, including myself. So what I do is write my stuff and then edit and edit and edit until it's reasonably passable."

—DAVID OGILVY[11]

- *Give it a rest.* The best advice we can give any creative person is *"Write hot. Edit cold."* In other words, if you're on a roll, keep going. Don't worry about word count, style, or even content. Write what's on your mind. Then put it away. Watch TV. Go jogging. Do anything but think about your ad. After a decent interval, look at your copy. Most people think, "Jeez, that's awful. What was I thinking?" So start the process again, this time with more focus and insight.

- *Adjust your work habits.* Everyone has a time when they're most creative. Unfortunately, it's usually not during the typical 9-to-5 workday. That's why it's important to write hot and edit cold. When you get an idea, jot it down no matter where you are. If you feel like writing a thousand words at 2 A.M., that's great. Edit as long as you can stay awake and then e-mail it to work.

- *Get help.* Most good writers are excellent proofreaders—of other people's work. They are usually criminally sloppy when it comes to their own writing. For proper editing, you need diligent, objective, and independent proofreaders. Don't rely on a computer spell-checker. *Ewe may halve the write spelling butt the wrong meaning.*

- *Mark it up.* Whether you're editing your own work or another writer's, document the problems or change them. This requires printing a hard copy and scribbling comments just like your great grandparents did. We've included a selection of editing marks in the appendix. Use these when you're proofing your copy.

- *Read it out loud.* You'll hear about this again when we talk about radio, but it applies to print as well. Sometimes just hearing your own words

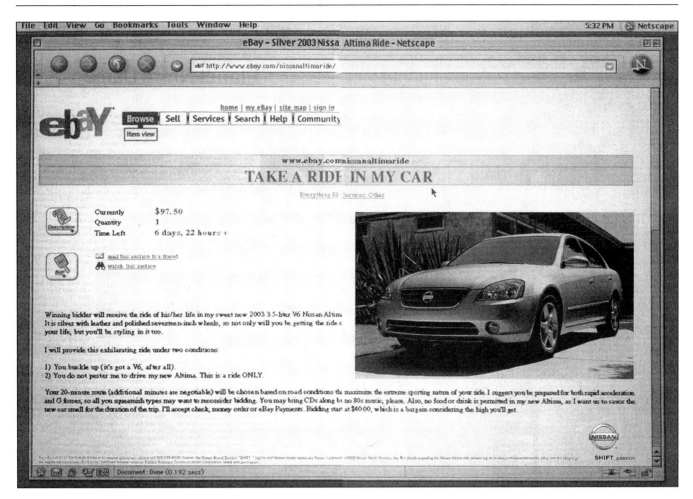

8.10. Here's another case where the copy is part of the graphic. This is a spread ad in a magazine. The features and benefits of the car are cleverly wrapped into the eBay format, with the kicker "This is a ride ONLY."

brings awkward construction right to the fore. When it's doesn't sound right, it won't read right.

- *Don't stop.* We can't think of a single project that we couldn't do better the second or third time (including this book). If you have the luxury of time, keep improving your copy. Replace weak words. Cut out the deadwood. Say it better with fewer words. Keep polishing that copy 'til it shines.

Who's Who?

Charles Brower—Charles Brower, influential chairman of BBDO, one of the leading ad agencies in the world, is noted for stating, "The good ideas are all hammered out in agony by individuals, not spewed out by groups."[12] Brower gained less notoriety in the early 1960s by firing Ronald Reagan from his role as spokesman for BBDO client General Electric, which helped propel Reagan into a new career—politics.

Janet Champ—Janet Champ started her career in advertising as the 15th employee, the receptionist, at Wieden + Kennedy. But Champ had a dream and the talent and passion to back it up. Over her 15 years at W+K, she worked on several accounts, including Nike, Coca-Cola, Microsoft, Neutrogena, and every women's brand that happened to show up. For seven years she, along with her partner Charlotte Moore, created the influential (and, at that time, ground-breaking) Nike "Women's Fitness Campaign," receiving numerous awards and recognition, including Cannes, One Show Best of Shows, National Addys, and two consecutive Kelly Awards for best national print campaign (making her the only writer in the history of the Kellys to do so). She was also recognized by the *National Women's Law Review,* the National Woman's Health Board, and the Office of the U.S. Surgeon General for the TV spot "If You Let Me Play." She was also named *AdWeek* Copywriter of the Year and has the painful distinction of having been sued by the surviving Beatles for the use of their song "Revolution" in the first TV spot she ever worked on. Since 1999 she has been a freelance copywriter trying to do good, instead of evil.

Jim Durfee—Jim Durfee, copywriter and cofounder of the Ally & Gargano agency, is one of the leaders of the Creative Revolution. A&G's philosophy was that advertising is a product, not a service. "A product," Durfee said, "is something that is molded, produced, thought out and set out before the person: 'We have made this for you, we think this will help.' A service is hat-in-hand and through the side door. It was a completely different attitude toward what an agency was and what an agency made."[13]

Ed McCabe—Ed McCabe has profoundly influenced the field of advertising. For more than four decades, his ads broke new ground for such clients as Volvo and Perdue chicken. Many of today's most creative advertising professionals follow his innovative teachings and examples. He cofounded Scali, McCabe, Sloves, Inc. and helped build the company into the 10th-largest ad agency network in the world. For 10 years after leaving Scali, McCabe, Sloves, he was CEO of McCabe & Co. At the age of 34, he was inducted into the Copywriters Hall of Fame, the youngest to be so honored.

Notes

[1] Quoted in Erik Clark, *The Want Makers: Inside the World of Advertising* (New York: Penguin, 1988), 56.

[2] Designers and Art Directors Association of the United Kingdom, *The Copy Book* (Hove, UK: RotoVision, 2001), 120.

[3] John Caples, *Wall Street Journal* ad, 1978.

[4] Quote from the Clio Awards Web site, http://www.clioawards.com/html/wsj/dusenberry .html (accessed December 20, 2004).

[5] Quote from James Simpson, ed., *Contemporary Quotations* (Binghamton, NY: Vail-Ballou, 1964), 83. Brower was president of BBDO when he made this statement in 1958.

[6] Quoted in Denis Higgins, *The Art of Writing Advertising: Conversations with Masters of the Craft* (Lincolnwood, IL: NTC Business Books, 1990), 93.

[7] Quote from the Clio Awards Web site, http://www.clioawards.com/html/wsj/riney.html (accessed December 20, 2004).

[8] Caples, *Wall Street Journal* ad.

[9] Quoted in Higgins, *The Art of Writing Advertising,* 118.

[10] Quoted in Designers and Art Directors Association of the United Kingdom, *The Copy Book,* 120.

[11] Quoted in Higgins, *The Art of Writing Advertising,* 83.

[12] Quote from the Brainy Quote Web site, http://www.brainyquote.com/quotes/authors/c/charles_brower.html (accessed June 27, 2005).

[13] Quoted in Randall Rothenberg, "The Advertising Century," *Advertising Age,* March 29, 1999, http://www.adage.com/century/Rothenberg.html (accessed June 27, 2005).

Print

We're using magazines and newspapers to start our section on writing for each of the major media for various reasons. Let's begin with magazines.

Magazines

A magazine ad is an ideal palette for applying all the creative strategies and tactics we've discussed in previous chapters. Magazines also present a lot of creative opportunities based on the variety of sizes, shapes, and multiple page combinations. Finally, a magazine ad is a perfect size and shape for your portfolio—small enough to fit anywhere, large enough for long copy and to make a design statement.

Why magazines?

From a creative standpoint, magazines offer many advantages. Specifically:

- *Magazines are selective.* Some magazines are devoted to very narrow interests, such as water gardens or old Porsches. Many general-interest publications print special editions based on region, occupation, or income.

- *In most cases, the printing quality is much better than in any other medium.* Four-color ads really pop. And when you run inserts, the sky's the limit for the number of inks and varnishes.

- *Magazines usually last longer than other media.* Weekly, monthly, and quarterly publications get passed around and reread. Your ads are seen longer and more often by more people.

- *Magazines can add prestige.* Publications such as *Architectural Digest* reach an upscale market. So if you're selling expensive cars, jewelry, or real estate, upscale magazines are the perfect choice.

- *Many magazines offer value-added services to advertisers.* For example, many business publications have "bingo cards" in the back where a reader can circle a number to get literature. Others offer advertisers their lists for direct mail or market research databases.

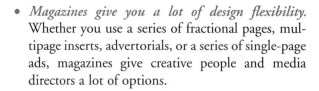

- *Magazines give you a lot of design flexibility.* Whether you use a series of fractional pages, multipage inserts, advertorials, or a series of single-page ads, magazines give creative people and media directors a lot of options.

- *Magazines are integrated with the Internet.* Most major magazines also have Web sites, which opens all kinds of promotional and cross-promotional opportunities for print and online advertisers.

Why not?

Here are a few reasons magazines may not be the ideal place for your ads:

- Even though magazines have a higher pass-along rate and hang around a little longer than other media, they still get dumped in the garbage, and all those ads are gone for good.

- Magazines are a relatively expensive way to get information. Many people just click on the online versions of their favorite publications to get feature articles or news reports.

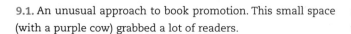

9.1. An unusual approach to book promotion. This small space (with a purple cow) grabbed a lot of readers.

9.2. Although advertising has always appeared in magazines, it wasn't until after World War I that creative concepts began to pair dramatic graphics with intriguing headlines for specific target audiences. This ad was written by Helen Lansdowne Resor, considered one of the greatest copywriters of her generation.

- Even weekly magazines can't stay current in this all-news-all-the-time world. Closing times may be two months for some publications, so your ad may be hopelessly out-of-date by the time it runs.

- Magazines can be very expensive for advertisers. Sure, you get the CPM (cost per thousand) you pay for, but at $150,000 a pop in some magazines, you'd better have a killer ad.

- The more popular the publication, the more competition you have from other ads. It's easy to get lost in the clutter of the top-selling consumer magazines.

Types of Magazines

Some texts on advertising list dozens of types of publications. Let's keep it simple by limiting the discussion to a few broad categories, starting with the most familiar.

Consumer

Thousands of titles clog newsstands and mailboxes, ranging from *AARP* (the largest-circulation magazine) to *Zink* (a rather obscure city lifestyle magazine). At last count, a recent *Standard Rate and Data Consumer Magazine Advertising Source* (SRDS) listed more than 3,000 publications. Rather than listing all the hundreds of categories and special editions, let's just say there's a magazine for everything and everybody. The more specialized the readership, the more focused the advertising should be.

Business

Outside of *Advertising Age* and *Business Week,* you probably can't name too many business publications. However, if you checked *SRDS* (Volumes 1 and 2) you'd find more than 8,500 titles. Look around. Just about everything you can see, hear, smell, or touch is covered by a trade magazine that addresses how it's made or sold. Business publications can be further divided into many categories. As with any publication, a thorough understanding of the readership is the key to creating an effective ad.

Professional journals

Magazines for professionals such as doctors, lawyers, and accountants are even more specialized. They usually feature scholarly articles, and many are peer reviewed to provide added legitimacy. Many allow advertising, which is focused on readers but does not have to be as deadly serious as the editorial content.

Agricultural

Like the family farm, agricultural publications are fading from the landscape. Most successful farmers run large, factorylike operations. The major difference between agricultural and other businesses is that farmers are buying industrial products with their own money (or rather the bank's money).

In-house/specialty

Many companies build goodwill with their customers by creating specialty magazines. Most car and many boat companies use these publications to reinforce a positive ownership experience (which is a fancy way to say they want to keep

9.3. Fractional pages let you stretch the budget. When you can't control the whole page it's critical to make sure your ad doesn't have to fight with other ads or strong editorial images.

their hooks in customers so they keep coming back). A lot of these books allow advertising from other companies. These publications also offer advertisers a lot of opportunities for cross-promotion and special offers. In addition, because the audience is so specialized, you can afford to run very targeted and thus more powerful ads.

9.4. If your budget dictates small-space ads, you can still be creative. This little ad has a lot of impact in more ways than one.

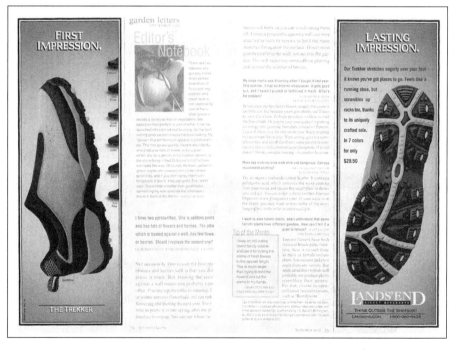

9.5. Facing vertical half pages dominate the whole spread without paying for it. Notice the parallel construction in the headlines and the well-connected editorial content.

Magazine Ad Formats

The basic unit for magazines is the page. Rates and dimensions are based on whole pages, multiple pages, and fractional pages. Some of the variations include the following:

- *Spreads:* Usually two facing pages.

- *Half-page spreads:* Usually a horizontal format on both sides of two facing pages with editorial above or below the ad.

- *Half-page vertical or horizontal:* Usually the outside half of the page if vertical, usually the bottom half if horizontal.

- *Quarter-page or third-page fractional:* Depending on the publication, this could be in a corner or outer edge of the page.

- *Island:* This ad "floats" on the page surrounded by editorial.

- *Advertorial:* This is all advertising; however, a portion of the ad looks like the editorial content of the particular magazine but features your message.

- *Inserts:* Many magazines allow inserts, which can be single page (front and back) or multiple pages. The number of pages allowed depends on the magazine and of course the production budget.

9.6. The bottom half of this spread looks like a traditional ad. The top half looks like editorial except the message is all about the advertiser. That's why it's called an *advertorial*. It's a useful technique when you can't get good cooperation from an editor to provide a story.

Creative and Media Teamwork

Magazines offer so many combinations that coordinating a media schedule with creative can be a challenge. Ideally, the creative should influence the specific media buy. For example, a series of fractional ads followed by a spread in a single issue may have more impact for a particular concept than a series of three single-page ads over three different issues. However, sometimes a media director may get the best deal on a format that doesn't fit the creative proposal. Then everybody has to decide: Is the idea worth the extra cost, or do you change the idea? Production costs also affect the creative-media partnership. For example, an eight-page insert may be very expensive to produce. But it could be designed to break out into a series of single-page or spread ads for future use to help stretch the media budget.

WORDS OF WISDOM

"We don't have readers anymore. We have thumbers, browsers, window shoppers through printed media. The image stops the thumber. The words seduce him to stay."

—MARTY COOKE[2]

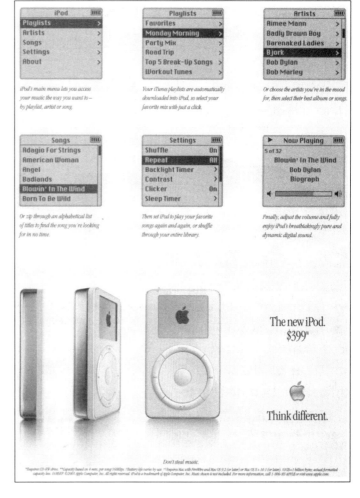

9.7. Apple launched their wildly successful iPod with the typical "Mac look" in a four-page insert. The images show the various screens available.

1,000 songs in your Mac.

Apple's award-winning iTunes™ software makes it easy to put your entire music collection right on your Mac. You can rip MP3s, create playlists and burn custom CDs all from one refreshingly simple interface. And now iTunes 2 offers even more features – like MP3 CD burning, crossfading and an equalizer. iTunes makes it simple and fun to build your very own digital music library on your Mac. Now, imagine having all of that incredible music with you wherever you go – even when you're away from your Mac.

1,000 songs in your pocket.

Presenting iPod.™ The first MP3 player to pack a mind-blowing 1,000 songs** and an 8-hour battery† into a stunning 6.5-ounce package you can literally take everywhere. But iPod™ isn't just a revolution in portability, it's also a revolution in simplicity. Just plug it into your Mac and all of your iTunes songs and playlists are automatically downloaded into iPod at blazing FireWire® speed. With iPod, it's that easy to take your entire music collection with you wherever you go, in the pocket of your choice.

9.7. (Continued, inside spread) . . . Today Apple sells more iPods than Macs.

Magazines and Campaigns

WORDS OF WISDOM

"You can entertain people in print. You can make print emotional. And you can sell your product. Print copy can cover all the small differences that add up to a big reason for buying a specific brand."

—**HAL RINEY**[3]

Magazines and campaigns seem made for each other. You can have a campaign within a single issue with multiple insertions. The periodic nature of magazines also fits many campaign strategies. Since readership of various magazines transcends demographics, it's natural to run ads in several magazines to maximize impact.

Magazines also fit well as part of an integrated marketing campaign. Here are just a few examples:

- Include a music or interactive CD-ROM as an insert in a magazine.
- Use cross-promotion with a compatible brand to cosponsor a contest, sweepstakes, or special offer.
- Run a series of short-copy ads that direct readers to a Web site for more detailed information.
- Use tear-out mini-inserts that include coupons.
- If it will fit within a magazine, include product samples in your insert.

9.8. Folded insert inside magazine.

9.9. Unfolded insert. Magazine size indicated in black.

9.10. A die-cut insert. The dark area represents the actual magazine page. When pulled out, the insert reveals a larger-than-life bottle. The other side describes a sweepstakes with cross-promotion partner *Golf Digest.*

WAR STORY:

FINDING THE LAST PAIR OF EARTH SHOES ON EARTH: TURNING PERCEPTION INTO REALITY FOR ROLLING STONE

When the creative team at Fallon McElligott Rice developed the long-running "Perception/Reality" campaign, the easy part was selling it to the client. The hard part was finding the right props. After literally designing the concept on a napkin, the agency team developed a number of "counterculture" (perception) symbols to contrast with yuppie (reality) images. Thus began a series that came to include such pairings as rolling papers/Post-it Notes, real mouse/computer mouse, psychedelically painted Volkswagen bus/new Mustang sports car, and Earth Shoes/Nike running shoes. In the case of the shoe execution, a practical problem presented itself: Where do you find mint-condition Earth Shoes when the brand had long been defunct? The agency was having no luck. Then, driving home from the office one day, art director Nancy Rice was passing the University of Minnesota campus and happened to spot someone at a bus stop wearing a fresh-looking pair of the shoes. She pulled over and collared the guy before he could board his bus. After explaining her mission, she learned that the fellow had a closet full of the shoes. "He must have been there for the closeout sale," says Rice. Anyway, problem solved.[4]

Where to Find the Best Magazine Ads

The Magazine Publishers of America present the Kelly Awards for the best magazine advertising each year. Winning a Kelly is a major accomplishment, and all the top creative shops compete.

"In the good shops, you learn how to write first. And that means print. You don't have thirty seconds; you don't have music; you don't have special effects; it's you and the reader and you have to capture his or her attention, right there and then."

—HELAYNE SPIVAK[5]

How to win a Kelly

When asked what it takes to win a Kelly Award, Mal MacDougall, chief creative officer of Christy MacDougall Mitchell, gave the following advice:

> Keep it simple. Don't try to be crazy. Don't try to go to your computer and think you can do something off the wall. Do something within a very narrow strategy. The narrower the better. The strategy is a very short sentence; the soul of the brand you're trying to talk about. Simplicity is what's going to work. You cannot win a Kelly award with a complicated message. Get to know who is really reading that magazine. Decide whom you really want to talk to. Narrow it down to a tiny few people. Then you know exactly who is reading this golf magazine, fishing magazine, fashion magazine or gardening magazine. Make your message simple, clear and aim it right at them.[6]

Here are a few of the winners of recent Kelly Awards:

Calling it transportation is like calling sex reproduction.

9.11. Porsche Cars North America/ Carmichael Lynch, Minneapolis. (The headline reads: "**Calling it transportation is like calling sex reproduction.**")

9.12. Altoids Curiously Strong Sours/Leo Burnett Company, Chicago.

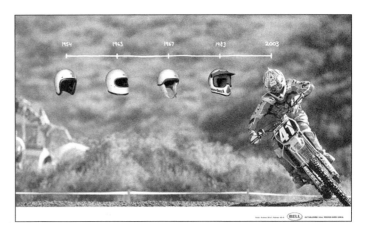

9.13. Bell Sports Inc./Crispin Porter + Bogusky, Miami.

9.14. Apple Computer/TBWA\Chiat\Day, Los Angeles (Grand Prize winner, 2004).

The other major awards competitions also offer magazine categories, often several categories. Check out their Web sites and awards books for the latest winners.

Newspapers

What's black and white and read all over? Not necessarily newspapers. Today they use almost as much color as magazines. Read all over? Not anymore. Readership has dropped off drastically, especially in people under 35. Still, in terms of advertising dollars spent, newspapers are second only to television.

Why newspapers?

From a creative standpoint, newspapers offer many advantages. Specifically, they are:

- *Local:* They fill in small niches so you can pinpoint advertising in a city or suburban area.

- *Timely:* Ads can be changed within hours of appearance; they can promote short-term events.

- *Widespread in their coverage* (although readership is declining).

- *Controlled by the readers:* They can scan, skip, or plod through paper (allows for long-copy ads).

- *Well suited for co-op opportunities:* National advertisers develop ads and help pay for them.

- *Specialized:* They include supplements and special-interest sections (sports, features, and so on).

- *Believable:* They offer news and sports first; entertainment is secondary.

- *Convenient:* Papers can be taken anywhere—trains, restaurants, bathrooms.

- *Large size:* A newspaper page offers a huge canvas for your ad. A full-page magazine ad is only a fraction of the size of a full-page newspaper ad.

Why not?

Here are a few reasons newspapers may not be the ideal place for your ads:

- *Short life span:* The flip side of timeliness. Yesterday's newspaper is, well, yesterday's news.

- *Hasty reading:* Other than Sunday morning, most people don't take the time to read the paper. Many people spend more time with the crossword puzzle than with the news.

- *Poor reproduction:* Printing quality has improved greatly, but a color ad in newsprint can't match the quality in a glossy magazine. Inserts let you control quality, but they can be expensive.

Newspaper readership trends

Current trends indicate newspapers are skipping a generation. Young adults are turning away from the news media their parents and grandparents relied on for information about their neighborhood, city, region, and world. The trend started 30 years ago but has accelerated since the late 1990s. Newspapers have beefed up their entertainment, gossip, and nightlife reporting. About 33% of U.S. families led by someone age 25 to 34 bought a daily newspaper in 2001 compared with 63% in 1985, according to the Bureau of Labor Statistics. This absence of youth has been blamed for shrinking circulation at many dailies of as much as 1% to 2% per year. The average age of a newspaper reader is 53.[7]

Newspaper Advertising Defined

Categories

Newspapers can be categorized in a number of ways:

1. *Frequency of publication:* daily, weekly
2. *Size of market:* national, regional, local
3. *Circulation:* paid (general newspaper) or controlled (shopper)
4. *Audience:* general interest, special interest/ethnic group, trade
5. *Size:* broadsheet (8 columns × 300 lines) or tabloid (5 columns × 200 lines)

Types of newspaper advertising

-   *Display ads:* For our purposes, these are the only ones worth discussing.
-   *Classified:* Cars, real estate, employment, personals.
-   *Public notices:* All text and all business.

9.15. Newspapers are made for black-and-white ads, but they don't have to be boring. Ballet lovers are going to go anyway, so why not attract some new blood?

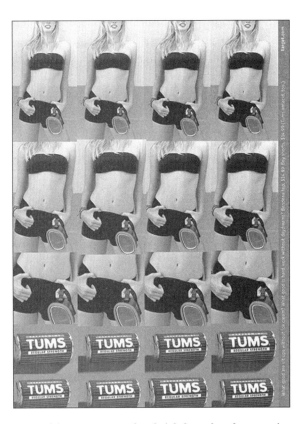

9.16. This was part of a brightly colored campaign for Target stores (it's really purple), which shows that newspaper ads can be as visually interesting as magazine ads.

"There's no better place for a young writer than in retail advertising. You learn the limits of aesthetics. You discover the world has no time for self-indulgence. You have to write ad after ad, and meet deadlines that force you to be fast. And every ad is judged on the basis of sales—period."

—Tom McElligott[8]

Newspaper ad formats

The basic unit used to be the agate line or column inch, line = 1/14th inch × 1 column wide. Now the Standard Advertising Unit (SAU) is used for national as well as local. Rates are calculated by the column inch, which is 1 column wide × 1 inch deep, no matter how many lines per inch. *Chicago Tribune* = 8 columns wide × 310 lines deep = 2,480 lines per page. Tabloids = 5 columns × 200 lines = 1,000 lines per page.

Retail Advertising

About four out of every five dollars spent in newspapers goes to retail advertising. Retail is also called "local" advertising; however, with national chains running traditional-looking retail ads in national newspapers like *USA Today*, it doesn't seem proper to call them local.

Retail is different from other advertising in the following ways:

- *Urgent:* Consumers act on it quickly ("Buy me today or you miss your chance"). It works quickly or not at all.

- *Price oriented:* Most national magazines do not feature price; most retail newspaper ads do.

- *The cheaper the merchandise, the more elements in the ad:* Tiffany's does not have 24 different items with prices in their ads like Wal-Mart.

- *The store personality is very important:* What is the personality—bargain prices (Wal-Mart), service (Nordstrom), reliable (Sears), long established (Jewel Osco), classy (Lord & Taylor)? Remember, the merchandise can be the same at every store, so making the store image different is the key.

In *Creating the Advertising Message,* Jim Albright states:

One of the biggest problems for a copywriter engaged in retail advertising is the fact that the ad runs today and tomorrow you're judged on your copy by how many actual sales are made. This is tough stuff, as opposed to a Pepsi campaign that may have to run a year before it's known whether your idea was any good.[9]

The biggest challenge in designing retail advertising is organizing the various elements. You may have two, four, or a dozen different products featured in an ad. How do you arrange them in an attractive layout that stresses the brand, price, and store personality? When it comes to writing the copy, consider the following guidelines:

1. *Tailor the copy to the customer:* Your tone should be in keeping with the price of the products, the clientele of the store, and the types of products.

2. *Be brief:* Just the facts.

3. *Use direct benefits if you can:* Mention features if you must.

Retail buzzwords

Retail has its own special jargon. You've grown up with it, but you may not know that many of these terms have special legal meanings and can be used only in certain ways:

- *Special purchase:* Not normally offered for sale.
- *Comparable value:* Use for special purchase (a special purchase cannot have a regular price).
- *Originally priced:* Retailer will discount price and not return to the original higher price.
- *Regularly priced:* Retailer has reduced the price temporarily but will reinstate the original price.

9.17. If you don't list specific products, concentrate on the store's image.

9.18. Multiple products, nicely arranged with a distinctive Bloomingdale's look. Check out the grid pattern.

Be careful when stating percentage discounts. Watch out for misleading statements such as these:

- **"Up to 50% or more"**: It could be misleading.
- **"Half price sale"**: Half of what?
- **"Save 50% off manufacturer's list price"**: Misleading. Can you really use the manufacturer's list price?

When you write a multi-item ad:

- Write a strong selling headline that expresses the commonality of the products and/or use a subhead that groups the products.
- Write an opening copy block that sells the items as a whole and sets the tone for the entire ad.
- Write strong selling subheads for each item.
- Write short copy blocks for each item with the main selling points for each.
- Pay attention to the graphic relationship of items—if you emphasize everything, you emphasize nothing.

National Newspaper Ads

Most national newspaper ads are like magazine ads. However, if it's a daily paper you can change the message every day if necessary. For large retailers with multiple outlets you obviously can't list every store location, but you can convey a store's personality.

National newspapers are also ideal for corporate image, public service, and open-letter advertising. In fact, national newspapers are great vehicles for any message you want to convey quickly to a large audience.

9.19. This national ad appeared in *USA Today*. It looks like a local retail ad except there is no listing of store locations.

9.20. This ad, designed by a student, promoted USPS insect stamps.

9.21. The front part of a four-page color insert in *USA Today* for Target. Actual size is about 17 × 22 inches. You can't see it here, but 10 products and prices are mentioned in the fine print at the bottom. (Did you notice the reference to "wants" and "needs"?)

National inserts

When you want the best color reproduction or really want to make a spectacular splash, you can produce full-page (or larger) inserts. *USA Today* has included some huge inserts. One for a hotel chain in Florida folded out to 20 × 48 inches. Sometimes advertisers insert whole sections in newspapers. Many readers pull out these inserts and keep them like brochures.

Newspapers and Campaigns

Newspaper advertising can fit very well into an overall campaign strategy. You can maintain continuity with other creative elements plus you have the flexibility to make rapid adjustments. For example, you may want to use TV and magazines to establish an image for a product but use newspapers to promote its price or guide readers to local retail stores. Many tourism accounts show beautiful images of their destinations in color magazine ads and run price promotions in small black-and-white ads in the Sunday travel sections of local newspapers.

9.22. MINI continues to blur the lines between traditional media, PR, and promotion. With their "Batboy" tabloid series, they blended newspapers (if you can call WWN one), outdoor and guerrilla marketing, gaining far more awareness than print advertising alone could provide.

WAR STORY:

BATBOY'S JOYRIDE: HOW MINI TWISTED THE TABLOIDS

The creative team at Crispin Porter + Bogusky continues to twist traditional definitions of media. In their view, "Everything is media." So it's no surprise they found a new way to use newspapers. Copywriter Bill Wright explains:

> *Weekly World News* is a supermarket tabloid, with stories about aliens and Elvis and aliens who look like Elvis and such. Now, we knew that our consumer probably didn't read it. But, we knew that almost everyone buys groceries at the supermarket and when you go through the checkout line, there it is. So my partner and I had this idea to buy the front cover as outdoor, which is a totally different way to think of media. The people at *Weekly World News* were into the idea, and I wrote a cover story about a rogue chimpanzee that steals a MINI and goes on a three-state joyride. And the *Weekly World News* people said, well, this is good, but we have this Batboy franchise, a recurring half-human, half-bat character, and would it be okay if he steals the MINI instead of a chimpanzee. And we asked, can he still go on a three-state joyride? And they agreed to that.

> What's really cool is that WWN kept updating the story; how Batboy and his stolen MINI were seen here, and how he was almost captured but got away, and that went on for the rest of the summer. And we never had to pay for any of that extra publicity.

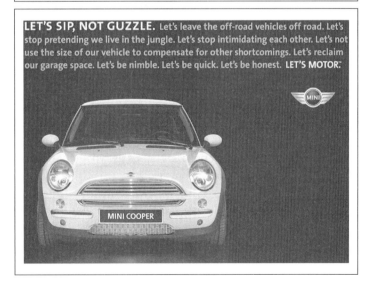

9.23–9.25. MINI does it again! This series of newspaper ads certainly has a family look, but it also features well-written copy and simple but memorable designs.

Making Your Newspaper Ads Work Better

The guidelines for writing good newspaper ads are basically the same as for other media. But note a few special rules for retail:

- Establish a store character: A store is also a brand.
- Use a simple layout: Sometimes fine detail is lost in newsprint.
- Use a dominant element if you can.
- Let white space work for you (or negative space if your ad is in color).
- State the price or range of prices (especially for retail).
- Specify branded merchandise (especially for retail).
- Urge your readers to buy now (especially for retail).

Where to Find the Best Newspaper Ads

The Newspaper Association of America presents the Athena Awards for the best newspaper ads of the year. Fortunately, the association displays the winners on its Web site (naa.org), including work by students. You'll also find great newspaper ads in the *Communication Arts Advertising Annual*. And don't forget to keep checking *USA Today* for spectacular inserts.

Who's Who?

Marty Cooke—Marty Cooke has created some of the most visually striking ads in the business. He is a strong advocate of letting the visual do most of the heavy lifting. He stated, "I'm not a frustrated art director. I am a misunderstood copywriter."[10] He also likes to "play with the keyboard" by turning words upside down, using abbreviations ("Reeboks let U.B.U."), and using icons as typography: "Anything to make the words more visual."[11]

Helen Lansdowne Resor—Helen Lansdowne Resor provided the creative spark in the early days of J. Walter Thompson. As the first female copywriter to write and plan national advertising, she opened the door for many women in advertising as she was constantly creating new ways to attract readers. She brought a woman's point of view to

9.26. This award-winning ad celebrates the birthday of the Minnesota Zoo. Note the simple idea and use of white space. Get the point?

advertising, addressing clients' conventions as she managed and supervised two-thirds of the business in the JWT New York and Boston offices. She was a revolutionary inventor of a new style in advertising. Among her many achievements is one of the greatest slogans of all time for Woodbury's soap—"The skin you love to touch."

Tom McElligott—Tom McElligott and creative partner Pat Fallon started out with a freelance business called Lunch Hour. After winning several awards, the pair launched their own shop in 1981. They quickly recruited art director Nancy Rice and account executive Fred Senn, and the legendary Fallon McElligott Rice was born. Thanks to award-winning creative and rapid acquisition of blue-chip accounts, such as US West, FMR was named Ad Agency of the Year just three years after its founding. A short time later, Rice left and McElligott jumped ship when Fallon sold a majority share to Scali McCable Sloves, an Ogilvy & Mather subsidiary.

Nancy Rice—Nancy Rice was a founding partner in the fabled Fallon McElligott Rice agency. Shortly after its founding, FMR began a meteoric rise in creative recognition and account growth, including Agency of the Year honors. Rice worked on such groundbreaking campaigns as *Rolling Stone* ("Perception/Reality") and Coleman. She later joined DDB Needham Chicago as senior vice president and group creative director. Working with numerous high-profile clients from Anheuser-Busch to General Mills, Rice's group has garnered an extensive list of awards, including gold and silver medals in the One Show, Clios, and Athenas. She was the first woman elected to the Advertising Hall of Fame.

Helayne Spivak—Helayne Spivak now runs a consulting company (HRS Consulting) and is still considered one of the most accomplished leaders in the ad business. She has run some of the world's top creative departments: At Young & Rubicam, she was chief creative officer; at J. Walter Thompson, she was worldwide creative director. She has won nearly every major honor the industry offers, including numerous Clio Awards and the Gold Award at the Cannes Advertising Festival.

WORDS OF WISDOM

"I approach print [advertising] as entertainment. After all, reading should be entertaining."

—HELAYNE SPIVAK[12]

Bill Wright—Bill Wright is vice president, creative director at Crispin Porter + Bogusky, one of the hottest creative shops in the 2000s. Since joining CP+B in 1995 as the 37th employee, Wright has contributed on just about every account that's ever walked through the agency. The list includes MINI, IKEA, Virgin Atlantic Airways, Schwinn, Giro Helmets, Burger King, Gateway, the Golf Channel, And 1 basketball shoes, and the "Truth" antismoking campaign. His work has been recognized by the One Show (including the most recent Best in Show), *Communication Arts, Archive Magazine,* the Clios, Cannes, Show South, the London International Advertising Awards, the Radio Mercury Awards, and the CBS program *World's Greatest Commercials.*

Notes

¹ Quote from the Clio Awards Web site, http://www.cliowards.com/html/wsj/chiat.html (accessed December 20, 2004).

² Quoted in Designers and Art Directors Association of the United Kingdom, *The Copy Book* (Hove, UK: RotoVision, 2001), 26.

³ Quote from the Clio Awards Web site, http://www.clioawards.com/html/wsj.riney.html (accessed December 20, 2004).

⁴ See Judy Warner, "Best Spots: Hill, Holliday John Hancock," *AdWeek*, November 9, 1998, http://www.adweek.com/aw/creative/top20_20years/top20_10.jsp (accessed June 28, 2005).

⁵ Quote from the Clio Awards Web site, http://www.clioawards.com/html/wsj.spivak.html (accessed January 10, 2005).

⁶ Quoted in "Advertising & PIB: Kelly Awards," Magazine Publishers of America Web site, http://www.magazine.org/advertising_and_pib/kelly_awards/winners_and_finalists (accessed June 28, 2005).

⁷ This information comes from the Center for Interactive Advertising Web site, http://www.ciadvertising.org/studies/student/99_fall/theory/tseng/practitioner (accessed June 28, 2005).

⁸ Quote from the Clio Awards Web site, http://www.clioawards.com/html/wsj/mcelligott/html (accessed December 20, 2004).

⁹ Jim Albright, *Creating the Advertising Message* (Mountain View, CA: Mayfield, 1992), 227.

¹⁰ Quoted in Designers and Art Directors Association of the United Kingdom, *The Copy Book*, 26.

¹¹ Quoted in ibid.

¹² Quote from the Clio Awards Web site, http://www.clioawards.com/html/wsj/spivak/html (accessed January 10, 2005).

Out-of-Home

We used to call this outdoor advertising. But what do you call signs inside an airport terminal, posters in a subway station, or three-dimensional displays in a shopping mall?

So we're using the term *out-of-home* to cover all advertising that's seen outside the home but is not in the point-of-sale category. That's not a nice, neat definition, but bear with us. We think this will make sense by the end of the chapter.

Why Out-of-Home?

From a creative standpoint, out-of-home offers many advantages. Specifically, out-of-home is:

- *Flexible:* The location, timing, structure, and dimension of the concept give you a lot of options.

- *A high-impact medium:* Nothing gives you a bigger canvas.

- *Exclusive:* You can select a specific location.

- *Economical:* Low cost per impression.

- Ideal for *establishing brand image* and *building rapid awareness.*

- Ideal for *promoting packaged goods.*

- Effective for *reinforcing existing brands.*

- Effective because, in many cases, your message is *always on display.*

- A medium that *combines selling with entertainment.*

- A medium that *quickly conveys a concept,* so out-of-home ads *look good in your portfolio.*

Why Not?

- You usually can't change the creative quickly.
- In most cases, you can't provide detail.
- You have to tell the whole story in about five seconds or less for billboards.
- Your message may be on display 24/7, but you're paying for off-peak times too.
- In most cases, you're limited to certain urban areas/country roads.
- People hate the idea of billboards, because most of them are ugly and stupid (we mean the billboards).

Posters and Bulletins (aka Billboards)

People in the outdoor advertising business don't talk about "billboards." The two main types of outdoor displays are the *painted bulletin* and the *outdoor poster.* The difference is the way they are displayed—posters use sheets of preprinted paper glued to backboards, and bulletins traditionally have used hand-painted images. Today, painted bulletins have given way to Superflex vinyl-coated fabric that gives them almost magazine-like quality. For simplicity's sake, we'll use the layperson's term *billboards.*

WORDS OF WISDOM

"I'm afraid the poor old billboard doesn't qualify as a medium at all; its medium, if any, is the scenery around it."

—Howard Gossage[1]

Posting companies offer a variety of sizes, usually described in poster terms, such as 36-sheet, 30-sheet, 24-sheet, and 8-sheet. A typical 36-sheet poster is 48 feet wide by 14 feet high—about a 3.5 to 1 ratio. Painted bulletins typically have a 2.5 to 1 ratio.

For layout purposes, all you have to know is that billboards are very wide and not very tall. So if you're using an 8½ × 11–inch sheet of paper and your design is 10 inches wide, it should be about 4½ inches high to have a 2.5 to 1 ratio. The reason we mention this here is that too many students treat billboards like magazine ads. When you start thinking about how they are different, it opens up a lot more creative opportunities. Which means they are much better suited to show a hot dog than a wedding cake.

Beyond the dimensions, billboards are available in several different formats or combinations of formats:

- *Standard static boards:* Your basic poster or bulletin that fits within the limits of the sign's borders.
- *Extensions:* Part of your image violates the boundaries of the board.
- *Motion boards:* These can be motorized images on a static board with sliding panels that reveal a totally different message, usually another advertiser.
- *Illuminated boards:* The board can be lighted for night viewing or, more dramatically, to include neon, moving lights, and selective spot lighting.
- *Three-dimensional boards:* You can add dimensional objects to and around the board, such as a car crashing through the middle, people sitting on the top edge, or parts of the poster removed to reveal the backing framework.

10.1. A student designed this standard static board.

10.2. A double side-by-side extension with both sides working together to convey a common message. With a brand as strong as Coke, you don't need a lot of copy.

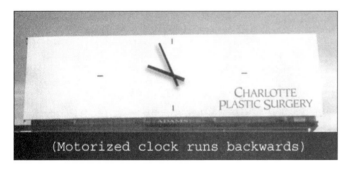

10.3. This motion board literally turns back time.

10.4. Outdoor signs can be used to give directions and valuable information, such as in this student-designed billboard.

10.5. This illuminated billboard looks like a neon sign in a bar.

10.6. As in real estate, the secret to cool outdoor advertising is location, location, location.

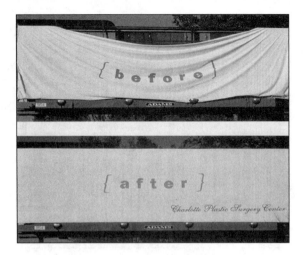

10.7. A fixed location actually offers creative opportunities. The first board with the saggy "before" captures attention. When it's replaced by the taught "after" and the advertiser's name, it all makes sense.

10.8. This anti-smoking board uses a combination of three dimensions and extensions (vultures looking at a smoker). With such a strong visual, you don't need copy.

Transit

Transit advertising also has its own special terminology. To make it simple, think of transit as advertising that goes on the outside or inside of things that move and at the places where you wait for things that move. Examples of transit advertising include:

10.9. Inside bus card: Consider treating it as more than a mini-billboard. You can use more copy and a more detailed concept.

- Inside and outside bus cards
- Outside bus murals
- Bus shelters and benches
- Kiosks
- Train, bus, and subway stations
- Airports
- Mobile billboards: car, truck, and trailer ads

Inside bus cards

Many times these are treated like mini-billboards, but keep in mind, you have a captive audience. Bored bus riders have a lot more than five seconds to get the message. So your copy can be a little longer and your images more complex than on billboards. Typical sizes of inside transit cards are 11 × 28 inches and 11 × 14 inches.

Transit shelters

These glass-and-metal cubes lend themselves to some very creative treatments aimed less at the people who wait there than at the people who pass by.

10.10. Transit shelter: There's no rule that you have to stay within the box.

10.11. Transit bench: Like a billboard, except people sit on it (and in front of your message).

Bus panels and murals

We've come a long way from just slapping a flat sign on the side of a bus, even though that's still common. However, some of the most striking transit advertising results from full-wrap murals, which completely envelope the bus.

10.12. Here's one way to put people in the seats. This can make for some pretty interesting combinations, depending on who rides the bus.

10.13. Back panels provide some creative opportunities too. This was part of a student-designed public service campaign.

Side and back panels can be very creative too. Remember that a bus is like a moving billboard, bringing your message to people on the street and in their cars. It has to be brief, striking, and entertaining, especially to drivers stuck behind or next to a bus in heavy traffic.

10.14. Careerbuilder.com offers hope to high-rise office workers in tough economic times.

10.15. Mobile billboards: If you own the truck, you can literally drive the message home.

Wall Murals

If you want a more permanent location without the dimensional restrictions of a billboard, consider a wall mural or wallscape. These are usually painted on the sides of brick buildings in large cities. Good locations are very limited, since you need a relatively tall (but not too tall) building next to an open space so people can see the mural. Usually it's an older building, which means it may not be in the most prestigious part of town. Even with all these restrictions, there are creative opportunities.

10.16. Wall murals work well with long-running campaigns promoting brand identity, as with Sauza's "Life is harsh" theme.

10.17. If you look closely at this 3-D wall mural you'll see a little slide coming out of the window.

Posters

Posters can be a creative person's best bet to pad a portfolio and win awards. Technically all you have to do is print one, post it somewhere, and *voilà,* you've produced a real-world advertisement, seen by someone other than your roommate.

  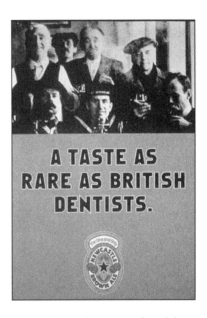

10.18–10.20. Because the posting can very selective, you can do things creatively you wouldn't dare with mainstream advertising.

10.21. In an attempt to reach a younger, urban audience, some advertisers use "wild postings," which look like random placement on abandoned buildings and construction fences. Some are intentionally covered with fake graffiti.

WORDS OF WISDOM

"Billboards are most effective if you can say these two magic words: 'Next Exit.' If you can't, they work best as a reminder of your other marketing."

—**JAY CONRAD LEVINSON**[2]

Out-of-Home and Campaigns

Out-of-home advertising is usually used as a secondary medium. Billboards and posters are great reminders of a slogan, logo, package, or other aspect of a total campaign. Keep the two key aspects of campaign continuity in mind when using out-of-home. Can you extend the message by using out-of-home, and can you repeat the theme created for out-of-home?

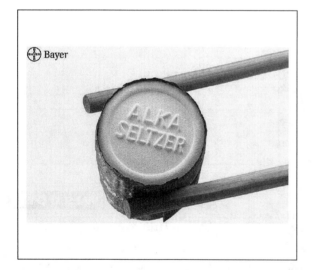

10.22–10.25. Repeatability in a campaign using posters. Although this was created in Mexico, the visual metaphors work all over the world.

IT'S OUT THERE: HOW NYNEX BROUGHT THE YELLOW PAGES OUTDOORS

Until the late 1980s, the most creative image of the Yellow Pages involved a pair of walking fingers ("Let your fingers do the walking"). That changed when Chiat\Day's "Human Cartoons" appeared for NYNEX. TV commercials and print ads showed silly visual puns, such as uniformed Marines dancing to a driving beat ("Rock Drills") and train conductors sitting on fancy sofas drinking tea ("Civil Engineers"). Outdoor ads played off the TV work. At the onset, images of a floppy-eared blue bunny multiplied across the streets of Manhattan for two weeks. Then came identical posters answering the riddle ("Hair Tinting") and using the campaign's familiar tagline,

"If it's out there, it's in here." Creative Director Bill Hamilton's fondness for the pitch is evident—"It's one of the best, most interesting things I've worked on"—as he remembers the evolution of the idea. Chiat\Day first created billboards that offered rational reasons consumers should prefer NYNEX's Yellow Pages. "But people didn't care about them until they needed a plumber or a pizza," says Hamilton, now senior creative director, J. Walter Thompson, New York. "There was no loyalty factor." Former NYNEX exec Susan DeFlora, now senior specialist, market communications at Bell Atlantic, said she realized how much impact the ads were having when she saw "a parking lot attendant with a blue bunny in his little kiosk . . . people are still talking about it."[3]

When you are developing concepts for a campaign, you might want to go with out-of-home first. Nothing crystallizes a concept like a billboard. If you can communicate that One Thing with one billboard, you've got something you can build on.

Where to Find the Best Out-of-Home Ads

Each year the Outdoor Advertising Association of America presents its OBIE Awards to the best in out-of-home media. The association's Web site also features a huge library of great outdoor ads over the years—649 examples for 2003 alone. As always, the *Communication Arts Advertising Annual* shows some pretty cool stuff.

"Outdoor boards are an event, not just an ad . . . don't do something that's just 'okay.' A billboard's size only magnifies how 'OKAY' your idea is. Be outrageous."

—LUKE SULLIVAN[4]

Tips and Techniques

The following recommendations are based on the collective wisdom of outdoor advertising professionals and our personal experience. They're not hard-and-fast rules, but factors you should consider when you're creating out-of-home advertising:

- *Be telegraphic.* The rule of thumb for billboards is nine words or fewer, with the emphasis on fewer. Some say six words is the limit. Keep in mind that someone driving by has about five seconds to get it.

- *Think big.* You've got an ad that can be seen from 500 feet away. The images and the type should be huge.

- *Go for a strong visual/verbal connection.* Think metaphors and visual puzzles. Many times you don't even need copy.

- *Stick with one main idea.* Above all, keep it simple!

- *Take advantage of location.* A sign on the side or back of a bus can be different from a static billboard because it's constantly in motion. The message on a billboard can be very local.

- *Use all caps for short headlines and uppercase/lowercase for longer heads.* Using all caps makes long copy harder to read.

- *Use short words when possible.* They're easier to read and you can get more on a billboard.

- *Use bold colors, not pastels.* You're trying to attract attention. That's why you see so many yellows and reds in billboards. Even white space draws attention, as long as it surrounds a bold color.

- *Use few elements.* Remember, keep it simple!

- *Use product package instead of words.* Show the Coke bottle or can, not the words Coca-Cola.

10.26. In this example the headline shows the product and spells it out. The red background and bright yellow letters also attract attention.

10.27. When you use more copy, upper- and lowercase is usually easier to read than all caps.

10.28. Metaphor, visual puzzle . . . whatever you call it, you don't need a lot of copy to tell people you can go topless in a Beetle.

Who's Who?

Howard Gossage—Howard Gossage influenced a generation of copywriters with innovative and often unconventional approaches to marketing communications. He began his copywriting career at age 36 in San Francisco. Success soon followed with award-winning work for Land Rover, Paul Masson wines, Rainier Ale, Eagle shirts, and Qantas airlines.

Notes

[1] Quoted in Luke Sullivan, *Hey Whipple, Squeeze This: A Guide to Creating Great Ads* (New York: John Wiley, 1998), 82.

[2] Jay Conrad Levinson, *Guerilla Marketing Attack* (Boston: Houghton Mifflin, 1989), 109.

[3] See Judy Warner, "Best Spots: Hill, Holliday John Hancock," *AdWeek,* November 9, 1998, http://www.adweek.com/aw/creative/top20_20years/top20_10.jsp (accessed June 28, 2005).

[4] Sullivan, *Hey Whipple,* 80.

Direct Mail

Direct response. Direct marketing. Direct mail. Direct me to a new chapter. It's all a little confusing. Even to experienced marketing professionals. Everyone will give you a little different spin, but here's the easiest way we've found to figure it all out:

Direct marketing covers the whole universe of sending a message directly to a consumer. According to the Direct Marketing Association (DMA), the three purposes of direct marketing are to:

- Solicit a direct order

- Generate a lead

- Drive store traffic

American companies spent more than $200 billon on direct marketing in 2004—about an even split between business-to-business and consumer. This generated sales of about $2 trillion.[1]

Direct response is a marketing transaction between the seller and buyer with no intermediary (such as a retailer or distributor) involved. The information from the seller to the potential buyer can be distributed in a number of different ways. For example:

- Television programming: As in home shopping programs and infomercials.

- Television commercials with toll-free phone numbers ("Operators are standing by").

- Interactive television commercials/programs: Click on the icon to buy the product.

- Magazine ads with coupons, toll-free phone numbers, and Web sites promoting direct sales.

- E-mail solicitations: These can range from the sleaziest spam to respected permission marketing programs.

- Telemarketing: A direct call from some boiler room precisely timed to interrupt your dinner or favorite TV program.

- Internet: Search engine marketing, whole Web sites, and advertising on Web sites.

- Direct mail: From the advertiser to the consumer/customer.

It's *direct* because the recipient of the advertising message *responds* directly to the sender of that message.

Direct mail is a marketing communication tool that enables direct response as well as other kinds of transactions. Direct mail is "simply a delivery medium, one very effective way for sellers to interact—and transact—directly with buyers."[2] For example, a clothing catalog mailed to a consumer may prompt a visit to a local store. Another recipient may make a direct purchase from the catalog center. Simply put, *direct mail puts the advertising message in your hands,* and, unlike other forms of print media, it has no competing messages (advertisers or editorial) attached to it.

Table 11.1 shows some examples of how direct mail works. Note that every one of these examples ends with an action. Direct marketing not only invites, it also provides recipients with the means to take real, measurable, physical action. In fact, "without a response mechanism, it's not direct marketing—it's merely advertising."[3]

TABLE 11.1   How Direct Mail Works

Purpose	Ask for	Process
Nonstore selling	An order	Send mailer → send money → get stuff
Retail store sale	Action	Send mailer → visit store → get stuff
Increase event attendance	Action	Send mailer → buy tickets → attend event
Research	Information	Send mailer → send back information

Why Direct Mail?

From a creative standpoint, direct mail offers many advantages:

- *It's specific.* With good data, an advertiser can zero in on specific demographics and lifestyles to create a more powerful message.

- *It's direct to an individual*—as close as you can get to one-on-one marketing.

- *It can be high impact.* If you correctly tap those wants and needs, you provide something of real value to the recipient.

- *It's flexible.* You can use virtually anything you can mail flat or put in a container.

- *It can be localized.* A mailer for a nationally advertised brand can include the names and addresses of local retailers.

- *It can generate sales where there are no stores.* In other words, it generates a direct response.

- *It can help gather information.* Given the right incentives, many people send back mail surveys.

- *It can be used to encourage trials of new products.* Samples and discount coupons help launch many new products.

- *It delivers instant results.* You know almost immediately if your mailing is successful, based on direct sales, phone orders, return of reply cards, or other measurement methods.

- *It can be used as part of an integrated marketing program.* For example, requests for information in a magazine ad are fulfilled by sending direct mail; you can direct people to a Web site for more detailed and interactive messages.

Why Not?

- Your direct mail is only as good as your mailing list (garbage in, garbage out).

- People hate it: It's unwanted, mistrusted, and, in some cases, feared.

- Companies misdirect and screen mailings: Remember, about half of all direct marketing is for B2B.

- It's difficult to create economical and effective direct mail that doesn't look like "junk mail."

- It's costly: The cost per thousand is very high in most cases. Elaborate print pieces and three-dimensional mailers can be very expensive to produce, and postage prices keep climbing.

Database Marketing

We can't stress this enough: *The value of your direct mail depends on the quality of your mailing list.* The most creative concept ever devised is no good if it goes to the wrong person. The better the list, the more on-target your creative message will be. The more you know, the more personal the message, and, with the possible exception of e-mail, direct mail is the most personal form of marketing communication.

Some of the information you might need to develop your message is listed below. The importance of these categories will vary depending on the type of product, marketing situation, price points, buying cycle, and other variables.

- Income

- Residence

- Age

- Gender

- Marital status

- Children in household

- Occupation

- Education

- Vehicles owned

- Recreational vehicles owned (boat, snowmobile, etc.)

- Recreation/leisure time choices

- Vacation choices

- Health/disabilities

- Propensity to buy

- Current or former customer status

Where to get information to build your database

You may wonder when you pick up a stack of junk mail, "How did they get *my* name?" If you're a direct mail marketer, you will *never* have an accurate, up-to-date mailing list. Ever. But you can try to make it as accurate as possible so the names on your list better match the profile of the people you want to reach. Sources of information include the following:

- Magazine/newspaper subscriptions

- Warranty card submissions

- Web site visits

- Coupons

- Toll-free phone numbers

- Literature requests

- Show registration

- Credit card holders

- Opt-in lists

- Compiled lists and custom selects

Rather than go through the intricacies of database management, we will assume you will employ the tips and techniques we offer below *after* you have secured information about your intended direct mail recipients.

Types of Direct Mail

Several categories of direct mail formats are available. The choice depends on the budget (production and postage), content, type of product, purchase cycle, and response mechanism. We describe below the three main types of traditional direct mail (TDM) plus Internet direct mail (IDM).

11.1. Even the most brilliant of direct mailers will fail if sent to the wrong people.

Source: Illustration by Dan Augustine.

Envelope mailers (letter package)

Anything you put into an envelope applies. It may be as simple as a letter or as elaborate as 10-piece multicomponent mailer. Keep in mind that every component has a purpose, even the envelope itself. The basic components can include a letter, a brochure, and a reply device, such as a prepaid reply card.

You want the outer envelope to say, "Open me." You can do this several ways:

- *Teaser copy:* It could be a special offer or some twist on the message. For example, one envelope for a Florida resort said, "Open carefully: contains white sand, dolphins, seashells and coconut palms."

- *Blind envelopes:* These are usually standard-sized envelopes that suggest normal business or personal correspondence rather than direct mail advertising. Sometimes a stamp is used rather than a meter stamp to make it look more like personal mail.

- *Official envelopes:* These look like government correspondence, a check, or a telegram. While you might get some immediate attention with these, you're more likely to annoy people by deceiving them.

- *Personalized copy:* Sometimes this is effective; other times it may offend people who wonder, "How do they know so much about me?"

Flat self-mailers

A self-mailer contains the mailing address on some part of the piece itself rather than on an envelope. Some traditionalists don't like self-mailers. They claim a letter package will always outpull a self-mailer. A letter is more personal, while a

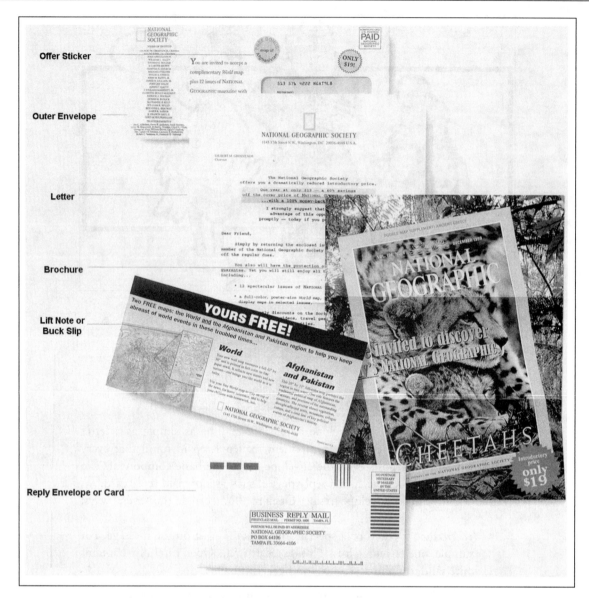

Offer Sticker

Outer Envelope

Letter

Brochure

Lift Note or Buck Slip

Reply Envelope or Card

11.2. The anatomy of an order solicitation letter package: A lot more can be involved than a letter and an envelope. Each component plays a key role in getting the recipient to return the reply card or pick up the phone. It's like having a mini-campaign in each envelope.

self-mailer shouts, "I'm an ad!" However, a well-designed self-mailer can be cost efficient and effective from a creative standpoint. Types of self-mailers include:

- Postcards
- Folded mailers—one fold, two folds, and multifolds
- Brochures and pamphlets
- Newsletters

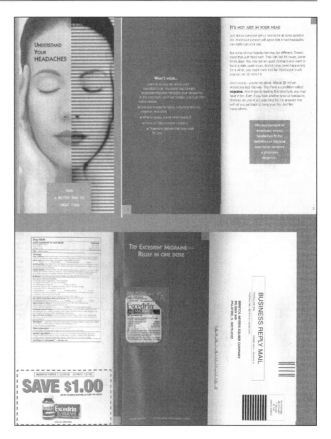

11.3. Jumbo postcards are an economical way to get your message out. Treat them like billboards on the front and provide more detail on the back. They're great for campaigns or a series of mailers.

11.4. Excedrin Migraine created this self-mailer to send to people who requested more information from their Web site and magazine ads. The multipage brochure contains a lot of facts about migraine headaches. It also includes a coupon, product sample, and business reply card.

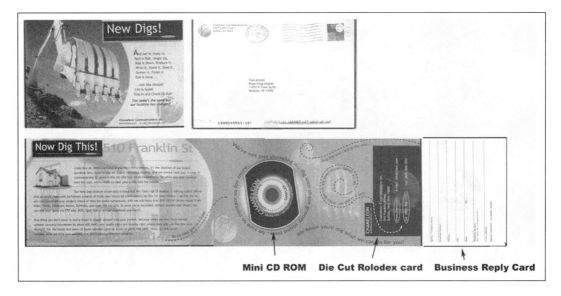

11.5. When folded up, this self-mailer is about the size of a standard postcard. Unfolded, it reveals its selling message plus a CD-ROM, Rolodex card, and business reply card.

Dimensional mailers

Some of the most innovative (and expensive) direct mailers are three-dimensional. Basically, they can be anything that can be mailed or shipped. Many times the box will include a separate item, sometimes called a *gadget*. This may be a sample, a premium item that might have some use, or something totally off-the-wall that makes a selling point. The limits to 3-D mailers are governed only by your imagination and your budget.

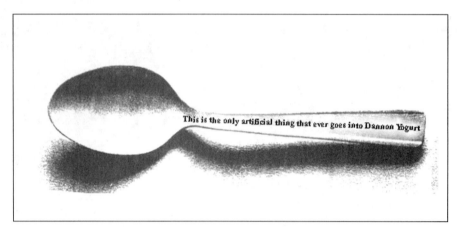

11.6. Three-dimensional mailers don't have to be elaborate or expensive. For the small cost of an imprinted plastic spoon, Dannon made a big impression.

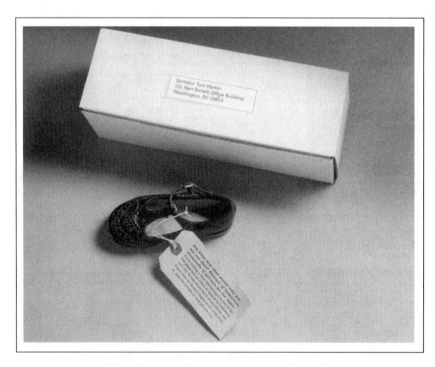

11.7. This student-designed 3-D mailer was sent to members of Congress, urging them to vote for anti–land mine legislation. The box contained a single small shoe formerly worn by a child whose leg had been blown off by a land mine.

11.8–11.9. An award-winning self-promotional 3-D mailer sent to prospective clients by an ad agency. Inside the box: a personalized letter, a brochure, and a stuffed "Adversaurus Rex" representing the agency's nonevolving competitors.

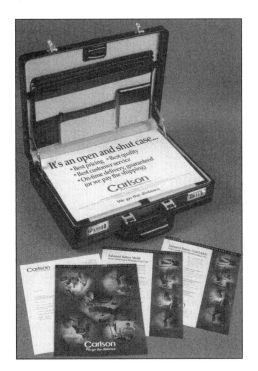

11.10. Since the number of customers may be much smaller, business-to-business direct mailers can be very high impact. Here, the company sent prospects a leather briefcase filled with product literature and a personalized cover letter from the company president.

11.11. This multiple-element mailer was sent to retailers who carry the Jensen line of audio components. Inside the box were a cover letter, product literature, a reply card, a high-quality pen, and a new road atlas.

"There are few things as certain as the effects of lumpy mail. If there's a mysterious bulge in a letter, it will get opened. . . . when it comes to mail, . . . 'lumpy lives.'"

—CONNIE O'KANE[4]

Internet direct mail

IDM should not be confused with ordinary e-mail. E-mail marketing has been so abused by spammers that legitimate marketers face more daunting obstacles than simply creating credible messages. Still, reputable firms have been successful, even in the face of spam filters and increasing frustration with unsolicited e-mail messages. Like TDM, IDM is used to generate leads or orders. However, since IDM's delivery system is different from TDM's, the copy approach also varies. The following are some tips for IDM that emphasize how it differs from traditional direct mail creative tactics:[5]

- The e-mail FROM line should show someone the readers will trust. If it's for a customer, be sure to put the company's name in the FROM line. For example, "FROM: Briggs & Stratton Customer Service Department."

- You should treat the SUBJECT line like envelope teaser copy. You have to give the prospect some reason to open the e-mail. For example, "SUBJECT: Try the New Update for Your Macromedia Project."

- Your first paragraph or two should contain a mini-version of your whole e-mail. So instead of carefully spreading out your AIDA (attention-interest-desire-action), you should try to get all these elements in early. Online users have little patience in general, and they need to understand your whole offer fast.

- Avoid using "hard-sell" techniques. These tend to produce poor results. Readers on the Internet expect to see information on the benefits and how to order, but the tone must remain helpful. If it's too slick, your e-mail will be trashed.

- *Always* remember to include a Web-based response form. Many online users prefer to keep the entire transaction online.

- Premiums and sweepstakes work great online. You have the opportunity online to animate your premiums in action or even make them interactive.

- Avoid the word *free* in the SUBJECT line. *Free* is too blatantly promotional a word for people to bother opening your e-mail. Besides, many online users now employ spam filters that work to screen out messages with *free* in the SUBJECT line.

- Try to make your headline different from your SUBJECT line. Your best benefit up front usually does the trick. Injecting a news feel and some self-interest doesn't hurt either.

- *Always* include an opt-out statement! The only thing more powerful than goodwill toward your company is ill will.

- For IDM, shorter is better. If some of your prospects require more information before they make purchasing decisions, include a click-through to an expanded version of your e-mail.

- With IDM, you can use viral marketing techniques. Prospects can pass your messages on to others they think would be interested.

WHAT THE BUCK WERE WE THINKING? THE JOYS AND PAINS OF E-MAIL MARKETING

Johnathan Crawford is founder and CEO of Data Dog Marketing, a Milwaukee-based firm that provides integrated marketing programs for retailers, member organizations, and the B2B industry sector. Crawford is a 25-year veteran of the advertising and marketing business with a background in radio, outdoor, print, and e-marketing. Some of his client biggies have included the Sharper Image, Burger King, and Tyson Chicken. He told us this story:

I was working for a Chicago firm that developed e-mail marketing programs for a variety of national companies. The e-mail medium was still somewhat young and there was a lot of learning to do, but we were ahead of the curve in many areas. One of those areas was using data to determine the content of the e-mail.

A small portion of the data and e-mail addresses we had collected for a client were from a promotion called "Buck Head" (a suburb of Atlanta), and this was an insignificant issue until our data linking went haywire. Due to a variety of reasons, we accidentally sent 50,000 e-mail messages to people addressed with "Dear Buck Head" (instead of Dear First Name).

We realized this mistake approximately seven seconds after clicking the "send" button. Talk about panic. Once you click send, it's all over, done, it's "out the door." If it's wrong, you're basically stuck with the results. Well, 50,000 people were addressed as "Buck Head," and because that sounds very close to an expletive some of us periodically use, that had an impact. Some people complained, others were amused. The client wasn't amused, but we were able to quickly send out a short apology e-mail making light of our mistake and explaining how it happened.

Direct Mail and Campaigns

The two campaign dynamics of repeatability and extendibility apply beautifully to direct mail advertising.

Repeatability with multiple mailings

Each mailing has to stand alone, but collectively several mailings may trigger the action you desire. The following are examples of how multiple mailings can create a greater response rate:

- *Numbered series of mailers:* Recipients get clues in each mailing and need to save all the mailings in the series to claim a prize.

- *Repetition of the same mailer:* Assumes that recipients may miss some of the mailings or need to be hammered repeatedly with the same message.

- *Multiple format mailings:* A series of flat mailers with business reply cards. If recipients continue sending back the cards, indicating interest, they receive a 3-D mailer with a premium.

11.12–11.14. Two examples from a series of eight jumbo postcards promoting an auto parts company. The third sample shows the back side with more detailed information.

Extendibility with integration in a campaign

Direct mail can be integrated into a campaign in a number of ways. For example:

- Direct mailers with product samples and coupons encourage the recipient to visit a retailer.

- A reader sees a magazine ad and calls for more information, and the fulfillment house mails product literature.

- A new brand image campaign is launched with print, television, radio, and outdoor. Direct mail is used to provide detailed product information that can't be conveyed in the other media.

11.15–11.16. MINI Cooper sent this mini-book to people who wanted more information on their cars.

11.17–11.19. A great example of direct mail used in a promotional/PR campaign. BMW donates $1 to breast cancer research for every test-drive mile driven. The campaign not only raises money for a good cause, it also gets people into BMW dealerships.

Tips and Techniques

The Direct Marketing Association, as well as many others, uses a process known as AIDA to explain how direct marketing works. The acronym AIDA stands for

- Attention
- Interest
- Desire
- Action

These elements are not unlike the *awareness, comprehension, conviction,* and *action* components of the DAGMAR model we discussed in Chapter 1. The main point is the last: *action.* You don't spend the time and effort to create direct mail just so the recipients are aware of your brand. You want them to take action, preferably *now.*

The following are some general tips for all direct mail. Below, we discuss some special applications in more detail:

- *Get attention:* Some 44% of mail is never opened. If you're using envelopes, do something to make your recipients open them. If it's a self-mailer, use a strong headline to invite further action.

- *Be personal:* Your database has given you the information, now get to know the recipient. Don't write to the masses, write to the individual—and nothing is more individual than direct mail.

- *Stimulate action:* Cover all areas of the transaction. If it's a direct sale, provide a toll-free number, Web site, or other means to spur immediate action. If the sale is through a retailer or dealer, get the recipient to visit the store right away.

- *Study your own mail:* What do you open? What attracts your attention? Why? Can you apply that to the mailings you create?

- *Measure it:* You'll know if your mailer worked or not by the response rate and ultimately sales. Agree on a reasonable return objective with the client.

- *Test it:* If you have two or more different approaches, do a split run. Measure the results and figure out why one pulled more response than the other.

- *Don't tell every detail in the mailer:* This is especially important if it doesn't cover the whole transaction.

- *Think campaigns:* Each mailer in a series should stand on its own and work with others. Got a great idea? Can you come up with a whole series of other great ideas?

- *Use simple language and avoid advertising jargon.*

- *In retail-oriented mailings, repeat the name of the product or store often.*

- *Use captions for illustrations:* People usually read picture/captions before body copy.

The fine art of writing a cover letter

Even experienced copywriters sometimes have a hard time writing a good cover letter as part of a direct mail campaign. A cover letter is an introduction, a sales pitch, and a proposal for further action all in one. Cover letters are typically one-page documents and, in most cases, have a beginning, middle, and end—usually an introduction saying who you are and why you're writing, followed by a sales pitch for what you have to offer, and then a closing in which you propose steps for further action. These three components often amount to three or four paragraphs, but there are no ironclad rules about how to break up the information. Phillip Ward Burton offers some good advice for cover letter writers in *Advertising Copywriting.*[6] We've paraphrased a few of his suggestions:

Cover letter outline: 7 steps

1. Promise a benefit in the headline or first paragraph—lead with your strongest sales point.

2. Enlarge on your most important benefit.

3. Tell the reader what he or she is going to get.

4. Back your statements with proof and endorsements (testimonials).

5. Tell the reader what's lost if he or she doesn't act.

6. Rephrase the benefits in your closing offer.

7. Incite action—set a time limit ("Buy now").

Cover letter style: 7 steps

1. Start with short opening paragraph—four lines or shorter.

2. No paragraph should be longer than eight lines.

3. Vary the length of paragraphs.

4. Use deep indents and center bullet points.

5. Close with a two- to three-line summary.

6. Don't forget the envelope (teaser).

7. Don't forget a follow-up letter—reinforce the message/refine your data mining.

Using gadgets

Some creative types tend to think of gadgets as silly, undignified devices to get attention. However, what's important is the recipient's reaction, not your personal preference. If you use a silly gimmick like dice, a pocketknife, or cheap

Letter	Annotation
Dear Jack:	*Personalize with name and other information.*
Here's how you can keep your Sea Ray 230 looking showroom fresh—above and below the waterline.	*Promise a benefit up front.*
During the boating season, you work hard to keep your Sea Ray 230 looking shipshape. But when you haul it out in the fall, you know you're facing many long hours of scrubbing that green slime off the bottom. It won't come off with a pressure washer. And don't think about using harsh acid cleaners on your fiberglass hull.	*Enlarge on that benefit.*
Here's a better way.	*Vary the length of sentences and paragraphs.*
New **BoteBrite** hull cleaner cuts through that grungy bottom grime to restore your boat's original color and shine. Without hard scrubbing. Without abrasives. Without dangerous acids.	*Tell the reader what he/she is going to get.*
Just spray **BoteBrite** on the bottom of the boat—wait 15 minutes—and rinse with a garden hose. That's all there is to it!	
• **BoteBrite** is a unique detergent that dissolves organic stains from algae and dirty water. • **BoteBrite** will not damage fiberglass, plastic, metal, or your driveway when used as directed. • **BoteBrite** is easy to apply and even easier to clean up.	*Use deep indents and bullet points to call out key features/benefits.*
BoteBrite has been approved by the industry's leading manufacturers, including Sea Ray. It's safe, easy to use, and effective against tough bottom stains.	*Back your statement with proof or testimonials.*
We hate to admit this boating season is coming to an end. After you pull out for the season, will you spend a weekend scrubbing and breathing chemical fumes? Or spraying on **BoteBrite** and rinsing off a whole season of crud in just minutes?	*Tell the reader what's lost if he/she doesn't act. Rephrase benefits.*
For a limited time, we're offering a *Buy 2–Get 1 Free* deal on **BoteBrite**. Just bring the attached coupon to any **BoteBrite** retailer before September 30 and get a free 16-oz. bottle of **BoteBrite** when you buy two 16-oz. or larger sizes.	*Incite action.*
When it's time to clean your boat this fall, take it easy. Use new **BoteBrite** for fast, safe, and effective bottom cleaning.	*Close with a benefit summary.,*

Figure 11.1. Sample Letter

sunglasses gets the recipient to take action, great. Hold your nose and collect your check. You've done your job. If, on the other hand, your clever little give-away is seen as cheap, cheesy, or insulting, you've not only lost a potential sale, you've damaged your client's image.

Here are a few examples of gadgets that have worked to generate strong positive responses and ultimately sales:

- A "changeable" mailer in which the image shifted from a camel to a water softener control to convey the message of "the ultimate water saver."

- A pair of sunglasses to exemplify "cool" savings from an air conditioner company.

- An imprinted golf umbrella from a bank to demonstrate that "we've got you covered."

- A telephone inserted into a bed of live sod to make the point that "we know your turf, give us a call."

Groan if you must. However, the right gadget to the right customer gets attention and may stimulate action. Once again, we paraphrase Phillip Ward Burton for advice on using gadgets:[7]

- A gadget won't sell a product that can't be sold on its own merits.

- Be sure the gadget fits the message/audience (avoid gags).

- Don't make a gadget more important than the product's name.

- Don't let your personal like/dislike influence your choice.

The best advice: Know your target audience. Will a cheap gimmick generate a response or turn off a sale? If you have the luxury of time and budget, you could do a split run test.

Business-to-business direct mail is different

While the goal of both is to encourage taking action, B2B and consumer direct mail take different paths to get there, as Table 11.2 illustrates.

Testing is necessary, but make sure you know what you're measuring

John Caples was one of the first to blend creativity with scientific evaluation of advertising copy. Direct mail was the perfect laboratory for his studies. By using split runs, he could measure the effectiveness of headlines, body copy, and sales promotion offers. He measured results by examining the number of responses and, most important, sales. Today direct mail—whether it is snail mail or e-mail—is still one of the most easily measured forms of marketing communication. When you have a client who insists on testing your direct mail concepts (and they

WORDS OF WISDOM

"Testing is the kernel of direct marketing. The truth is that every major direct marketing business that succeeds does so largely by testing—or a run of exceptional luck."

—**Drayton Bird**[8]

TABLE 11.2   **Differences between Consumer and B2B Direct Mail**

Consumer Direct Mail	Business-to-Business Direct Mail
High quantities: This means you have to pinch pennies. Reducing weight to lower mailing costs or eliminating an element could save thousands of dollars in a mass mailing.	*Low quantities:* This means you may be able to increase the quality and thus the impact of the mailing piece. Some mailings are so tightly targeted, you may only need to mail a few dozen to get the desired return.
Lifetime value: Some consumer clients are willing to give up short-term return on investment for long-term gains. So they are not very concerned with break-even points on their mailings if they can gain market share overall.	*Lead generation:* This is usually the goal. Typically it's a two-step transaction, so the mailer facilitates a sales call or request for more detailed product literature.
Break through the clutter: The main challenge is to get the recipient to pull your mail piece out of the stack of "junk" he or she receives every day.	*Get past the gatekeeper:* Businesspeople get piles of "junk" too. But most companies screen the mail, so only a few select pieces reach the right people. The higher the level, the tighter the screening.

should), make sure you help define what's measured. That way the client can't come back and say, "This just didn't work." Also, work with the client to identify roadblocks that may affect the success of your efforts—such as lack of stores, poorly handled customer service, new competitive sales promotion, and other factors over which you have no control from a creative standpoint. Your client may have read one or more of the hundreds of books and Web sites that profess to offer the secrets of effective direct marketing. Most offer cookbook-like formulas for success, but very few talk about brand image, synergy with other media, integrated communication, and resonance—mainly because these factors can't be measured as easily as sales from a direct mail campaign.

Where to Find the Best Direct Mail Advertising

The DMA recognizes the best direct marketing communication efforts in several categories with the ECHO Awards. For a list of current ECHO winners, visit the DMA Web site (the-dma.org/industryawards/echo). The other major awards also honor direct mail, as does the *Communication Arts Advertising Annual.* The John Caples International Awards also recognize the best in direct marketing every year. Entries are received and awards are bestowed on creatives from more than 40 countries worldwide. Check out recent winners, tips for submitting entries, and other useful information online at caples.org.

Who's Who?

Drayton Bird—Drayton Bird was worldwide creative director of Ogilvy & Mather Direct, the world's largest direct marketing agency. He went on to found what became the United Kingdom's largest direct marketing agency. With more than 40 years of experience in direct marketing and advertising, Bird wrote and published *Commonsense Direct Marketing, How to Write Sales Letters That Sell,* and *Marketing Insights and Outrages*—all best sellers. He also writes regular columns for marketing/advertising publications in the United Kingdom, United States, Malaysia, India, and Europe.

John Caples—Often called the father of direct response advertising, John Caples was one of the most influential copywriters of all time. He spent a lifetime researching the most effective methods of advertising. His direct approach for writing headlines cut through the clutter and grabbed the readers, pulling them into the ad. Caples penned one of the most famous headlines ever written: "They laughed when I sat down at the piano but when I started to play!"

Notes

[1] Direct Marketing Association, "Findings and Analysis from the DMA 2001–2002 Economic Impact Report" (press release), June 10, 2002, http://www.the-dma.org/cgi/disppressrelease?article=339 (accessed June 30, 2005).

[2] Walker Marketing, "You've Got Mail," n.d., http://www.walkermarketingagency.com/articles_content_frame.asp?articleID=26 (accessed June 30, 2005).

[3] Ibid.

[4] Connie O'Kane, "Direct Mail with Promotional Products," *Imprint* (publication of the Advertising Specialty Institute), 2002, available on Printable Promotions Web site, http://www.printablepromotions.com/Articles/DirectMail.htm (accessed June 30, 2005).

[5] This list is adapted from Aran S. Kay, "Internet Direct Mail Is Different: 14 Things to Remember," n.d., http://www.professionalcopy.ca/emails.html (accessed June 30, 2005).

[6] Phillip Ward Burton, *Advertising Copywriting* (Lincolnwood, IL: NTC Business Books, 1991), 163.

[7] Ibid.

[8] Drayton Bird, *Commonsense Direct Marketing,* 3d ed. (Lincolnwood, IL: NTC Business Books, 1994).

Radio

First, a little background noise . . . To really understand radio, you need to talk to your grandparents. That's the last generation whose families gathered in their living rooms to listen to radio programs. Whether it was Jack Benny, the Green Hornet, a fireside chat by FDR, or a Brooklyn Dodgers game, people stopped to listen. Radio wasn't in the background. It was the focus of home entertainment.

Read a dozen textbooks and you'll find nearly everyone calls radio "theater of the mind," a description that originated during the so-called Golden Age of Radio. Not having visual references, people believed what they heard. Clip-clopping wooden blocks were hoofbeats. Paper crinkled next to the microphone became a raging fire. Music, sound effects, and multiple voices created vivid mental pictures. And, unlike modern radio, there was no competition. People sought out radio and listened attentively.

Copywriters who work in radio today face many new challenges, the biggest one being people don't listen. You need to find a way to break out of the audio wallpaper that radio has become. From a copywriting standpoint, radio presents a perfect opportunity for you to flex creative muscles in totally new ways. You're using words, music, and sound instead of pictures. When you're the writer/producer, the radio commercial is your baby, and the art director can't save your lame idea with a great layout.

Why Radio?

For advertisers and the people who write the ads, radio offers many unique advantages:

- *It's everywhere and it's free.* There's nothing to buy (other than a radio) and no effort to find programming.

- *You can stimulate immediate action.* And, you know if your spots are successful.

249

- *It supports local retailers and national brands.* You can combine national campaign themes to support local stores.

- *It features segmented markets.* You can personalize your messages. Radio has become a very personal medium, so you can tailor specific messages to reach specific demographics.

- *Radio personalities sell.* Well-known voices have built-in credibility with key listener demographics.

- *It offers creative opportunities.* It's the ultimate creative challenge to create visuals with music, voice, and sound effects.

Why Not?

- Radio is usually a background medium. Not everyone selects your station as they do with magazines or newspapers.

- It's hard to control listenership. While you can select station demographics, you can't be sure they're listening.

- It can have high production costs. The expenses of talent, music, production studios, and residuals (the fees you pay the talent each time a spot runs) can really add up.

- It's not good for providing product information—you need other media to give consumers details.

- It imposes time constraints. How much can you really say in 15, 30, 60 seconds?

- Satellite radio, one of the fastest-growing media choices, is virtually commercial free.

12.1.

Source: Illustration by Dan Augustine.

Creative Challenges and Opportunities

Years ago, the Radio Advertising Bureau ran an ad featuring a fish smoking a pipe, with the headline, "I saw it on the radio." Although the expression "theater of the mind" has been overused (and can also be used to describe paranoid schizophrenia), you should never forget that radio gives you advertising's biggest palette to create your visuals. As Jewler and Drewniany comment: "Seasoned radio writers will remind you that radio is a visual medium, in which the audience sees whatever the writer makes them see. The better the writer knows radio, the more the audience will see."[1] If you can use words and sounds to make listeners "see" in their minds, just think how easy it will be to write a TV spot where they can see with their eyes.

In most cases, the copywriter plays a big role in production. In smaller shops, he or she may be the sole decision maker for production—the person who selects the talent, music, sound effects, and production studio. As writer/ producer, you supervise the recording and editing sessions, making sure everything matches your vision. While you certainly have input from the account exec, creative director, and client, most of the decisions are up to you. To pull this off, you need a clear vision of the finished product. You have to communicate exactly what you need to the production engineers and talent. If it isn't making sense to them, you have to listen to their ideas to make it better. However, don't get trapped into production by committee.

We'll discuss this in more detail later, but we should mention that a copywriter needs to think of production in terms of campaigns. The continuity factors, such as music and voice talent, should be available and affordable if you want to repeat your commercials in a series.

> **WORDS OF WISDOM**
>
> "[We're] bring[ing] the audience closer into the commercial. Radio is wonderful as a medium for doing that. It's so one-to-one. So personal."
>
> —DICK ORKIN[2]

Terminology and Classifications

You can categorize radio commercials in a number of ways. We'll use the terminology explained below, even though the terms *type, style, genre, format,* and *technique* can be interchanged at will.

Format

Radio production has its own language and style of writing. The following example script covers some tips for writing radio commercials.

Sample Radio Script

ANNCR:	(POMPOUS ANNOUNCER VOICE) This is another bogus example to help students write better ads. When you write words to be spoken, put them in lower-case. When you write directions or add--
SFX:	(DOOR SLAMMING)
ANNCR:	--sound effects, use uppercase in parentheses. (ASIDE) By the way, you're late. When--
STUDENT:	(INTERRUPTS) What about music?
MUSIC:	BEETHOVEN'S FIFTH SYMPHONY IN AND UNDER
ANNCR:	(ANNOYED) As I was saying, when you add music you have to indicate when it comes in and out and if it goes under the voice-over. Another--
STUDENT:	(INTERRUPTS) No. I mean music, Mr. Announcer Dude.
MUSIC:	BLACK SABBATH'S "PARANOID" IN AND UP
ANNCR:	(SHOUTING OVER MUSIC) Be careful not to mix the music too loud or you'll drown out the announcer.
MUSIC:	OUT
ANNCR:	(STILL SHOUTING) And another thing--(RETURNS TO NORMAL VOICE)--and another thing, when a word is underlined, the announcer should give it more emphasis. But don't underline more than one word. Also, when an announcer sees a double dash--he knows it's for a dramatic pause.
STUDENT:	Are you going to tell us words are like perfectly proportioned peach pits?
ANNCR:	You're spitting on the mike. Try to avoid alliterations or too many P, S, and K sounds. And keep it clean. No swearing.
STUDENT:	Damn straight. Any other words of wisdom, Mr. Announcer Dude?
ANNCR:	Yes. Read your commercial out loud and time it. This one is at least 10 seconds too long.
STUDENT:	(WHISPERS) Seventy seconds if you ask me.

Types of commercials by production

Radio commercials can be categorized by the way they're produced; for example:

- *Fact sheet* (sometimes called "rip and read" in the radio biz): It's nothing more than a script read by a single announcer. Fact sheets are used a lot in co-op advertising, where a manufacturer provides commercials to dealers who fill in the blanks and send them to the radio stations.

- *Live script/live production spot:* They're usually done on location, such as at a car dealership or event. Typically a radio station personality comes on the air from the remote location. Many times the personality will interview a store owner and customers and interact with the studio-based disc jockey.

- *Production spot:* This type involves the recording and editing of one or more of the following key elements: voice, sound effects (SFX), and music. Sometimes production spots include a mix of a nationally produced spot and local content. Figure 12.1 shows how this works.

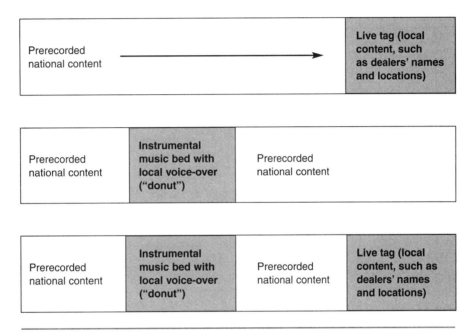

Figure 12.1. Mixes of National and Local Content in Radio Spots

Styles of commercials

Most production commercials fall within four styles (or genres, or basic themes): news, drama, comedy, and music. Certain styles work better for specific situations, as Table 12.1 shows.

Creative techniques for radio commercials

Within a style or genre you have a lot of flexibility. Every textbook offers a little different take on the various options. In Table 12.2, we've simplified it a bit and narrowed the list down to a select few creative techniques. More important, we list examples of their applications, so you have a better feel for the right technique for the right creative situation.

The following examples show how you can use three of these techniques. While the printed word can't possibly convey all the nuances of the talent, sound effects, and music, you can get a good idea what award-winning spots look like on paper.

TABLE 12.1   Commercial Styles and Their Uses

Style/Genre	Situation
News	Announce a sale, event, special prices, grand opening, new product introduction
Drama	Serious problem, personal conflict, dramatic situations
Comedy	Humorous tone, funny situations, parody of news or drama
Music	Full jingle, jingle with donut, music as the main element of the commercial

TABLE 12.2   Creative Techniques and Their Applications

Technique	Variations/Applications
Straight announcer	Serious news style
	Humorous read
	Distinctive accent
	Voice modification (fast or slow)
Dialogue/interview	Two or more characters (slice of life)
	Announcer-consumer interaction
	Authority figure/consumer
Dramatization	Mini-play
	Reenactment
	News/historical event
	Outrageous situation (comedy)
Testimonial/case history	First-person testimonial
	Story about person's experience
	Celebrity endorsement
Music dominant	Full jingle—original music
	Jingle with "donut" for voice segment
	Popular music
	Adapted popular music—new lyrics
Combinations	Any of the above so that one component is not dominant

Dialogue/interview

This "man on the street" interview by Mal Sharpe takes a deadly topic and makes it fun.

Example: Dialogue/Interview

CLIENT: *Forest Hills Mortuary*

TITLE: *"Detroit"*

SHARPE: Where are you from, by the way?

MAN: Detroit Michigan.

SHARPE: You're from Detroit. You're living here now?

MAN: No, I've only been here one day.

SHARPE: Do you realize that the Forest Lawn mortuaries are within your reach financially?

MAN: Forest Lawn mortuaries?

SHARPE: What's wrong?

MAN: What do I want to do with that? I'm from Detroit.

SHARPE: You can go back to Detroit and tell all the people that last year at Forest Lawn, almost one-third of all the mortuary arrangements cost under six hundred dollars. Detroit wants to hear that.

MAN: I don't know why Detroit would want to hear that.

SHARPE: What else do they have to listen to?

MAN: What does Forest Lawn mean to Detroit?

SHARPE: What does Detroit mean to Forest Lawn?

MAN: Nothing.

SHARPE: But you are excited to learn that--

MAN: No I'm not. I'm from Detroit. I come here on vacation. Why would I want to learn about mortuary services? You're the first person out here who's talked to me and now you talk to me about mortuary services.

SHARPE: You want to know about mortuary services. That's why you came out to Los Angeles.

MAN: No, no, I come out to forget about death. I come out here to live a little.

SHARPE: Yeah, well, I can understand that being from Detroit. It is exciting to know though, that last year at Forest Lawn almost one-third of all the mortuary arrangements did cost under six hundred dollars. That is exciting right?

MAN: Not to me it isn't.

SHARPE: Why?

MAN: I'm from Detroit.

Dramatization

Not all commercials are funny. This one, edited from interviews and actual location recordings, conveys the drama of the South-Central Los Angeles riots in 1992 following the acquittal of the police officers charged in the Rodney King beating. Sponsored by the League of Women Voters, the commercial captures some of the chaos of the riots and two voices from the area: Tim Lee, a Korean dry cleaner, and Otis Arnold, an African American pharmacist.

Example: Dramatization

CLIENT: *League of Women Voters*

TITLE: *South Central*

PILOT: (RADIO TRANSMISSION FROM HELICOPTER)—engage OCD, you've got one, two, three, four, five, six fires burning.

ANNCR: South Central Los Angeles. April twenty-ninth, nineteen-ninety two. What was it like to really be there?

LEE: Almost all the customers' clothes were stolen. Broken windows. They busted down the door.

ANNCR: Tim Lee works at his uncle's dry cleaners.

LEE: It hurts. Makes me think there's a lot of racism in this country. The main thing I think is the misunderstanding.

DISPATCHER: (RADIO TRANSMISSION) Life force 50. Life force 50. We need help. We've got shots fired.

ANNCR: Otis Arnold runs a pharmacy on Florence Avenue.

ARNOLD: Most of the going businesses here, particularly around this area, were destroyed.

ANNCR: So where do we go from here?

ARNOLD: I think basically, if we need change, the place to do it is at the ballot box.

LEE: Registering to vote is good thing. I think everyone should do it.

ANNCR: Vote for peace. Vote for change. But vote. This message was brought to you by the League of Women Voters and this station.

Testimonial/Case History

These can be real, using actual stories with ordinary people or celebrity talent. Or they can be spots that seem realistic but are produced for laughs, as in the admittedly fake testimonial for Priceline online travel services on the opposite page.

Production Considerations

Production and media costs

Even though radio usually costs a lot less than television, costs can quickly get out of control. As a writer, you should know how budget constraints will affect your concept. As a producer, you need to know how much you can do in the studio and when to stop fooling around and lay down some tracks. Keep in mind the factors listed in Table 12.3, which start with the cheapest and get more expensive as you move down. Don't forget day-part considerations, since a drive-time schedule can transfer more money from production into media.

Example: Testimonial

CLIENT: *Priceline*

TITLE: *"Family Crisis"*

MUSIC: GUITAR IN AND UNDER

GEORGE: Hi, my name is George. Uh--a little while back my sister called me up.

ANNCR: Another fake testimonial for Priceline-dot-com.

GEORGE: The deal was she was fighting with her husband again and she was really upset, so I said what I think Earl needs is a punch in the nose.

ANNCR: George had a family emergency. But he didn't have a lot of extra cash.

GEORGE: Air fares were way too steep for me to go across the country just to punch a guy in the nose.

ANNCR: So George got online and went to Priceline-dot-com, where you name your own price for airline tickets.

GEORGE: The process was real easy, real simple—and the service is free.

ANNCR: In just one hour, George's offer was accepted and he was on his way. Priceline is perfect for families, students, seniors, any leisure travel on a budget.

GEORGE: And so I flew to my sister's and punched my brother-in-law in the nose and then flew back home—all for less than I thought possible.

ANNCR: Try Priceline today. Visit Priceline-dot-com or call one-eight hundred-Priceline.

GEORGE: You know this marriage was saved with Priceline.

TABLE 12.3   Factors Affecting Production and Media Costs

Music	Voice Talent	Sound Effects	Editing	Media Costs
Stock music: You may have to pay a fee based on how it's used, where it's used, and how many times you use it.	*Staff announcer:* Sometimes the radio station will provide free talent if you pay for airtime.	*Stock effects:* Millions of sound effects are available on disc. You either buy the disc or pay for use of the effect.	*Simple digital editing:* Software is available for most home computers to handle simple cut-and-paste edits.	*"Fire sale":* Some stations have holes in their schedules that force them to offer super-cheap airtime—usually at times when no one is listening anyway.
Original music: Either a "buy-out" for unlimited exclusive use (usually more expensive) or residuals based on how, where, and when it's used.	*Nonunion talent:* A flat or negotiated fee based on how, where, and when it's used.	*Studio effects:* Created from electronic or physical items to imitate the real thing.	*Small recording studio:* If you need to mix multiple tracks with moderately sophisticated effects, you'll probably need professional equipment and/or expertise.	*Off-peak time:* Just about anytime other than drive time is going to be cheaper. People may have their radios on at work from 9 to 5, but only as background.

(Continued)

TABLE 12.3 **(Continued)**

Music	Voice Talent	Sound Effects	Editing	Media Costs
Popular music: You'll have to pay for the rights to use it. Price is negotiated based on how, where, and when it's used.	*Union talent: Scale* is a published rate based on how, where, and when union talent is used and may include residual and other fees. *Scale +* is added onto standard scale and also includes additional fees. *Celebrity talent:* Price is negotiated based on a number of factors, including how, where, and when it's used. Ultimately the talent weighs money vs. image.	*Location sound:* Take the recorder out in the field to get the real thing.	*Fully equipped audio studio:* For the best recording, mixing, and editing, you'll have to rely on trained audio engineers running state-of-the-art boards. Tell 'em what you want, then sit back and watch the magic.	*Drive time:* This is the highest-cost time, when people are captive in their cars going to and from work. Drive-time costs can be 10 times higher than costs for other day parts.

It takes talent to cast talent

As Luke Sullivan says: "Casting is everything. In radio, the voice-over you choose is the star, the wardrobe, the set design, everything all rolled into one. It's the most important decision you make during production."[3]

Where to start: When you're a beginning writer, the list of people who can and will help you is rather limited. Let's see: There's you, your roommate, your significant other, and the crazy guy who works the late shift at the Quickie Mart. Not much of a choice, is it? Just for timing and testing purposes, any voice will do. But before you actually record the spot, think carefully about talent. Perhaps you can work with other beginning writers who are really into broadcast—people who work at the campus radio station or broadcast students. Check out your school's drama department. Those trained actors could be natural voice-over talents. If you're looking for the proverbial man on the street, take your recorder down the street and find him. The point is, don't take the easy way out and record your friends the night before a radio assignment is due.

In the real world, when you work for a shop that's able to pay talent, your possibilities open up considerably. If you're not familiar with specific voice talent, you can get demo CDs from talent agencies. Most voice talents are capable of many different styles, so listen carefully. If you're looking for multiple voices, you don't have to select them from the same agency or even have them work face-to-face, thanks to the beauty of digital editing.

WORDS OF WISDOM

"Production is where 90 percent of all radio spots fail."

—LUKE SULLIVAN[4]

When you pick your talent, depending on the budget, you may want to hold an audition, especially if you have to sell the client. Many voice talents will do free auditions with your copy. You don't even have to be there. You'll listen to a phone patch and they'll send you the MP3 via e-mail. It's a great way for a lot of people to listen to a lot of voices. (Beware of selecting talent by committee, though.)

Spend some time considering the voice talent. Even if you just need a straight announcer, there are many styles. Some sound "authoritative"; others are warm and friendly, with "a smile in their voice." The casting of character talent is especially critical. Be very specific about the voice tone, inflection, accent, and timing. You might need to write casting specs to help the talent agent find the perfect voice.

Keep a file of voices you'd like to use for future commercials. However, don't lock yourself into the voice *du jour*—you know, the guy who's suddenly doing every commercial on the air. No matter how great you think your commercial is, it will start to sound like all the others.

Timing is everything

Beginning writers sometimes have a hard time with the immutable time constraints of radio. They write beautiful 45-second spots and can't cut them down to 30s. Or they pack in a lot of useless filler to stretch them to 60s.

How to make your creativity fit? One way is count the words. If you have a 60-second straight announcer commercial, you should have between 130 and 160 words. As you approach that 160-word limit, your announcer is likely to talk faster, so the whole spot seems frantic and poorly planned. A 30-second announcer spot should be between 60 and 75 words. The announcer will thank you if your word count runs a little on the short side.

The best way to make your spot fit is to time it! Get a stopwatch (don't try to use your wristwatch) and read the commercial the way you'd like it delivered, leaving room for music and/or sound effects that will take time. If you time out at 60 seconds, it's too long—because nine times out of ten, you'll read it faster than a professional. Try to give the announcer and producer a few precious seconds to play with.

Is This Funny?
(Comedy in Commercials)

Few topics are less humorous than a dissertation on comedy. If you are naturally funny, you don't have to be told how to make people laugh. If you're not gifted with a funny bone, chances are no textbook can tell you how to use humor effectively. However, most people can appreciate humor in advertising, even if they can't deliver it. After toiling to write a funny commercial, you may find that drama or music may be a better way to go. Or you may discover that you have a gift. You'll never know until you try.

So, what's funny? Comedienne Carol Burnett said, "Comedy is tragedy plus time."[5] Most comedic situations are about pain or the threat of pain—physical or mental. That pain can be as obvious as dropping a piano on a person's head or as subtle as a mildly embarrassing situation.

Rejection is one of our most powerful psychological fears. So being exposed as stupid, uncaring, socially inept, weak, uncool, or just different can be very painful. And even a threat of rejection brings that pain to the forefront. But it's only funny when it happens to someone else, and then you need some distance in time or space to minimize the tragic effect.

The following commercial is for a local sporting goods retailer in Michigan. This spot proves you don't have to be a big chain with a huge production budget to produce an award-winning commercial. It's also a good example of using pain as a comedic device.

Example: Pain as Comedy

CLIENT: *Gordo's Snowboard Store*

TITLE: *"Snow Down the Crack"*

MUSIC: GENTLE GUITAR INSTRUMENTAL IN AND UNDER

MEDIC: As a ski patrol emergency medic I've seen it all. And the thing that I encounter the most, year after year, is snow down the crack. This occurs when a snow boarder is sitting in the snow trying to get in or out of their bindings. In this position, snow easily gets in the back side of their pants, and in a matter of seconds, they get snow down the crack. Oftentimes, a victim, unable to bear the pain, will scream out, "I've got snow down my crack." It's so frustrating because there's nothing you can do. You just have to wait it out and hope for the best. The good news is it's completely avoidable . . . by simply going to Gordo's Snowboard Store in the Maple Hill Mall in Kalamazoo. You can buy external high back step-in bindings for only a hundred and forty nine dollars. So call Gordo at three-four-nine-eighty-three-twenty-eight, and see what he can do for you this winter. And bring an end to the senseless pain of snow down the crack.

When you're writing radio, first listen to a lot of commercials. Then, think about what makes them funny. We did, and we found some common threads in hundreds of funny radio commercials:

Be outrageous. While radio is theater of the mind, it can also be theater of the absurd. Stan Freberg was a master of using radio to turn the absurd into memorable commercials. To demonstrate the power of radio, one of his spots conjured up images of draining Lake Michigan and filling it with the world's largest ice cream sundae. The helicopter bringing in the giant cherry was the perfect way to top off the commercial.

Do something unexpected. Remember the "twist" in Chapter 4? That's what we're talking about here. You introduce a topic, sound effect, or musical cue, and then take the listener in an unexpected direction. You can also take a seemingly straight commercial out of the ordinary with twisted copy. The deeper you get into it, the more it twists. Avoid the trap of giving away so much that the listener is ahead of the twist. Sometimes the gimmick is too obvious. It's as if you're saying, "Here's the joke . . . get ready . . . here it is . . . the joke is coming . . . and bingo, here's the punch line you already knew." In the following example, you don't know what the grunting and groaning is all about until you're almost at the end.

Example: Sound Effects as Twist

CLIENT:	Whitney Farms Organic Fertilizer
TITLE:	"Giant Tomato"
SFX:	BIRDS CHIRPING/OUTDOOR SOUNDS
GARDENER:	(SERIES OF GRUNTS, GROANS AS IF SHE'S LIFTING SOMETHING VERY HEAVY) Ugggh! Oooooofffff! Aaaaaagh! (GRUNTS CONTINUE UNDER)
ANNCR:	We can't promise you wealth. We can't promise you romance. But if you feed your soil Whitney Farms natural organic fertilizer, we can promise you one thing . . .
GARDENER:	(GROANS COME UP) Aaaaaaaagh! Whoooooooooo!
ANNCR:	. . . the biggest, ripest tomatoes you've ever grown.
GARDENER:	(EXHAUSTED) I give up. This tomato is just too big.
ANNCR:	Whitney Farms natural plant foods. Maybe you really do have a green thumb. Available at garden centers everywhere.

Use detail. The combination of sound effects, music, and voice can provide a rich visual image. Radio can't provide detailed information about the product itself, but used the right way, details can make a commercial funnier and more memorable.

Example: Detail

CLIENT:	*Axe Deodorant body spray*
TITLE:	*"Cherry"*

SFX:	PHONE RINGING AS HEARD BY CALLER
OPERATOR:	(AUTOMATED ATTENDANT STYLE VOICE) Welcome to the Axe deodorant body spray automated ordering system. To choose the right scent of Axe, select the woman you wish to attract. For real women, press one, for blow up dolls, press two. If you are attracted to lunch meats or are calling from a rotary phone, please stay on the line.
SFX:	PHONE BUTTON TONE
OPERATOR:	You have chosen--real women. For American women, press one. For Icelandic—
SFX:	PHONE BUTTON TONE
OPERATOR:	For skimpy field hockey skirts, press one. For chocolate sauce bikini, press two.
SFX:	PHONE BUTTON TONE
OPERATOR:	Choose one special feature. Press one for double jointed. Press two for tongue that can tie cherry stem into knot.
SFX:	PHONE BUTTON TONE
OPERATOR:	You have selected—American woman—with Adam's apple—
SFX:	MULTIPLE PHONE BUTTON TONES
OPERATOR:	Correction—you have selected American woman—wearing skimpy field hockey skirts—with tongue that can tie cherry stem in knot. Your match is Apollo. Spray Axe Apollo under your arms and across your chest and soon you will--score. Enjoy the Axe effect.
ANNCR:	Axe deodorant body spray. Coming April Twenty-Fourth.

Combine extreme situations with realistic dialogue. Some of the funniest commercials feature the most outrageous situations but use downplayed dialogue. Some of the most annoying commercials are just the opposite. The example on the page opposite is a rare case of three-way dialogue that works beautifully. The casting, timing, unscripted expressions, overlapping of lines, and subtle sound effects combine to make an outstandingly well-produced and funny spot. There is no way to convey this spot in print. You have to hear it to appreciate it.

Comedic formulas

Some experts advise copywriters to avoid formulas. Others offer them as guidelines. Whichever direction you take, you should at least learn how to recognize

Example: Extreme Situations

CLIENT:	*Yahoo.com*
TITLE:	*"Substitute"*

SFX:	DOOR OPENS
KEVIN:	Mom? Dad? I'm home. Hey, who are you?
NEW KEVIN:	I'm Kevin. Who are you?
KEVIN:	Mom!
SFX:	FOOTSTEPS ENTER
MOM:	Kevin! Where have you been?
KEVIN:	I was in Europe, remember?
MOM:	Oh, that's right.
KEVIN:	Yeah--who's this guy?
MOM:	Oh, we hadn't heard from you in so long we got a new Kevin.
KEVIN:	You replaced me?
MOM:	Oh, don't be silly. New Kevin has a hairpiece.
NEW KEVIN:	You can tell?
MOM:	Uh huh.
NEW KEVIN:	Oh, look at the time, mom. I'm goin' on break.
KEVIN:	Break? Wait, wait. You're paying this guy to be me?
MOM:	Well, he is a really good Kevin.
NEW KEVIN:	Actually my name is Ron.
MOM:	He always lets us know where he is.
KEVIN:	Hey, what happened to all my trophies?
MOM:	Oh, we gave those away. They were giving New Kevin an inferiority complex.
NEW KEVIN:	You could tell that too? I love you mom.
MOM:	Ahhh!
KEVIN:	I love you, too.
MOM:	Yeah, yeah.
ANNCR:	Let 'em know you're still alive with Yahoo Mail. It's free, easy to use and you can access it anywhere, even Europe, Kevin. Yahoo Mail. Do you—Yahoo?
MUSIC:	Yahoo-ooooo (signature line)

some of the most commonly used comedic formulas, three of which are illustrated in Figure 12.2 on page 264.

Again, think about the commercials you find funny. Then analyze them for their structure. Chances are they will fit one of these three formulas. But keep in mind, it's not the formula that makes it funny, it's the content. Don't write a commercial to fit a formula. Instead, consider whether using some of the techniques in the formulas would make your commercial any better. If not, forget the formulas.

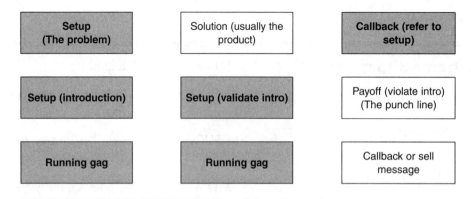

Figure 12.2. Common Comedic Formulas

Types of comedic devices

While we've made the case that comedy involves pain or the threat of pain—either physical or mental—that's not enough to construct a humorous commercial. The following are some of the most common comedic devices used:

- Normal person in comic environment
- Comic character
- Special powers (magic/supernatural)
- Ensemble cast—dialogue driven (tough for radio)
- Slapstick
- Satire (attack substance)
- Parody (attack style)

Comedy checklist

- Don't lose your humanity. Relate to other people. While you may be inflicting pain on another person, get the listener to say, "Hey that could be me."
- Does it sell the product or at least reinforce the brand name? Will people be able to remember the company that's risking its brand on your sense of humor?
- Are you making fun of the people who use the product or the product itself? You can have fun with a product or brand, but you can't make fun of it.
- Did you create a one-joke concept? Can your theme be extended throughout the campaign?
- Do you have the right talent to pull this off?
- Does anybody else get it besides you? If you have to explain why it's funny, it's probably not.

Do you really think this is funny?

Discuss the premise of your commercial with a friend who's totally unfamiliar with the concept. If you have to explain why it's funny, you've got problems. If other people see the humor in your premise, read the spot. If they fall over laughing, that's a good sign. But you still have to sell something, even if you have the funniest commercial ever written. Blending in a message, establishing a brand, and still having an entertaining concept is the ultimate challenge. As Luke Sullivan says, "Being funny isn't enough, you must have an idea."[6]

Above all, you have to be honest with yourself. If you're not funny, face it and move on. Most people aren't funny, and those who are funny are probably a little screwed up in other parts of their lives. If after all your introspection you find that your sense of humor just doesn't come out in your commercials, try a new tactic.

A Word or Two About Dialogue

Some writers forget how real people actually talk. In their effort to cram the client's name and as many features and benefits as they can into 60 seconds, they turn ordinary folks into aliens from Planet Schlock. Here are the three biggest problems with radio dialogue.

Problem: Consumers become salespeople

You've heard commercials where neighbors, friends, spouses, or whatever launch into spirited and highly detailed conversations about laundry detergent, motor oil, or feminine protection products. It usually starts with one person stating a problem. The other person comes up with a solution with lots of reasons why it's so great. The first person is instantly convinced and relieved that the problem is finally solved.

- *Solution: Use the announcer for the sales pitch.* Let the characters talk like real people and let the announcer do the heavy lifting. People expect an announcer to deliver a sales message, whether it comes at the end or separates the dialogue.

- *Solution: Use an "authority" figure.* This can be a salesclerk, doctor, teacher, or anyone who is expected to know more about the product than the consumer. While the authority may be better suited to pitch the product, you still need to keep the conversation real.

Problem: Stilted language

Even if characters don't become salespersons, many radio commercial conversations sound awfully fake. In reality, people interrupt, step on each other's lines, slur words, say "uhh" and "umm," and are generally pretty inarticulate.

- *Solution: Write the way people talk and allow ad-libs.* If you listen closely to some of the best dialogue commercials, you'll notice people hesitate, overlap each other's lines, use contractions and sentence fragments, and, in general, talk the way real people talk. To do this right, you need the right talent and the flexibility to let them ad-lib. Give the talent the general premise and have them improvise as they rehearse. The announcer can be as polished and articulate as you like, but keep him or her out of the conversation.

- *Solution: Read it out loud.* This is good advice for any radio spot, but especially for dialogue. Read both parts yourself or have someone else read with you. If it sounds phony, keep trying until it sounds natural.

Problem: Gaps in conversation

Slight pauses between lines ruin many dialogue commercials. In real conversations, most people don't wait a beat before answering a question or responding in a conversation. Sometimes they take a dramatic pause, but more often they start answering while the other person is finishing, so that words overlap. Dialogue should not be a tennis match where everything happens on either one side or the other.

- *Solution: Compress.* Whether you do it in the actual recording or in editing, look for ways to close the gaps. That does not mean you want the spot to be one breathless run-on sentence, but go for good natural flow—in other words, the way real people talk.

The following spot does a good job with natural-sounding dialogue and separates the sales message from the conversation.

Example: Realistic Dialogue

CLIENT: *Minnesota Dept. of Public Health*

TITLE: *"Classified Ad"*

SFX: PHONE RINGS

CLERK: Good afternoon, classified ads.

EXEC: Ummm. I wanted to put an ad in the paper.

CLERK: What would you like your ad to say?

EXEC: I want it to read--lost--tobacco executive's soul.

CLERK: (PAUSE) What?

EXEC: Uh. I've lost my soul.

CLERK: What will the rest of the ad say? Just give me the general—

EXEC: The general gist of it is--I'm a corporate tobacco executive and responsible for promotions like giving free cigarettes away to kids during recess in other countries--stuff like that.

CLERK: Oh my goodness.

EXEC: I'm sorry. I missed what you said there.

CLERK: I just--the idea of somebody giving away free cigarettes at recess--it almost knocked me off my chair.

EXEC: Yeah, so I guess you can understand why I feel emptiness inside.

CLERK: Uh-huh. So are you planning on staying with the company?

EXEC: Well, yeah, I mean, it pays really well.

ANNCR: Corporate tobacco knows that if they don't get you hooked before age 18 they probably never will.

Give Me a Jingle

As we discussed in Chapter 6, music can tie a whole campaign together with one catchy jingle. Some copywriters hate jingles more than the people who have to listen to them. Luke Sullivan advises not to resort to using a jingle.[7] But as Jewler and Drewniany note: "Not everyone agrees with that. . . . A catchy jingle can make a lasting impression in our minds. For example, there's a good chance you can sing the lyrics to 'Oh I wish I were an Oscar Meyer wiener'"[9] (at least if you're over 30).

Most original music is not all that memorable, or if it is, it's remembered for being annoying. Maybe that's why you hear so many recycled popular songs in commercials today. As Bendinger notes, "One of the best ways to connect with a target is by playing the music he or she was listening to at about the age of 14."[10] It's all about resonance.

Tips and Techniques

- If you forget every other tip, remember this: *Keep it simple.* One main idea per commercial. Preferably one main idea per campaign.

- *Get to the point early and stick with it.*

- *Identify SFX creatively, don't label them.* For example, if you use a thunderstorm effect, don't have a character say, "Uh-oh. Looks like we're having a thunderstorm." Use something like "Looks like we're stuck inside all day."

- *Use music to evoke a place or mood.* For example, mariachi music in the background says you're in Mexico so the announcer doesn't have to.

- *Consider using no music or SFX.* Depending on the voice talent, the power of the spoken word can be very compelling.

- *Repeat the client's name.* Some people say you should do this at least three times, more if it's retail. We don't have a magic formula, but if you do repeat the brand or store name several times, make sure it flows naturally and isn't forced.

- *Capture attention early.* The first five seconds are critical, whether it's drama, comedy, or music.

- *Use voices to create visuals.* For example, an old lady with soft, kind voice is a loving grandma. The same voice that's harsh is a witch. Remember the importance of casting specs.

- *Try building your commercial around a sound.* For example, one commercial was about putting a cat in a clothes dryer, and in the background for the whole commercial you heard a mewing cat and a thumping dryer.

- *Create extreme pictures with words.* Don't be afraid to have an outrageous premise.

- *Give yourself time.* Try to do a 60-second spot rather than 30. You have more time to do creative things because your announcer has more time to make the sales pitch.

- *Make sure your copy is tailored to the market.* A hip-hop music bed is not going to work on a classic hits station.

- *Use action verbs.* Go back to Chapter 8 and review the section on power writing. The same principles apply to radio.

- *Avoid using numbers,* especially long phone numbers and street addresses. Instead, feature the Web site where all that information and more is available.

- *Help your announcer.* Keep the copy a little shorter and watch for hard-to-pronounce words and awkward phrasing. Listen to the announcer if he or she has suggestions for making it sound better.

- *Don't overdo the SFX.* Just because you have a 10-disc library, you don't have use it all.

- *Trust your audio engineer.* When he or she says it's not working, find out why. The engineer has produced a lot more spots than you have.

- *Don't use any other brand name unless the ad is a cross-promotion.* It's hard enough for people to remember your brand name.

- *Write the whole spot and read it out loud* before you decide it's not going to work.

- *Go easy on the hype.* Watch out for ad jargon (advertising-ese).

Example: It's All Bad!

CLIENT: *Bike Barn*

TITLE: *"Spring Bike Sale"*

MUSIC: HEAVY METAL ROCK IN AND UNDER

BOB: Hey dude. Where'd you get that great bike?

DIRK: Oh hi Bob. I got it at the new Bike Barn. That great new bike shop in town.

BOB: No way! They got a great new bike shop in town?

DIRK: Way. They got lots of great bikes like Trek, Schwinn, Fuji and Cannondale.

BOB: No way!

DIRK: Way. And their friendly staff knows how to set you up with the bike that's just right for you. Plus their service is second to none. If you need a bike you gotta go to the new Bike Barn.

BOB: That sounds like a great idea, dude. I better get over to the Bike Barn to get my new bike. Where are they?

DIRK: Right off Highway Forty-Four in Auburn. Well I got to break in this new bike. Catch you later dude.

BOB: Later dude.

MUSIC: OUT

ANNCR: Get your new bike at the New Bike Barn. Highway Forty-Four and Eighty-Fourth Street in Auburn. Or call Two-Oh-Two-Three-Four Five-Nine-Eight-Seven-Nine or visit w-w-w-bike barn-dot com.

Tip for novice writers:
Don't write like one

Radio is tough to write and even tougher to produce. When given a radio assignment, most students and beginning copywriters fall into the familiarity trap. They write commercials that sound just like the ones they grew up with, plus they write them using dialogue and situations they think are tailored to young adults. See the example on page 268. That was an actual commercial. Only the client's name has been changed to prevent a lawsuit. That spot actually sounded worse than it reads. First, there's no hook. Nothing catches the listener's attention. Next, the dialogue is lame. Not only is it entirely banal, you've got the characters acting like announcers. Real people don't talk that way. Third, in a feeble attempt to get in tune with the audience, this commercial, written by college students for college students, reads like some 60-year-old's attempt to be hip. Finally, although you can't tell by reading it, the voices, music choice, sound quality, mixing, and all the other production values were atrocious.

WORDS OF WISDOM

"Quick, do something good on radio before someone catches on and makes it as difficult as it is everywhere else."

—ED MCCABE[11]

Example: A Campaign Hero

CLIENT: *Bud Light*

TITLE: *"Hawaiian Shirt Pattern Designer"*

ANNCR: Bud Light presents . . . Real American heroes.

SINGER: Real American heroes.

ANNCR: Today we salute you, Mr. Hawaiian shirt pattern designer.

SINGER: Mr. Hawaiian shirt pattern designer.

ANNCR: You provide us with colorful lounge wear capable of hiding any stain we can dish out.

SINGER: Gettin' sloppy.

ANNCR: Who else can create flowered shirts that are still so unmistakably masculine?

SINGER: Oh!

ANNCR: A single shirt that matches every pair of pants we own and really sets off a white belt.

SINGER: Lookin' good now.

ANNCR: Sure, women say they hate them. But deep inside they're all swooning for the big kahuna.

SINGERS: Ooohhh kahuna.

ANNCR: So crack open a cold Bud Light Mr. Hawaiian shirt pattern designer. Your shirts may not be made in Hawaii, but Taiwan is an island too.

SINGER: Mr. Hawaiian shirt pattern designer.

ANNCR: Bud Light. St. Louis, Missouri.

Radio and Campaigns

Radio commercials and campaigns are made for each other. Because radio can be relatively inexpensive, you can run a lot of commercials to support the campaign theme. Using the same music and voice talent burns that brand name into the listener's mind. When a concept works, it can run for years, as long as it keeps working. The Motel 6 campaign with Tom Bodett mentioned in the War Story below is a prime example. Another good example is Bud Light's "Real American Heroes," which evolved into "Real Men of Genius." Both have used the same basic format for years, winning awards and reinforcing an already strong brand. In the example on page 269, notice how many times the Bud Light name is worked into the spot as well as the seamless interaction of announcer, singers, and music.

WAR STORY:

SEEING THE LIGHT AT MOTEL 6

In 1986, David Fowler, creative director from the Richards Group advertising agency in Dallas, was listening to NPR on his pickup truck radio. He chanced upon a folksy monologue by a humorist named Tom Bodett and thought the style might work for his clients. As it turned out, Richards Group was the agency for Motel 6, a no-frills motel chain that was getting lost in the clutter of competitive advertising. Fowler convinced Motel 6 that Bodett's laid-back style and dry humor would work. And did it ever! After 12 years of award-winning commercials featuring Bodett, Motel 6 revenues grew 283%. In the first series of spots, Bodett had a little extra time, so he threw in the line "We'll leave the light on for you," which

became one of the all-time great radio taglines. Here's one from a series of spots:

MUSIC: (MOTEL 6 THEME UNDER THROUGHOUT)

TOM: Hi, Tom Bodett for Motel Six. You know Blind Cave Salamanders never see the light. Course, they also end up with transparent skin and dark holes instead of eyeballs—plus they're kind of sticky. And you don't want that do ya? So c'mon and see the light, save your money and your skin. Call One-Eight Hundred-Four-Motel-Six, and we'll leave the light on for you.[12]

Where to Find the Best Radio Commercials

The Radio Advertising Bureau posts a great Web site (rab.com) loaded with resources. It's also one of the sponsors of the Radio-Mercury Awards, which honor the radio spots of the year in several categories. Looking back at the past several years of Mercury winners, we've noticed the following trends:

- Extreme situations
- Mock testimonials
- Off-color humor (to some people)

- Realistic dialogue
- Catchy music

Check out the Radio-Mercury Awards Web site (radiomercuryawards.com) and decide for yourself.

Who's Who?

Stan Freberg—Stan Freberg fathered "abnormal" or comic advertising in the late 1950s through the 1970s. His spoofs of Madison Avenue on his CBS radio show convinced Howard Gossage to use Freberg's warped sense of humor for real commercials. His ads "that don't take themselves so damn seriously" won awards and sold Contadina tomato paste, Pacific Airlines, Chun King foods, Jeno's pizza, Sunsweet prunes, and Heinz Great American soups. Freberg established, and exploited, advertising's fun potential.[13]

Dick Orkin—Dick Orkin first broke into radio with syndicated comedy serials such as "Chicken Man" and "The Tooth Fairy." With his distinctive voice and off-the-wall sense of humor, it wasn't long before Orkin was in high demand to write and produce comedy radio spots. Through his partnership with Bert Bertis, Orkin won scores of awards for his radio commercials. Later, he cofounded the famous Radio Ranch in Hollywood. In 2002, Orkin was inducted into the NAB Radio Hall of Fame.

Notes

[1] A. Jerome Jewler and Bonnie Drewniany, *Creative Strategy in Advertising,* 7th ed. (Belmont, CA: Wadsworth, 2001), 158.

[2] Dick Orkin, president of the Radio Ranch in Los Angeles, California, in an audio clip (track 19) available at the Radio Marketing Bureau's Web site page advertising the CD *Radio Renaissance,* http://www.rmb.ca/asp/creative-radiorenaissance.asp (accessed July 5, 2005).

[3] Luke Sullivan, *Hey Whipple, Squeeze This: A Guide to Creating Great Ads* (New York: John Wiley, 1998), 142.

[4] Ibid., 145.

[5] Quote from QuoteWorld Web site, http://quoteworld.org/author.php?thetext=Carol+Burnett (accessed July 5, 2005).

[6] Sullivan, *Hey Whipple,* 132.

[7] Sullivan, *Hey Whipple,* 139.

[8] Quoted in Jewler and Drewniany, *Creative Strategy in Advertising,* 168.

[9] Jewler and Drewniany, *Creative Strategy in Advertising,* 160.

[10] Bruce Bendinger, *The Copy Workshop Workbook* (Chicago: Copy Workshop, 2002), 279.

[11] Quoted in Sullivan, *Hey Whipple,* 139.

[12] Quoted in Jewler and Drewniany, *Creative Strategy in Advertising,* 172.

[13] See *Advertising Age*'s "Web Version of the 1999 'Advertising Century' Report," 1999, http://www.adage.com/century (accessed July 5, 2005).

Television

When most of us decided to become advertising practitioners, there was one prime reason—television. Television offers the glamour of show business plus the impact to make or break a brand virtually overnight. Creating a major TV ad campaign not only lets millions of people see your work, it may also shape pop culture for years. As Luke Sullivan says, "Great print can make you famous. Great TV makes you rich."[1] No other medium does a better job of delivering those three motivators—Fame, Fortune, and Fun.

As television matured, advertisers learned to stretch the creative boundaries of the medium, often influencing pop culture. Considered by many as the best TV commercial of all time, Apple's "1984" showed a bleak monocolor totalitarian world (IBM computers) that was liberated by a colorful woman with a sledgehammer (Apple Macintosh).

13.1. Howdy Doody, 1954. In the early days, characters in programs often read the commercials.

13.2. Apple Macintosh, "1984."

13.3. With interactive TV, you can use your remote to shop online, place a bet, make phone calls, download music, send an e-mail, . . . and even watch television programs.

Why Television?

In addition to the above considerations, television offers other creative advantages:

- *Impact:* With the exception of the Internet, no other medium does a better job of combining sight and sound.

- *Universal access:* Almost everyone has a TV. Most American homes have three or more sets. TV is the great disseminator of pop culture.

- *Huge audience:* More than 140 million people watch the Super Bowl each year. But even the lowest-rated late-night show attracts millions of viewers.

- *Segmentation (programming, time of day, cable/satellite):* Specialized programming makes it easier to deliver highly targeted commercials.

- *Integrated marketing:* TV is ideal to promote a promotional campaign. It's perfect for cross-promotion. With advancing technology, TV and the Internet are becoming a seamless entertainment and information medium.

Why Not?

- *Time limits:* Except for some cable channels and infomercials, you are limited to 10-, 15-, 30-, 60-, and 120-second messages. While it's easier to show and tell on TV than on radio, you still have to make every second count.

- *High cost:* Some Web sites offer cheap TV commercial production for as low as $1,299 a spot, but according to the American Association of Advertising Agencies (AAAA), the average production cost is more than $330,000, with director's fees alone averaging more than $21,000.[2] And the cost of airtime has started another upward spiral after a couple of flat years.

- *TV commercials are the most intrusive form of advertising:* Everyone says they hate commercial interruptions. It's when people go to the bathroom, get a snack, or just groan about "another stupid commercial."

- *Technology might stifle creativity:* Some people spend a lot of money on TiVo just to avoid commercials. If an advertiser insists on per-inquiry TV to increase efficiency, chances are the spot will be very hard sell, with lots of phone numbers and Web site titles in it.

Creative Challenges and Opportunities for Beginning Writers

A storyboard is not a rough layout. It's much more difficult to convey your idea for a TV commercial than it is for print. A storyboard or script is only a very rough approximation of the finished spot. A storyboard "is only a map of the TV spot. It simply refers to it, the way a map of Colorado refers to the state itself."[3]

You don't have the equipment or talent. While production of video programs has been made much easier, most students and novice writers still don't have the facilities to produce good-quality commercials. The same scarcity of professional talent we described in the radio chapter makes TV production doubly difficult for beginners.

You don't have the experience. The production of good TV requires knowledge of the medium, including what's possible for a given budget as well as experience of what works and what doesn't. Very few beginning writers have that knowledge and experience.

You watch TV without really seeing it. Young people write what they know. And they know TV better than any other advertising. George Felton cites research that shows a 20-year-old in the United States has already seen 800,000 TV commercials.[4] Why is that a problem? Because most beginning writers fall back on the tried-and-true commercial concepts they grew up with. As with radio, they tend to make the actors into pitchmen, use forced advertising jargon, create unrealistic situations, and in general don't break out of the established commercial molds.

It won't fit in your book. TV does not work very well in most portfolios. Usually, your best TV spot is worse than the weakest print ad. Besides, most portfolios are better suited for flat print work, not broadcast. Even scripts and storyboards interrupt the visual flow of most books.

How to solve those special problems

Concepting. Really study the commercials you see. What makes them funny? Why do you remember them? Then analyze them—how do they handle transitions between scenes, camera angles, lighting, sound effects, music, titles—everything that makes a commercial great? The rest of this chapter offers some ways you can analyze commercials and, we hope, use that information to create your own great commercials.

You may have to limit your concepts to spots you can shoot and produce. You probably can't visit or even simulate some exotic location, indoor shoots present problems without proper lighting, you're not going to have blue-screen or other computer-generated effects, and you're not going to get a movie star for your spot. Be realistic about what you can accomplish if you're planning to actually produce the spot.

Conveying your concept. Computers can help you produce professional-looking print ads. They can also help you put together a good-looking storyboard. Stock photos and scanned images work well in storyboards. If you're showing a progression of scenes using the same characters, you'll probably need to shoot your own still photography. Whether you use photos or marker renderings (hand-drawn art), make sure your storyboard captures the key frames to convey the concept of the commercial.

Talent. You can solve the problem of finding talent the same way as with radio. If you just need bodies, it's pretty easy. If you need someone who can really act, you might want to work with theater students or someone with professional experience.

Postproduction. Since the advent of camcorders, shooting a commercial has not been the problem. The trick has been editing. Now with iMovies, Premiere, and other video editing software, it's easier than ever to make your own commercials. It still takes time, talent, and experience to know how to do it right. Make sure you have the patience to review every frame of your commercial for days until you get it right. The temptation is to say, "It's good enough!" but it usually never is. Also keep in mind, even the slickest production can't save a weak concept.

Showing it. If you have a great TV commercial, you can import it into a PowerPoint or Flash program. You can also mix in your print and radio samples to make a multimedia portfolio. If you don't have produced spots, you can put storyboards in your book, but they have to be as good as your print work.

Technology and Trends That Affect the Creative Process

New technology is changing TV as we know it. Some of these technological advances will also change the way you will develop commercials. The following are some of the current trends.

Interactive TV (ITV). The lines between computers and television continue to blur. Some folks say interactive television will make it all commercially viable. With ITV, when a little **i** pops up during a commercial, a viewer has the option to accept or decline a special offer, such as a coupon or merchandise incentive. "You can play along with game shows, vote in live polls, learn trivia tidbits, get game stats and purchase items just by pushing a button on your remote control."[5] With interactive TV, a subscriber clicks on a banner ad that reveals a full-screen, full-motion commercial for the advertiser's product and is then taken to that company's Web site. Advertisers submit their current banner ads and TV commercials, and the interactive network converts their materials to the advertising product. Some current click-to-video advertisers are Ford, Maytag, Hewlett-Packard, and Volvo Cars of North America.[6]

Digital video recorders (DVRs). With a DVR and a service like TiVo, you can record a program on a hard drive rather than analog tape. According to TiVo, you can find and record by title, actor, team, or keyword. You can also control live TV by pausing, rewinding, and using the slo-mo and instant replay features. TiVo makes it much easier to skip over the boring parts of programs, like the ads. In fact, some TiVo subscribers use the service mainly to screen out commercials.

Per-inquiry TV (PITV). With a PITV campaign, the client only pays for the inquiries it receives. PITV firms pay TV stations to produce a direct response for an advertised product or service. Instead of paying the media's airtime costs, the firm prepays for a specified number of inquiries that the media agrees to generate. PITV commercials are specifically tailored for the clients' brands, products, and services while they also encourage viewers to call a toll-free number or visit a Web site for additional information. In most cases, PITV works better for stimulating immediate demand than for building brand image over time.

High-definition TV (HDTV). Promised for years, broadcast HDTV has become a reality in most markets, delivering up to five times the resolution of traditional TV. We won't get into technical issues such as numbers of pixels, compression, and bandwidth, but from a creative standpoint, you should know the screen size is wider and narrower than traditional TV, which may affect your concept. Also, since the detail approximates what's achievable in 35mm film, viewers will see every tiny detail in your commercial. If you're using an aging actor or actress, you might need better makeup people.

Television Commercial Directions and Terms

Terms you'll need to know (for more, see the appendix):

Angle shot   A camera shot taken from any position except straight on.

Crawl   Graphics (usually copy) move slowly across the screen.

CU (close-up)   A camera shot that shows the actor's head and shoulders.

Cut   An instantaneous transition from one scene to another.

Dissolve   A fade-in of a new scene over the fade-out of a previous one.

Dolly (in or out)   A slow frame change accomplished by moving the camera forward or backward.

DP (director of photography)   The person in charge of the shoot.

ECU (extreme close-up)   Shows the actor's face or specific features such as hands. Can also be used to show a package or product feature.

Follow shot   The camera follows the movement of the subject without moving itself.

Full shot   The actors and entire background are all in the scene. Also called a *wide shot* or *cover shot*.

Grip   The person who does most of the grunt work on a commercial shoot.

In   The point at which a sound effect or musical segment is inserted. The effect stays "in" unless otherwise directed.

In and under   The effect or music is introduced and layered under other sound effects or voices.

Jump cut   A cut to the same scene without a change of angle or framing.

MCU (medium close-up)   The actor is shown from the waist up.

Mortise   Placing another image in part of the frame. Also called frame-in-frame.

MS (medium shot)   The actor's whole body is in the frame.

OC (on-camera)   The person on-camera is speaking. Also called *SYNC*.

Open   The opening scene of the commercial. The first thing a viewer sees.

Out   The point at which a sound effect or musical segment is deleted.

Pan (left or right)   The camera moves from a set position along a horizontal arc.

Pan with   The camera moves at the same speed as a moving person or object so the person or object stays in the center of the frame as it moves.

Scroll   Graphics or titles move up the screen.

SFX   Sound effects.

Slo-mo   Slow motion.

Still   Photograph or nonanimated art. Also referred to as a *slide*.

Super   Graphics or titles are superimposed over the background images.

SYNC   You can see the person on camera as he or she is talking.

Tilt (up or down)   Camera movement from a set position along a vertical arc.

Truck   A slow frame change accomplished by moving the camera sideways.

Voice-over (VO)   The actor is speaking off-camera. You cannot see the actor speak.

Whip shot   A fast pan shot blurring the action on the screen.

Wipe   An optical effect in which a line or object appears to move across the screen, revealing a new picture. A *page wipe* simulates turning a page to reveal a new scene "under" the previous scene. A *clock wipe* reveals a new scene in clockwise motion.

Zoom (in or out)   A fast move in or out accomplished with a zoom lens on a fixed camera.

How to Show Your Concept

You have several ways to convey your concept for a TV commercial. The one you use depends on the stage of development and conceptual ability of the person approving it.

Script

This is the most basic and often the only method you need to show your concept. It's written in the same way as a radio script, except there is a column on

Client: VISA

Product: Visa Card

Title: "Torino"

Time: 30 seconds

VIDEO	AUDIO
OPEN ON SLIDE OF VISA LOGO	
CUT TO WIDE SHOT OF TORCHBEARER RUNNING ON ROAD, MOUNTAINS IN BACKGROUND	MUSIC: UP AND UNDER ANNCR: (VO) In the Italian Alps . . .
CUT TO MS BOBSLED RACE STARTING	SFX: CROWD SOUNDS ANNCR: (VO) . . . is a place where people will go faster . . .
CUT TO MS SKI JUMPER, ZOOM TO WIDE SHOT	SFX: CROWD SOUNDS ANNCR: (VO) . . . and fly farther than ever before.
SLOW DISSOLVE TO WIDE SHOT CALGARY SKYLINE AT SUNSET	ANNCR: (VO) The place is Torino, home of the 2006 Winter Olympics . . .
CUT TO MS GIANT SLALOM SKIER	SFX: SKIING SOUNDS ANNCR: (VO) . . . where a lifetime of work will be measured in seconds.
CUT TO MCU GOALIE STOPPING PUCK	SFX: HOCKEY SOUNDS, CROWD SOUNDS ANNCR: (VO) But if you go, bring your camera . . .
DISSOLVE TO ECU HAND HOLDING VISA CARD OVER TICKETS	ANNCR: (VO) . . . and your Visa card . . .
CUT TO WIDE SHOT OF LUGE RACER ON TRACK	SFX: LUGE RACING ANNCR: (VO) . . . because the Olympics don't take place all the time . . .
CUT TO MCU FIGURE SKATER	ANNCR: (VO) . . . and this time . . .
CUT TO CU SPEED SKATER	SFX: SPEED SKATING, CROWD ANNCR: (VO) . . . they don't take American Express.
DISSOLVE TO MS SKATER AFTER RACE	MUSIC: OUT
SUPER TITLE: It's everywhere you want to be.®	ANNCR: (VO) Visa. It's everywhere you want to be.
VISA CARD/OLYMPIC SYMBOL	

the left for VIDEO that lines up with the AUDIO column on the right. As with radio, the directions and effects are in CAPS.

Storyboard

For more detail, you can create a storyboard, with pictures of key scenes from beginning to end. The audio and video directions are under each frame. A storyboard can be sketched by hand or created with photography. Storyboards really help the producer, director of photography, and postproduction crew, as well as the client, understand the spot.

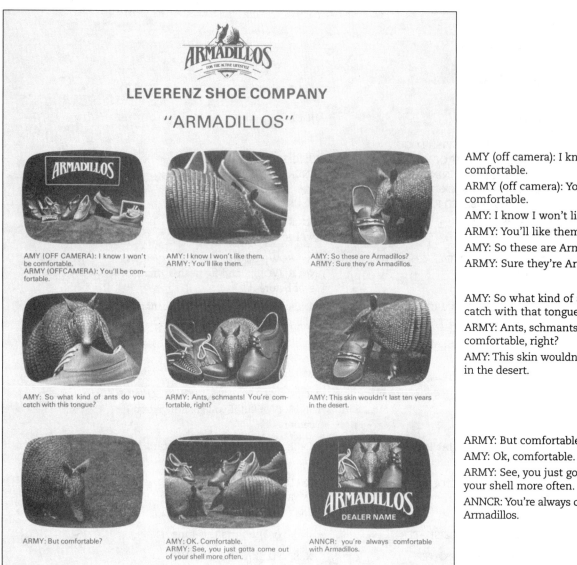

LEVERENZ SHOE COMPANY

"ARMADILLOS"

AMY (OFF CAMERA): I know I won't be comfortable.
ARMY (OFFCAMERA): You'll be comfortable.

AMY: I know I won't like them.
ARMY: You'll like them.

AMY: So these are Armadillos?
ARMY: Sure they're Armadillos.

AMY: So what kind of ants do you catch with this tongue?

ARMY: Ants, schmants! You're comfortable, right?

AMY: This skin wouldn't last ten years in the desert.

ARMY: But comfortable?

AMY: OK. Comfortable.
ARMY: See, you just gotta come out of your shell more often.

ANNCR: you're always comfortable with Armadillos.

AMY (off camera): I know I won't be comfortable.
ARMY (off camera): You'll be comfortable.
AMY: I know I won't like them.
ARMY: You'll like them.
AMY: So these are Armadillos?
ARMY: Sure they're Armadillos.

AMY: So what kind of ants do you catch with that tongue?
ARMY: Ants, schmants! You're comfortable, right?
AMY: This skin wouldn't last ten years in the desert.

ARMY: But comfortable?
AMY: Ok, comfortable.
ARMY: See, you just gotta come out of your shell more often.
ANNCR: You're always comfortable with Armadillos.

13.4. Storyboard.

13.5. A key frame from the famous (some would say infamous) Miller "Catfight" commercial.

Key frame

This should be the most memorable scene of a commercial. It may be the "punch line" or "payoff frame" in a spot. Think of the single image that a newspaper or magazine might use to describe a TV commercial and you'll know what we mean.

Scenario

This is a brief description of the commercial concept. Typically, it starts with "We open on a . . ." The scenario can describe scenes in more detail and can also work in marketing and creative strategies.

CLIENT: *Pepsi*

TITLE: *"Bear Identity Theft"*

TIME: *30 second*

In this spot, we show a twist on identity theft, with thirsty bears looking for Pepsi to drink with the food they ransack from a cabin. We open on a medium wide shot of two large grizzly bears roaming through the snowy wilderness. They break into a log cabin looking for food. Rummaging through the cabin, they raid the refrigerator, open a cooler, and find an empty Pepsi bottle. Cut to an extreme close-up of the bear's paws grabbing sunglasses and cartons of Pepsi. Cut to a clerk at mini-mart cash register who asks for ID. The bear gives him a check and driver's license showing a bearded man who looks sort of like a bear. Cut to a medium close-up of the bear in a cap, sunglasses, and flannel shirt. The clerk nods and says OK. Cut to a wide shot of the bears running away from the store, on their hind legs, carrying the Pepsi. The announcer says, "Nothing goes better with leftovers than an ice-cold Pepsi. It's the cola." Super the Pepsi logo.

13.6.

Production Considerations

Why TV is so expensive

Clients who are new to television advertising wonder why it costs so much to produce a spot. To estimate the cost of a major production accurately, it's necessary to consider all the expenses, including the following:

- Preproduction
- Location scouting and related travel
- Studio rental
- Sets and set construction
- On-location site
- Equipment rental
- Videotape and videotape duplication
- Production crew
- Producer, director, writer, and creative fees
- On-camera talent
- Fees for insurance, shooting permits, contingencies, etc.
- Online and offline editing
- Advertising, promotion, and publicity
- Research and follow-up
- Materials, supplies, and miscellaneous expenses

Plus the agency has to make some money. So there are costs for casting, vendor sourcing, scriptwriting, production supervision, and, of course, media commissions.

Shot selection

13.7. Wide or long shot.

13.8. Medium shot.

13.9. Close-up.

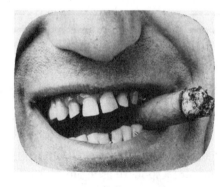

13.10. Extreme close-up.

Talent can make a commercial or break the bank

Most on-camera and voice talent in major productions belong to either the Screen Actors Guild (SAG) or the American Federation of Television and Radio Artists (AFTRA). Working with union talent means you will pay a set session fee. Depending on where and how the spot airs, you will pay for the principals' reuse or residual fees. Rates differ for network and spot market

Transitions between scenes

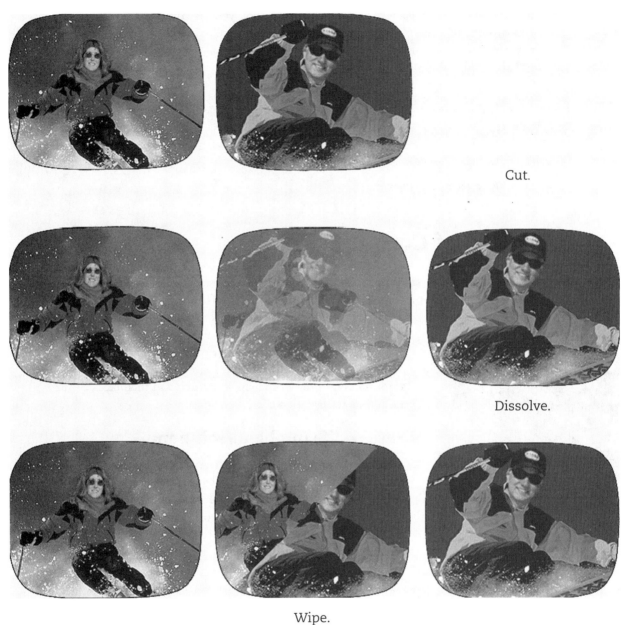

Cut.

Dissolve.

Wipe.

13.11.

use—the more markets, the higher the fee, and you'll pay residuals for each cycle the ad runs. Add to that agent fees (10%) plus pension and welfare fees (12.1%), and you're looking at a lot of expenses. Keep in mind, all these fees are for scale, the lowest price tier. Celebrity talent is negotiated with agents and lawyers and can range from nothing (if the talent really believes in a cause) to millions per spot.

Ways to cut costs

As a beginning writer, you're not concerned about the high cost of TV production. However, if you want to actually produce a spot, you may quickly see that your wonderfully complex concept can't be done as you've written it. Here are a few ways you can get more into your spot with less effort and less money:

- Reduce the number of actors on-camera.

- Reduce the number of scenes.

- Use a stock photo or stock video to show a specific location.

- Use stills rather than shooting new video.

- *Keep the concept simple.*

Styles of Commercials

Describing different kinds of commercials won't make you creative. However, if you start to analyze the various styles of commercials, you'll see a pattern. You may begin to understand why they are moving, or funny, or hard selling. A lot of the styles blend together, so you may have a celebrity in a problem/solution format or a vignette with a strong musical theme. We don't offer the following list of styles as formulas, but rather to help you watch and then create commercials with a critical eye and ear.

13.12. What's in your wallet? Not this guy if you use a Capital One card.

Slice of life (problem/solution)

In the so-called Golden Age of Television, many commercials featured a slice of life (which was more often a parallel universe) in which a frustrated housewife couldn't solve some kind of cleaning problem. A helpful neighbor, announcer, or cartoon character told her about the advertised product and, like magic, her problems were over.

Today's commercials are not quite that cheesy, but they're still using problem/solution formats. For example, a Capital One campaign showed some of the threats of high credit card fees, represented by marauding Vikings, Mongol hordes, abominable snowmen, and avalanches. The solution was provided by flashing the Capital One bank card, which made the threat disappear, usually by attacking a noncardholder.

Demonstration

It didn't take advertisers long to figure out that TV is a natural to show a product being used. Especially one that moves. Demonstrations have also been very effective in showing what a product can do. One of the best demonstrations was a wordless commercial for Cheer that showed a funny little guy putting a dirty napkin into a clear bowl of cold water, adding Cheer, swirling it all around, and pulling out a clean napkin. The following arc various types of demonstrations:

- Straight product in use

- Torture test

- Comparison to competitor

- Before and after

- Whimsical demonstration—exaggerated situation

13.13. Some SUVs are shown driving in winter. But this one is shown plowing under the snow. In fact, we never even see the product, only the exaggerated benefit. Only in a Jeep.

13.14. Citibank produced a great series of commercials about identity theft. In each one we hear the voice of the thief while we see the victim. This one talks about a stolen card used to buy a leather bustier that "lifts and separates."

Spokesperson (testimonial)

Ordinary person. You don't have to be famous to pitch a product, although if you do it right, you might become famous.

Character actor. Some brands are associated with a single character, created just to promote that brand. For example, Mr. Goodwrench used Stephen Colbert as a kind of annoying reporter to get the inside scoop on service technicians.

Corporate spokesperson. Whether it's the CEO or an actor, some companies use the same person to represent them on TV. Richard Branson is the personification of Virgin airlines, records, cell phones, and whatever else he's selling today. In the 1980s Chrysler chairman Lee Iacocca effectively convinced millions to bail out his company and buy his cars and came back in 2005 to hype discounts. Dave Thomas, the founder of Wendy's, brought a warm, lighthearted touch to hundreds of his commercials. Several years after his death, Wendy's still used his image in commercials.

13.15. In early 2004, Pepsi ran a joint promotion with iTunes. The TV spot featured real people who were caught illegally downloading music. The background music—"I fought the law and the law won."

13.16. The lonely Maytag repairman finally retired. Seems he didn't have much to do anyway.

13.17. Following Cliff Freeman's breakthrough "Where's the Beef?" commercials, Dave Thomas's folksy commercials help propel Wendy's to the number three spot among burger chains.

Celebrity. This is perhaps the oldest technique in television advertising, borrowed from decades of use in print and radio. Whether it's a sports figure, cartoon character, or movie star, a celebrity can gain immediate attention and shine some of his or her limelight on the product. As we discussed previously, make sure the celebrity has some logical connection with the product, even if it's indirect. For example, Willie Nelson did commercials for H&R Block. What's the connection? Years ago Willie had some problems with the IRS. A good tax preparer could have helped him stay out of trouble with the feds.

13.18. Yo, it's you, Yao. Although his English was minimal, some funny wordplay worked well for this spot for Visa.

13.19. He used to be a real stiff, but now Frank is pitching Osteo Bi-Flex for arthritis pain.

13.20. Two superstars combine their special powers in a series of ads for American Express. In addition to TV, Jerry Seinfeld and Superman have teamed up on the Amex Web site.

13.21. In the four years of using the duck, Aflac has seen sales increase 20%, and consumer awareness has shot to 90% from 12%. The duck is more popular than Ronald McDonald and the Energizer Bunny.[7]

Story line

This may be a mini-movie, with a beginning, middle, and end. And like many movies, the ending may be ambiguous, as in the 2003 Volkswagen Jetta commercial. The commercial opens with a bride preparing for her big day. The action cuts to a frantic young man in his Jetta, obviously in a hurry. He is becoming more frantic and frustrated with each delay. Finally, he arrives at the church and bursts in to the surprise of the bride . . . and the groom. You're led to believe that he's late for his own wedding. The ending is left open. Does he stop the wedding? Does the bride run away with him? And, some might ask, what does any of this have to go with a Volkswagen Jetta?

13.22. The viewer is led to believe that the frantic Jetta driver is late for his own wedding. But as he arrives at the church we see something else. It's not only a good story line, but it also has an enigmatic twist.

Vignettes

These are usually made from a series of short clips that are strung together, usually with a strong musical track to hold it all together. Vignettes can be used to show different people using the same product or a variety of products with the same brand. A good example of using vignettes is the global "i'm lovin' it" campaign for McDonald's. The initial spots showed a wide variety of ages and races. An example of different products for the same brand would be some Honda corporate spots that show cars, lawn mowers, motorcycles, generators, and all the other products that Honda makes.

13.23. TBWA\Chiat\Day created this "musical" commercial for Nike with vignettes of NBA stars bouncing a ball in time with the music.

Musical

It's hard to separate music as a category, since it's so integral to commercials today. However, we'll consider this as a unique type when music is the dominant factor of the commercial. Over the years, Pepsi has been a leader in musical spots, merging brand awareness, celebrity talent, and lots of singing and dancing. Some of the top names associated with the brand are Michael Jackson, Madonna, and Britney Spears, none of whom are strangers to controversy.

Creative Techniques for TV Commercials

The MTV influence

In the early 1980s, MTV changed the way we look at music. The hottest directors experimented with a new genre and did things never before tried in television or movies. Music videos have kept evolving since then and still represent cutting-edge creativity. The lessons learned have been applied to commercials, first on MTV and later in mass-market programming. The following are some of the creative techniques pioneered by music videos that have found their way into mainstream commercials:

WORDS OF WISDOM

"Much of the messy advertising you see on television today is the product of committees. Committees can criticize advertisements, but they should never be allowed to create them."

—David Ogilvy[8]

- Hyperkinetic images

- Quick, jerky cuts rather than slow, sensible segues

- Short, disjointed vignettes rather than whole stories

- Tightly cropped, partial images instead of whole ones

- Combinations of live action, animation, typography, film speeds, and film quality

Other trends in commercial concepts

Edginess. The availability of adult content on cable and the general erosion of old taboos have led to an increasingly raunchy attitude in television commercials. American commercials are still pretty tame compared to European television, but it's not uncommon to see ads for previously restricted products and themes. Until the 1980s, you couldn't show a woman wearing a bra in a commercial. Compare that to the Victoria's Secret spots of today. While the backlash to Janet Jackson's Super Bowl flashing created talk about toning down content, don't expect that to have any long-term effect on commercials.

Market segmentation. The availability of cable and satellite in more areas lets programmers fine-tune their content for specific markets. Likewise with commercials. You'll see commercials on some cable channels you'd never see on broadcast TV.

Brand image versus content. Attention spans are shorter and people are bombarded with more messages than ever. So a lot of TV advertisers have given up trying to provide any features and benefits. Instead they focus on the brand character—the product and the people who use it.

The power of sports celebrities. Certain athletes transcend their sports and become household names, even to people who have never seen them play. Michael Jordan was a prime example in the 1980s and 1990s. Tiger Woods has that potential as long as he keeps winning.

Humor in TV

The commercials people remember most seem to be the funny ones. Probably 9 out of the top 10 Super Bowl spots each year are funny. As with radio, don't start out to create a funny television spot. You may have a good joke, but it's not a commercial unless it sells something. Luke Sullivan offers some excellent advice for writers who want to make their mark with humorous TV spots: "Don't set out to be funny. Set out to be interesting. I find it interesting that the Clios had a category called Best Use of Humor. And curiously, no Best Use of Seriousness."[9]

What Makes It Funny?

Some of the funniest commercials include at least some of the following elements:

- *The unexpected:* Throw in a surprise ending, a twist, a zinger, something they don't see coming. Many times that unexpected ending involves pain—physical or mental.

- *Pain/risk of pain:* The old formula of tragedy plus time works for TV even better than radio because you can show it as well as tell it.

- *Exaggeration:* Making things extremely bigger, smaller, faster, or slower than expected can be humorous. So can giving animals human traits or vice versa. Extreme behavior can be funny too.

What Makes It Good?

You need more than a funny situation to make a good commercial. Many humorous ideas fall flat because of poor production. The best humorous commercials need all three of the following:

- *Good direction:* The writer and director need to know when to use a wide shot, when to zoom in, how many scenes to use, and all the other intangibles that make a good spot great.

- *Attention to detail:* Do the sets look real? Are little kids dressed like real children? Are the props accurate for the time frame depicted? Little things mean a lot, and they show.

13.24. What makes it funny? This commercial for travel insurance has all three elements—the unexpected, pain, and exaggeration. (The wife's attempt to vacuum crumbs off her sloppy husband's chest has some disastrous results.)

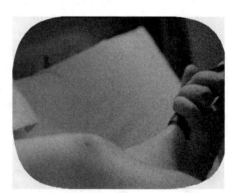

13.25. What makes it good? Attention to detail, good direction, the right talent, and tight editing. Plus, as you'll see in the following War Story, a good client and some fast thinking by the copywriter.

- *Talent/acting:* This is perhaps the most critical element. The same qualities that make a great comic actor different from a clown apply to commercials. Remember that with TV you can show subtle expressions and nuances in close-ups. You don't need the broad gestures of a stand-up comic or stage actor.

- *Editing:* Well-executed postproduction makes a huge difference. The timing and transition of scenes can turn a "cute" concept into a truly funny commercial.

WAR STORY:

THINKING ON YOUR FEET WHILE WORKING IN A VACUUM

Jeff Ericksen is a copywriter and creative director at BVK, one of the biggest agencies in the Midwest. In this story he tells how to turn a potential disaster into a great commercial:

Insurance is boring. Therefore, insurance advertising must be even worse. Not so. In creating a television campaign for Travel Guard Insurance we had the benefit of working with an incredibly insightful client who knew that when all others zig, you have to zag. They also understood that not having a huge media budget, their one campaign would have to do the work of ten. They wanted to stand out. Cool.

In doing research for the project we came across a number of very odd but real claims travelers had filed. This led us to the platform and copy line, "For the things you can't imagine when traveling, there's Travel Guard Insurance." With this as our starting point, we created even more bizarre scenarios in which Travel Guard could save a vacationer's day. One approved commercial had airport baggage handlers trying on people's clothes and "borrowing" items like toothbrushes to highlight baggage protection. Another spot featured a couple on a romantic bike ride in Italy. When the man's eye wanders to another woman, he ends up sailing over some bushes, showing the need for emergency medical coverage. But it's the third one that proved to be most interesting.

Here's the concept: a guy is using one of those vacuum packing systems to get ready for a trip. He notices the device's superior sucking power, so he

decides to put it down his pants. Cut to him doubled up on the floor as the paramedics come to take him away, thus showing the need for trip cancellation coverage. Funny . . . sure. Not a chance in hell it'll get approved . . . wrong. The client loved it. Sold.

Now the real fun begins. Two days before the shoot the director and I are in the hotel bar talking about some last-minute issues when we get a call. The vacuum spot has to die. Did some VP get cold feet? Were the People for the Ethical Treatment of Penises planning a boycott? Nope. It turns out legal discovered the underwriters of the insurance policy would not cover any self-inflicted wounds. So now what?

With locations picked, talent chosen, schedules made, and crew hired there was a lot set in stone and paid for. Never willing to give up, we looked at the hand we were dealt. We have a guy, a bedroom location, and a vacuum packer. Now here's where the lesson lies. . . . It seems the most successful people in advertising are the ones who can think on their feet, see opportunity in the face of disaster and always believe there's a solution.

In the end we created a spot where a wife was packing for a vacation while a lazy husband lies on a bed eating cheese puffs. Noticing the man with crumbs on his chest, the wife starts to vacuum them off. Unfortunately for him, yet hilarious for us, the hose gets stuck on his nipple, nearly ripping it off. The spot ends with the man in the hospital with a protective cone over his nipple, foolishly eating cheese puffs again, afraid his wife will notice.

Spot airs. Sales rise. Client is happy. All is right with the world.

Tips and Techniques

Aside from the general advice for humorous spots listed above, the following tips apply to nearly all commercials. These are offered as rules of thumb and not as hard-and-fast guidelines you must follow. However, experience shows that you can have a lot better results if you heed most of them when you are critiquing commercials.

- *Get immediate attention.* The first 3 to 10 seconds are critical. Make the first couple of seconds visually interesting.

- *Stick with one main idea.* Keep it simple. Don't try cramming more than 2–3 scenes per 10 seconds or more than 10 scenes per 30. If you're using vignettes, you might need a lot more.

- *Think about brand awareness.* Show the product and involve characters with it.

- *Use titles to reinforce key points.* But not so many that the viewer feels like he or she is reading the commercial.

- *Think visually.* Consider how you want to move within a scene, transition between scenes, change scenes.

- *Don't forget synergy.* Don't show what you're saying or say what you're showing.

- *Audio is still important.* Use music/SFX to describe place or mood.

- *Make every word count—count every word.* Rule of thumb is about 2 words/sec and about 60 words for a 30-second spot. That's less than radio.

- *Give the viewers some credit.* Let them complete the creative equation. Don't overexplain. They'll remember it better too.

- *Keep conversation real.* Dialogue should be natural, not forced. Let the announcer be the salesperson, if you have to have one.

- *Don't save it all for the ending.* A commercial should be entertaining through the whole spot. Don't have a sloppy buildup to a punch line.

- *Rely on your experts.* Your director, art director, lighting and sound technicians, and editor can make you look like a genius. Let them!

- *Think in campaigns.* Make your commercial compatible with, but not identical to, the other elements. It should not be a video version of the print ad. Think in terms of extending a concept without repeating the same idea in subsequent spots.

- *Study great commercials.* Look for style, camera angles, editing techniques, and so on. Understand what makes them great.

WORDS OF WISDOM

"Advertising has become MTV lazy. You know, sound bites, spectacular effects, great music—but no real idea. We forget the key to advertising effectiveness isn't technique, it's intelligence."

—HELAYNE SPIVAK[11]

TV and Global Campaigns

Because it delivers the highest impact, television is often the centerpiece of a campaign. The tagline and music theme are usually launched on TV and then carried over to print and radio. For multinational brands, the challenge is to create a striking brand image that appeals to people all over the world. In other words, creative globalization.

In late 2003, McDonald's rolled out their "i'm lovin' it" global campaign. They developed a slogan and images that were meant to be used everywhere they do business. The campaign was driven by television commercials that used vignettes, usually in urban settings—a 180-degree shift from the white suburban background of previous television ads. The spots featured popular artists such as Justin Timberlake and the now ubiquitous "Dah dah dah dah dah" jingle. Despite some critics' reviews, McDonald's credited the new campaign with helping turn their flagging business around.

About six months later, they launched a new series of commercials. According to Larry Light, McDonald's executive vice president and global chief marketing officer, "The new advertising . . . clearly demonstrates that our 'freedom within a framework' global marketing philosophy is working."[12] In a 2004 press release, McDonald's announced:

WORDS OF WISDOM

"You have only 30 seconds [in a TV commercial]. If you grab attention in the first frame with a visual surprise, you stand a better chance of holding the viewer. People screen out a lot of commercials because they open with something dull. . . . When you advertise fire-extinguishers, open with the fire."

—**DAVID OGILVY**[13]

> According to research conducted by McDonald's, in six-month's time total advertising awareness of the "i'm lovin' it" campaign in its top 10 countries has reached 86 percent overall, including 89 percent awareness among young adults and 87 percent among moms.
>
> "The popularity of 'i'm lovin' it' is remarkable," said Bill Lamar, Chief Marketing Officer, McDonald's USA. "It translates clearly and effectively to every language and culture and has really caught the attention of our customers here in the U.S."[14]

Of course McDonald's says they're lovin' the new TV campaign. But other people are not so sure. Bob Garfield in *Advertising Age* says McDonald's commercials "aren't meant to be advertising, so much as jingle-conveyance mechanisms—much as McDonald's fries convey oil and salt. Yeah, that's it: This stuff is to advertising as McDonald's is to food—a Crappy Meal that stays with you whether you like it or not."[15]

Political Commercials: TV Advertising at Its Best and Worst

Unfortunately, most political campaigns today launch full frontal assaults on their opponents with the subtlety of a sledgehammer. It wasn't always that way. In 1964,

PLAYING GOD

Mike Trinklein is a former professor at Idaho State University and a working professional film and television producer. His business partner in Boettcher/Trinklein Media, Steve Boettcher, has won five Emmys and has produced feature programs seen on NBC, CBS, PBS, and ESPN, to name a few. Mike relates a few of the crazy things that happened during one commercial shoot:

You shouldn't try to one-up Michelangelo. That's the lesson we learned from a commercial we produced for a national Lutheran church body. The spot required re-creating the famous Sistine Chapel painting where God reaches out to create Adam. Re-creating the Sistine Chapel with live actors was a bigger undertaking than we expected. For example, in the painting, God is floating in an impossible position (appropriately). So we were saddled with the task of building a system of pulleys and belts to twist, contort, and support our plus-sized thespian. When we finally got our actor into position and framed the close-up, we discovered an unexpected casting problem. He was of German ancestry. Don't misunderstand, I'm German—as is my business partner (and pretty much everyone else in greater Milwaukee). The problem is we Germans all have stubby fingers. Michelangelo painted God with long, elegant fingers. It just didn't match.

Nonetheless we pressed onward and shot the first reel of film. We had hired a new assistant cameraman who claimed he was an expert on the Arriflex movie camera we were using. With the first few hours of shooting under our belt, we handed this new hire the film magazine and asked him to remove the film and load another reel. A bit of explanation here: Reels of film are put in a light-tight magazine and then snapped onto the camera. After shooting, the exposed film must be removed in a 100% dark environment—or it's ruined. Typically, camera operators put the entire magazine in a black bag, zip it shut, then stick their hands in special holes which grip tight around their arms to prevent light leaking in. Then they feel their way around to change the film. It's tricky. Once you put your hands in the bag and open the magazine, it's the point of no return. You must get the film into a light-tight can or all is lost. If you pull your hands out in the middle of the operation, well—it's like a surgeon who has just cut out the bad heart. He can't say "oops" and ask for a "do-over."

Anyway, our guy stuck his hands in the bag and soon started contorting his face. Then he began sweating. More contorting. Then the impossible happened. He pulled his hands out of the bag! Light was pouring in. I rushed over to seal up the arm holes as fast as I could (apparently I thought I was faster than the speed of light). Before we could question (or pummel) the camera assistant, he slinked away and ran out the door—never to be seen again.

What did we learn? First, casting requires more than just looking at head shots. Second, hire experienced crew people—for film shoots (or heart transplants).

a single commercial for Lyndon Johnson ran only once but created a buzz that helped assure his election. In the commercial, as a little girl was picking petals from a daisy, the audio played a countdown to a nuclear missile launch, with the final scene showing an ominous mushroom cloud. The commercial from Doyle Dane Bernbach never mentioned his opponent but implied we'd all be safer with LBJ's finger on the nuclear trigger.

Twenty years later, Hal Riney and other creative superstars were enlisted to help reelect Ronald Reagan. Their "Morning in America" commercial featured soft-textured vignettes that portrayed an improving economy and renewed national pride. Positive images of new home owners, kids raising the flag, and newly married couples were backed by a rich musical score and Riney's own folksy yet authoritative voice. As a former commercial pitchman, Reagan knew the power of good advertising. With Riney's help, he got it—and a second term.

13.26. Although it ran only once, DDB's famous "Daisy Girl" spot for Lyndon Johnson is considered one of the great political ads of all time.

Checklist for Your TV Commercial

When you've finished your script or storyboard, let it rest, if you can. Then come back to it and check the following:

- Does the video tell the story without audio, and how well?
- Did you specify all the necessary directions? Could a director take your script and produce the spot?
- Do the audio and video complement each other, and are they correctly timed for each other?
- Are there too many scenes (can some be omitted)? Do you need more scenes?
- Have you identified the product well?
- Does your script win attention quickly and promise an honest benefit?
- Have you provided a strong visualization of the One Thing that will linger in the viewer's memory?

13.27. Hal Riney's series of commercials for Ronald Reagan portrayed an America that was safe, financially secure, and confident of its future.

- Could a competitive brand be substituted easily and fit well?
- Is it believable?
- Are you proud to say you wrote it?[16]

Presenting Your TV

OK, your spot meets all the requirements in the checklist. Now you're ready to show it to the boss. It's not a print ad that you can just hand in. You have to sell it. The following is a pretty good procedure for presenting a TV commercial, especially to a small group.

- If it's a stand-alone concept, review the creative strategy and state the One Thing you want to convey.

- State your main creative theme for the commercial.

- Describe main elements—music, effects, actors.

- Walk through the video portion; describe what's happening.

- Hit the key visual points, with emphasis on the key frame.

- Once the visual path is established, go back and read the copy.

- Summarize the action in a brief scenario.

Where to Find the Best TV Commercials

Most people consider the Super Bowl to be, well, the Super Bowl of advertising. To see the best spots from the past several years online, check out superbowl-ads.com, ifilm.com, adcritic.com, and usatoday.com. Many others sites feature good commercials as well. Most of the major awards programs post their TV winners on their Web sites, and you can see the year's best in the *Communication Arts Advertising Annual* in storyboard form.

Here are some trends we noticed over the past few Super Bowls. Depending on the viewer, they are either delightfully edgy or totally tasteless:

- *Animals:* It's a real zoo. We've seen a donkey, a zebra, horses, dogs, and chimps (and that's just Bud); other animals include bears, cats, lizards, ducks, turtles, monkeys, cheetahs, and wolves, to name a few.

- *Crude humor:* Some find this kind of slapstick humor hilarious. In 2004 some of the top-rated Super Bowl commercials featured a crotch-biting dog, a flatulent horse, an oversexed monkey, and unintentional bikini waxing (again, all for Budweiser).

- *Stereotypes:* Whether you are offended or find them humorously on target, many commercials (especially for beer) featured insensitive, clueless guys, beautiful but ditzy women, silly old people, and hip-hop culture images of African American males.

Who's Who?

Jay Chiat—Jay Chiat founded Chiat\Day, the agency that gained fame with its unique Apple Computer and Honda work. Chiat added research-based account planning, preached ideas rather than technique, pioneered (and later abandoned) the virtual office, utilized satellites and interactive video, helped found the Advertising Industry Emergency Fund, and drove his agency to $1 billion-plus in billings by the 1990s. C\D's "breakthrough" Apple Macintosh commercial, "1984"—created by art director Lee Clow, written by Steve Hayden, and directed by Ridley Scott—won every industry honor and award. Chiat also led efforts to bring minorities into advertising.[17]

Lee Clow—Lee Clow was the art director and creative force behind some of the most influential advertising of his generation. His work for Chiat\Day and later TBWA\Chiat\Day includes the famous Apple "1984" spot as well as the Taco Bell Chihuahua, Nike "Air Jordan," and the Energizer Bunny. Dan Wieden of Wieden + Kennedy, another creative giant of the modern era, described Clow this way: "Lee Clow's heart has been pumping this sorry industry full of inspiration for longer than most its practitioners have been alive. He is the real thing. He is indefatigable. I hate him."[18]

Cliff Freeman—Cliff Freeman used outside-the-box creative vision to build recognition and brand awareness. His agency's unique approach attracted the general media coverage that transformed advertising into popular icons. Freeman gained fame with the still-popular Mounds/Almond Joy candy bars ("Sometimes you feel like a nut . . . sometimes you don't") and Wendy's "Where's the Beef?" campaigns. His own agency, opened in 1987, brought forth Little Caesars's "Pizza! Pizza!" Freeman's distinctive work has brought him numerous major awards along with "most remembered" and "most popular" honors.[19]

Hal Riney—Hal Riney achieved creative excellence by getting people to like his clients. His work for Saturn cars, Bartles & James, President Reagan, and others celebrated a unique American spirit that was confident yet at times self-effacing. While working at the San Francisco office of Ogilvy & Mather, he was part of the First Tuesday team, which created ads for Ronald Reagan's reelection effort. In 1986, he took over the office, renaming it Hal Riney & Partners, and went on to mastermind GM's Saturn introduction with dazzling success.

Notes

[1] Luke Sullivan, *Hey Whipple, Squeeze This: A Guide to Creating Great Ads* (New York: John Wiley, 1998), 103.

[2] See the AAAA Web site at http://www.aaaa.org.

[3] George Felton, *Advertising: Concept and Copy* (Englewood Cliffs, NJ: Prentice Hall, 1993), 193.

[4] Ibid., 195.

[5] "The Future of Advertising," n.d., http://advertising.about.com/od/planning/a/interactivetv.htm (accessed July 6, 2005).

[6] Ibid.

[7] "Aflac Duck's Paddle to Stardom: Creativity on the Cheap," *Wall Street Journal,* July 30, 2004, B1.

[8] David Ogilvy, *Confessions of an Advertising Man* (New York: Ballantine, 1971), 70.

[9] Sullivan, *Hey Whipple,* 56.

[10] "Jeff Goodby's Creative Rules," from *Advertising Age,* January 29, 2001, available on the Center for Interactive Advertising Web site, http://www.ciadvertising.org/student_account/spring_02/adv382j/eoff/ultimategoodby/creative.html (accessed July 6, 2005).

[11] Quote from the Clio Awards Web site, http://www.clioawards.com/html/wsj/spivak.html (accessed January 10, 2005).

[12] Quoted in McDonald's Corporation, "McDonald's Rolls Out New "i'm loving' it" Commercials" (press release), May 12, 2004, http://www.media.mcdonalds.com/secured/news/pressreleases/2004/Press_Release05122004.html (accessed July 6, 2005).

[13] David Ogilvy, *Ogilvy on Advertising* (New York: Random House, 1985), 111.

[14] Ibid. Quoted in McDonald's Corporation, "McDonald's Rolls Out New "i'm loving' it" Commercials" (press release), May 12, 2004, http://www.media.mcdonalds.com/secured/news/pressreleases/2004/Press_Release05122004.html (accessed July 6, 2005).

[15] Bob Garfield, "Why McDonald's New Ads Are Like the Food," *Advertising Age,* May 17, 2004, http://www.adage.com/news.cms?newsId=40503 (accessed July 6, 2005).

[16] Phillip Ward Burton, *Advertising Copywriting* (Lincolnwood, IL: NTC Business Books, 1991), 258.

[17] "Jay Chiat," in "Top 100 People of the Century," *Advertising Age,* March 29, 1999, http:/www.adage.com/century/people010.html (accessed July 6, 2005).

[18] Quoted in Karen Lee, "The Lowdown on Lee Clow: Advertising's Chief Creative Maven of the Last Quarter Century," 2000, available on the Center for Interactive Advertising Web site, http://www.ciadvertising.org/student_account/ fall_00/adv382j/klee/Lee_Clow/Lee_Clow.htm (accessed July 6, 2005).

[19] "Cliff Freeman," in "Top 100 People of the Century," *Advertising Age,* March 29, 1999, http://www.adage.com/century/people098.html (accessed July 6, 2005).

Internet

I magine you're an advertising executive in the early 1940s and someone tells you about a wonderful new kind of technology that will revolutionize advertising as we know it. This new invention is called "television" and it's kind of like radio with pictures. After squinting at a blurry black-and-white image on a six-inch screen, you'd probably write it all off as an interesting little gimmick, but not worthy of any changes in your thinking about marketing or advertising.

That's where the Internet was about 10 years ago—a fascinating concept with a lot of possibilities, but not something any mainstream advertiser would consider. Then came commercialization of the Web and the dot-com revolution of the late 1990s. Almost everyone jumped in headfirst. The number of Web sites increased exponentially, and online advertising revenues skyrocketed. Almost as quickly as it boomed, a lot of it went bust by 2001.

Today, online advertising has achieved a solid comeback and appears to be headed for long-term, sustained growth. The reasons include the following:

- Advertisers now have realistic goals for online results.

- Online use is more measurable, so online advertising is more accountable.

- More consumers are online, and the number keeps growing.

- The growth of broadband makes rich content more practical and affordable.

- The Internet and television are merging to provide a seamless interactive entertainment and information medium.

- Advertisers have accepted that the Internet is a critical component of an Integrated Marketing Communications strategy and not an afterthought.

To understand why the Internet and online advertising are important to your career in marketing communications, look at these numbers:

- The number of Americans online reached 150 million in 2003, making it the fastest-growing medium ever.[1]

- The average Internet surfer spends 11.5 hours online a month.[2]

- The ratio of users is evenly split—50/50—between male and female.[3]

- Most of users are in the most desired age demographic: 76% are 18–49.[4]

- Many users, 44%, make more than $50,000 a year, and 71% have some college, a college degree, or an advanced degree.[5]

- Market penetration of high-speed connections has reached 40% and will reach 60–70% within two years.[6]

Why the Internet?

In addition to the statistics listed above, the Internet is desirable for a copywriter for several reasons:

- *It's always on.* It provides entertainment and information 24/7, anywhere in the world.

- *It's personal.* Perhaps the most personal medium ever.

- *It's dynamic.* The use of video and audio plus print generates more impact.

- *It's a Web.* Links provide easy access to marketing partners for co-op and cross-promotion opportunities.

- *It fits into a campaign.* You can make a Web site the flagship of your campaign and promote it with other media.

- *It's a data mine.* Whether visitors provide data consciously or you get it under the radar, you know who's visiting your site.

- *Almost everyone is connected.* The digital gap is closing fast. The Internet is not just for rich folks anymore. The proliferation of hot zones makes Internet access even more widespread.

Why Not?

Most of the following drawbacks will be solved in the near future through better technology. But right now, the Internet is not the final solution.

- You need a computer. While devices like cell phones are making Internet access even easier, the majority of consumers can't take advantage of rich media.

- Not everyone has broadband. A lot of customers still connect through dial-up.

- Attention spans are shrinking. People don't want to wait for rich media to load. That means you have to grab attention in a few seconds and hold it.

- Measurement is better than with traditional media, but still not as good.

- You are limited to the size of a computer screen. No matter how it's displayed, you still can't touch and feel it.

What happens 10 years from now?

The Internet started out as the Wild West—a lot of opportunity but no rules. While no one can predict exactly how the Internet will change, we can make a few reasonable assumptions. Dan Early, president of Ascedia, Inc., a major Web site development and interactive marketing firm, offers these predictions:

- Devices will change for advertising, providing more opportunity for video and text messages.

- Messaging formats will be richer.

- Online advertising will be mainstream and incorporated as part of general marketing communication strategy.

- Message delivery will have greater global impact.

- Agencies will need to integrate cross-platform communications to include the Web, and advertisers will seek strong one-stop shopping from their agencies.

- Technology will allow consumers to block ads even better than they can today.[8]

Terminology

The list of computer- and Internet-related terms is growing almost as fast as processor speeds. New terms and acronyms appear every day. Just when you think you've mastered the lingo, a totally new set of terms emerges. The following are a few key terms you should know:[9]

Ad clicks   The number of times users click on an ad banner.

Bandwidth   Usually measured in bits per seconds (or megabits per second), bandwidth defines how much information can be sent through a connection. The bigger the bandwidth, the faster you get data. Anything over 300 kilobytes per second (kps) is considered high speed. Traditional dial-up is 56 kps, ISDN is 128 kps, DSL can range from 192 kps to 1,500 kps, cable is 1,000 kps, T1 is 1,540 kps, and T3 ranges from 3,000 to 45,000 kps.

Button   An Internet ad smaller than a banner.

Click-through   The percentage of ad views that resulted in an ad click.

Content management system (CMS)   A CMS uses a central database as the repository of all text and images. Rather than building separate pages with dedicated content for each page, the CMS selects images and assembles the page. This is especially useful for sites that may use the same images but different translations of text. It also allows nontechnical people to access data and update portions of their Web sites without going back to a programmer.

Cost per click (CPC)   Used to price advertising online. Advertisers pay Internet publishers based on the number of clicks a specific ad banner gets. Rates usually range from 10 to 20 cents per click.

Hits   Every time a Web server sends a file to a browser it's recorded as a hit. This is actually a poor measurement of traffic because every item on the page is registered in the hit count. For example, if two graphics are on a page, three hits are recorded (one for each graphic and one for the page itself).

Impressions (or **ad views**)   The number of times an ad banner is downloaded and seen by visitors; corresponds to net impressions in traditional media. (*Note:* You can't tell if an ad was actually loaded, which has been a major problem in online advertising measurement.)

Interstitial ad   Appears in a separate browser window while you wait for a Web page to load. These usually contain larger graphics and more streaming presentations than standard banners. While they generate more impact, many users complain that they interrupt access to destination pages.

Jump page (or **splash page**)   Click on a banner and you're sent to the jump page, which can be used to promote special offers or measure the response to the ad.

Rich media   Advanced technology used in Internet ads, such as streaming video, interactive applets, and special effects. High bandwidths allow faster transfer rates, which allow rich media.

Site map   This can be shown as a schematic, organizational chart, or text outline. It organizes all the content of a site by subject, which not only helps developers and content providers but also helps viewers find information on the site.

Sponsorship   In the Internet world, sponsorship is when an advertiser pays to sponsor content, usually a section of a Web site or an e-mail newsletter. The sponsorship may include banners or buttons and possibly a tagline.

Streaming video   Basically, it's video on demand that's made possible by high-speed connections.

WORDS OF WISDOM

"The Web is a process, not a project. It's a living and breathing thing that requires a commitment. The Web affects all marketing communications and operations of a business."

—DAN EARLY[10]

Web Site Design

As Dan Early points out, Web development partners should generate ideas, not just take orders. That's why we're seeing a shift from the title and role of "Webmaster" to "interactive marketer."

As a copywriter you may be involved in Web site design in several ways, ranging from developing a total site to writing a headline for a banner ad. No matter what your role, you're probably going to need some help. Just as you can't produce a radio or TV commercial without some technical assistance, the same is true of Web site development. You may have the big picture for the site, but you need to know if your ideas are practical and affordable. For example, we had a client who wanted to introduce his home page for a university with a "hologram" of the university president, who would float onto the page (presumably like an angel) and introduce each section. We relied on our Web developers to tell the client that his vision was "interesting" but not technically feasible given his tiny budget.

Your role in Web site development begins with your understanding the client's wants and needs as well those of the customers. What does the client want to accomplish? Do they want an e-commerce component? Is this site only for information? Do they have opportunities to include video or 360-degree movies?

If you are Web savvy, you may be able to "walk the walk" as well as "talk the talk." But even if you're a budding Bill Gates, you may want to rely on some technical expertise from programmers and Web site designers. You should ask someone with more experience if your ideas are (a) technologically feasible, (b) affordable for your client's budget, and (c) original. Chances are your ideas were inspired by what you've already seen on the Internet.

Planning

When you determine what the client wants and what they can afford, you (and your Web site development partners) need to start laying out the Web site—not only the content, but also how it's all connected. To do this you need to do two things:

1. Identify the main sections and subsections of your Web site.

2. Link them all together in a diagram called a *site map*.

The site map is the master plan for the client, the creative team, and the technical team. It should identify all the main components of the site and out-line the logical navigation of the Web site. If your goal is to never be more than two clicks from anywhere on a site, you need to have a navigational path in mind. When someone starts playing "what if" games, get out the site map and see where those new ideas fit.

In many ways, a site map is like a company's organizational chart. There is a hierarchy, with the home page at the head and various major sections reporting to it. Each major section has subsections, and, as in a well-run company, a com-mon operating procedure (in Web terms, *universal navigation*) is the common thread through every section.

A site map for a traditional site with discrete pages will look differently from one for a site with a content management system. Rather than repeat pages in each section, a CMS site connects those sections to a central database.

Designing the site

When developing the look and feel of a Web site, you have two main considerations:

1. *Template:* the organization of elements and backgrounds

2. *Content:* what goes into the template

Janine Carlson, director of strategic marketing and principal at Icon Communications, points out the greatest challenge facing online marketers: "You can't be satisfied with getting a reaction. You have to spark an interaction. One is simply a split-second exchange with your audience. The other opens the door for an ongoing relationship. And that should be the goal for anyone working in advertising or marketing."[11]

Think campaigns. Your pages have to work individually and cumulatively. Make sure your design has the same look and feel throughout the Web site, even though many pages will have different functions. Most designers start with the most complicated page. If you can make that work, the simpler pages will be easier to lay out.

Design at different levels. Your site map is usually headed by the home page, which should set the tone for the whole site. Then the next level, or first-level, pages are used to hold content for the main sections. Each of these first-level pages has buttons or links to second-level pages, which in turn may have links to third-level pages, and on it goes. Your first-level and subsequent pages should have the same look and feel as the home page, even though they have different functions. This does not mean they have to look exactly the same, but consider font size, colors, graphic style, and all the other design elements that hold together a campaign.

Prioritize. To paraphrase Howard Gossage, people read what interests them, and sometimes it's a Web site. But there is a limit to what they are willing to read, and Web site visitors have short attention spans. There's just too much to see on any given site, so it's natural to jump around. It's critical to put the most important information up front and display it prominently. For example, if e-commerce is an important marketing activity, make sure the casual visitor is directed to that section of the site.

Don't forget the navigation. Think about how a visitor finds his or her way around your Web site. *Primary navigation* on a home page directs visitors to the major sections or first-level pages. *Secondary navigation* directs visitors to content inside a specific section. *Universal navigation* is on all pages—for example, links to the home page, "search," or "contact us."

Keep it simple. Besides overdesigning a Web site from a graphic standpoint, you can also overdo the technology. Too much movement is annoying and pulls readers away from the text. Don't use technology for its own sake. Instead, concentrate on strategy: what you want to accomplish, not how cool you can make it.

A Web page template is basically a table—a grid pattern (see Figure 14.1). This is how the page is built, but it doesn't always indicate that the final appearance has to be a perfectly symmetrical grid layout. The navigation sections can go anywhere on the page, and the main content can be anything that fits in the window.

Static or active?

Until fairly recently, most Web sites consisted of hard-coded *static* pages. Some sites have thousands of pages of text and visuals linked together. The content and templates are locked together on each page. This not only makes for more complicated navigation, it also produces a lot of redundancy, especially if text and

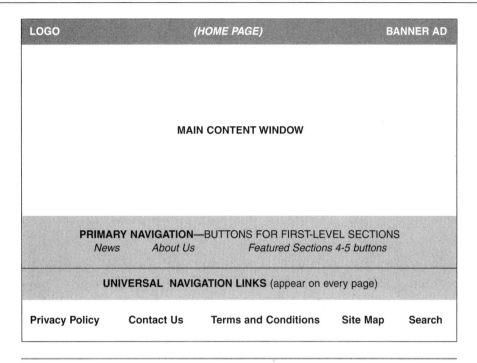

LOGO (HOME PAGE) BANNER AD

MAIN CONTENT WINDOW

PRIMARY NAVIGATION—BUTTONS FOR FIRST-LEVEL SECTIONS
News *About Us* *Featured Sections 4-5 buttons*

UNIVERSAL NAVIGATION LINKS (appear on every page)

Privacy Policy **Contact Us** **Terms and Conditions** **Site Map** **Search**

Figure 14.1. Web Page Template

graphic elements can be used on multiple pages. However, a static site makes sense for many reasons.

Active content uses a CMS with information in a central database. The content is separated from the template, which makes changing content much easier, since you are not changing the background.

Dan Early offers the guidelines listed in Table 14.1 for deciding on a static or active Web site design; he also notes that "successful sites find the balance between both active and static content."[12]

Writing the content

While most of the basic writing guidelines we've presented in Chapters 6, 7, and 8 apply, writing copy for Web sites also has its own set of rules. First of all, people do not like to read online—mainly because it's harder to read a screen than the printed page. Instead, they scan copy, much the same way they look at full-size newspapers. Bold headlines and pictures catch their eye and may draw them into the copy for more detail. In many cases, visitors print pages to read later rather than wade through a lot of text on-screen.

Here are a few tips for writing Web site content that people will want to read:

- *Call out key words.* Use boldface and/or color to highlight important words. But don't overdo it. You still want to make it easy to read.

- *Use subheads to break up major copy blocks.* Since people scan rather than read, make sure your subheads have some meaning related to the body copy. Don't be so cute with your subheads that visitors miss the point of your content.

TABLE 14.1   **When to Use Active and Static Content**

Use Active Content (database driven)	Use Static Content
When it provides value in site maintenance	When content does not change often
When content interacts with the user experience and specific applications	When content does not interact in other phases or applications
When content requires unique searching functions	When content is not always online
When you're publishing content for multiple locations as well as online	

- *Keep it simple.* Stick with one main idea per copy block or paragraph. Don't introduce too many new ideas per section. In some ways a text-heavy Web site is like a bad PowerPoint presentation—too much copy on two few slides.

- *Convert paragraphs to bullet points.* This is especially critical if you have several key features and/or benefits. Make it easy to see the key copy points.

- *Limit your text links.* The beauty of the Web is the ability to navigate within and to other sites. However, too many links interrupt your message. You don't want to hook readers and then lose them to another topic or even another Web site, which may take them to yet another destination.

- *Lead with the main message, then drill down.* This is the inverted-pyramid style of journalistic writing. You state your main message up front and gradually add more detail to support that message. Many times, the opening paragraph will be enough to hook the readers or at least get them to download the whole message.

- *Keep it short.* The rule of thumb is to use half as many words as you would for a comparable print piece. As we mentioned, people read text on-screen much more slowly than they read print.

- *Avoid scrolling.* If at all possible, try to keep a short block of text within a window, so readers don't have to scroll down. Since people don't like to read online, they really hate to take any special effort to read even more text.

Programming the site

As we mentioned earlier, various disciplines are involved in providing Web content and making it functional. While you, as a writer or designer, may not handle the actual programming, you still need to be aware of some technical issues that will affect the content you create.

Operating systems. While Web site content is usually created on a Mac or Windows operating system, some programming is done on Unix or Linux machines. A site created on one OS may look different on another, so it's important to test the site on every popular OS.

Screen size. The screen size is measured in pixels. The height of the image in pixels times the width gives you the screen's resolution. The most common screen resolutions are 640 × 480, 800 × 600, and 1,040 × 780. On the same size monitor, the lower the resolution, the larger the images. So what does this mean? When you create a template and the content, it has to fit the lowest common denominator, which rules out high-resolution photos and images larger than 640 × 480 for a 15-inch monitor.

Browser-safe colors. Your operating system may make millions of colors available, but only 216 are considered safe for all operating systems and browsers. Make sure you stick with this palette.

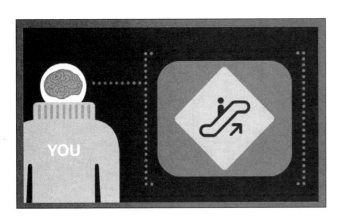

14.1. MINI Canada created a very simple-looking interactive personality test that matches the tone of their other advertising efforts.

Browser selection. Browsers make viewing a Web site possible. Two products account for more than 90% of the browser market: Microsoft Internet Explorer and Netscape, which is owned by America Online and Sun Microsystems. The other fraction is divided among a few minor players. While all browsers basically operate the same way, make sure your site works with older as well as recent versions of Netscape and IE.

Additional software requirements. One of the problems with rich-media Web sites is some visitors may not be able to see that really cool video. So you have to make additional software available through your site. These applications may include Flash, Real Media, QuickTime, Microsoft Media Player, or several others. Without installing them on their computers, your visitors may not be able to take advantage of all your site's functions.

Personal portals

In the past two or three years, much discussion has focused on the idea of personalized portals as the "latest thing" in Web technology. The scope of personalization and the impact it has on Web organization and costs vary widely. The personal portal is the access or interface layer to all the back-end services and technology for communicating to and from individuals.

A simplified personal portal can be an access point for user interfaces that lets users connect and interact with the functions and resources on the network they need most often. Many of these sites have names that begin with the word *My*, such as "My Yahoo" or "My eBay." The purpose is to give visitors the ability to customize the content they see and how it is displayed. If you produce a lot of new content regularly, a portal model may be a great way to serve the needs of a number of diverse Web audiences.

14.2. Budweiser keeps their very detailed site fresh with new videos, promotions, and music features. They also mention something about beer.

The more detailed the personal portal, the stronger the direct link to the visitor. However, some extremely complicated portals require a great deal of technology to make them functional. What's more, the nature and amount of personal information may be hard to obtain. People are becoming less willing to give out personal information over the Web. The amount of transcoding needed for the different user devices to intercommunicate across networks, combined with the various application processes, can be prohibitive in terms of labor, timing, and cost.

Online Branding

As online marketing becomes more integrated into a total marketing communication campaign, Web site development has to consider the impact on brand image. For most consumer brands, a Web presence enhances their brand identity and positive brand image. You can animate the logo, use Flash to add motion to the name, create interactive programs that involve the brand, and use cross-promotional opportunities on the Web. Dan Early offers some guidelines for online branding:

- *Identify the brand attributes that can be applied online.* What are the goals for the brand, and how can they be achieved on a Web site or in online advertising?

- *Be specific within the medium.* If you can, differentiate the brand using techniques specific to the Web. Don't use the same broad brush for all media.

- *Develop the branding strategy and apply it to the Web.* Consider messaging, experiences, interactions, relationships, the tone/voice.

- *Coordinate with all other marketing efforts.* No Web site is an island, regardless of the touch point.

- *Be willing to evolve.* Each medium, including the Internet, has its own abilities and attributes that evolve and change to support brand building online.[14]

WAR STORY:

MINI WANTS TO KNOW WHAT'S IN YOUR HEAD

MINI Canada commissioned a graphically simple interactive "inkblot" test (using MINI silhouettes) that was fun for the participants and useful to the client. Steve Mykolyn, creative director for TAXI, the design and development firm for the site, explains:

To put the audience in the right frame of mind, we began with a lengthy Flash intro using relaxing music and a soothing voice-over. We then showed four inkblots and asked them to choose from a list of responses (the first three of which were obviously nonsensical and the fourth was the only "real" one). Basically, a task that could've been accomplished in under five seconds took almost four minutes—our true source of pride on this project.

This is one of those projects that turned out so well that it seemed as if the clients were as concerned about padding our portfolios as we were. But that's really not the case. We worked hard to make sure the piece reflected the mischievous MINI branding and that it was entertaining enough for users to actually want to hear more from MINI. This piece met each of their initial objectives and has been a huge success from a viral standpoint. The program will continue with further e-mails to deliver specific info to users based on their choices of performance or value. It's currently being translated into at least three other languages for use in other countries; we're still waiting to see how they pull off the "MINI Driver" joke in Russian.[15]

Internet Advertising

While the Web site is a marketing communication element, it's also a media vehicle, the same as a magazine or newspaper. In other words, it conveys advertising. Online advertising hit a speed bump in 2001 after the dot-com collapse and aftermath of 9/11, but it has been rising steadily since then.

Online advertising has a different set of rules and terminology than print. Because ads can include audio and video, they can have a much greater impact than static print ads. As Internet media expert Bruce Morris states: "Bandwidth and serving power are the limiting factors for doing some really wacky and visually exciting advertising on the Internet. But you can pack quite a bit into a 468 × 60 Web banner if you use your imagination and some cool tools."[16]

TABLE 14.2   Standard Internet Ad Sizes

Type of Ad	Pixels
Full banner	468 × 60
Full banner with vertical navigation bar	392 × 72
Half banner	234 × 60
Leaderboard	728 × 600
Micro button	88 × 31
Skyscraper	120 × 600
Square button	125 × 125
Vertical banner	120 × 240

Banner ads

Banner ads have been the staple of Internet advertising. The most common size is 468 × 60 pixels, and they usually appear at the top of a commercial Web page. They are priced on a cost per thousand (CPM) page basis. Prices vary based on targeted sites and whether the banners are static or pop-up, ranging from $1 to $50 or more. According to Bruce Morris: "Banners are not terribly good for generating traffic but have a powerful branding effect. Matching site content to banner ad subjects can certainly increase their power."[17]

Rich-media banners

Newer technology lets you go beyond the ordinary banner ad to add drop-down boxes, sound-on mouse-overs, animated bits, and even interactive games. Rich-media banners and badges provide advertisers with ways to present additional content and interaction within traditional ad sizes, including 468 × 60, 120 × 240, and 125 × 125. Rich-media banners and badges offer a great deal of flexibility. According to studies, they can also lead to significant increases in response, brand perception, and recall—for instance, a Wired/Millward Brown Interactive study found a 340% increase in banner click rates when rich media was used.[18]

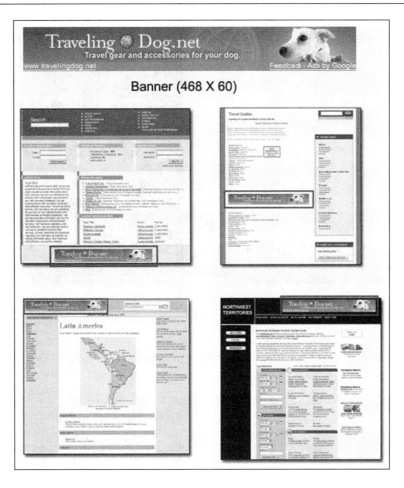

14.3. Banner ads can appear anywhere on a page, but most often they are at the top. While static banners are losing their impact, the potential for rich-media enhanced banners is huge.

14.4–14.5. Skyscraper left (120 × 600), skyscraper right.

14.6. Leaderboard ad (728 × 90).

14.7. In-line rectangular ad (300 × 250).

14.8. In-line ad, bottom-right text wrap.

Interstitial ads

Interstitial ads are whole-page ads or little boxes that pop up mysteriously after you click a link but before you see what you want to see. Interstitial ads run between the pages of a Web site, just like commercials run between parts of a TV program. Some play in the main browser window, while some play in new, smaller windows; some are precached, while some stream ad content as it plays; some provide the ability to create very rich ads, while some focus on smaller, faster-loading ads. Whatever the format, nearly all interstitial ads perform well, as measured by both click-through rates and brand recall.[19]

A recent study found that interstitials are nearly twice as effective as banner ads for increasing ad recall and conveying the advertiser's main message. Click-through rates are, on average, five times those of banner ads. However, consumers find interstitials twice as irritating as banners.[20]

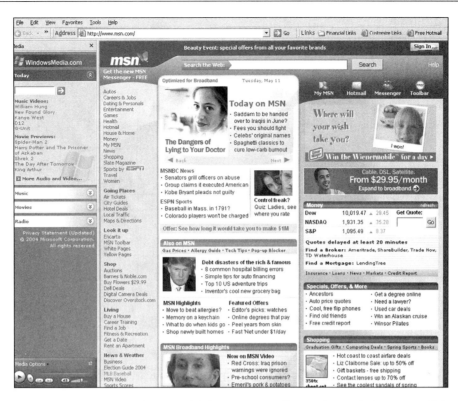

14.9. Oscar Mayer used a banner ad in browsers to call attention to their contest. Click on the ad (upper right), and it takes you to the contest detail page.

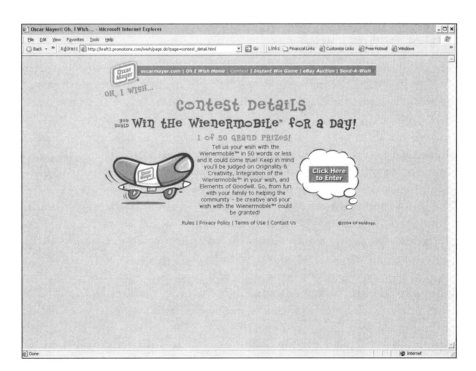

14.10. You may already be a wiener ... or at least you could have won the Wienermobile for a day in the Oscar Mayer interactive online contest.

14.11. This interstitial ad is 510 × 425 pixels and features a movie of the vehicle with links to product pages, an interactive contest, and the Mazda corporate site.

Out-of-banner ads

New technology has opened up a number of opportunities for moving images out of the traditional banner ad grid—literally out-of-the box thinking. Some of these ads fly across the page, appear from a tiny point to fill the screen, and develop into messages from the site visitor's cursor. Software programs such as Director and Flash provide the ability to embed interaction, video, and audio within the files. Shockwave is best suited for campaigns that want to utilize out-of-banner real estate, such as applets, trading cards, and games. Viral marketing and strong brand interaction are two of the key strengths of these ads.

A floating ad moves across the Web page that hosts the ad. Types of floating ads include DHTML sponsorships, in which advertising objects "fly" across the page on a preset course; cursor sponsorships, in which the cursor turns into an advertising image; and scrolling ads, in which an advertisement moves up and down the edge of a page as the user scrolls up and down. Floating ads give the advertiser and publisher the flexibility to achieve nearly any effect. However, as this is one of the more daring types of online advertising, advertising and content must be balanced on any given page. Floating ads (especially DHTML and cursors) are best run for short periods to create brand awareness—running them for longer periods can bring negative user feedback.[21]

14.12. This ad created in Flash is transparent and floats over the Web page. Three frames of a quick animation are shown above. The ad promoted *The Cat in the Hat* movie as well as a contest promoting Sierra Mist.

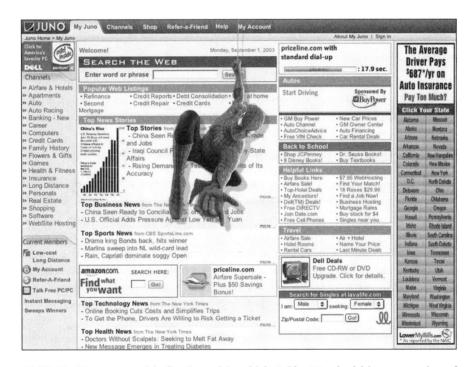

14.13. Blockbuster ran this floating ad in which Spider-Man had his own version of the web.

Digital coupons

Digital coupons give you special deals on the Web. Coupons may be tied to specific promotions or offer discounts on regular-priced merchandise. Like traditional coupons, they are incentives to buy now and allow advertisers to measure the response.

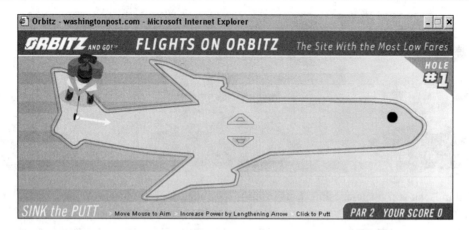

14.14. Orbitz has used interactive pop-ups with great results. Even people who find pop-ups annoying take time to play games such as "Dunk the Punk" and "Sink the Putt."

Sponsorships

If you sponsor a section of a site, you can integrate your advertising and branding elements a bit more unobtrusively than you can with just a banner at the top. You may get a bit more exposure and can get closer integration with content.[22]

Pay-per-click/pay-per-sale

In the early days of the Internet, nobody knew what they were getting because metrics (measurement standards) were so bad. That led to pay-per-click (PPC) and pay-per-sale (PPS) advertising. Basically, the advertiser is charged more money but is paying only for the people who see the ad or, in some cases, actually buy something online. However, there is very little benefit when a visitor clicks on a banner, sees it for a second, and then leaves. In a *Web Developer's Journal* article, Bruce Morris says: "These deals usually suck. Advertisers are probably better off forgoing such deals and keeping their site visitors hanging around longer."[23]

Paid ads in e-mail newsletters

There are hundreds of thousands of online newsletters. Many allow advertising at very modest fees. Click-through rates are in the 1–3% range.

Those annoying pop-ups

You know what they are. You hate them. So why do advertisers keep using them? For the same reason you get junk e-mail. It's a percentage game. Enough people will notice them, click on, and get stuck. MSN has banned pop-up advertising on their browsers. Others are following suit. Pop-ups, like junk e-mail, are being easily filtered.

Tips and Techniques

Dan Early offers these guidelines for creating online advertising:

- Recognize that this is the fastest-growing advertising segment: You need to understand it.

- Understand the technology as well as the marketing.

- Limit clutter (include fewer than 16 elements).

- Use larger ad sizes.

- Use larger brand logos.

- Use logo and product shots in the first frame.

- Add the human element (people like to see people).

- Build frequency.

- Stay up-to-date. Commit to it![24]

Other Online Marketing Communication

Search engine marketing

Search engine/keyword marketing is the hottest online advertising trend. It's inexpensive, with a very low cost per lead (as low as 29 cents versus almost $10 for direct mail).[25]

Optimization is one of the big buzzwords in interactive marketing today. It refers to getting your site moved closer to the top of a search protocol. So when you enter "NWBC" in Google for "Norwegian Wooden Boat Company" you don't get "Northwestern Business College." We won't get into a technical explanation of how this works. But there are a couple terms to know. The first is *META tags,* which tell Web *spiders* what information to grab for a search rather than having the spiders capture the first few sentences or paragraphs and deciding how to prioritize the content. With META tags you can have the robot display your Web page description the way you want it displayed (within reason, of course). You can also help people find your Web page by providing keywords that describe your page and help drive traffic to your Web site. Combining META tag indexing protocols with pay-per-click gives you more budget control to reach a very targeted audience.

Today the World Wide Web has more than three billion pages, so search engines must use very complex algorithms to sort out data quickly and accurately. When your site is competing with all the other sites in a search engine, getting top listing can be a challenge. The odds of top-of-the-page display increase dramatically when you pay for premium placement. Top placement spots in the keyword search are sold to the highest bidder or priced on a PPC basis.

You should consider search engine marketing as a form of advertising and/or a key component of your Web site development costs. The only way to guarantee a top listing is to pay for it! Make sure your Web design budget allows for paid search engine placement, including fees and the time required to design and maintain the search engine marketing program. In addition, you need to do the following:

- Put your most important and descriptive keywords first.
- Use the most popular keywords in the body text of the index page.
- Include popular keywords in the title tag, because that tag is indexed by every search engine.
- Don't repeat your keywords, or it will look like spam.
- Avoid doing the whole site in Flash. Embedding Flash allows the page to be indexed.
- Use META description and keyword tags on your index page.
- Use 25 words or fewer for keywords.

Buying keywords

To ensure top placement in search engines, you can buy keywords. Just so you know, all the good ones have already been sold or are very expensive. Most legitimate marketers buy words associated with their brand or product category. Others buy words that casual surfers are looking for (usually related to porn) to get their messages moved to the top of search lists.

Paid listing in portal sites

You pay a flat fee or a percentage of the sale to a portal site such as Google or Lycos. Your listing appears when a visitor selects a category.

Permission-based marketing

Permission-based marketing (PBM) supports one-to-one marketing efforts or correspondence campaigns. Unlike spam, permission based e-mail means that the recipient has voluntarily agreed to receive messages and announcements in order to be informed. A well-run PBM program can save a lot of time and money over producing printed materials and mailing them in a direct mail campaign. Recipients feel more in control, since any legitimate e-mail campaign allows the recipient to opt out. Opt-in mailing lists hit very specific demographics. These can be people who really want to see your ads because they're already customers or people who are considering your product versus the competition. In addition, if the recipient follows links within the e-mail, these can lead directly to a Web page where they can access additional information. It is also possible to keep track of recipients' responses using click-through tracking technology.

Rich mail

Rich mail allows graphics, video, and audio to be included in the e-mail message. When you open up a rich e-mail, your e-mail client automatically calls up your Internet connection and launches an HTML page in your browser. E-mail clients that are offline will invite you to click on the link when you have your Internet connection open again. If your e-mail client does not support graphics, you will receive the e-mail in text only.[26]

Opt-in e-mail ads

These are stand-alone ads, not attached to a regular e-mail message. These are sent to people who have volunteered to receive the information (they have "opted in").

Weblogs (blogs)

Weblogs are popular with the highly desirable, young, Internet-savvy demographic. Blogs are loosely structured, free-form sites that have so far not been commercialized extensively. A recent study of 17,159 blog site visitors found 61% are over the age of 30 and 40% have household incomes of $90,000 or above—clearly not an audience that advertisers should ignore.[27]

The popularity of blogs has drawn the attention of marketers, sometimes with less-than-stellar results. Dr. Pepper showered teen bloggers with gifts and indoctrinated them on how to blog its new Raging Cow beverage. The plot backfired, with a well-publicized boycott and global media covering the debacle.[28]

Nike, on the other hand, made no secret of its commercial intent with the "Art of Speed" on the gawker.com blog. Nike commissioned 15 talented young filmmakers to interpret the idea of speed. Over the course of 20 days, this

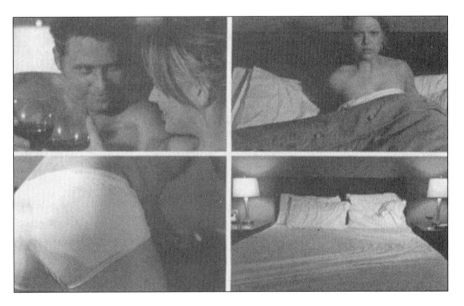

14.15. This "commercial" for Tide with Bleach shows rather graphically how stained tighty whities can kill the mood. While not officially commissioned by Procter & Gamble, the fake spot was seen by thousands through viral marketing and Weblog appearances.

14.16. Blogs are by nature anticommercial. However, when you create content that interests the viewers, such as Nike's "Art of Speed" film series, viewers accept it as more than a crude attempt to co-opt the blog culture.

Weblog introduced these innovative directors, their short films, and the digital technology behind the scenes. Nike is not the only net-savvy marketer taking advantage of the blog upswing. Microsoft has MSN Blogbot and Oxygen Media launched a blog to promote its *Good Girls Don't* program. Google Adwords sponsored links and ads through BlogAds. Whether blogs will develop into a viable medium for big brands depends on whether they can learn how to use the sites in the same spirit as their readers.[29]

Promoting the Web Site

So now you have a really cool Web site or some great ads on other sites and you want people to see them. Aside from search engine marketing, how do you increase traffic? If you keep in mind that the Internet should be part of an integrated marketing campaign, you have several ways.

Linking strategies. The more links that point to your site, the more traffic you'll experience. One of the easiest ways to get complementary sites to link to yours is to provide links to theirs. Another way is to join a *Web ring,* with each member site linking to the next member down the chain. You can also join a *banner exchange:* For every two banners displayed on your site that promote other businesses, one of your banners will be shown on another member site.

Viral marketing. As with word-of-mouth advertising, viral marketing encourages others to carry your message, using their own network of relationships. HotMail accounts are a good example. You get free e-mail, but every message reminds each recipient to sign up for a HotMail account. Another example is a postcard promoting a movie that you might want to send to a friend. Many online articles feature little envelope icons that make it easy for readers to send the articles to friends (along with all the surrounding advertising). Some innovative video producers create very edgy fake commercials for real products to show off their talents. These videos create a viral buzz as friends e-mail to their friends, with the intention that someone will contact the original producer.

Public relations. When your online news release is picked up by print and/or Internet publications, you'll get a lot of "free" publicity. Of course, there is some cost to prepare the copy, and you need a newsworthy message. When done correctly, your online news release generates editorial support that you can't match with traditional advertising.

Traditional media. Most people still get their marketing messages through traditional media. But, as we mentioned before, print and broadcast should work hand in hand with the Internet. For example, you may have a short-copy ad with prominent URL that tells a complete story. Some catalog service centers may only be working 12-hour shifts, but their Web shopping pages are open 24/7.

Networking. Newsgroups provide networks of similar-minded people who might be interested in your Web site. While it's rude to barge in and promote your site, you may want to check out likely groups and participate as a member. But always include your URL in your signature.

Where to Find the Best Online Marketing

You can choose from dozens of sites that recognize the "best" interactive work in various categories. Any awards for last year's work will probably be hopelessly out-of-date. A better idea is to just keep using the Internet. You'll see exciting new stuff all the time. The rules keep changing. The creative just keeps getting better. Bookmark what you like and keep surfing.

Note: We have made every effort to provide information about online communications that is as up-to-date as possible. However, the Internet is a moving target. Technology advances at a rapid rate, and, with it, marketing challenges and opportunities change radically. Likewise, by the time this book is published, we may have missed including in "Who's Who?" for this chapter the latest interactive superstar or may have featured someone who's changed careers (it happens a lot in this segment). All of which is a long way of saying, This is what we know at the time of publishing. Much of it may already be obsolete.

Notes

[1] As reported in June 2003 by eMarketer, http://emarketer.com.

[2] As reported in 2003 by A. C. Nielsen.

[3] Amanda Lenhart et al., *The Ever-Shifting Internet Population: A New Look at Internet Access and the Digital Divide* (Washington, DC: Pew Internet & American Life Project, 2003), 6; available online at http://pewinternet.org/pdfs/PIP_Shifting_Net_Pop_Report.pdf (accessed July 8, 2005).

[4] Ibid.

[5] Ibid.

[6] Steve Moss, senior sales director, national field sales, MSN; remarks made during the panel discussion "On-Line Advertising: Turn Virtual Exposure into Real Results," American Advertising Federation National Conference, Dallas, TX, June 14, 2004.

[7] Ibid.

[8] Dan Early, president, Ascedia, Inc., "Interactive Marketing Overview," lecture presented at Marquette University, Milwaukee, WI, November 6, 2003.

[9] Many items in the following list are adapted from the "Ad Resource Glossary," 2003, available at http://www.tkb-4u.com/advertising/adglossary.php (accessed July 8, 2005).

[10] Early, "Interactive Marketing Overview."

[11] Quoted in A. Jerome Jewler and Bonnie Drewniany, *Creative Strategy in Advertising,* 7th ed. (Belmont, CA: Wadsworth, 2001), 221.

[12] Early, "Interactive Marketing Overview."

[13] King Hill, principal marketing strategist, DigiKnow, Inc.; remarks made during the panel discussion "On-Line Advertising: Turn Virtual Exposure into Real Results," American Advertising Federation National Conference, Dallas, TX, June 14, 2004.

[14] Early, "Interactive Marketing Overview."

[15] "Interactive Annual 10 Winners," *Communication Arts,* 2004, http://www.commarts.com/ca/interactive/cai04 (accessed July 8, 2005).

[16] Bruce Morris, "Internet Ad Types," *Web Developer's Journal,* April 22, 1999, http://www.webdevelopersjournal.com/columns/types_of_ads.html (accessed July 8, 2005).

[17] Ibid.

[18] Beth Cox, "Study Finds 340% Click Rate Boost with Rich Media," ClickZ Network News, March 22, 1999, http://www.clickz.com/news/article.php/83721 (accessed July 8, 2005).

[19] Verovi, "Banner Ads, Rich Media Ads, Flash Ads, Layer Ads and More," 2002, http://verovi.com/banner_ad_rich_media_ad_flash_ad_design.html (accessed July 8, 2005).

[20] Ibid.

[21] Beth Cox, "Study Confirms Effectiveness of Interstitial Ads," ClickZ Network News, May 17, 1999, http://www.clickz.com/news/article.php/12_118931 (accessed July 8, 2005).

[22] Verovi, "Banner Ads."

[23] Morris, "Internet Ad Types."

[24] Early, "Interactive Marketing Overview."

[25] Morris, "Internet Ad Types."

[26] Verovi, "Banner Ads."

[27] "Weblogs Reach Desirable Target Audiences," June 14, 2004, on Adrants Web site, http://www.adrants.com/2004/06/weblogs-reach-desirable-target-audiences.php (accessed July 8, 2005).

[28] John Heinzl, "Dr Pepper/Seven Up Cowed by Web Plan," *Globe and Mail* (Toronto), March 13, 2003, http://www.globeandmail.com/servlet/story/RTGAM/2003013.wpitc313/BNstory/Technology (accessed July 8, 2005).

[29] "Nike-Gawker Deal Tests 'Art of Speed' Online Feature," *Advertising Age,* June 14, 2004, http://www.adage.com/paypoints/buyArticle.cms/login?newsId=40773&auth=(accessed July 8, 2005).

Promotions and Point of Purchase

O K, time to review some definitions. *Promotion* is one of the Five Ps of marketing. In its strictest definition, all marketing communication is a form of promotion. However, in this text we'll call it *sales promotion* and define it as an activity that stimulates purchases by adding a *short-term additional value* to a product or service. In other words, the advertiser is bribing you to buy something quickly. That bribe may be as basic as a discount or as lofty as a donation to a worthy charity.

Sales promotions. Most (but not all) sales promotions have specific short-term goals. They are designed to produce results quickly. Once the promotion is over, sales can slip, sometimes prompting an unending chain of new sales promotions.

In some professions, sales promotions are still rare—you probably won't see a plastic surgeon advertising a free tummy tuck with every nose job. However, the use of sales promotion is increasing, even in the service sector. Many marketers have seen diminishing returns from their traditional advertising efforts. Sales promotions, for both trade and consumer, give their sales that extra boost. This is especially common in the cutthroat world of package goods, where the only perceived differences between products are in the promotions. Traditionally, three-fourths of the total marketing communication budget for package goods goes to trade and consumer promotion, while the rest goes to traditional advertising.[1]

Sales promotion is actually more of a product than an advertising medium. To be successful, promotions must be promoted, usually by traditional media, such as television, magazines, and newspapers, as well as by Web sites and other so-called nontraditional media.

Point of sale (POS) or point of purchase (POP). This is a display for a product or service at the establishment where that item is sold. For example, a table tent promoting a brand of beer in a bar or restaurant, a freestanding display for a brand of lunch meat in a grocery store, or a poster for high-performance tires in an auto parts store. The difference between point of sale and other out-of-home advertising is that POS promotes an immediate purchase in the place where it appears.

Public relations. The term *public relations* covers any nonpaid information from a third party that mentions an identified product or service. There are many kinds of PR, and we're not going to address them here. Instead, we'll focus on the publicity aspect of PR and how it applies to promotion and Integrated Marketing Communications. Examples include event sponsorship, donations to causes, charitable foundations, and other good things companies do that deserve positive mention. PR can also be used to announce a sales promotion activity.

Why Sales Promotion?

For a copywriter, sales promotion offers many advantages, especially when it's integrated into a total campaign. Some of these advantages are as follows:

- *It's fast.* Sales promotion accelerates the selling process and maximizes sales volume.

- *It can cover the whole distribution channel.* Targeted promotions reach wholesalers, retailers, and consumers.

- *It can help retain customer loyalty.* Promotions provide a way to stay in touch with current customers and to give them incentives for continuing their relationship with a brand or business.

- *It can increase early adoption.* You provide an incentive for a customer to try a product for the first time. With the proliferation of new brands, incentives shorten the path from awareness to action.

- *It's measurable.* In most cases sales promotion is designed for short-term sales increases, not long-term brand image. You get results (or lack of results) almost immediately.

- *It supports retailers.* The growth of *account-specific marketing,* or *co-marketing,* requires customized sales promotion programs for retail chains. For example, Sony might offer a promotional program just for Best Buy stores.

- *It fits the consumer's expectations.* On the plus side, consumers are receptive to promotions. On the minus side . . . that's coming later.

- *It fits into an integrated marketing campaign.* To be successful, most promotion needs to be promoted by traditional media.

Why Not?

For each of the major advantages, there is a flip side:

- Because of their short-term, price-oriented nature, most sales promotions do not help build long-term brand equity.

- Although incentives can help retain customer loyalty, they can also encourage brand switching. If a brand has no perceived advantage, the consumer will base the purchase on price (or added value).

- Retailers are demanding more, and they are getting it. So in addition to slotting allowances, retailers are demanding more generous account-specific marketing programs that often include expensive sales promotion programs.

- Customers not only respond to promotions, they expect them. Automakers would love to get out of the endless chain of rebates, discounts, and other incentives. But when one offers them, the others follow suit until the whole industry suffers.

- Most promotions can't stand alone. So the advertiser has to weigh the short-term increase in sales against the cost of the incentive and the cost to advertise it. Sometimes an advertiser will settle for break even, or even a small loss if it means retaining a retail account or gaining market share. For example, an automaker may offer very generous year-end deals just to say they're the number one seller in the rest of their advertising.

Types of Sales Promotions

Consumer sales promotions

With the exception of long-term PR tactics such as sponsorships, most consumer sales promotion is considered to be *non–franchise building*. Promotions are intended to jump-start sales and do almost nothing to build brand image. Another purpose is to gather information (give us the data and we'll give you a prize). Either way, the ultimate goal is to stimulate action. Examples of sales promotions include the following:

- *Contests/games:* The consumer actively participates in some way by writing an essay, taking a quiz, or engaging in some other mental activity that would not challenge a first grader's intellect. In return for providing some marketing data, you have a one-in-a-gazillion chance to win something.

- *Sweepstakes:* These involve chance more than contests do. Just enter and you may already be a winner. Sometimes you don't have to do anything except wait for your prize. The laws governing contests and sweepstakes vary from state to state. In mid-2004, Pepsi announced a chance to win a billion dollars. Although no purchase was necessary, you can bet the winner probably bought some Pepsi along the way.

- *Product giveaways:* Buy the product and you might get the next one free. Fast-food restaurants and soft drinks use this quite a bit. You have to buy something first, but you have a better chance of winning.

- *Samples:* You can get them in the mail, in magazine inserts, or from little old ladies in the supermarket. You can give away more than pills, perfumes, and fabric softener sheets. A few years ago AOL gave away millions and millions of CD-ROMs in every imaginable way.

- *Coupons:* Essentially these are little slips of paper that ensure a discount. They are distributed in a number of ways: traditionally, in magazine and newspaper ads; in freestanding inserts (FSI) in newspapers; in direct mail packs (such as Val-Pak); and online, in a form that consumers print at home.

- *Discounts:* These are temporary price reductions. *Temporary* is the key word, because a permanent price reduction creates no urgency to buy.

- *Bonus packs:* The consumer gets more of a product at the regular price. For example, detergent boxes may be bundled in a buy-one-get-one-free promotion. Bonus packs provide more value to the consumer. However, if the consumer is already a loyal customer, there is no incremental value to the manufacturer.

- *Rebates:* Consumers are offered money back if they mail receipts and packaging to the producer. This requires more effort, and the seller bets that a large percentage of people will not bother. If they do, they have to provide information for the seller's database. Many times, prices listed contain "after rebate" in the fine print.

- *Premiums (merchandise):* Instead of money back, the consumer gets stuff. It can be as simple as the toy in a Happy Meal (marginally harder to digest than the food) or as elaborate as thousands of dollars in water toys with the purchase of a new boat. Premiums can also be intangible items, such as frequent-flier points.

- *Loyalty programs:* These reward customers for continuing to purchase the same brand of a product or service. Airline frequent-flier plans are the most obvious form of loyalty program. But retailers such as grocers, discount stores, and electronics stores, where customers shop frequently, also use loyalty programs. Many consumer packaged goods companies are also developing frequency programs that award points for purchases. The points can be redeemed for gifts, such as merchandise, or for discounts.

- *Cross-promotion:* Some products just seem to complement each other. If so, they can work together to multiply their promotional dollars. For example, a cookie company may offer coupons for milk. Other times the lead brand in a promotional campaign will bring in partners. For example, BMW's test-drive program to raise money for breast cancer also included Harmon Kardon and Michelin, which are used in BMW cars. In 2004, Pepsi teamed with Apple to promote free iTunes with purchase of Pepsi.

- *Product placement:* Some companies specialize in placing their clients' products on game shows as prizes. Others concentrate on getting their clients into movies and TV shows. For example, in *ET: The Extra Terrestrial* the hero was lured with Reese's Pieces because M&M's would not pay for product placement. Short-term sales of Reese's Pieces skyrocketed. So when you see a character reach for a box of Cheerios, drink a Coors, or drive a new Jaguar, it's no coincidence. Product placement is negotiated with the producers and can run into hundreds of thousands of dollars. The blending of advertising and entertainment is so pervasive, it's created a new category of promotion called "Madison and Vine." Recent examples include what seemed like a nearly two-hour infomercial for FedEx in the movie *Castaway,* promos for Donald Trump's various enterprises on *The Apprentice,* and sponsors' products used as rewards on *Survivor.* With more people tuning out traditional 30-second commercials, placement within programs ensures that viewers see the products.

15.1. How many brands can you cram into one promotion? This sweepstakes combines Levi's, JCPenney, *The Apprentice,* and Donald Trump, who has done a great job of branding himself.

15.3. Tango is a popular orange drink in the United Kingdom. Their "Shout Down Non Drinkers" promotion targeted 15- to 24-year-old males. The goal was to increase awareness and market share. Tango drinkers were given a *premium*—a free telescopic megaphone for shouting at people who don't drink Tango. This was supported with TV, radio, outdoor posters, and sandwich boards on college campuses as well as the Tango package. If anyone tried something like this in the United States, the "shouters" would find a new place to put their megaphones.

15.2. BMW's Mountain Driving Tour targeted visitors at ski resorts. The goal was to encourage test-drives. Think of the incentive as a $50,000 product sample. Prospects filled out a form (for BMW's database) and were given the keys for a test-drive as long as they wanted. The promotion was promoted with outdoor displays, ads, radio, local concerts, and POP displays in bars and restaurants.

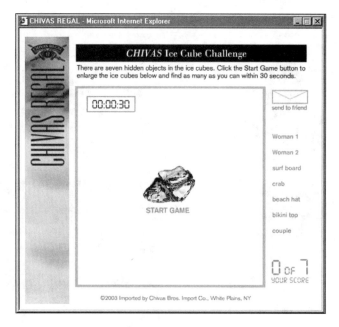

15.4. The Internet is an ideal medium for *interactive contests*. Visitors can take as long as they want to participate, and the results are immediate. This promotion for Chivas Regal was advertised in magazines and called out in banner ads on the Chivas Web site.

Almost all of the consumer promotion types described above need the support of other forms of marketing communication (even the sample lady in the supermarket has some kind of signage). All of the media we discuss in this book, plus packaging and public relations, can be used to promote promotions.

Trade sales promotions

If you're a manufacturer, how do you motivate your sales staff, move product through distributors, and encourage retailers to stock your brands? Trade sales promotion is used for business-to-business products and for wholesale transactions for consumer goods. Some trade sales promotions include the following:

- *Financial incentives:* Lower interest rates, reduced freight costs, price discounts, and extended payments can encourage retailers to stock up on products. Some of these include *slotting allowances* to provide shelf space, *buying allowances* to reduce the introductory price, and *promotional allowances* for short-term promotions. These allowances are usually meant to be passed on to the consumer, but some retailers pocket the savings and charge full retail prices, which does not help to move the product. To counter this, some packaged goods companies have dropped their everyday prices and cut back on trade allowances. *Push money*—also known as "spiffs"—can be an extra commission paid to sales force, wholesaler, or retailer.

- *Trade contests:* Salespeople, wholesalers, and retailers receive rewards for increasing their sales. The more you sell, the more you get. These often involve travel incentives, such as a trip for two to Hawaii or tickets to a major sporting event.

- *Sales support:* The manufacture provides displays, posters, counter cards, signage, and other point-of-sale items. Products sell better with attractive displays, which are often accompanied by price deals. The manufacturer may also provide special promotional literature for the dealer to hand out.

- *Training programs:* The manufacturer trains the distributor or dealer employees in selling the product.

- *Trade shows:* Manufacturers display their products, salespeople meet and greet potential customers, distributors and wholesalers check out new lines, and everybody sees what the competition is up to. Trade shows can be small regional events with nothing more than a few 10-by-10-foot or major extravaganzas such as the Consumer Electronics Show, which generates worldwide coverage. Some manufacturers spend millions every year on trade shows—for elaborate booths, celebrity talent, high-profile events, extravagant banquets, contests, and handouts. Trade shows provide a lot of opportunity for creative people. Dozens of details require creative planning: the booth design itself; displays, posters, handout literature, event planning, preshow promotion, and premium selection; audio and video displays; and more. In a way, a trade-show booth is a campaign in itself, with components that work individually and cumulatively to convey a single message.

- *Cooperative advertising:* Basically, the manufacturer helps the retailer pay for advertising its products. Sometimes the ads are provided, and all the retailer has to do is slap a logo and address on the bottom. In many cases, the co-op ad is similar to the national brand advertising done by the manufacturer. Other times, the manufacturer provides images and copy that the retailer uses to build its own ads. If you ever have to produce co-op ads, always keep the intended media in mind. For example, don't try to convert an elaborate four-color magazine ad into a black-and-white co-op ad for a local newspaper.

Like consumer sales promotions, trade promotions usually have to be supported with some form of marketing communication, usually print advertising, direct mail, and the Internet.

Promotional Strategy and Tactics

Promotional strategy stems from marketing objectives. For example:

- Get 20% of Brand X users to try Brand Y within three months.

- Get 40% of current Brand Z users to increase purchases from 5 to 10 packages per month within six months.

- Expand distribution for Brand A from 40% to 80% in all X-Mart chain stores within one year.

You need to first have a clear idea of what the client wants to accomplish before you create a promotional program.

15.5. In this contest for Sony salespeople called "Fuel Your Fantasy," merchandise and travel incentives were offered in return for increased sales. Sell more, get more. This 3-D direct mailer announced the promotion.

15.6. Trade shows, whether for business, consumers, or institutions, bring potential customers directly to the sellers.

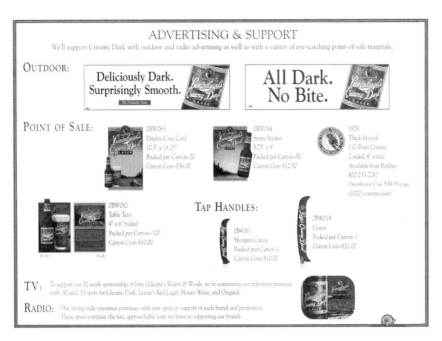

15.7. *Promoting the promotion.* It's important to let your retail customers know you're supporting the brand. This beer company highlighted their advertising and sales promotion program on the back of a sell sheet.

Components of the promotion

Assuming you know the client's objectives, you need to follow these steps:

1. *Think campaigns.* If the promotion is part of a total campaign, make sure your sales promotion will fit the way the product is positioned in the market, the brand image, the target audience, and how it is sold.

2. *Develop a promotional theme.* It's like a tagline. Use some of the guidelines for taglines in Chapter 7. Ideally, your promotion theme ties into the total campaign, as in Budweiser's "True Music" summer promotion.

3. *Consider the incentive.* What will you offer that adds value to the product or service and encourages quick sales? As with the theme, you have to consider the target audience and brand image. For example, a free trunkful of frozen pizzas may get a prospect into a Hyundai dealer but it probably won't motivate a potential Audi customer.

4. *Promote the promotion.* Once you have determined the theme and the incentive, how do you let people know? Your promotion of the promotion also depends on the target audience and brand image. Using multiple media, such as the Internet and print, provides for more interaction and greater involvement with the product.

15.8. Just a few examples of freestanding and countertop displays. The only limits are your budget and your imagination.

Tips and techniques for promotion

- Use a memorable theme.
- Relate to the product attributes (brand image).
- Keep it simple.
- Make the benefit (reward) clear.

Point of Sale/Point of Purchase

It doesn't matter what you call it—POS or POP—it refers to some kind of display in the store that sells the featured product or service. The display can be used to support a promotion, or it can be a more permanent reminder of a brand, such as a neon beer sign.

Types of POP

- In-store posters
- Banners—indoor or outdoor
- Counter/shelf displays
- Freestanding displays/kiosks
- Signs (floors, shopping carts, shelves, shelf talkers, end caps, counter cards)
- Table tents/menu inserts
- Lighted signs/neon
- Interactive displays (computer)
- Motorized/video displays

Tips and techniques for POP

- Keep it simple.
- Relate to the product attributes (brand image).
- Use primary colors/bold graphics.
- Keep headlines and copy short.
- Use memorable themes.

Promotional Public Relations

A dedicated public relations practitioner would probably be outraged to see PR relegated to a subhead in a discussion of promotions. We do not mean to dismiss the value of public relations. In fact, we believe PR should be the foundation of most marketing communications plans. In this context, however, we will discuss public relations in terms of creative strategy, with special emphasis on how public relations can fit into a promotional campaign.

Good deeds get good press, even if you have to buy it

One function of public relations is getting credit for the good things your company does. So many promotional PR efforts concentrate on charitable acts. For example, your promotion could be about donating money to research against diseases such as breast cancer, supporting national parks, building local

15.9. POP display used to promote Miller beer. (Until a few years ago, most beer companies avoided association with motor vehicles. As you can see, those concerns don't apply anymore.)

playgrounds, and cleaning up river walks. In addition to doing the good deed, you need to promote it through publicity releases and editorial contacts as well as traditional and nontraditional media.

Event Marketing and Sponsorships

Event marketing and sponsorships are specialized forms of promotion that link a company or brand to a specific event or a themed activity. Event

15.10. Ford Motor Company said they were passionate about preserving the beauty of our national parks. So they retrofitted some old buses with clean-burning propane fuel systems. Then they promoted that good deed using public relations and print advertising.

marketing and sponsorship are sort of like public relations because they can be long-term goodwill efforts that can enhance brand image. Marketers often participate in event marketing by associating their product with a popular activity such as a sporting event, concert, fair, or festival. In event sponsorship, a company develops sponsorship relations with a particular event and provides financial support in return for the right to display a brand name, logo, or advertising message and be identified as a sponsor of the event.[2] Examples include the following:

- Corona Beer presents Jimmy Buffett in concert

- The Nextel Cup NASCAR series

- The Rose Bowl presented by AT&T

- The Virginia Slims Tennis Tournament

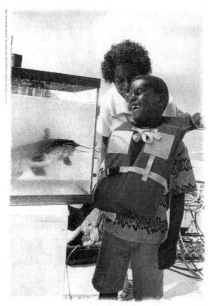

THERE'S BEEN A LOT OF TALK about the environment lately. But out on Chesapeake Bay, sailing around on a vintage skipjack, a group of school kids are learning that when it comes to the environment, actions speak louder than words.

Myrtha Allen, Environmental Sciences teacher at P.S. 405, Baltimore, explains, "Most of my kids are city born and bred. They live in apartments, they get their milk in cartons, their eggs in those styrofoam containers. They were about as interested in the environment as they are in homework." She smiles at a nearby eight-year-old. "And who can blame them? Some of them, like Jawan here, had never even seen a live fish before."

That's where the Chesapeake Bay Foundation stepped in. Since 1966, when it started in Annapolis, Maryland, with a rented fishing trawler and little else, the Foundation has taken more than 300,000 students out into the Bay to experience the environment first hand. And at the same time making them aware of how important their contribution is to the future of the planet.

Myrtha puts it simply. "To get these kids wanting to clean up the world, we've got to get their hands dirty."

And they do. They get very dirty.

"Oh yeah," chuckles Myrtha, "we do it all. Once we threw a net in just to see what we'd get. When we pulled it up, sure enough there were the milk cartons, the soda cans, the egg containers. And flapping around in the middle of it all was this big, cranky striped bass. You should've seen their faces.

"We took 20 little consumers out on a boat that day. We came back with 20 budding environmentalists."

At Toyota, we're proud that through the support we give to the Foundation more kids like Jawan will be able to experience our fragile environment first hand. And hopefully start playing an active part in preserving it.

Is the program working? "These kids are organizing neighborhood recycling drives,

they're writing letters to Senators. Take a look at these posters some of my students have been doing."

The classroom walls are alive with crayon and pencil. Bright orange crabs. Smiling oysters. Families of ducks.

And one poster that stops everyone. It's of a smiling little boy holding hands with a big striped bass. And boldly scrawled above both their heads is one word: "Brothers".

And it's signed by Jawan. Age eight.

TOYOTA
INVESTING IN THE INDIVIDUAL

"IT WAS THE FIRST FISH Jawan had seen that WASN'T SURROUNDED by french fries."
MYRTHA ALLEN, Teacher

15.11. Toyota wanted everyone to know they donated to the Chesapeake Bay Foundation, a group dedicated to educating kids about cleaning up the bay.

Event marketing has become very popular in recent years for several reasons:

- It creates experiences for consumers and associates a company's brand with certain lifestyles and activities.

- It provides opportunities to distribute samples as well as information about a marketer's product or service or to let consumers actually experience the product.

- It gives marketers access to large numbers of consumers at a relatively low cost and can be an effective part of a grassroots marketing program.[3]

Promotion in IMC

All through this chapter we've stressed that promotions can't exist in a vacuum. Sales promotion techniques usually work best when used in conjunction with

15.12. NASCAR: the hottest sports marketing venue today. The cars are moving billboards watched by 150,000 fans at the track and millions more at home. Plus the sponsors tie in national and local promotions with each race. The drivers become spokespersons for the brands.

advertising. Conversely, a consumer sales promotion program can enhance the effectiveness of an ad campaign. When properly planned and executed to work together, sales promotion and advertising can provide a *synergistic effect* that is much greater than the response that would be generated from either promotional element used alone. Proper integration of advertising and sales promotion requires the coordination of several decision areas:

- Budget allocation
- Coordination of advertising and promotion themes
- Media support and timing[4]

Guerrilla marketing

The behind-the-scenes maneuvering reflects an axiom of 21st-century advertising. In this cluttered marketing environment, simply buying TV time isn't enough.[5] In the 1980s, the term *guerrilla marketing* came to represent a number of nontraditional MarCom tactics used to gain awareness without spending a lot of money (at least not as much as for traditional TV advertising). The current campaign for Aflac is a prime example. Their duck icon is supported with a relatively modest $45 million ad budget. But the behind-the-scenes effort multiplies the impact. In four years, awareness of the company has grown from 12% to more than 90%. The following blurb from the *Wall Street Journal* describes how it works: "Creating a breakout ad character is in some measure a matter of luck and circumstances, but Aflac

WORDS OF WISDOM

"[Guerrilla marketing] requires that everyone who deals with your customers remember the Golden Rule for Guerrillas: ALWAYS TRY TO THINK LIKE YOUR CUSTOMER."

—JAY CONRAD LEVINSON[6]

"JUST DO IT"—BUT NOT ON T-SHIRTS

Through his leadership at Nike and Starbucks, Scott Bedbury redefined the "consumer brand relationship." He told us some of the pitfalls of overpromoting a brand:

Around 1996 when the Nike brand was white hot, the company went through a "swooshification of planet earth" phase in which Nike lost some brand discipline. It seemed that the more Nike swooshes on something, the better. Big, garish swooshes everywhere on shoes and apparel. Up to that point we had always been restrained and subtle with our trademark, careful about oversaturation. It was a critically valuable, irreplaceable brand asset. I think this damaged Nike somewhat. Nike eventually saw its folly and cut way back and even introduced a swooshless logo for a time. Back in August 1988, when Nike launched "Just do it," some people started creating pencils, pouches—all kinds of school supplies and even drink stir sticks with "Just do it" on them. Did it belong on that? I had to impale myself on the project and stop it. We knew "Just do it" was good but we didn't know how long it would last. We had to refrain from tacking it on everything—it was just wrong for the brand, no matter how much money it would make. These sorts of decisions have enabled that campaign to survive for almost two decades.

lowered its odds considerably by supplementing its TV ads with a well-orchestrated, behind-the-scenes guerrilla public- relations campaign. Instead of simply buying lots of TV ads, a team of four ad and marketing executives are focused on getting the duck on TV at no cost to Aflac."[7] Some of their actions have included handing out plush duck toys to people on the outdoor set of *The Today Show,* sponsoring a water tank for synchronized swimmers on David Letterman's show, getting coverage on CNBC (which ran the commercials for free as part of a news story), and lobbying consumers to vote for the duck in a Yahoo/*USA Today* poll on favorite ad icons.

Now that advertising costs are on the rise again, and clients are looking to get more for their dollar, it makes sense to consider innovative ways to outsmart the competition rather than outspend them.

Who's Who?

Jay Conrad Levinson—Jay Conrad Levinson is the author of a wildly successful series of books about "guerrilla marketing" tactics. He cites many examples of unconventional marketing and communications programs that generated spectacular results. Typically, these guerrilla tactics use existing marketing communication tools, such as direct mail or outdoor, but in highly targeted, very creative ways.

Notes

[1] George E. Belch and Michael A. Belch, "Sales Promotion," in *Advertising and Promotion: An Integrated Marketing Perspective,* 6th ed. (New York: McGraw-Hill, 2003), 510–61.

[2] Ibid.

[3] Ibid.

[4] Ibid.

[5] "Aflac Duck's Paddle to Stardom: Creativity on the Cheap," *Wall Street Journal,* July 30, 2004, B1.

[6] Jay Conrad Levinson, *Guerrilla Marketing Attack* (Boston: Houghton Mifflin, 1989), 146.

[7] "Aflac Duck's Paddle to Stardom: Creativity on the Cheap," *Wall Street Journal,* July 30, 2004, B1.

Business-to-Business

16

Some beginning copywriters dread business-to-business (B2B) assignments. The products aren't fun. The target audience is deadly serious. You're mostly stuck with trade magazines and collateral pieces. And worst of all, nobody will see your ad except a few thousand industrial buyers. In two words: *bor–ing.*

Many creative directors tell their young writers, "There are no boring products, only boring advertising." But many times, you don't know enough about a product to make it interesting. Too often even the clients don't know why anyone should buy their products. So they settle for a sterile recitation of facts and figures. While it doesn't take a rocket scientist to figure out beer, soap, or toilet paper, you have to know something about your subject when you're writing business advertising. Sometimes you have to know more about the market, the customers, and the product than the client does. However, many business-to-business marketers don't see the need for an account planner or even primary research. Too many think, "Who knows the market and customer better than me? So don't give me all that phony baloney about branding, image, resonance, and the like. We make a good product. Just let people know where to get it."

Another creative drawback of B2B has been the rigid formulas dictated by so many old-school ad managers. Although it's taken a while, business advertising has finally broken a lot of the old rules that handcuffed creatives. As Jim Albright notes: "It took business-to-business writers a long time to figure out that the purchasing agent who reads

"I don't know who you are.
I don't know your company.
I don't know your company's product.
I don't know what your company stands for.
I don't know your company's customers.
I don't know your company's record.
I don't know your company's reputation.
Now–what was it you wanted to sell me?"

MORAL: Sales start **before** your salesman calls–with business publication advertising.

McGRAW-HILL MAGAZINES
BUSINESS • PROFESSIONAL • TECHNICAL

16.1. This McGraw-Hill classic makes the case for business publications. The little man in the chair has long since retired, but his message is even more appropriate today.

Purchasing Weekly during the day also reads *Time* at night and watches TV. Once that thought took hold, business-to-business advertising took its place as a creative area of advertising that looks up to no one."[1]

While writing good B2B copy can be a challenge, it also presents a great opportunity, especially for entry-level writers. Rather than being stuck with a small piece of the account, you're more likely to work on a whole campaign. You might be able to work out a whole integrated plan that uses a lot of fun promotional and Web components in addition to print ads and collateral. You can probably work in some cool guerrilla marketing ideas. Some clients love that, since they think they're getting more for their money. In *Hey Whipple, Squeeze This,* Luke Sullivan praises B2B ads: "Trade ads are just as important to your client's economy as its consumer work, and they're usually a better gig than a consumer campaign."[3]

Why B2B Is Different

- The customer is buying products with his or her company's money.
- Traditionally, the copy has been more factual and less emotional than what's usually found in consumer advertising.
- In general, the emphasis is on generating immediate response rather than on long-term brand building.
- Ad budgets are usually much smaller than with mass-appeal consumer products, restricting many creative options.
- Most business products are not sold retail, which means they are either sold direct to buyers or through dealers or distributors.

Why B2B Is the Same

- Business customers still have wants and needs—saving money, success, self-esteem. Sure, they want facts, but ultimately it's about making more money and feeling good about it.
- The copy and design principles discussed in previous chapters apply to business readers, maybe even more than they do with some consumer products.
- The Internet is just as important, and in some cases even more important, as a communication source and as part of an Integrated Marketing Communications campaign.
- Branding for business products and services is becoming hugely important, especially as companies merge and change affiliations. Sometimes the brand name is the only constant.
- Even though the numbers of business customers may be smaller, using traditional mass media such as television, radio, outdoor, and newspapers may be an effective way to reach them.
- Companies do not buy products and services. People do.

16.2. The main message is the headline. The supporting facts are between the lines.

16.3. This insert was printed on a piece of sandpaper, so it not only got a lot of attention, it was also a great product sample.

16.4. This tasty ad is actually a testimonial for Cisco Systems wireless technology.

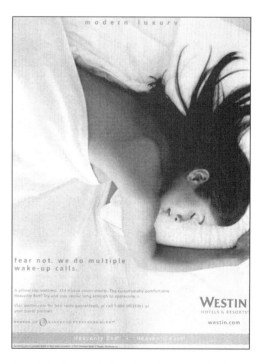

16.5. Westin wants to attract women business travelers (and by the looks of this visual, we think a few businessmen too).

16.6. Publicly held corporations spend a lot of money trying to polish their image. Corporate image ads reassure investors, vendors, customers, and employees that a company is in good financial shape—or a least on the right path to recovery. In this ad, GM took the bold step of admitting their cars used to be lousy, but, of course, now they're great.

Don't Forget Those Wants and Needs

A salesperson who just got rejected by a heartless purchasing agent may disagree, but business buyers are human. They may use economic rationales, but they still have wants and needs similar to those of other consumers. For example:

- An office manager responds to a direct mailer from an office supply store that offers free delivery. This saves her time, so she can get more work done; she can save her company money, which makes her look good to the boss, which might mean she gets a raise. All of which satisfies her needs.

- A factory manager sees an ad for a robot that stacks boxes on pallets in minutes, saving valuable time and labor. This will save his company a lot of money, making him look good, which may mean a promotion and more money. (Starting to see a pattern?)

- A doctor reads a brochure, sees a medical journal ad, and checks a Web site for a new blood-thinning drug. She gets more information from a sales rep, including research reports. She prescribes the drug, not because she'll make more money, but because her need is to help her patients. Sometimes business is about more than making money.

Agricultural Advertising: It's Another Animal

Some of the hottest creative shops have taken on ag clients and won a ton of awards. Not only shops in the Midwest, but some of the leading agencies in California, New York, and Virginia. Someday you just might work on an ag account, so here are a few tips:

- Successful farmers are college-educated businesspeople and should be treated as such, not as bib-overall-wearing hicks. Appeal to their business sense, not to the nostalgia of a small family farm that disappeared years ago.

- Farmers are extremely sensitive to detail and very concerned about being up-to-date. Show a 10-year-old tractor, CRT computer monitor, or out-of-date satellite dish in your ad and you've killed your sales message.

- You can have fun with the product, but never mock the farmer's country, profession, or lifestyle.

- Be careful with claims. If anyone recognizes BS, it's a farmer.

Business-to-Business and Campaigns

Many B2B marketers have discovered that magazines may not be the primary method to reach their customers. Using Integrated Marketing Communications for B2B makes sense because customers are easier to define and locate. All the IMC components listed in Chapter 2 apply to business-to-business. Because the number of key customers is sometimes very small, you may be able to create expensive high-impact communication tools that generate higher response rates. As with consumer advertising, you need to think of how many different ways you can reach a customer. Do you go for a few high-impact "rifle shots" or use a lot of different marketing tools? Here are some examples:

- A Japanese engine manufacturer wanted potential customers to recognize their commitment to the U.S. market. So they sent a large box to the nation's top industrial engine buyers. On the box lid was the slogan, "Take a Power Trip." Inside was a high-quality garment bag embroidered with the company logo. In the pocket of the bag were vouchers for two plane tickets to the company's North American headquarters in California. Also enclosed were a cover letter from the U.S. general manager, product literature, and a corporate brochure. Each mailing cost about $200, but when compared to millions of dollars in engine sales, it was very economical. Just as important, salespeople from the engine company called potential customers after the big boxes arrived. You can be sure the prospects remembered the mailer, which made it much easier for the sales force.

- A manufacturer of construction equipment launched a new line of telescopic material handlers. They used print ads but also produced a series of sell sheets, full-line brochures, head-to-head comparisons with other brands, a walk-around guide to help salespeople sell the machine, a feature/benefit video, an operational video showing applications and attachments, an interactive multimedia program to show potential customers, a co-op advertising kit, a dealer sales kit, a point-of-sale displays for dealers, a complete trade PR program on CD-ROM, and oversize posters and motorized displays for trade shows. The company's dealers had the tools they needed to sell to their contractor customers, who were also very familiar with the new products after seeing the ads and direct mailers.

16.7. This manufacturer wanted customers to know that comparing their dealer-installed controls to mass-merchandised products was like comparing apples to oranges. They promoted the message through a series of trade magazine ads and a direct mail campaign. The final mailing was a box of ripe apples. They also handed out apples at a trade show and used the apple/orange theme in their trade-show booth.

- A marketer of veterinary products launched a line of products to help vets treat ear problems in dogs. They produced a magazine insert that folded out to form a poster for the vet's exam rooms. They ran spread and single-page ads in professional journals. The company offered audiocassettes about building a clinic's business by using these new products. A direct mail kit included a 100-page technical guide. They provided handouts for clinic customers and even ran ads in consumer publications to encourage dog owners to visit their vets.

Here's one way to sum up the use of IMC for business-to-business campaigns: Imagine that in order to get a sale, you have to open a big iron door. Run a few magazine ads, and you're throwing pebbles at that door. Use all the integrated marketing tools at your disposal, and you've got a big boulder that'll knock that door wide open.

Collateral

Collateral is a big catchall category that includes printed material used for personal selling, handouts, and sometimes direct mail. The materials can be as elaborate as a coffee-table book featuring the illustrated history of a company or as cheesy as a black-and-white single-page flyer stuck under your windshield. Collateral includes, but is not limited to, the following items:

- Product brochures

- Corporate image brochures

- Catalogs

- Sell sheets

- Capabilities brochures

- Personal selling kits

- Trade-show handouts

- Annual and quarterly reports

While virtually every consumer product uses some kind of collateral, much of it is done by a design firm or collateral agency other than the agency of record. However, in most cases, business-to-business collateral is often integrated into a total communication program developed by one agency or design firm.

When you're writing collateral pieces, especially multipage brochures or a series of pieces, keep the following tips in mind:

- *Have a theme* and carry that theme throughout the brochure, whether it's a graphic or text theme (or both).

- *Think of the brochure as a campaign*—each major element has to work by itself and collectively with other parts of the brochure.

- *Appeal to wants and needs of the readers.* To do this you have to know and understand the intended target audience.

- *Think visually.* Even technical pieces need good, attention-getting graphics.

- *Pay attention to typography,* especially for copy-intensive pieces.

- *Stretch your thinking.* Consider gatefold, pockets, inserts, die cuts, windows, and other creative devices to liven up the design.

- When penciling out a design, don't forget that in most cases you have to *think in terms of four-page units* (unless you have one or more gatefold pages).

There are no other rules for collateral, except following good design and copywriting practices. Other than budget, there are no restrictions on paper stock, number of colors, binding technique, or paper size.

Many businesses have drastically cut back on printed literature. Instead, they put their literature on their Web sites as PDF documents so customers can download them. This not only saves a lot of money in printing costs, but there's no inventory and you can make changes whenever you want. If printing quality

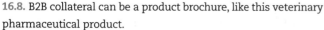

Soothe the savage beast.

Panolog Cream Veterinary

Nystatin/Neomycin Sulfate/Thiostrepton/Triamcinolone Acetonide Cream

On The Move
PCA
POTASH COMPANY OF AMERICA

16.8. B2B collateral can be a product brochure, like this veterinary pharmaceutical product.

16.9. Corporate capabilities brochures show companies in their best light.

16.10. By law, annual reports have to report the numbers, but everything else is open to creative license.

is not an issue and you don't need a salesperson to walk a prospect through the literature, it makes a lot of sense.

Another trend is the bundling of interactive programs with product literature. For example, we had a client who was selling very comprehensive management software. Rather than printing a 20-pager showing all the screens and reports, we produced a mini-CD-ROM with an interactive product demo. This was inserted in a pocket of a simple 6-pager. The CD could also be used for handouts, personal selling, and direct mail, as well as integrated into the client's Web site and other interactive programs.

"Nontraditional" Has Gone Mainstream

Internet for business

Many B2B clients adopted the Internet long before consumer brands did. Whether it's used strictly for information or for direct selling, the Internet provides B2B marketers with tremendous advantages over "traditional" media, including the following:

- Provides more detailed information than you can fit in an ad.

- Shows streaming video, animation, and interactive media.

- Includes links to co-op partners and/or affiliated companies.

- Provides updated product information that can be downloaded.

- Delivers company news; announces new promotions and special offers.

- Sets up merchant accounts for direct sales.

- Identifies dealers, shows their locations, and provides links to their sites.

- Tracks inquiries, builds databases, and establishes customer relationship management programs.

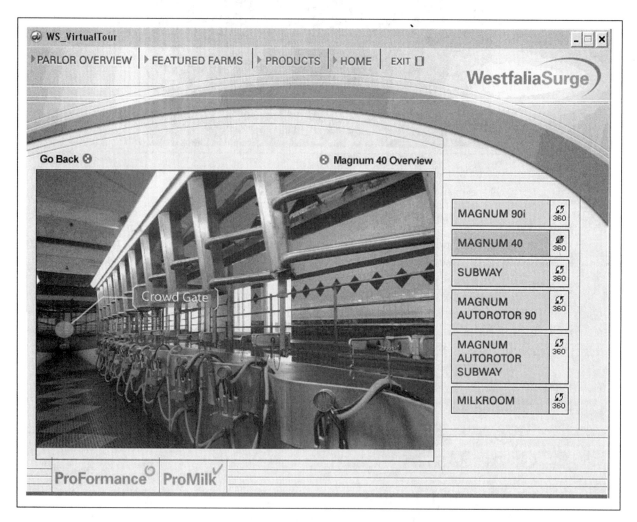

16.11. This award-winning interactive program lets dairy farmers take a virtual tour of several high-tech milking parlors with 360-degree movies, interactive product demos, literature downloads, video clips, animated fly-throughs, and farmer testimonials. It was credited with selling $5 million worth of parlors in just three months.

Interactive

You can't show animation in a magazine. You can't get a video into a brochure. Or can you? With new innovations in interactive technology, you can put virtually any image, still or motion, on a CD-ROM or DVD and insert it into a publication. Or mail it. Or hand it out at a trade show. The only limits are your imagination, your budget, and disc space. But with 4.7GB available on a DVD, you have a lot of room for creativity.

WAR STORY:

FAST TALKING AND FAST THINKING FOR BUSINESS ADVERTISING

When Ally & Gargano took over the Federal Express account in 1974, the package carrier was struggling to differentiate itself from bigger firms like UPS. At that time, very few consumers used overnight package services. The primary audience was businesspeople. The agency developed one of the great taglines of all time, "When it absolutely, positively has to be there overnight." The One Thing: Federal Express is fast. Now, how do you show it?

The creative team of Patrick Kelly and Mike Tesch found their answer while watching a guy billed as the "World's Fastest-Talking Man" on a TV show. They paired the fast-talking character actor John Moschitta with director Joe Sedelmaier to create a series of very funny and hugely successful commercials. Sedelmaier described how it worked: "There is no time to build character in a commercial so you have to find characters." Back then comedy was put down in business advertising. It was thought that it really didn't work. "People would remember the jokes but not the product," Sedelmaier said. "We had one of those fortunate

circumstances where the client and the agency were really with it."

In "Fast Talker" and others, viewers connected with irreverent office workers, laughing not at them, but with them. "It was a decidedly new tactic in business communications," said Mike Tesch. "It took guts in those days to laugh at yourself," he said. Nonetheless, viewers responded favorably, relating to the ludicrous situations time and time again. "It wasn't just humor. It was comedy."[4]

16.12. The "Fast Talker" was one of 80 FedEx commercials directed by Joe Sedelmaier. Ally & Gargano took on FedEx in 1974 with an ad budget of less than $400,000. By 1987, when the agency lost the account, FedEx was a household name billing $20–25 million.[5]

Business broadcast

When business advertisers finally realized their customers listen to the radio on the ride home and watch TV at night, they started using consumer tactics to reach business buyers. If you're selling goods or services that can be used by a wide assortment of businesses, broadcast makes sense.

Business video

When broadcast doesn't make sense, or you need more time to tell your story, video is the answer. Whether it's packaged in VHS or DVD or included as part of an interactive CD-ROM, video is a proven business-to-business medium. Even if the product doesn't move or a service can't be pictured, you can show testimonials of satisfied customers.

Other Business IMC Opportunities

Many business-to-business accounts have small budgets compared to consumer products. However, for the creative team, that can provide a lot more opportunity, since they may be responsible for most, if not all, of the campaign. When this happens, the creative team can develop marketing communications tools that are truly integrated. From a creative standpoint, you can have a lot of fun with:

- Sponsored events
- Sports marketing
- Sales promotions
- Contests, sweepstakes
- Trade-show booth design
- Sales meetings
- Specialty advertising
- Cross-promotion with consumer brands

Where to Find the Best B2B Advertising

The Business Marketing Association sponsors local and national competitions covering all facets of business marketing communication. The association's Pro-Comm Awards recognize the year's best work. You'll also find some great B2B ads in the *Communication Arts Advertising Annual*. For agricultural advertising, the year's best work is honored with the National AgriMarketing Association's NAMA awards. Other specialty markets also honor the best advertising within their categories.

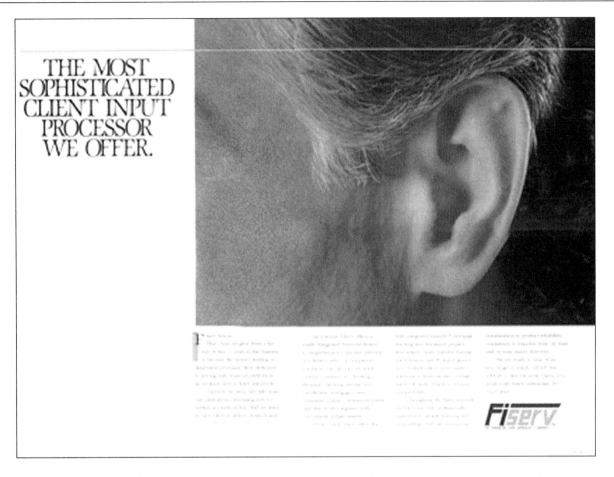

16.13. How do you show something as obscure and technical as financial data processing services? Forget the technology and concentrate on listening to customers.

Who's Who?

Joe Sedelmaier—A successful Chicago-based art director-producer, Joe Sedelmaier opened a film production studio in 1967 and began developing clutter-cracking commercials that featured offbeat, one-of-a-kind nonactors. Sedelmaier's zaniness was evident in his work for Wendy's ("Where's the Beef?") and Federal Express ("Fast Talker"), creating public and industry cutting-edge "buzz."[6] Although he became a hot director for many well-known consumer brands, Sedelmaier's early work included business-to-business clients, such as a chain of office furniture stores.

Notes

[1] Jim Albright, *Creating the Advertising Message* (Mountain View, CA: Mayfield, 1992), 232.

[2] Luke Sullivan, *Hey Whipple, Squeeze This: A Guide to Creating Great Ads* (New York: John Wiley, 1998), 83.

[3] Luke Sullivan, *Hey Whipple, Squeeze This: A Guide to Creating Great Ads* (New York: John Wiley, 1998), 83.

[4] See Judy Warner, "Best Spots: Hill, Holliday John Hancock," *AdWeek,* November 9, 1998, http://www.adweek.com/aw/creative/top20_20years/top20_10.jsp (accessed July 11, 2005).

[5] Ibid.

[6] "Joe Sedelmaier," in "Top 100 People of the Century," *Advertising Age,* March 29, 1999, http://www.adage.com/century/people/people063.html (accessed July 11, 2005).

Selling It

In Chapter 1, we said one of the copywriter's roles is selling his or her ideas to the client. You could opt to just slide your ideas under the client's door and run away, hoping the client will like them. However, in selling your ideas, you're also selling yourself, ensuring gainful employment, and building some very valuable self-esteem.

Presentations

People learn a fear of public speaking in kindergarten. Most people, even gifted public speakers, never get over that naked fear of standing in front of an audience. The difference is that gifted public speakers have the ability to channel that fear into positive energy.

17.1.

At the risk of sounding like an ad for Toastmasters: The ability to present your ideas in public is a skill you'll use all your life, whether you're an advertising executive or just offering a toast at a wedding. While you may dread presenting your work to your peers or outside reviewers, the presentation can be the fun part of a creative effort.

The new-business pitch

Here are some tips offered to students competing in the National Student Advertising Competition sponsored each year by the American Advertising Federation. While they apply to a high-level formal new-business pitch, most of the tips work for informal presentations as well.

- *Your insight of the target audience will drive your presentation.* It's very simple—who are you talking to/what will you tell them/how will you deliver the message/how do you know it will work?

- *Don't memorize.* Know your material and speak from the heart, not from memory.

- *Know what you're saying.* Don't read from note cards. If you need note cards, sneak a peek before you begin speaking, but don't have them in your hand when you're talking.

- *It's possible to be professional and look as if you're having fun.* You should not be deadly earnest or too flippant. It's easier to tone down an over-the-top presentation than to punch up a boring one.

- *Don't be a slave to your graphics.* PowerPoint slides or Flash programs should highlight your verbal presentation, *not* replace it. Don't read from your slides. Don't have so much copy that your audience won't want to read the slides. If you have a lot to say, use more slides.

- *Start with an idea.* Tell how that idea relates to your recommendations, keep using that idea throughout your presentation, and come back to it at the end. Tell 'em what you're gonna tell 'em, sell 'em, then tell 'em what you told 'em.

- *If you have a theme, use it early and often.* Weave it through your presentation.

- *Eye contact is important.* Use "eye bursts," where you look at an individual audience member for two to three seconds at a time. Find the "head nodders"—people who are listening and agreeing with you. (These should be your nonpresenting teammates.) They'll give you confidence.

- *If you use a stunt or a gimmick, make sure it fits.* It should complement your theme and recommendations. Don't use a gimmick just to be different.

- *Get technical help.* If you're not confident of your technical ability, make sure you have someone who is an expert at setting up the equipment.

WORDS OF WISDOM

"Learn how to present. I've seen great ideas slip between the cracks just because they were poorly presented. If you have a flair for the dramatic, use it. If you don't, get one."

—**PHIL DUSENBERRY**[1]

- *Aim for a tone that's "cocky but humble."* In other words, be confident and enthusiastic, but also self-effacing when necessary. Don't come across as a know-it-all. Refer to your research as the basis for your opinions rather than your superior intelligence. Don't be afraid to use a little humor, if it can be naturally worked into the presentation. Don't tell "jokes" or make your humor seemed forced.

- *Remember, the first minutes of your presentation are critical.* This is when you set the tone of your presentation. The introduction grabs attention. It should instantly engage the audience.

- *Don't apologize for poor-quality visuals, video, audio, etc. (Why present poor quality in the first place?)* Don't say, "You probably can't tell from this layout," or "I'm not a good artist, so bear with me" or any other admission of poor quality. All the reviewers will hear is that you didn't care enough to give it your best effort.

- *Practice. Practice. Practice.* You may be sick of your presentation, but the audience is seeing it for the first time. Their enthusiastic reception will make all your hard work worthwhile.

- *Ask for the business.* You're not there to just entertain them.

WORDS OF WISDOM

"At the end of a presentation, it's not your brilliant strategy or clever ideas that win the business. It really depends on whether the client thinks you're the kind of people they want to hang around with."

—JOHN MELAMED[2]

When presenting as a team

In many ways, your team is also a campaign. You must be strong presenters as individuals, but you should also have a cumulative effect. Your transitions from presenter to presenter should be seamless. You should appear as a cohesive team, with members who all like each other (or at least give that appearance). If you like each other, chances are the audience will like you.

- *Trust your teammates.* Support them. Have faith in each other's abilities. Then you can concentrate on your part of the show.

- *Don't be afraid to interact.* A total team approach is much more effective than four or five individuals making separate presentations.

- *Practice with the nonpresenting members of your team as surrogate reviewers or clients.* Have them critique your presentation—watching for eye contact, hand movement, entry and exit, voice inflections, presentations of visuals, and other parts of your presentation that you can't see from the stage.

Distinctive presentations

You have to find the right blend of entertainment and serious business information. Here are some methods others have used to open up their presentations:

- *Ask a question.* One winning presentation opened with, "Your house is burning down. Your family is safe, but you only have time to get one possession from your house. What would it be?" Or more generically, "What's the most important thing in your life?"

- *Start with a video.* If you use a video, it should be short and crisply edited, with a clear message. Remember, this sets the tone for the whole presentation.

- *Make a series of statements.* Each team member states an opinion, or a misconception, about the client or its products. Follow with, "That's what people told us . . . and this is how we plan to change their minds."

- *Describe your target audience.* A day in the life. "Let me introduce you to . . . (name of people)." Or some other compelling way to draw the audience in.

Handling Q&A

Sometimes the outcome of a presentation depends more on how you defend your work than on the quality of the work itself. Here are a few tips for dealing with questions.

How you answer is just as important as what you say

- Treat each question as an opportunity, not as a criticism of your effort. Sometimes reviewers just want to see how you defend your work. If you get too defensive, vague, or impatient, your attitude may turn them off. (They are much more sensitive to this than you may realize.)

- Answer the question! You should be able to explain calmly and confidently why you did what you did. Don't be a politician. (If you can't defend what you did, then you made the wrong decisions.)

- Pay attention to your tone of voice. Just like your physical motions, your tone of voice says a lot about you. Be sure to answer questions in a strong, consistent tone. Don't act offended, impatient, or flustered.

- Avoid wavering or talking too softly, mumbling, or speaking too quickly.

Thinking on your feet

- A good thing to remember before answering a question is to take a deep breath, think for a second, and then begin to answer. This will help you calm your nerves and will give you the opportunity to "look before you leap" when it comes to answering important questions.

- Repeat the question or ask the client or reviewer to clarify a part of it. This gives you and your teammates more time to think about an answer.

- If you start an answer, finish it! Don't taper off and leave a question unanswered. Your teammates will instinctively jump in to finish your sentence and try to bail you out.

- Even if a question comes out of left field, don't act surprised. It may seem very logical to the reviewer. For example, if someone asks you why you didn't do something, you could say, "We looked into that, but our research indicated that some other approaches would work better" or "We studied a lot of ways to do this and found this was the most cost-efficient way to achieve our objectives."

- Don't say, "That's a good question," because it's code for "We never thought of that and don't have the answer."

- Don't change the subject and give an off-target answer. Think for a second, then answer the question to the best of your ability. If you sense the reviewer is not satisfied, simply ask, "Did I answer your question?"

- Don't argue, but don't automatically cave in. You had reasons for making these decisions. The reviewers don't necessarily disagree, but they want to see how you defend your work.

Anticipate questions

- You are so close to your work that it's hard for you to understand why someone doesn't get it. Think about the early phases of your planning. What questions did you ask yourselves? Why did you do things that way? Those are some of the questions others will also have.

- Practice for the questions. Try to come up with the toughest possible questions, no matter how "stupid" you think they may be. No doubt you will be asked some "stupid" questions.

- Have outsiders look at your book and presentation and invite their questions and comments. Don't be surprised if people are not as crazy about your ideas as you are. Encourage constructive criticism. It's good practice for handling reviewers.

Final words

- Believe in what you're presenting. It may not have been your original idea. You may not even agree with some of the approaches, but sell it like it's the only solution possible.

- Know your presentation. Don't memorize it. Come across as convincing, not as overrehearsed.

- Don't worry about mistakes. You're judged more by how you recover from a mistake than by the flawlessness of your presentation.

- Get enough sleep the night before.

- A little tension helps. The audience never notices those butterflies.

Avoiding Death by PowerPoint (or Flash)

Like any powerful tool, presentation software can be deadly in the wrong hands. The following are a few tips and techniques to give your presentation a little more zip:

- *Be original.* PowerPoint gives you a ton of clip art, but you don't have to feel obligated to use it. Cheesy clip art says you are as lazy and amateurish as most clients. They expect *you* to be the creative person.

- *Less copy/more slides.* Think of slides as billboards. Keep copy short. Use bullets rather than paragraphs if you can. Don't load up the whole slide with copy.

- *It's important to import.* Take advantage of the software's capabilities. Bring in sounds, video, experiment with transitions and custom animations.

- *Be consistent.* Once you create a background and style and select a font, stick with it. Pay close attention to consistent positioning of text on the slide and consistent use of punctuation and upper- and lowercase.

- *Keep it simple.* Even though you have a lot of choices in transitions, type effects, and animation schemes, don't feel compelled to use all of them in one presentation. Stick with one or two styles.

- *Don't read your slides to the audience.* Look at the audience, not the screen. The audience should look at you first and the screen as a background to reinforce your presentation.

- *Leave something for the leave-behind materials.* Your visual presentation should function as a reminder, not a finished document. Just hit the key points.

- *Use a remote control.* Advance your slides with a wireless "clicker." You can keep this in your pocket and the slides will change behind you like magic. Don't stand in front of the screen and point the clicker at the computer like you're casting a spell. (We've even seen people pointing it at the screen!)

- *Mix it up.* If you have to give a long presentation, especially for a new-business pitch or advertising campaign, don't rely entirely on PowerPoint. When the lights go down, so does the energy level. Take a break every now and then. You can show work on posters. Distribute handouts. Walk into the audience. Do anything to break up the monotony of staring at that screen.

- *Don't be blinded by the light.* If you're working with a front-projection system, try to position your screen on one side of the stage, so you can keep presenters from staring into the light.

- *Proof positive.* Have someone other than the presenters proofread the slides, preferably from a hard copy. Few things are more embarrassing than having a room full of people see a typo on your slide.

- *Remember, mistakes aren't fatal.* You're human. So you may forget to change a slide on cue. Or you may speak out of order. Or a technical glitch may screw up a transition. It happens. Don't let it throw you. Calmly try to sort it out without disrupting your presentation. You might be able to skip over it. But if it's critical, you might have to take a break and fix it. The main thing is not to freak out.

- *Know your equipment.* If you have to borrow computers and projection equipment, make sure you're comfortable with them. Every computer and projector is a little different. Don't assume everything will work just fine.

- *Have a Plan B or even a Plan C.* Anticipate what could go wrong from both technical and personal standpoints. For example, one student presentation involved tossing an orange from one presenter to another. If she caught it, fine. If she dropped it, she had an "ad-lib" line ready to use.

- *Practice. Practice Practice.* Did we mention you should practice? There is no substitute for being prepared.

WAR STORY:

PRESENT(ING) TENSE: A LESSON IN HOW NOT TO SHOW YOUR WORK

In grad school, I had two jobs—moving furniture and writing copy for a local ad agency. Both paid $5 per hour. After one disastrous presentation I thought hauling sofas held more promise.

I had prepared a full campaign for a local tourist attraction, including TV, radio, print ads, brochures, signs, promotional events—the works. The agency art director worked up some really nice layouts based on my ideas. So far so good. The president of the agency decided that the genius behind this campaign should present it at a local Chamber of Commerce luncheon. After lunch I gazed at 20 sleepy old men anxious to get back to their insurance agencies and hardware stores, and I knew they had no interest in the brilliant ideas of

a 23-year-old ad intern. It was deer-in-the-headlights time. As I stumbled through the layouts, forgot the rationale, and lost my place a half dozen times, I was turning as red as the checkered tablecloths. Those who weren't glancing at their watches or putting on their coats stared at me with a combination of pity and disgust. Sort of like looking at road kill. After a 15-minute train wreck of scattered layouts and disjointed rationale, I sat down to a thunderous ovation of dead silence. During the long, long ride back to the agency, the president's only comment was, "Well, I would have presented it a little differently."

Lessons learned: Never go into a presentation unprepared. Know your audience. Believe in your topic. And always have a backup plan, like moving furniture.

—Tom Altstiel

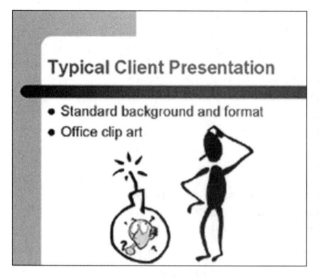

17.2. Even though PowerPoint gives you a lot of clip art, think of alternatives. Anything is better than those little blob people.

17.3. A slide from a student presentation using custom background and simple but eye-catching graphics.

17.4. Audiences want to be entertained. They don't want to read your slides.

17.5. Keep it short and simple, even if you need more slides.

17.6. Above all, keep it clean and simple with consistent and easy-to-read text.

17.7. In case you've missed our point during the past 17 chapters: *Keep it simple,* and please remember, if you emphasize everything, you emphasize nothing.

Notes

[1] Quoted in Maxine Paetro, *How to Put Your Book Together and Get a Job in Advertising* (Chicago: Copy Workshop, 2002), 152.

[2] John Melamed, executive with the Cramer Krasselt ad agency, "How to Make Winning Presentations," lecture presented at Marquette University, Milwaukee, WI, February 10, 2004.

Appendix

Copy Platform
(Creative Strategy Statement)

Product (Service) _____

The Product (or Service)

A. Primary features/benefits in order of importance (remember "So whats?")

Feature   Benefit
1. _____   1. _____
2. _____   2. _____
3. _____   3. _____
4. _____   4. _____

B. Exclusive or unique product (service) attributes

_____

C. Can product claims be substantiated?

_____

D. Parent company name important? _____ Why?

_____

E. Brand value: High status _____   Low status _____
   No brand image _____

The Consumer

A. Demographics (age, sex, education, income, occupation, geographic distribution)

_____

_____

_____

B. Psychographics (lifestyle, attitude, personality traits, buying patterns)

_____

_____

_____

C. Needs fulfilled by buying this product or service

_____

_____

_____

The Marketplace

A. Major competitors/rank in market/market share

1. _____ / _____ / _____
2. _____ / _____ / _____
3. _____ / _____ / _____

B. Competitive advantage/disadvantage of product (service)

Competitor   Our advantage (disadvantage)

_____   _____

_____   _____

_____   _____

C. Position of product (service) in market
Parity product (no perceived competitive advantage)

_____

New product category (first of its kind)

_____

Significant improvement over similar products

_____

D. Pricing position (compared to competition)
Premium priced _____   Comparably priced _____
Low priced _____

Creative Strategy

A. The "One Thing": If you could say one thing about this product or service: _____

B. Significant facts or statistics about product, consumer, or market

_____

_____

_____

Copyediting and Proofreading Symbols

Begin paragraph	¶	Years ago we invested in a small Seattle-based coffee…
Set in italics		Isn't it interesting how the English countryside… (ital)
Set in caps		Try the hotpockets. they're breathtaking. (cap)
Set in lowercase		Is it an Evil Petting Zoo? (lc)
Insert period, comma		No, Mr. Powers, I expect you to…. ⊙ / ⌃
Insert question mark		Why won't you die?
Insert apostrophe		It got weird, didn't it?
Insert hyphen		Do you like your quasi futuristic outfits?
Insert quotes		When a problem comes along, you must zip it.
Put in space		Are they angry seabass? #
Close up		Crikey! I've lost my mojo.
Set in boldface		I'm from Holland. Isn't that weird? (bf)
Insert word		He kind of looks like baby. ⌃ a
Delete word		No, this is me in a a nutshell.
Delete and close up		Moove over rover. This chick is taking over.
Leave as it was		A ~~trillion~~ is more than a billion… stet
Transpose		I call it the Parsons Allen Project. (tr)
Spell out word		Who does number ② work for? (sp)
Copy on next page		more
End of copy		### or —30—

Additional Radio Terms

AFTRA   American Federation of Television and Radio Artists, one of the two main unions for voice talent.

ANNCR   Announcer.

Board   Electronic control panel for recording, mixing, and editing.

Boom mike   Microphone on long extension, over announcer's head.

Buyout   Total payment to talent for one-time use, as opposed to residual payments.

Cans   Slang for announcer's headphones.

Compression   Electronic removal of dead air between words.

DAT   Digital audiotape.

Dead air   No sound between words or sound effects.

Demo   Demonstration recording for reviewing or auditioning, not meant for airing.

Donut   Nonvocal musical segment or sound effect that allows an announcer to read copy over it.

Double donut   Usually a commercial with a musical intro, announcer segment, musical middle, announcer segment, and musical close.

Fade   Gradually reduce (fade out) or increase (fade up) volume.

Flight   Time frame during which a commercial runs.

In   Introduce music or effect.

Out   Music or effect is deleted abruptly.

Nonlinear   Segments recorded out of sequence and assembled digitally.

Phone patch   Review of recording over phone lines instead of in the studio.

PD   Public domain (music with no royalty fees, as in classical music).

Punch in   Insert rerecorded segment into commercial to replace a segment.

P&W   Pension and Welfare, additional payments made to SAG/AFTRA talent.

Quarter track   Analog recording tape with four channels (two each direction).

Residual   Payment made to talent after the initial run of the commercial.

Reverb   Reverberation, an echolike effect.

SAG   Screen Actors Guild, one of the two main unions for voice talent.

Sample   Digital recording and re-creation of music or sound effect.

Segue   Gradually lead into a new segment of a commercial.

SFX   Sound effects.

Slice of life   Simulated real-world situation, usually using dialogue.

Spot   Commercial.

Spot market   A local media buy rather than network.

Stage whisper   Whisper that's loud enough to be easily heard and understood.

Stinger   Musical effect to provide emphasis, usually at the end of a jingle.

Swell   Expansion of copy to fit a specific segment (e.g., translation of English to Spanish usually accounts for a 20% swell due to the increase in words).

Tag   End of a commercial, usually with the name of store locations, hours, or other information.

Take   Reading of a segment of copy at one time; each reading is a take. Most commercials involve several takes.

Talent   Announcer, actors, singers, or musicians in a commercial.

Talk back   The button an engineer or producer uses to communicate with talent in an isolated booth.

Under   Reduce the volume of music or an effect so you can hear the announcer.

Up   Raise the volume of music or an effect.

Voice of God   Conversation with someone "off-camera," usually with an effect such as an echo.

White noise   Undefined noise such as static.

Additional Television Terms

Accelerated montage   Sequence edited into progressively shorter shots to create a mood of tension and excitement.

Ambient light   Natural light surrounding the subject, usually understood to be soft.

Aspect ratio   Ratio of the width to the height of the film or television image. The formerly standard Academy aperture is 1.33:1. Wide-screen ratios vary. In Europe 1.66:1 is most common; in the United States, 1.85:1. Anamorphic processes such as CinemaScope and Panavision are even wider, 2.00:1 to 2.55:1.

Asynchronous sound   Sound that does not operate in unison with the image, or sound belonging to a particular scene that is heard while the images of the previous scene are still on-screen, or that continue over a following scene. *Also* diegetic sound whose source cannot be seen on screen or sound unintentionally out of sync with the image track.

Backlighting   Main source of light is behind the subject, silhouetting it, and directed toward the camera.

Bird's-eye shot (or **overhead shot**)   Wide shot taken from high above the action.

Blue screen (or **green screen** or **chroma-key**)   Shooting a subject in front of a blue or green background so the image can be superimposed over another background. The camera can be adjusted not to pick up blue or green, so, in effect, you have a blocked-out image on clear background.

Boom   Traveling arm for suspending a microphone above the actors and outside the frame. See also **Crane**.

Bridge   Passage linking two scenes either by continuing music across the transition or by beginning the sound (including dialogue or music) of the next scene over images of the previous scene (also called *sound advance*).

Bridging shot   Shot used to cover a jump in time or place or other discontinuous changes.

Continuity editing   Technique whereby shots are arranged in sequence to create the illusion of a credible chronological narrative. Often contrasted with *montage editing*.

Crane   Mechanical arm used to move a camera through space above the ground or to position it in the air. A *crane shot* allows the camera to vary distance, angle, and height (also called *boom shot*).

Crosscutting   Intermingling the shots of two or more scenes to suggest *parallel action*.

Cutaway   Shot inserted in a scene to show action at another location, usually brief; most often used to cover breaks in the main take, as in television and documentary interviews. Also used to provide comment on the action (e.g., by cutting away from scenes of explicit sex or extreme violence).

Day for night   Practice of using filters to shoot night scenes during the day.

Depth of field   Range of distances from the camera at which the subject is acceptably sharp.

Detail shot   Usually more magnified than a close-up; shot of a hand, eye, mouth, or subject of similar detail.

Drive-by shot   View of person, object, or place from a camera located on a moving vehicle as it passes by.

Dub   Rerecord dialogue in a language other than the original or record dialogue in a specially equipped studio after the film has been shot.

Dupe   Print a duplicate negative from a positive print or print a duplicate reversal print; also the term for a print made in this manner.

Establishing shot   Generally a long shot that shows the audience the general location of the scene that follows, often providing essential information and orienting the viewer.

Fast motion (or **accelerated motion**)   Film is shot at less than 24 frames per second (i.e., the camera is undercranked) so that when it is projected at the normal speed actions appear to move much faster; often useful for comic effect.

Final cut   Film in its final state, as opposed to *rough cut*.

Flashback   Scene or sequence (sometimes an entire film) inserted into a scene in "present" time that deals with the past.

Flash forward   Scene or shots of future time. See **Flashback**.

Flash frame   Shot of only a few frames in duration, sometimes a single frame, which can just barely be perceived by the audience.

Focus pull   Pull focus during a shot in order to follow a subject as it moves away from or toward the camera.

Follow shot   Tracking shot or zoom that follows the subject as it moves.

Frame   Any single image on the film. Also refers to the size and shape of the image on the film, or on the screen when projected, or to the compositional unit of film design.

Freeze frame   Freeze shot achieved by printing a single frame many times in succession to give the illusion of a still photograph when projected.

FX   Effects.

Gaffer   Chief electrician, responsible to the director of photography; responsible for all major electrical installations on the set, including lighting and power.

High key   Type of lighting arrangement in which the *key light* is very bright, often producing shadows.

Intercutting   See **Parallel editing.**

Key light   Main light on a subject. Usually placed at a 45-degree angle to the camera-subject axis.

Mask   Shield placed in front of the camera lens to change the shape of the image. Often used in POV (point of view) shots (e.g., looking through binoculars or a keyhole).

Master shot   Long take of an entire scene, generally a relatively long shot that facilitates assembly of component closer shots and details. Because the editor can always fall back on the master shot, it is also called a *cover shot.*

Match cut   Cut in which the two shots are linked by visual, aural, or metaphorical parallelism. Famous example: At the end of *North by Northwest,* Cary Grant pulls Eva Marie Saint up the side of Mt. Rushmore; match cut to Grant pulling her up to a Pullman bunk. (Do not confuse with jump cut.)

Montage editing   Technique of arranging shots in sequence to create connotations and associations rather than a standard chronologically unfolding narrative. See also **Continuity editing.**

Parallel action (or **parallel montage**)   Narrative device in which two scenes are observed in parallel through *crosscutting.*

Parallel editing   Narrative construction that crosscuts between two or more lines of action supposed to be occurring simultaneously. Usually restricted to particular sequences in a film, *crosscutting* can also occur between lines of action that are thematically related rather than simultaneous.

Postproduction   Increasingly complex stage in the production of a film that takes place after shooting has been completed; involves editing, addition of titles, creation of special effects, and final sound track, including dubbing and mixing.

Preproduction   Phase of film production following the securing of financial backing but preceding shooting; includes work on the script, casting, hiring crews, finding locations, constructing sets, drawing up schedules, arranging catering, etc.

Reaction shot   Shot that cuts away from the main scene or speaker in order to show a character's reaction to it.

Rough cut   First assembly of a film, prepared by the editor from the selected takes, which are joined in the order planned in the script. Finer points of timing and montage are left to a later stage.

Shooting ratio   Ratio between film actually exposed in the camera during shooting to film used in the final cut. A shooting ratio of 10 to 1 or more is not uncommon.

Soft focus   Filters, Vaseline, or specially constructed lenses soften the delineation of lines and points, usually to create a romantic effect.

Subjective camera   Style that allows the viewer to observe events from the point of view of either a character or the persona of the author.

Swish pan (or **flick pan, zip pan, whip pan**)   Pan in which the intervening scene moves past too quickly to be observed; approximates psychologically the action of the human eye as it moves from one subject to another.

Sweep in (or **wipe in**)   Frame-by-frame revelation from blackout of complete image.

Sweep out (or **wipe out**)   Opposite of *sweep in.*

Synchronous sound   Sound whose source is visible in the frame of the image or whose source is understandable from the context of the image (e.g. source music).

Tracking shot (or **traveling shot**)   Generally, any shot in which the camera moves from one point to another sideways, in, or out. The camera can be handheld or mounted on a set of wheels that move on tracks or on a rubber-tired dolly.

Wild sound   Sound recorded separately from images.

What Agencies are Looking for in an Entry-Level Copywriter

Core competencies

- Working knowledge of QuarkXPress, Adobe InDesign, Adobe Photoshop, Adobe Illustrator, and/or Microsoft Excel

- Mastery of Word, WordPerfect, or other word-processing software

- Computer literacy, especially knowledge and use of the Internet

- Understanding of key advertising terms

- Understanding of agency structure, agency-client relationships, traditions of the advertising business

- Understanding of basic marketing principles

- Mastery of the English language, including correct grammar and spelling

Developed skills

- Recognize superior creative ideas and be able to explain why

- Find, assemble, and organize background research

- Develop a logical copy platform with prioritized copy points

- Develop attention-getting headlines

- Combine headlines and graphics into a single idea

- Write compelling, benefit-oriented copy

- Connect reader/viewer/listener with advertiser

- Create campaigns with elements that work independently and collectively

- Present ideas with confidence and enthusiasm

Personality

- Ability to accept criticism and use it to improve

- Leadership ability

- Team mentality—ability to work with art directors/account people

- Willingness to learn about clients' businesses

- Strong work ethic—not a 9-to-5 mentality

- Confidence without arrogance

What Happens When
You Obey All the "Rules"

Color photo of kid
and dog

Lots of white space

Benefit headline
with proven words

At last! Announcing the free advice
you've always wanted.

Who else would show you a new way how to do this?

You *can* have it all. Money. Sex. Fame. A corner office with a window. Just follow these easy steps. First, obey the "rules" for effective advertising design. Which rules? All of them! Next, do exactly what you're told…by everyone you work with. Then, wait for all the good things to come your way. That's all there is to it.

To get all the facts, send for our free book "How to Become a Rich, Famous Ad Person who Gets Lots of Sex <u>and</u> a Corner Office with a Window." Act now! Supplies are limited.

Strong call to action

Short sentences. Strong
appeal to wants and needs

Color logotype

AdHacks
If it smells, it sells

Rhyming slogan

www.send-us-your-bank-account-number.com

Prominent Web site

The Whole Book in One Page

- *Find the central truth in a product.* Discover the "One Thing" you can communicate. Look for that single adjective that defines a brand.

- *Don't write to the masses.* Talk to an individual. Find out how to satisfy his or her wants and needs.

- *Learn to write structured, well-crafted body copy.* People will read long copy if they are interested in the subject.

- *Write hot. Edit cold.* In other words, write with enthusiasm and let the words flow. Later, go back and edit ruthlessly. After you edit, cut another 20–30%.

- *Learn to write headlines.* The headline can be the most important words in the ad. Don't write a weak headline and try to support it with a subhead.

- *Learn to write theme lines.* Really good taglines or slogans can make a product.

- *Learn teamwork.* Learn to collaborate. Not just with art directors, but also account people and the client. Become valuable to the client, and you become valuable to the agency and the next agency.

- *Think visually.* Don't assume an art director will save your idea if you can't visualize it. Look for the visual-verbal connection. They work together— one does not describe the other.

- *Keep it simple.* That applies to both copy and design. When you emphasize everything, you emphasize nothing. Stick to one basic idea and make it work.

- *Think campaigns.* Think about different elements that work individually and cumulatively to convey the message. Think of how you can extend and repeat campaign components.

- *Learn how to present.* Be confident, persuasive, logical. If you're naturally funny, use it. If you're not, don't try to be. Defend your opinions but know when to back down (see *Learn teamwork*).

- *Accept menial assignments.* Be humble. Do everything. Absorb the experience and use it later. A good attitude is a major component of your success.

- *Continually upgrade your portfolio.* Don't put things in just because they were produced. Don't get sentimental. Weed out anything less than wonderful.

- *Accept criticism and use it to improve.* Develop a thick skin—creative directors, account people, clients, your peers will think they have a better idea. Throw a tantrum and you won't sell the *next* idea either.

- *Get involved in outside activities.* Read, pay attention to pop culture, take an interest in life outside of advertising and marketing.

Index

About the Authors

Tom Altstiel is Creative Director and Partner at Prom Krog Altstiel, Inc. (PKA), a Milwaukee-area marketing communications agency. He has been a copywriter and creative director at several Chicago- and Milwaukee-area agencies, working on accounts for consumer, business-to-business, and agricultural clients. He earned a Master's degree in advertising at the University of Illinois–Urbana/Champaign and has been teaching at Marquette University as an Adjunct Instructor since 1999. In 2003 he received the Dean's Recognition Award for Outstanding Part-Time Faculty, and in 2004 he advised the Marquette team at the NSAC finals in Dallas.

Jean Grow is Assistant Professor in the Department of Advertising and Public Relations at Marquette University. She earned her PhD from the University of Wisconsin–Madison and her BFA from the School of the Art Institute of Chicago. She has won numerous teaching awards, including placing third in the national Promising Professors Awards sponsored by the Association for Education in Journalism and Mass Communication. Although teaching is her passion, she continues to keep herself active in the ad business through her consulting firm, Grow Creative Resources. Prior to moving to Wisconsin, she worked in Chicago as an artists' representative; her agency clients included DDB Needham, Foote Cone & Belding, J. Walter Thompson, and Leo Burnett.